Linux® FOR DUMMIES® 9TH EDITION

by Richard Blum
and
Dee-Ann LeBlanc

WILEY

Wiley Publishing, Inc.

Linux® For Dummies®, 9th Edition

Published by
Wiley Publishing, Inc.
111 River Street
Hoboken, NJ 07030-5774
www.wiley.com

Copyright © 2009 by Wiley Publishing, Inc., Indianapolis, Indiana

Published by Wiley Publishing, Inc., Indianapolis, Indiana

Published simultaneously in Canada

For general information on our other products and services, please contact our Customer Care Department within the U.S. at 877-762-2974, outside the U.S. at 317-572-3993, or fax 317-572-4002.

For technical support, please visit www.wiley.com/techsupport.

Wiley also publishes its books in a variety of electronic formats. Some content that appears in print may not be available in electronic books.

Library of Congress Control Number: 2009931457

ISBN: 978-0-470-46701-5

Manufactured in the United States of America

10 9 8 7 6 5 4 3 2

WILEY

About the Author

Richard Blum has worked in the IT industry for more than 20 years as a network and systems administrator. During that time, he's had the opportunity to work with lots of different computer products, including Windows, Netware, Cisco, Avaya, different flavors of UNIX, and of course, Linux. Over the years, he's also volunteered for several nonprofit organizations to help support small networks that had little financial support. Rich is the author of several Linux-based books for total Linux geeks, and a couple of Windows-based books for programmers.

When he's not being a computer nerd, Rich plays the electric bass in a church worship band, and enjoys spending time with his wife, Barbara, and their two daughters, Katie Jane and Jessica.

Dedication

To my daughters, Katie Jane and Jessica. Remember: It's always a good time to learn new things (even when you're not in school).

Author's Acknowledgments

First, all praise and glory go to God, who through His Son makes all things possible, and gives us the gift of eternal life.

A special thanks to Dee-Ann LeBlanc for passing the baton of this series to me. It's amazing to think of the great authors who've been involved with guiding this series from the start. I'm glad to be able to build off of that tradition, and all your hard work.

Many thanks go to the great people at Wiley Publishing for their help and guidance in writing this. Thanks to Kyle Looper, the acquisitions editor, for offering me this opportunity, and Rebecca Senninger, the project editor, for helping keep the project focused and on track. Many thanks to Michael Wessler, the technical editor, for his tireless efforts at trying to make sure everything presented here was accurate and actually worked! Thanks also go to Carole McClendon at Waterside Productions for arranging this gig.

Finally, I'd like to thank my parents, Mike and Joyce Blum, for constantly stressing education over goofing off, and wife Barbara and two daughters Katie Jane and Jessica for their love and support, especially while working on this project.

Publisher's Acknowledgments

We're proud of this book; please send us your comments through our online registration form located at http://dummies.custhelp.com. For other comments, please contact our Customer Care Department within the U.S. at 877-762-2974, outside the U.S. at 317-572-3993, or fax 317-572-4002.

Some of the people who helped bring this book to market include the following:

Acquisitions, Editorial, and Media Development

Project Editor: Rebecca Senninger
  (Previous Edition: Linda Morris)

Acquisitions Editor: Kyle Looper

Senior Copy Editor: Barry Childs-Helton

Technical Editor: Michael Wessler

Editorial Manager: Leah Cameron

Media Development Project Manager:
  Laura Moss-Hollister

Media Development Assistant Project Manager: Jenny Swisher

Media Development Associate Producer:
  Shawn Patrick

Editorial Assistant: Amanda Foxworth

Sr. Editorial Assistant: Cherie Case

Cartoons: Rich Tennant (www.the5thwave.com)

Composition Services

Project Coordinator: Patrick Redmond

Layout and Graphics: Samantha Allen, Reuben W. Davis, Timothy C. Detrick, Andrea Hornberger, Ronald Terry

Proofreaders: Laura Bowman, Amanda Graham, Jessica Kramer

Indexer: Palmer Publishing Services

Publishing and Editorial for Technology Dummies

  Richard Swadley, Vice President and Executive Group Publisher

  Andy Cummings, Vice President and Publisher

  Mary Bednarek, Executive Acquisitions Director

  Mary C. Corder, Editorial Director

Publishing for Consumer Dummies

  Diane Graves Steele, Vice President and Publisher

Composition Services

  Debbie Stailey, Director of Composition Services

Table of Contents

Introduction

*W*elcome to the fascinating world of open-source software that is Linux. In this book, we introduce you to the wonders of the Linux operating system, originally created as a labor of love by Linus Torvalds in the early 1990s. Our goal is to initiate you into the rapidly growing ranks of Linux users and enthusiasts busily rewriting the rules for the operating system marketplace.

If you've contemplated switching to Linux but find the prospect too forbidding, you can relax. If you can boil water or set your alarm clock, you too can become a Linux user. (No kidding!)

When this book appeared in its first edition, Linux was an emerging phenomenon that was neither terribly well known nor understood. In this edition — for a new generation of Linux users — so much material is available that we have steered this particular title toward what Linux is and how you can make the best use of it on your desktop. To that end, these pages contain various online resources, tips, and tricks, as well as more general instruction. If you're looking for material on servers, *Linux All-In-One Desk Reference For Dummies* by Naba Barkakati (Wiley Publishing, Inc.) can serve your needs.

In this book, we keep the amount of technobabble to a minimum and stick with plain English as much as possible. Besides plain talk about Linux installation, boot up, configuration, and software, we include many examples, plus lots of detailed instructions to help you use your very own Linux machine with a minimum of stress or confusion.

We also include with this book a handy DVD-ROM that contains image files for both Ubuntu 9.04 (the most popular workstation Linux distribution around) and Fedora 11 (a project sponsored by Red Hat, the leading Linux vendor). To find out what exactly is included on the DVD-ROM, see Appendix B. If you have no idea of what we're talking about, don't worry. You'll know soon enough!

About This Book

Think of this book as a friendly, approachable guide to tackling terminology and the Linux collection of tools, utilities, and widgets. Although Linux isn't terribly hard to figure out, it does pack a boatload of details, parameters, and *administrivia* (administrative trivia, in UNIX-speak). You need to wrestle those details into shape while you install, configure, manage, and troubleshoot a Linux-based computer. Some sample topics you find in this book include the following:

- Understanding where Linux comes from and what it can do for you
- Installing the Linux operating system
- Working with a Linux system to manage files and add software
- Setting up Internet access and surfing the Web
- Customizing your Linux desktop
- Managing Linux system security and resources

Although it may seem, at first glance, that working with Linux requires years of hands-on experience, tons of trial and error, advanced computer science training, and intense dedication, take heart! It's not true! If you can tell somebody how to find your office, you can certainly build a Linux system that does what you want. The purpose of this book isn't to turn you into a full-blown Linux geek (that's the ultimate state of Linux enlightenment, of course); it's to show you the ins and outs that you need to master in order to build a smoothly functioning Linux system and to give you the know-how and confidence to use it.

How to Use This Book

This book tells you how to install, configure, and customize a Linux desktop system. Although you can do most things in Linux these days by pointing and clicking, you still may want to try using Linux at the command prompt — where you type detailed instructions to load or configure software, access files, and do other tasks. In this book, input appears in monospace type like this:

```
rmdir /etc/bin/devone
```

When you type Linux commands or other related information, be sure to copy the information exactly as you see it in the book, including uppercase and lowercase letters, because that's part of the magic that makes Linux behave properly.

A failure to follow instructions exactly can have all kinds of unfortunate, unseemly, or unexpected side effects.

The margins of a book don't give you the same amount of room as your computer screen; therefore, in this book, some URLs and lengthy commands at the command prompt may appear wrapped to the next line. Remember that your computer sees these wrapped lines as a *single set of instructions,* or as a single URL — so if you're typing a hunk of text, keep it on a single line. Don't insert a hard return if you see one of these wrapped lines. We clue you in that it's supposed to be all one line by breaking the line at a slash mark or a natural word break (to imply "Wait — there's more!") and slightly indenting the overage, as in the following silly example:

```
www.infocadabra.transylvania.com/nexus/plexus/lexus/
           praxis/okay/this/is/a/make-believe/URL/but/
           some/real/ones/are/SERIOUSLY/long.html
```

Note that as you dig your way into and through this book — and other sources of Linux wit, wisdom, and inspiration that you're likely to encounter — you may find some terms used interchangeably. For example, you may see the same piece of software called a *program,* a *command,* a *utility,* a *script,* an *application,* or a *tool,* depending on the source, the context, and the author of the information you're consulting. To a large extent, you can treat these terms as interchangeable, and when an important distinction needs to be made among them, we point it out. Similarly, when you're working with various commands or configuration controls, you may also encounter terms such as *flag, switch, option,* or *parameter* used more or less interchangeably. In this case, all these terms refer to ways in which you can control, refine, or modify basic commands or programs to make them do what you want. Again, wherever distinctions and clarifications may be needed, we provide them.

Three Presumptuous Assumptions

They say that making assumptions makes a fool of the person who makes them and of the person about whom those assumptions are made. Even so, practicality demands that we make a few assumptions about you, gentle reader:

- ✔ You can turn your computer on and off.
- ✔ You know how to use a mouse and a keyboard.
- ✔ You want to install, configure, and/or use a desktop Linux system because you're curious or interested or it's your job to do so.

You don't need to be a master logician or a wizard in the arcane art of programming to use this book, nor do you need a PhD in computer science. You don't even need a complete or perfect understanding of what's going on in your computer's innards.

If you have an active imagination and the ability to solve rudimentary problems, that's even better — you have already mastered the key ingredients necessary to making Linux work for you. The rest are mere details and a bit of patience. We can help you with the details, but the patience is up to you!

How This Book Is Organized

This book contains six major parts, arranged in an order to take you from Linux installation and configuration through keeping a Linux desktop system up and running, if not purring like a cat in the sun! Most parts contain three or more chapters or appendixes, and each chapter or appendix contains modular sections. Whenever you need help or information, pick up this book and start anywhere you like, or use the Table of Contents and the index to locate specific topics or key words.

Following is a breakdown of the book's six parts and what you find in each one.

Part I: Getting Your Feet Wet

This part sets the stage and includes an overview of and introduction to the terms, techniques, and software components that make Linux the raging software tiger that's so ready, willing, and able to do its thing. To be a little more specific, we start out with a Linux overview that explains what Linux is, where it came from, and how it works. Next, we tackle the various tasks and activities involved in preparing for and installing Linux on a computer. After that, we tell you how to give Linux the boot — not to get rid of it by any means, but rather, to fire up your brand-new system to reach the heights of computing ecstasy. Finally, we help you find your way around the desktop and tweak it some to your liking.

Part II: Getting Up to Speed with Linux

In this part, you find out the basics of how to work in Linux. You discover where various things are stored in your Linux filesystem and how to navigate your way through it. After you can find your way around, you'll see how to find your way *out* of the system and connect to the Internet.

Part III: Getting Things Done

Linux includes a great many facilities and capabilities, so after you get past the initial installation and configuration, you probably want to use your system to _do_ something. Here's where the doing begins! In this part of the book, you find out how to use Internet tools like Web browsers (Firefox!), e-mail, instant messaging, and more. Then you discover how to edit text files, and then go whole hog with word processors and other office suite programs thanks to OpenOffice.org. The fun stuff is in this part too, like how to use audio and video in the Linux world, and how to access software and formats that you're told are only available to Windows users.

Part IV: Junior Administrator Boot Camp

In this part of the book, you discover how to take care of your system. You see how to handle various file formats, how to install new software, and most important, how to keep your system updated so it's not vulnerable. You also find out about basic system administration tasks like creating and managing user accounts, caring for your filesystem, setting up printing, and more. Then you find out a bit about keeping your Linux system secure. **_Hint:_** As with any operating system, the most important thing is keeping it up to date!

Part V: The Part of Tens

In this book's grand climax, we sum up and distill the essence of what you now know about Linux and its inner workings. Here, you have a chance to revisit some key troubleshooting tips and tricks for Linux systems, along with setting up a Samba server so you can share files with another computer.

Part VI: Appendixes

This book ends with a set of appendixes designed to sum up and further expand on this book's contents. Appendix A delivers groups of Linux commands, complete with syntax and explanations, arranged according to their function. Appendix B lists details about what's on the _Linux For Dummies,_ 9th Edition, DVD.

Icons Used in This Book

Within each chapter, we use icons to highlight particularly important or useful information. You find the following icons in this book:

The Tip icon flags useful information that makes living with your Linux system even less complicated than you feared it might be.

We sometimes use this icon to point out information you just shouldn't pass by — don't overlook these gentle reminders. (The life, sanity, or page you save may be your own.)

Be cautious when you see this icon — it warns you of things you shouldn't do. This icon is meant to emphasize that the consequences of ignoring these bits of wisdom can be severe.

This icon signals technical details that are informative and interesting but not critical to understanding and using Linux. Skip these paragraphs if you want (but please come back and read them later).

Where to Go from Here

This is where you pick a direction and hit the road! *Linux For Dummies,* 9th Edition, is much like *1001 Nights* because it almost doesn't matter where you start. You look at lots of different scenes and stories as you prepare yourself to build your own Linux system. Although each story has its own distinctive characters and plot, the whole is surely something to marvel at. Don't worry — you can handle it. Who cares whether anybody else thinks that you're just goofing around? We know that you're getting ready to have the time of your life.

Enjoy!

Part I
Getting Your Feet Wet

The 5th Wave   By Rich Tennant

Before installing Linux, Dwayne prepares to partition the hard drive.

In this part . . .

This part includes an introduction to the development and capabilities of the Linux operating system. We also cover the terms and tools that make Linux what it is, along with detailed step-by-step instructions about what it takes to prepare your computer for Linux and to install either the popular Ubuntu or Fedora on your very own computer. From there, you find out how to address particular trouble-shooting problems, and then we take a tour of the desktop and find out how to customize it. By the end of this part, you've installed the Linux system and have some basic ability to navigate around your new desktop.

Chapter 1

Getting Acquainted with Linux

Ford, you're turning into a penguin. Stop it!

— Arthur Dent

Welcome to the world of Linux, the operating system developed by more than a thousand people around the world! In this chapter, you find out about Linux itself — what it is, where it comes from, and why it gets so much attention in the news these days. Prepare to have your assumptions challenged about how software *must* be developed and sold, and open your mind to new possibilities.

Is Free Really Free?

Understanding Linux requires a radical shift of thought regarding the way that you acquire and use computer software. (**Note:** By *radical*, we mean getting to the root of the matter, rather than putting on beads and camping out in the administration building.) Your first step toward shifting your mind-set is to alter your general connotation of the word *free* to represent *freedom*, rather than *free lunch*. That's right; you can sell "free" software for a fee . . . and you're encouraged to do so, as long as you relay the same freedom to each recipient of the software.

Don't scratch your head too hard; these concepts are tough to grasp initially, especially when you consider the conditioning you've received from the commercial software industry's marketing departments. Perhaps you don't know that when you purchase most proprietary, shrink-wrapped software, you don't actually *own* the software. Rather, you're granted permission to use the software within the bounds dictated by the licensor.

Linux also has a license. However, the motives and purpose of the license are much different from those of most commercial software. Instead of using a license to restrict use of the software, the GNU General Public License (GPL) that Linux uses ensures that the software will always be open to anyone. No company can ever own or dictate the way in which you use or modify Linux — although they can have their own individual copyrights and trademarks on their various brands of it, such as Red Hat and Novell. In essence, you already own Linux, and you can use it for anything you like, as long as you propagate the GPL freedoms to any further recipients of the software.

Linux: Revolution or Just Another Operating System?

Before going any farther into Linux, we need to get some terminology out of the way.

An *operating system* is the software that runs your computer, handling all interactions between you and the hardware. Whether you're writing a letter, calculating a budget, or managing your recipes on your computer, the operating system provides the essential air that your computer breathes. Furthermore, an operating system isn't just one program; it consists of hundreds of smaller programs and utilities that allow us humans to use a computer to do something useful. You then run other programs (such as your word processor) on top of the operating system to get everything done.

Linux has been accused of being "just another operating system." On the surface, it may appear so, but if you look deeper, you can see that this isn't so. The Linux project is a flagship leading the current trend toward open-source and free (as in "freedom," not "free beer") software within the computing industry. A rock-solid operating system because of the model under which it was (and continues to be) developed, Linux represents much that is good in software development.

Two fundamental distinctions separate Linux from the rest of the operating-system pack:

- Linux is licensed under the unique and ingenious *GNU General Public License,* which you can read about in the next section.
- Linux is developed and maintained by a worldwide team of volunteer and paid programmers working together over the Internet.

Linux is great for many reasons, including the fact that the folks who built it from the ground up wanted it to be all the following:

- **Multiuser:** More than one user can be logged in to a single computer at one time.

- **Multiprocesser:** True *pre-emptive multitasking* enables the operating system's core to efficiently juggle several programs running at once. This is important for providing multiple services on one computer.

- **Multiplatform:** Linux currently runs on more than 24 *platforms* (hardware types), including 32- and 64-bit Intel-based PCs, Digital/Compaq Alpha, all variants of the Apple Macintosh, Sun SPARC, the Apple iPod, and even the Microsoft Xbox.

- **Interoperable:** Linux plays nice with most network protocols (languages) and operating systems, allowing you to interact with users and computers running Microsoft Windows, UNIX, Novell NetWare, Macintosh computers, and other groups that occupy smaller market niches.

- **Scalable:** As your computing needs grow, you can rely on Linux to grow with you. The same Linux operating system can run on a tiny electronic photo frame, a desktop computer, or a very large, industrial-strength server system.

- **Portable:** Linux is mostly written in the C programming language. *C* is a language created specifically for writing operating-system-level software and can be readily *ported* (translated) to run on new computer hardware.

- **Flexible:** You can configure the Linux operating system as a network host, router, graphical workstation, office productivity PC, home entertainment computer, file server, Web server, cluster, or just about any other computing appliance you can think of.

✔ **Stable:** The Linux *kernel* (the heart of the operating system) has achieved a level of maturity that makes most software developers envious. It's not uncommon to hear reports of Linux servers running for years without crashing.

✔ **Efficient:** The modular design of Linux enables you to include only the components needed to run your desired services. Even older Pentium computers can utilize Linux and become useful again.

✔ *Free!:* To most people, the most intriguing aspect of Linux is the fact that it's often available free of charge. How (the capitalists murmur) can anyone build a better mousetrap with no incentive of direct monetary return?

In this chapter, we intend to answer that last question for you. We also hope to paint a picture of the open-source software development model that created Linux.

So where did Linux come from?

Although programming of the Linux core started in 1991, the design concepts were based on the time-tested *UNIX* operating system. UNIX was developed at Bell Telephone Laboratories in the late 1960s. The original architects of UNIX, working back when there were few operating systems, wanted to create an operating system that shared data, programs, and resources both efficiently and securely — an ideal that wasn't available then (and is still sought after now). From there, UNIX evolved into many different versions; its current family tree is so complicated that it looks like a kudzu infestation.

In 1991, Linus Torvalds was a computer science student at the University of Helsinki in Finland. He wanted an operating system that was like the UNIX system that he'd grown fond of at the university, but both UNIX and the hardware it ran on were prohibitively expensive. A UNIX version called Minix was available for free, but it didn't quite meet his needs. So, Torvalds studied Minix and then set out to write a new version himself. In his own words (recorded for posterity on the Internet because this was in an early version of an online chat room), his work was "just a hobby, won't be big and professional like GNU."

Writing an operating system is no small task. Even after six months of hard work, Torvalds had made very little progress toward the general utility of the system. He posted what he had to the Internet — and found that many people shared his interest and curiosity. Before long, some of the brightest minds around the world were contributing to Linus's project by adding enhancements or fixing bugs (errors in the code).

Anatomy of an Open-Source Software Project

To the casual observer (and some corporate IT decision makers), Linux appears to be a freak mutation. How, after all, can something so complex and discipline-dependent as a computer operating system be developed by a loosely knit band of volunteer computer geeks from around the world?

Just as science is constantly attempting to classify and explain everything in existence, technology commentators are still trying to understand how the open-source approach can create superior software, especially in cases where no one is in charge. Often the reasons have much to do with the usual human desire to fill a need with a solution. When a programmer in the Linux world wants a tool, the programmer simply writes one — or bands together with other people who want a similar package, and they write it together.

GNU who?

Imagine software created out of *need* rather than projected profit. Even though UNIX ultimately became proprietary software, the motives for its creation were originally based on practical needs. What people usually refer to as *the Linux operating system* is actually a collection of software tools created with the express purpose of solving specific computing problems.

The speed of Linux's popularity also wouldn't be possible without the vision of Richard Stallman. Massachusetts Institute of Technology (MIT) has long held a reputation for nurturing the greatest minds in the technological disciplines. In 1984, Stallman, a gifted student and brilliant programmer at MIT, was faced with a dilemma — sell his talent to a company for a tidy sum of money or donate his gifts to the world.

Stallman set out on a journey to create a completely free operating system that he would donate to the world. He understands — and continues to live — the original hacker ethic, which declares that information wants to be free. This concept wasn't new in his time. In the early days of the computing industry, many advancements came from freely sharing ideas and programming code. Manufacturer-sponsored user groups brought the best minds together to solve complicated problems. This ethic, Stallman felt, was lost when companies began to hoard software as their own intellectual property with the single purpose of profit.

As you may or may not have gathered by this point, widespread and accessible source code is paramount to successful software development. *Source code* is the term for the human-readable text (as opposed to the unreadable cyber-hieroglyphics in an "executable" file) that a programmer types to communicate instructions to the computer.

Writing computer programs in binary is an extremely arduous task. Modern computer software is usually written in a human-friendly language and then *compiled,* or translated, into the computer's native instruction set. To make changes to this software, a programmer needs access to a program's source code. Most proprietary software comes only as a precompiled product; the software developer keeps the source code for those programs under lock and key.

After determining that his operating system would be built around the conceptual framework of UNIX, Stallman wanted the project name to distinguish his system from UNIX. So he chose the recursive acronym *GNU* (pronounced ga-*new*), which means "GNU's not UNIX."

To finance the GNU project, Stallman organized the Free Software Foundation (FSF), which sold free (that is, open-source) software to help feed the programmers who worked on its continuing development. (Remember, we're talking *free* as in *free speech,* not as in *free beer.*) Although this organization (and its goal of creating a complete operating system) was necessary and important, a much more important piece of the puzzle had to be put into place. The new software needed a license to protect it from big-business pirates — a concern still all too relevant today as a former Linux company tries to hijack ownership of decades of volunteer work from thousands of people around the world.

The *GNU General Public License* (GPL) is a unique and creative software license that uses copyright law to protect the freedom of the software user, which is usually the opposite of how a copyright works. Generally, a copyright is an enforceable designation of ownership and restriction from duplication by anyone but the copyright holder. When software is licensed under the GPL, recipients are bound by copyright law to respect the freedom of anyone else to use the software in any way they choose. Software licensed with the GPL is also known as copy*left* software (the reverse of *right*, get it?). Another way to remember the GPL is through its ultimate result: Guaranteed Public for Life.

While Stallman's work set the stage for Linux's rapid climb to popularity, the operating system he and his crew were working on took longer than expected. If you're interested in the completed version, go to `www.gnu.org/software/hurd/hurd.html`.

Who's in charge of Linux anyway?

As an open-source project evolves, various people emerge as leaders. This leader is known as the project's *benevolent dictator*. The benevolent dictator has probably spent more time than anyone else on a particular problem and often has some unique insight. Normally, the words *democratic* and *dictator* are never paired in the same sentence, but the open-source model is a very democratic process that endorses the reign of a benevolent dictator.

Linus Torvalds is still considered the benevolent dictator of the Linux kernel (the operating system's core). He ultimately determines what features are added to the kernel and what features aren't. The community trusts his vision and discretion. In the event that he loses interest in the project, or the community decides that he has gone senile, a new leader will emerge from amongst the very competent people working with him.

Einstein was a volunteer

Someone who is a volunteer or donates time to a project isn't necessarily providing a second-rate effort (or only working on weekends and holidays). In fact, any human-resources expert will tell you that people who choose to do a job of their own free will produce the highest-quality products.

The volunteers who contribute to open-source projects are often leaders in their fields who depend on community collaboration to get useful work done. The open-source concept is no stranger to the scientific community. The impartial peer-review process that open-source projects foster is critical in validating some new feature or capability as being technically correct.

Those who paint the open-source community as copyright violators and thieves often misunderstand — or outright ignore — these vital issues. Open-source programmers are very proud of their work *and* are also very concerned about their own copyrights, not wanting their work to be stolen by others — hence licenses such as the GPL. This concern creates an atmosphere with the greatest respect for copyright. Bandits who claim that they're "just being open-source" when they steal other people's hard work are grossly misusing the term to soothe their own consciences.

Many have also pointed out that if copyright is violated in open source, it's easy to tell. Watch the news and notice how often large software corporations are convicted of stealing other people's code and incorporating it into their own work. If the final product is open-source, it's easy for anyone to look and make sure nothing stolen is in it. As you might imagine, tracking down such copyright violations is much more difficult in a closed-source scheme.

Packaging Linux: The Distribution

A complete Linux system package is called a *distribution*. A Linux distribution contains the Linux kernel, the GNU project's tools, and any number of open-source software projects to provide diverse functionality for the system. By combining all the pieces into one package, you don't have to go hunting for the individual pieces across the Internet.

There are lots of different Linux distributions available to meet just about any computing requirement you could have. Most distributions are customized for specific user groups — such as business users, multimedia enthusiasts, software developers, or normal home users.

Each customized distribution includes the software packages required to support specialized functions, such as audio- and video-editing software for multimedia enthusiasts, or compilers and Integrated Development Environments (IDEs) for software developers.

The different Linux distributions are often divided into three categories:

- ✔ Core Linux distributions (more about the core in a minute)
- ✔ LiveCD test distributions
- ✔ Specialized distributions

The following sections describe these different types of Linux distributions, and show some examples of Linux distributions in each category.

A single Linux distribution often appears in several different versions to cover more ground. For example, Fedora releases both a full core distribution, as well as a LiveCD version that contains a subset of the full system. Many of the specialized Linux distributions (such as Ubuntu) are based on the Debian core Linux distribution. Ubuntu uses the same installation files as Debian, but packages only a small fraction of a full-blown Debian system.

Core Linux distributions

A *core* Linux distribution contains the Linux and GNU operating systems, one or more graphical desktop environments, and just about every Linux application that is available, ready to install and run. The core Linux distribution provides one-stop shopping for a complete Linux installation, no matter what your requirements are. Table 1-1 shows some of the more popular core Linux distributions out there.

Table 1-1	Core Linux Distributions	
Distribution	**Where to Find It**	**Description**
Slackware	www.slackware.com	One of the original Linux distribution sets, popular with Linux geeks.
Red Hat	www.redhat.com	A commercial business distribution used mainly for Internet servers.
Fedora	www.fedoraproject.org	A spinoff from Red Hat, designed for home use.
Gentoo	www.gentoo.org	A distribution designed for advanced Linux users, containing only Linux source code.
Mandriva	www.mandriva.com	Designed mainly for home use (previously called Mandrake).
openSuSe	www.opensuse.org	Different distributions for business and home use (now owned by Novell).
Debian	www.debian.org	Popular with Linux experts and commercial Linux product developers.

We use the Fedora Linux distribution in this book to illustrate how to work with a core Linux distribution.

In the early days of Linux, a distribution was released as a set of floppy disks. You had to download groups of files and then manually copy them onto disks. It would usually take 20 or more disks to make an entire distribution! Needless to say, this was a painful experience. Nowadays, with home computers commonly having CD and DVD players built in, Linux distributions are released as either a CD set or a single DVD. This makes installing Linux much easier.

The Linux LiveCD

While having lots of options available in a distribution is great for Linux geeks, it can become a nightmare for beginning Linux users. Most distributions ask a series of questions during the installation process to determine which applications to load by default, what hardware is connected to the computer, and how to configure the hardware. Beginners can often find these questions confusing. As a result, they often either load way too many programs on their computers or don't load enough and later discover that their computers won't do what they want them to do. Fortunately for beginners, there's a much simpler way to install Linux.

A relatively new phenomenon in the Linux world is the bootable Linux CD distribution, called a *LiveCD*. Most modern computers can start up by reading the operating system from the CD instead of the hard drive. This arrangement lets you see what a Linux system is like without actually installing it.

To take advantage of this feature, some Linux distributions create a bootable CD that contains a sample Linux system. Due to the limitations on the single CD size, the sample can't contain a complete Linux system, but you'd be surprised at all the software they can cram on there! The result is pretty cool: You can boot your computer from the CD and run a Linux distribution without having to install anything on your hard drive!

This is an excellent way to test various Linux distributions without having to mess with your PC. Just pop in a CD and boot! All the Linux software will run directly off the CD. There are lots of Linux LiveCDs that you can download from the Internet and burn onto a CD for a test drive. Table 1-2 shows some popular Linux LiveCDs that are available.

Table 1-2	Linux LiveCD Distributions	
Distribution	*Where to Find It*	*Description*
Knoppix	www.knoppix.net	A German Linux distribution, the first Linux LiveCD developed.
SimplyMEPIS	www.mepis.org	Designed for beginning home Linux users.
PCLinuxOS	www.pclinuxos.com	Full-blown Linux desktop workstation on a single CD.
Ubuntu	www.ubuntu.com	A worldwide Linux project, designed for many languages.
Slax	www.slax.org	A live Linux CD based on a subset of the Slackware Linux distribution.
Puppy Linux	www.puppylinux.org	A full-featured Linux distribution designed for older computers.

Some Linux LiveCD distributions, such as Ubuntu, allow you to install the Linux distribution directly from the LiveCD. This enables you to boot with the CD, test drive the Linux distribution, and then if you like it, install it onto your hard drive. This feature is extremely handy and user friendly.

We use the Ubuntu LiveCD distribution in this book to demonstrate using LiveCDs.

As with all good things, Linux LiveCDs have a few drawbacks. Because you access everything from the CD, applications run more slowly, especially if you're using older, slower computers and CD drives. Also, because you can't write to the CD, any changes you make to the Linux system will be gone the next time you reboot.

But advances are being made in the Linux LiveCD world that help to solve some of these problems:

- ✔ Copying Linux system files from the CD to memory to run faster
- ✔ Copying system files to a file on the hard drive to save them
- ✔ Storing system settings on a USB flash drive
- ✔ Storing user settings on a USB flash drive

Some Linux LiveCDs, such as Puppy Linux, are designed with a minimum number of Linux system files; they're copied directly into memory when the CD boots — and you can remove the CD from the computer as soon as Linux is done booting. Not only does this make your applications run much faster (because applications run faster in computer memory), it frees up your CD tray so you can use it for ripping audio CDs or playing video DVDs from the software included.

Specialized Linux distributions

Over the past few years, a new subgroup of Linux distributions has started to appear. These are typically based on one of the core distributions, but contain only a subset of applications that would make sense for a specific area of use.

Besides providing specialized software (for example, bundles of office products for business users), customized Linux distributions also attempt to help beginning Linux users by auto-detecting and auto-configuring common hardware devices. This makes installing Linux a much more enjoyable process.

Table 1-3 shows some of the specialized Linux distributions available and what they specialize in.

Table 1-3	Specialized Linux Distributions	
Distribution	*Where to Find It*	*Description*
Linspire	www.linspire.com	A commercial Linux package configured to look like Windows.
Xandros	www.xandros.com	A commercial Linux package preconfigured for beginners.
SimplyMEPIS	www.mepis.org	A desktop distribution for home users.
Ubuntu	www.ubuntu.com	A desktop and server distribution for school and home use.
PCLinuxOS	www.pclinuxos.com	A distribution focusing on home and office use.
gOS	www.thinkgos.com	A distribution designed for beginners, and pre-installed on some laptop and desktop systems.
Puppy Linux	www.puppylinux.org	A small distribution that runs well on older PCs.

That's just a small sampling of specialized Linux distributions. There are hundreds of specialized Linux distributions, with more popping up all the time on the Internet. No matter what your specialty, you'll probably find a Linux distribution made for you.

We use the gOS distribution in this book to see how some of the features in a specialized Linux distribution work. The gOS distribution includes the Google Desktop applet, which we discuss in Chapter 15.

Chapter 2

Prepping Your Computer for Linux

> *You got to be careful if you don't know where you are going, because you might not get there.*
>
> — Yogi Berra

One of the most important decisions you have to make when installing Linux is one that you make *before* you actually install Linux — that is, how you want to install it. That's right; it's not as easy as just tucking Linux onto your computer's hard drive and calling it a day. You can install Linux in many different ways; which one you pick depends entirely on your situation. But don't worry; with this chapter, you'll breeze through that decision.

Then, after you've made that important decision, we cover any preparation you have to do for that particular installation.

Choosing the Right Installation Approach

In this section, we give you a road map that tells you what's important for your particular situation. To install Linux permanently on an existing computer, you'll need to have an area of a hard drive already set up for it. There are three common ways to do this:

✔ Replace an existing operating system on the hard drive.

✔ Install Linux on a second hard drive.

✔ Partition an existing hard drive to include Linux.

And there are a couple uncommon solutions to installing Linux:

- ✔ Use a virtual-server software package to install Linux virtually.
- ✔ Add a partition as a normal file inside an existing Windows partition, and then install Linux as a Windows application.

If the thought of changing anything on your computer gives you hives, use a LiveCD *distribution* (see Chapter 1) to boot your computer into Linux without installing anything. Running Linux from a CD drive is slower (perhaps even painfully slow on an older computer), but nonetheless it works, and it gives you an idea of just what Linux is all about.

Replacing an existing operating system

If you have a spare computer that's only going to run Linux and nothing else, you're in luck! Replacing an existing operating system with Linux is the easiest way to install Linux on a computer. Most Linux installations even include an automatic process that guides you through converting a computer entirely to Linux. However, this is an all-or-nothing approach — you'll be replacing your existing operating system entirely with Linux!

If you *do* replace your existing operating system, be aware that when you're done, you won't have your original data files anymore! If you want to keep any files, you have to back them up to media that you can read from Linux. A USB flash drive is a great way to copy small amounts of data (up to 16GB or so) and move them onto your Linux system. For really large amounts of data, look into getting an external USB hard drive.

If you replace your existing operating system, you can skip the next section, "Preparing to Use Linux and Microsoft Windows Together." In fact, if you're feeling brave, you can skip right to Chapter 3 and start your installation. There's troubleshooting information in Chapter 22 as well.

Using a second hard drive or partitioning a hard drive

Installing Linux on a second hard drive — or, for that matter, partitioning your existing hard drive to run Linux — requires a *dual-boot* scenario: Both Linux and Microsoft Windows reside on hard drives (or partitions) in the same computer. When you boot the computer, a menu appears, asking you which operating system you want to use. You get to keep your original Windows applications and files, *and* use Linux — all on the same computer!

The scenario that many people prefer is to add a second, fresh hard drive on which to install Linux. This is by far the easiest solution for a dual-boot system, and one we recommend you use if at all possible.

If you're comfortable working with hard drives, you can always partition an existing hard drive to make room for Linux. *Partitioning* means having two or more logically separate areas on the same physical hard drive. The computer sees each partition as a separate disk. We tackle this process a little later in this chapter.

Just make a note of which drive is which as far as the computer sees them: You want to make sure that you leave your Microsoft Windows installation untouched. All you need to know is which drive (Windows or Linux) is first and which is second as far as the computer is concerned. You can find out about how to read the order information in the section "Partitioning an existing hard drive for a dual boot" later in this chapter. When you are sure you know which drive is which, proceed to the section "Double-Checking Hardware Compatibility" later in this chapter.

It's extremely important that you know *which* hard drive has your original Windows installation on it. When you load Linux, you don't want to accidentally install it over your original Windows drive! This is another reason it's important to back up any important files before starting this process. Accidents can (and often do) happen!

If you can't spare an entire hard drive for Linux and you already have Windows installed, you have to resize your current Windows installation. You need to work through this entire chapter.

Absolutely *DO NOT PROCEED TO CHAPTER 3* without at least reading the next section, "Preparing to Use Linux and Microsoft Windows Together." Sorry for yelling, but you can wipe out your whole Windows installation if you don't take precautions!

Other installing scenarios

If you absolutely don't want to dual-boot using your hard drive, you have three other options — we know we said that there were three approaches in total and adding three here brings us up to six, but give us a moment to explain.

You can use a *virtual server* software package, such as VMWare or Sun's VirtualBox (see Chapter 20) to install a "virtual" Linux machine that lives in a window inside your existing Windows installation. You keep your Windows disk as-is without any modifications. You just install Linux within the virtual area created by the VMWare or VirtualBox software.

You can also do the opposite — install only Linux on the computer and then use VMWare (see Chapter 20) to install a virtual Windows machine that lives in a window within your Linux installation.

If you take this approach, back up your original Windows files *before* installing Linux, and then restore them in the new Windows virtual machine.

Yet another option is a new feature included in the Ubuntu LiveCD. The *Windows Ubuntu Installer* (Wubi) is an application you can use to create the Ubuntu Linux partition as a normal file inside an existing Windows partition, after which it installs Linux *as a Windows application.* This cool new method lets you create a dual-boot scenario without having to partition any disks, and it's easily reversible (just uninstall Wubi).

Preparing to Use Linux and Microsoft Windows Together

If you're planning to run Linux and Microsoft Windows on the same machine, the odds are that you already have Windows installed and have been using it for some time. Because we hate to hear screams of anguish from new Linux users, take a moment to assess what you have and what you need. The following sections walk through the processes required to get your computer ready for a dual-boot environment.

On the off chance that you actually don't have Windows installed yet and still want dual-boot capability, you should install Windows *before* you install Linux. Otherwise, during installation, Windows overwrites the part of your hard drive that Linux uses to store its *boot menu.* (This factor can create a mess later when you want to boot back into Linux!) Then after you have Windows installed, return here.

Installing a second hard drive

Next to replacing the existing operating system, the second easiest way to get Linux onto a computer is to install a second hard drive. Many computers support multiple hard drives, whether chained together on the same disk cable or connected via multiple cables.

Usually you can determine how your disk controller is configured by looking at the BIOS setup screen for your computer. The BIOS setup screen controls the basic hardware configuration on the computer. Figure 2-1 shows an example of the disk-controller area on a BIOS screen.

```
                       PhoenixBIOS Setup Utility
   Main      Advanced    Security    Power    Boot    Exit

                                              Item Specific Help
   System Time:               [14:59:47]
   System Date:               [06/11/2008]
                                              <Tab>, <Shift-Tab>, or
   Legacy Diskette A:         [1.44/1.25 MB  3½"]   <Enter> selects field.
   Legacy Diskette B:         [Disabled]

 ▶ Primary Master            [VMware Virtual ID]
 ▶ Primary Slave             [None]
 ▶ Secondary Master          [VMware Virtual ID]
 ▶ Secondary Slave           [None]

 ▶ Keyboard Features

   System Memory:            640 KB
   Extended Memory:          396288 KB
   Boot-time Diagnostic Screen:  [Disabled]


 F1  Help    ↑↓  Select Item   -/+    Change Values    F9   Setup Defaults
 Esc Exit    ↔   Select Menu    Enter  Select ▶ Sub-Menu  F10  Save and Exit
```

Figure 2-1:
The BIOS hard drive configuration area.

How you get to the BIOS screen depends on your computer. All it takes is pressing a secret key (usually F12 or ESC) when your computer first starts. Sometimes the computer tells you on-screen what key to press to enter the BIOS. Other times you have to consult your owner's manual.

If you can't figure out your hard drive setup using the BIOS, you have to crack open your computer's case and take a look inside to see what you're up against. The standard disk-controller cards in most computers allow up to two devices per controller; often computers have more than one controller installed on the motherboard. If you see two cables with the long multi-pin connectors in them, you're in luck. If you see only one cable with an empty connector on it, you should be okay also.

The example in Figure 2-1 shows two hard drive controllers, called a primary and a secondary. The primary hard drive controller contains the hard drive that's used to boot the computer. Each hard drive controller can support two devices (called a master and a slave). This setup allows you to connect a total of four separate devices to the computer.

Besides the hard drive, controllers also support connecting CD/DVD drives. Be careful to take these drives into account when you evaluate your disk-controller situation.

After you get the second hard drive installed, you're ready to get going with Linux. Just skip to the "Double-Checking Hardware Compatibility" section to check on the rest of your computer hardware.

Partitioning from scratch for a dual boot

If you plan to install both Windows and Linux on your hard drive, *be sure to install Windows first.* While you're going through the Windows installation, you're asked to *partition* your hard drive (use the software to divide one large drive into smaller virtual drives). When you have your partitions ready, you have a place to put Linux.

Three types of partitions are available: primary, extended, and logical. A hard drive can have three *primary* partitions and one *extended* partition. Inside the extended partition, you can have up to 12 *logical* partitions — think of an extended partition as just a cardboard box that contains the logical partitions. Logical partitions hold data; extended partitions hold logical partitions.

Because we can't predict what software you want to install, we recommend having at least 10GB of space available for your Linux installation. More is always better because it gives you more room for downloads and even more programs, and, at the very least, you can install everything from this book's companion DVD-ROM into that 10GB.

Make a note of the partition you dedicate to Windows and the one you dedicate to Linux. Jot down which hard drive each partition is on (the first, second, third, and so on) and the number of each partition on the disk (first, second, and so on). You need this information when you're installing Linux.

You are not limited to a dual boot. You can have three or more operating systems on the computer if you have room.

Partitioning an existing hard drive for a dual boot

If you aren't starting from scratch for a dual boot, you probably need to make changes to your current installation. Before you change anything, be sure you collect some important information about your current setup — in particular, these two major things: (a) whether you have any unpartitioned space left on your hard drive(s) and (b) if you do, how much.

If you discover at least 10GB of unpartitioned space, you can skip straight to the "Double-Checking Hardware Compatibility" section later in this chapter. Otherwise, check out the "Making space" and "Defragmenting files" sections to make space for Linux.

You probably want *more* than 10GB of space. For example, if you download lots of multimedia content, you'll quickly eat up whatever was left after you installed your software. Practically speaking, 20GB might be a better amount to shoot for — *at minimum.*

Peeking at your partitions in Windows Vista

The Windows Vista operating system is more security minded than previous versions of Windows. No surprise that you have to use an account with administrative privileges to follow the steps. After you've logged into such an account, do the following:

1. **Open the Control Panel by choosing Start⇨Control Panel.**

   The Vista Control Panel opens.

2. **Select Classic View if necessary.**

3. **Double-click Administrative Tools.**

   The window displays the various administrative tools available in Vista.

4. **Double-click Computer Management.**

   The window displays the various tools available in Vista to manage your computer. (You may have to click Continue to get to this dialog box.)

5. **In the left pane, select Disk Management.**

   The Disk Management tool opens (see Figure 2-2).

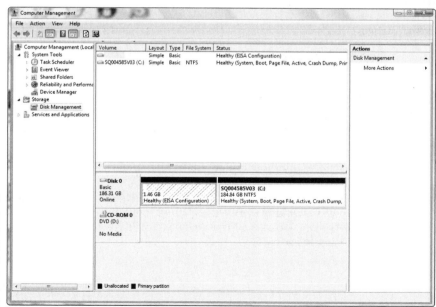

Figure 2-2:
The Windows Vista Disk Management tool.

If you look through the Disk 0, Disk 1, and Disk 2 listings, you see that one of the boxes says `C:` (which may be hauntingly familiar to Windows veterans). That's the Vista installation. You may also see some boxes that say `Unallocated`. They are free space that isn't being used for anything.

If you find an unallocated partition of 10GB or larger, make a note of which disk this partition is on and the numbered partition it occupies on that disk. You need that information to install Linux in Chapter 3.

If a tool says a partition cannot be resized, don't count that space toward your Linux installation. Do not try to resize Windows Vista partitions unless a tool specifically states that it can safely do so. You may damage the partition so Vista can't read it.

Peeking at your partitions in Windows 2000 and Windows XP

The Windows 2000 and XP operating systems only allow certain accounts to control and secure the files and folders; to get information about the computer's disk-space usage, first you have to be logged on as the Administrator (or use an account that has administrative permissions). After you log on, follow these steps:

1. **Open the Control Panel by choosing Start⇨Settings⇨Control Panel.**

2. **Open the Administrative Tools folder and double-click the Computer Management icon.**

3. **In the left pane of the Computer Management application, click the Disk Management folder icon.**

   Within a few seconds, the right pane displays the current status of the storage devices on your computer, such as the hard drive(s), CD drive(s), DVD/CD drive(s), and so on. Figure 2-3 shows the Windows XP Disk Management display; Windows 2000 users see a nearly identical view.

The important thing to look for here is the word *Unallocated* in the Disk listing. Unallocated partitions are not assigned to any operating system and are available for use in your Linux installation. Look in the Capacity, Free Space, and % columns. Here you can see how much space you've already used in each partition and how much you have available.

If you do find an unallocated partition, *and* it's 10GB or larger, you're all set. Make a note of which disk this partition is on and what its partition number is on that disk. You use that information when you install your Linux distribution in Chapter 3.

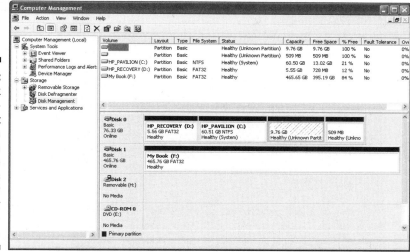

Figure 2-3:
Disk
Management
information
as seen
in the
Windows
XP
Computer
Management
tool.

Peeking at your partitions in Windows 98

Even though Microsoft no longer supports Windows 9*x*, an old computer that's running Windows 98 can make a good Linux box. Unfortunately, Windows 98 doesn't provide a graphical tool. Instead, Win98 uses FDISK, a command-line tool that indicates the partitions on your hard drive.

Be *very* careful in FDISK. You can wipe out your data if you make any changes with it. When you're exiting the program, *be sure not to save any changes*.

To find out the details about a computer's hard drive in Windows 98, follow these steps:

1. **Open an MS-DOS prompt window by choosing Start➪Programs➪ MS-DOS Prompt.**

2. **Type** FDISK **and press Enter.**

   In Windows 98, you can enter FDISK in uppercase, lowercase, or any mixed case you like as long as you spell FDISK correctly!

   You're very likely prompted to display large "disk" (drive) information — "large" is relative to what was a big hard drive at the time of Windows 98, which means a drive larger than 512MB. If you don't see the prompt, skip to Step 4, and the FDISK menu options will be similar to Figure 2-4.

3. **If you see the large disk prompt, choose Y at this prompt and then press Enter.**

   The FDISK menu options appear, as shown in Figure 2-4.

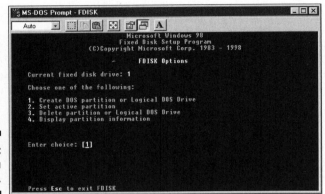

Figure 2-4:
FDISK menu
options.

4. **Display the current drive-partition information.**

    If you have more than one hard drive in your computer, FDISK displays a fifth menu choice so you can change between disks.

   Here's how to use the fifth menu choice to change to another disk:

   a. *Type 5 and press Enter.*

      The FDISK screen displays all the hard drives in your system.

   b. *Type the number of the disk you want and then press Enter.*

      The top of the FDISK menu screen displays the number of the drive that FDISK is working with.

5. **To display partition information for the disk number displayed, type** 4 **and press Enter.**

   Figure 2-5 shows an example of the Display Partition Information screen within FDISK.

   Figure 2-5 indicates that no free, unallocated disk space is available on the drive. If the disk had unpartitioned space, FDISK would display how much.

   If you have an extended partition on the disk, you'll have to dig deeper.

6. **To view the logical partitions within the extended partition, select the** EXT DOS **entry and press Enter.**

You can tell whether there's free space by totaling the Usage percentages for the drive.

- If the total is 100 percent, no space is available.

- If you have 10GB or more available, you have enough space.

Making space

Ultimately you may have to resize your partitions — for one of several reasons:

✓ You may have some unallocated space but less than 10GB of it.

✓ You may have 10GB of unallocated space, but it's broken up into numerous pieces across your drives and needs to be consolidated.

✓ You may not have any unallocated space at all (the most common reason).

In all these situations, you need to move data around to make room — not only to install Linux but also to store any files you want to keep in your Linux filesystem.

The key is to determine if you have extra space available on your existing C: drive that you can convert into a separate partition. All the Windows operating systems allow you to easily see how much space is available on the C: drive.

Windows XP, 2000, and Vista provide that information in the Computer Management tool; see the "Partitioning an existing hard drive for a dual boot" section, earlier in this chapter.

If you're bringing a venerable Windows 98 and 95 machine back to dual-boot life, use the Computer Management tool this way:

1. **Double-click My Computer to open the Computer Management tool.**

2. **Choose View⇨Web Page.**

3. **Highlight your first drive.**

   You see something like what is shown in Figure 2-6.

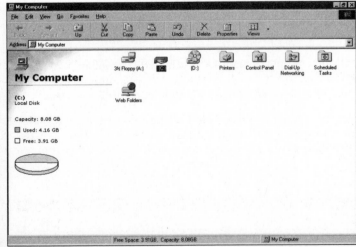

Figure 2-6:
Here's how much disk space is available on this Windows 98 user's C: drive.

Determining how much space is enough for your Windows setup — you don't want to shrink it so much that you run out of space in Windows — also involves taking a look at how you use your machine. Again, if you download and save a lot of multimedia stuff, it's wise to keep enough room around to accommodate your downloading habit.

If you find that your Windows drives are all too full and you have no room to spare (or you download and save too many audio, video, or graphics files), it may be time to save some of your files to CDs or DVDs so you can delete them from your hard drive. The other option is to add a second drive to the computer — if you're not comfortable doing this yourself, many stores will install a drive for you for a fee.

Defragmenting files

During the normal course of using your workstation, the Windows system writes pieces of files at random places on the hard drive. This can spread data out over the entire disk. Before you split the hard drive into partitions, you need to ensure that you don't lose any of the data that Windows strewed around the drive — and that includes both system and data files.

To make a cleanly partitioned hard drive, first you'll need to make sure that all your Windows data is moved toward the beginning of the hard drive. This is commonly done using a *defragmenting tool*.

Defragmenting is a common process in the Windows world. It's the process of realigning how files are stored on the hard drive. As Windows creates and removes files, file data gets split into various blocks scattered around the hard drive. Defragmenting reassembles the blocks so they form contiguous files, and puts those files in an equally contiguous area near the beginning of the hard drive area.

All versions of Windows include a utility for defragmenting the hard drive. You can get to the defragmentation utility from the Computer Management window. Just select the Disk Defragmenter option.

In Windows Vista, disk defragmenting happens behind the scenes, without any indication of what's going on. Windows XP provides a handy defragmenter window that shows progress as files are moved about, as shown in Figure 2-7.

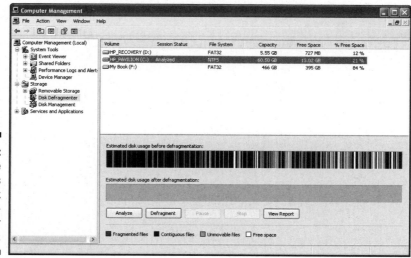

Figure 2-7:
The Windows XP Disk Defragmenter utility.

Figure 2-8 shows the Disk Defragmenter in Windows 98.

Often it takes more than one pass to get all the files into a common area. After defragmentation is complete, your files are in a contiguous area at the beginning of the disk space — and you're ready to partition the hard drive as part of the Linux installation.

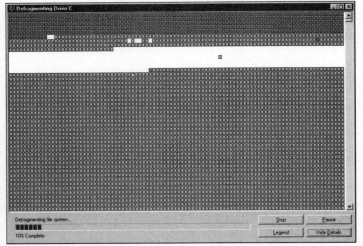

Figure 2-8:
The
Windows 98
Disk Defrag-
menter
utility.

Double-Checking Hardware Compatibility

If you're installing Linux on hardware you already own, just give it a try and then see what does and doesn't work. Parts of this section can help you out; they address fixing general hardware problems. Other chapters address more specific hardware issues such as sound cards (Chapter 13), wireless cards (Chapter 9), and so on. If you run into trouble, start in the specific sections dedicated to particular tasks, and then come here for more general help if you still haven't solved the problem.

The biggest problem areas are wireless cards and the *very* latest whiz-bang multimedia hardware — such as fancy new versions of video cards, sound cards, and image scanners. You can check hardware compatibility lists before purchasing new hardware, but they're of limited use because the hardware world changes so quickly. If you're interested in looking at a general list, go to the Red Hat Enterprise Linux listings at `http://hardware.redhat.com/hcl/`. (There's no official Fedora list.) Keep in mind that this list focuses on business equipment, so just because you don't see something listed there doesn't mean it's not supported.

Don't worry about whether particular devices have been *Certified* (heavily tested to make sure they work properly). *Supported* and *Compatible* are fine most of the time for a home user. Ultimately, the best way to tell whether a piece of hardware is supported is to do a Web search. Go to `www.google.com/linux` and do a Web search on the make and model of the hardware; include the word *Linux* in the search phrase. For example, you can search on "Innovision DX700T Linux" to find out how other people are faring with this particular brand and model of hardware. (No endorsement of any hardware mentioned as examples is implied here, of course.) Such a search is likely to show you what problems and successes people have run into with that particular piece of hardware.

If even thinking about computer hardware gives you dizzy spells, don't worry; you can find plenty of information on the Internet. A great place to start is `www.tomshardware.com`. Other places to look for information on how various devices work in Linux include the following:

✓ **Other Linux-oriented Web sites:** In particular, the generic Linux hardware list at `www.tldp.org/HOWTO/Hardware-HOWTO/`.

✓ **Vendor Web sites:** Many hardware vendors support Linux, but they don't make it easy to find information. In general, go to the vendor's forum for the piece of hardware, the FAQ for the hardware, or follow the Support links to look for downloads for Linux. Don't download what you find if there are downloads. The point is to look and see whether they exist. The *driver* (the software that tells the operating system how to use the hardware) for download might actually be included in your Linux installation. Only download the driver from the vendor if this is the only way you can get it.

If worst comes to worst, you might not find any information on the hardware in question involving Linux. However, this doesn't mean that the hardware won't work. Try it anyway if you already have the item. You may find that it works fine. Or you might not be able to use the very latest features, whereas the rest works just fine (for example, with a latest-generation video card, the newest fancy features might not work, but you can still use it as a generic SVGA at the very least).

✓ **The dreaded manuals:** When possible, keep your computer manuals (especially those for your video card and monitor) handy, just in case you need them for answering a question asked by the installer (most Linux users don't have to deal with this scenario, but some do).

Laptop considerations

The current distributions of Linux do very well on relatively new notebooks and laptops. (See www.linux-laptop.net for an excellent research site on how Linux gets along with various makes and models.) If your laptop is a common brand, you shouldn't encounter any problems installing Linux. However, laptops often contain WinModems. (Hardware labeled with the *Win* prefix is *only for Windows,* so it can't figure out what to do with Linux.)

If you plan to purchase a laptop for Linux, check out its modem and other hardware (such as network cards) to make sure they're not Win-branded. If the built-in or default hardware for the laptop is Win-labeled (or you discover, while researching the machine, that it *contains* a Win product, even one that isn't properly labeled), you might be able to switch the offending hardware for a PCMCIA (Personal Computer Memory Card International Association) card. This is a standard for laptops, and provides a way to plug in additional feature cards. Most current laptops contain at least one PCMCIA card slot to give you a place to slip in a PCMCIA card modem, network card, or combo modem-network card. As long as you stick with a common brand of PCMCIA card, it should work well with Linux.

If you need to find out exactly what hardware is in your machine, you have the following options:

- ✔ **Use an existing operating system to document your hardware.** If your computer is already running Windows, you can collect a lot of information from the Windows environment. Use one of the following methods, depending on your system:

  - *In Windows 98:* Choose Start⇨Settings⇨Control Panel⇨System⇨ Device Manager to access the dialog box shown in Figure 2-9.

  - *In Windows XP:* Right-click the My Computer desktop icon, and select Manage to open the Computer Management dialog box. Then choose the Device Manager menu to access the list of hardware installed on your machine (as shown in Figure 2-10).

    You can double-click each item within the Device Manager to display the corresponding details.

  - *In Windows Vista:* Choose Start⇨Control Panel⇨Device Manager to browse your hardware. A warning dialog box will appear; when it does, click Continue.

- ✔ **Download a hardware-detection tool.** If you don't have any diagnostic tools, you can download various hardware-detection tools, such as Dr. Hardware, from the Internet. The Dr. Hardware tool contains lots of information about what's inside your machine. This tool is shareware, and the usage and fee information is available from the Gebhard Software Web site at www.dr-hardware.com.

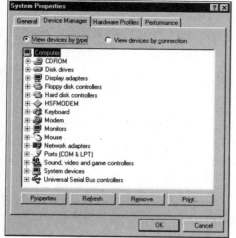

Figure 2-9:
In Windows
98, the
Device
Manager
gives you
information
on the hard-
ware you've
installed.

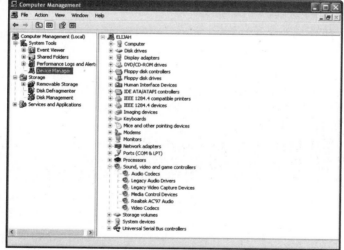

Figure 2-10:
The
Windows
XP Device
Manager.

✔ **Gather information by reading the screen when the computer starts.**
If your system doesn't contain any operating systems and you don't
have any of your system's documentation, you can resort to reading the
screen as your computer starts. On some systems, the video information is displayed from the BIOS as the computer boots. You may have to
reboot several times to read the information if it goes by too fast. Also,
some systems display the PCI components and their settings as the
system is starting up. You may have to reboot several times to gather all
the information.

You can try pressing the Pause-Break key on your keyboard (it should be near the Scroll Lock key) to freeze the scrolling during boot. You can then unfreeze it by pressing any key when you have finished reading.

✓ **Access the Basic Input/Output System (BIOS) information.** Stored in a small area of memory and retained by a battery, this is sometimes referred to as CMOS (Complementary Metal-Oxide Semiconductor), which indicates the type of computer chip that can store and retain information. The amount of information stored in the BIOS can range from very little to quite a lot. Some newer systems may display several screens of BIOS information about the computer's hardware.

If you choose to access the BIOS, make sure you do so *before any operating systems load.* Most manufacturers indicate the keyboard key (or key sequence) that gets you into the BIOS (or Setup) on-screen when the system is starting up — for example, `Press Del to enter Setup`. If you can't find the keyboard sequence, check the manufacturer's Web site. After you've entered the BIOS, you typically navigate around with the arrow keys, Tab key, or Enter key. Some BIOS environments also use the function keys; look for a list of function-key options at the top or bottom of the screen.

Be especially leery of labels on hardware boxes and Web sites that include the term *Win* (as in *Windows*). These components, such as *WinModems,* rely on Microsoft Windows to be able to function — even worse, the packaging may show nothing that suggests this limitation. Only a very slight chance exists that you can find a Linux driver for *Win* hardware. If you do find one, copy it to a storage device such as a CD or flash drive *before* you install Linux. If you can't find a driver and you need to use a modem, put down a little cash and get a modem that is supported properly. (For more information about WinModems in particular, see Chapter 8.)

Finally, Before You Get Started

The bootable first CD or DVD is the final thing you need to have handy before proceeding to install Linux. This book's DVD contains ISO images of both the Ubuntu LiveCD and the Fedora full distribution DVD. You need to copy these disc images to your hard drive before you burn them onto separate bootable CD or DVDs. If your computer doesn't have a DVD-ROM drive capable of burning discs, see Appendix B for various other options.

Now, before you go any further, there's one more thing we need you to do: Make sure you have access to help from the Linux online community. Go to the following sites and bookmark them so you can easily reference them if you need help:

- **The Ubuntu Project:** http://www.ubuntu.com
- **The Fedora Project:** http://fedoraproject.org
- **The gOS Project:** http://www.thinkgos.com
- **The Fedora Project Wiki:** http://fedoraproject.org/wiki/

  A *wiki* is a Web page (or collection of Web pages) maintained collectively, where anyone can make changes (or a group of designated people can, depending on how the wiki is set up). Wikis are becoming popular for generating community-based support sites because anyone with the desire to contribute can pitch in with a minimum of hassle.

- **The Ubuntu Project Wiki:** https://wiki.ubuntu.com
- **LinuxQuestions.org:** linuxquestions.org

Chapter 3

Installing Linux

· ·

· ·

Do, or do not. There is no "try."

— Yoda, *The Empire Strikes Back*

No longer are arcane glyphs and complex sorcerer's spells required to install Linux. The graphical installation is now quite easy to perform and will be familiar to you if you're coming from another graphical operating system, such as Microsoft Windows. This chapter provides the details.

The installer is actually pretty smart. You may find that you don't see exactly the same screens that we show in this chapter. If you see something unfamiliar or don't see a screen that we cover here, don't panic. The installer is just adjusting what it offers based on the hardware in your system and what you choose to install.

In this chapter, we show you how to install a Linux desktop on your personal computer. If you want to install a Linux server on your network, plenty of other books focus on servers. It is just not possible to cover both desktop and server functions to a satisfying depth in a book of this size.

Things to Consider Before You Begin Installation

There are two ways you can install Linux from the DVD-ROM included with this book:

- ✔ Copy the Ubuntu LiveCD ISO image from the DVD-ROM, burn it to CDs, and then boot from the CDs to install Ubuntu.
- ✔ Copy the Fedora full installation DVD image from the DVD-ROM, burn it to CDs, and then boot from the CDs to install Fedora.

To begin the installation from the CD-ROMs that you create from the ISO image, you may first need to change your system to start (that is *boot*) from a CD-ROM. Many systems today are configured to do this already, so you may not need to make any changes. For some systems, you need to press a key during the boot process to bring up a menu, which allows you to select which device to boot from. If your boot screen doesn't list the key to press, consult your system's owner's manual for more information.

In this chapter, we concentrate on three different installation methods — installing Ubuntu from the LiveCD image, installing Fedora from an installation DVD-ROM, and installing Ubuntu using the Wubi package. We selected these methods for two reasons:

- ✔ The Ubuntu LiveCD installation and the Fedora full-installation methods represent the two main ways to install most Linux systems.
- ✔ Covering the installation of every Linux distribution in existence would make this book into a set of encyclopedias.

Once you get the hang of installing Linux using these methods, you can tackle just about any Linux installation out there.

If you're installing another version of Ubuntu or Fedora, or a different distribution of Linux altogether, your screens *will* look different from what is shown in this book. Each Linux distribution's installation routine covers the same basic tasks, but the specific actions may be presented in a different order, or they may be customized to look different on-screen. For example, one distribution may present account creation before disk partitions; another may reverse the order of those two topics. Most distributions go through the same basic choices, so reading this chapter could still be helpful for something other than Ubuntu or Fedora.

Dealing with damaged CDs or DVDs

If your CDs or DVD appears to have a problem, what you do next depends on where you got the DVD or CDs. If the DVD came with this book, contact Wiley Customer Care at 877-762-2974 to get the disc replaced. Do not contact Red Hat's technical support to have the DVD replaced in this case.

On the other hand, if you burned your own CDs or DVD, you may be experiencing one of two different problems. First, the burn may have become corrupted; to solve this problem, try burning the disc again at a slower speed. If the newly burned disc also fails the media check, the file(s) may have become corrupted during download. To solve this problem, download the disc image again.

Installing from an Ubuntu LiveCD

The Ubuntu installation process is one of the simplest in the Linux world. Ubuntu guides you through all the steps required to set up the system, and then installs the entire Ubuntu system without prompting you for too much information.

You can start the installation process from two locations in the LiveCD:

- Directly from the boot menu without starting Ubuntu
- From the Install desktop icon after you start the Ubuntu system

Both locations start the same installation process, which guides you through seven steps of options.

Burning your image

The Ubuntu LiveCD and Fedora full installation supplied on the DVD-ROM included with this book are *ISO image files*. An ISO image file is a copy of a CD-ROM saved as a file. This is a common format used for distributing Linux distributions.

The trick is getting the ISO image burned onto a CD-ROM that you can boot from. You can't just copy the file over, you must use a CD-burning software package that can burn ISO images. Consult the directions for your CD-burning software to find out how to burn an ISO image to a CD-ROM disk.

If your particular CD-burning software package doesn't burn CD images, Ubuntu recommends InfraRecorder (`infrarecorder.source forge.net`), free CD image-burning software.

When you have a LiveCD in your hand, you can start the installation process. Just follow these steps:

1. **Place the Ubuntu LiveCD in the CD tray of your computer, and restart your computer.**

   Your computer boots from the Ubuntu LiveCD, and after you select the language you want to use, the main Ubuntu LiveCD menu appears, shown in Figure 3-1.

2. **From the menu, choose either to install Ubuntu directly (Install Ubuntu) or to try Ubuntu first by running it from the LiveCD (Try Ubuntu without Any Change to Your Computer).**

   The great feature about the LiveCD is that you can test-drive Ubuntu without having to mess with your hard drive — which can give you an idea of what will work and what won't. After you've completed your test drive, if you decide to install Ubuntu, just click the Install icon on the desktop.

Figure 3-1:
The Ubuntu
LiveCD boot
menu.

When you start the Ubuntu installation, the first window you get is the Language window.

3. **Select the language to use for the installation, then click Forward.**

   This selects the language Ubuntu uses to display text messages used during the installation process, plus sets the default language used when the operating system runs.

Choosing a default language doesn't necessarily mean that all applications running on the system will use that language. Each individual application may or may not detect the default language configured in Ubuntu.

The second window in the installation process allows you to select the time zone for your area.

4. Select a time zone and then click Forward.

This window allows you to select your location via either the map or the drop-down menu. Although selecting the time zone from the graphical map sounds like a good idea, it can often be a challenge, depending on how many cities Ubuntu recognizes around your particular city.

Next in the installation process is identifying the keyboard you'll use with the Ubuntu system. While this may sound like a simple option, it can get complicated if you have a keyboard that includes special keys. Ubuntu recognizes hundreds of different keyboard types, and it lists them all in the keyboard selection window.

5. Select a keyboard, then click Forward.

The Keyboard configuration window lists the different types of keyboards commonly used based on your country. Ubuntu provides a suggested option for you based on what it detects as your keyboard. This may or may not be right. If you want to fine-tune things, the lower portion of the window allows you to experiment. On the left side is a list of countries; on the right side is a list of the different known keyboard types used in the country selected. Select your country from the left-side list first; then select your keyboard type from the right-side list.

You can click in the right-side list and start to type the name of your keyboard type to jump quickly to that selection.

Under the two listings is an area where you can test the keyboard selection. Just type any special or unique characters available on your keyboard to see whether the setting you selected produces the proper characters.

The next step in the installation is quite possibly the most important, and the most complicated. You tell the Ubuntu installer exactly where to place the Ubuntu operating system on your system. One bad move here can really ruin your day.

The exact partition window you get during the installation depends on your hard drive's configuration. If you went through the steps in Chapter 2, you should be all set for this step. Figure 3-2 shows an example of what the partition window looks like.

6. Select a disk setup method and then click Forward.

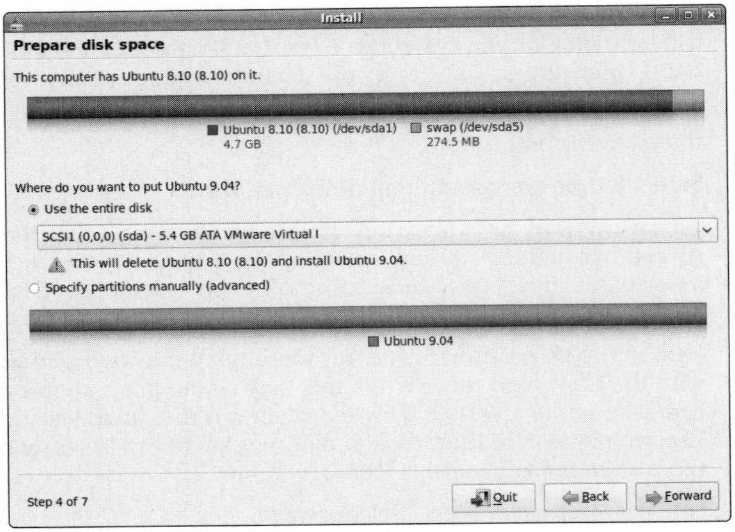

Figure 3-2:
The
Ubuntu disk
partition
window.

The Ubuntu disk partition window starts out with at least two possible selections:

- *A guided partition to install Ubuntu on the entire hard drive:* By default, Ubuntu offers a guided partition where it automatically reformats the entire hard drive on the system for Ubuntu. If you want to run an Ubuntu-only workstation, this is the quickest and easiest way to go. If you select this method, skip to Step 11.

  Be careful — this is the default installation option! When you choose to install Ubuntu on the entire hard drive, any previously installed operating system (and data) will be removed. Be sure to back up any important files you have before you do the Ubuntu installation.

- *A manual partition to create your own partitions:* If you select the manual partition process, Ubuntu turns control of the partition process over to you. It provides a partition utility, shown in Figure 3-3, for you to create, edit, or delete hard-drive partitions. The manual partition utility displays the current hard drives, along with any existing partitions configured in them. Each hard drive appears as a separate item in the partition listing and is assigned a device name (such as sda for the first hard drive and sdb for the second hard drive). You can manually remove, modify, or create individual partitions on any hard drives installed on the system.

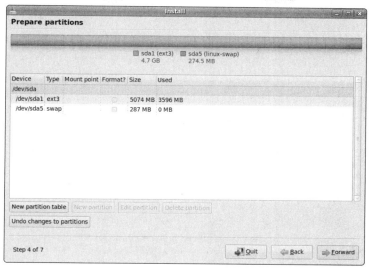

Figure 3-3:
The Ubuntu
manual par-
tition utility.

If you choose to partition an existing operating system, remember that bad things can (and often do) happen. Even though you plan on keeping the existing operating system, it's a good idea to make a complete backup of your existing operating system before performing the partition process.

If you're performing a manual partition, continue with Step 7.

Be sure you remember your disk-space requirements (determined in Chapter 2) to use here! We recommend at least 10GB of space for a minimal Ubuntu installation, 20GB would be better if you're planning on saving lots of image or audio files.

7. **If you're performing a manual partition, click the Edit Partition and Delete Partition buttons to manipulate the existing partitions on your hard drive.**

   To resize an existing Windows partition, select the partition from the partition list, and then click the Edit Partition button. You can then resize the partition to the amount you want to free up space (make sure you freed up the space as shown in Chapter 2) to create a new partition.

8. **When you have empty space on the hard drive, or if you have a second hard drive, click the New Partition button to create the new partition.**

   The Create Partition window appears, allowing you to select the size of the new partition. You can add the new partition to the empty space on the first hard drive, or add it to the second hard drive.

9. **Select a filesystem for your Ubuntu partition in the Create Partition window.**

   Part of the manual partition process is to assign a filesystem to each partition. A *filesystem* is a method used for storing and accessing files on the partition; lots of different filesystem formats are available. Unlike some other operating systems, Ubuntu supports several different filesystems. Table 3-1 shows the filesystem types available for you when creating disk partitions in Ubuntu.

Table 3-1	Ubuntu Partition Filesystem Type
Partition Type	*Description*
ext3	A popular Linux journaling filesystem (more about that in a minute) that is an extension over the original Linux ext2 filesystem.
ext4	The newest Linux journaling filesystem that makes improvements over the Linux ext3 filesystem.
ext2	The original non-journaling Linux filesystem.
ReiserFS	The first journaling filesystem supported in Linux.
JFS	The Journaled filesystem, created by IBM and used in AIX UNIX systems.
XFS	A high-performance journaling filesystem created by Silicon Graphics for the IRIX operating system.
FAT16	Older Microsoft DOS filesystem.
FAT32	Newer Microsoft DOS filesystem compatible with Microsoft Windows.
swap area	Virtual memory area.
Do not use	Ignore the partition, such as if you're going to install another operating system on it later.

The most common partition type (and the default used by the Ubuntu guided methods) is the ext3 format. This format provides Ubuntu with a *journaling filesystem* that records file changes in a log file before it attempts to commit them to the disk. If the system should crash before it can properly commit the data, the filesystem uses the journal (that is, the log file) to finish committing the pending files to disk; then it returns the disk to a normal state. Journaling filesystems greatly reduce file corruption in Linux.

10. If you're performing a manual partition, select the mount points for the partitions in the Create Partition window.

Ubuntu handles hard drives by plugging them into specific locations in the virtual filesystem (see Chapter 6). So, after you select a filesystem format for the partition, Ubuntu wants to know where to place the new partition in the virtual filesystem (called *mounting*). Table 3-2 lists the possible locations.

Table 3-2	Mount-Point Locations for Your Filesystem
Location	**Description**
/	The root of the Linux virtual filesystem.
/boot	The location of the Linux kernel used for booting the system.
/home	User directories for storing personal files and settings for individual applications.
/tmp	Temporary files used by applications and the Linux system.
/usr	A common location for multiuser application files.
/var	The variable directory, commonly used for log files.
/opt	Optional package-installation directory for third-party applications.
/usr/local	A common alternative location for installations of optional multiuser packages.

If you create just one partition for Ubuntu, you must mount it at the *root mount point* (/). If you have additional partitions available, you can mount them in other locations within the virtual filesystem by specifying them individually. Be careful, as you need to make sure you leave enough disk space for each mount point. For example, the /home mount point will contain all of the files used by individual users on the system. That could be a lot if you store lots of files.

Don't forget to allocate a partition for the swap area, even if you already have lots of physical memory installed on your system. The standard rule is to create as large of a swap area as you have physical memory. Thus, if you have 2GB of physical memory, create a 2GB partition and assign it as the swap area.

Up next in the installation process is the login ID window, shown in Figure 3-4.

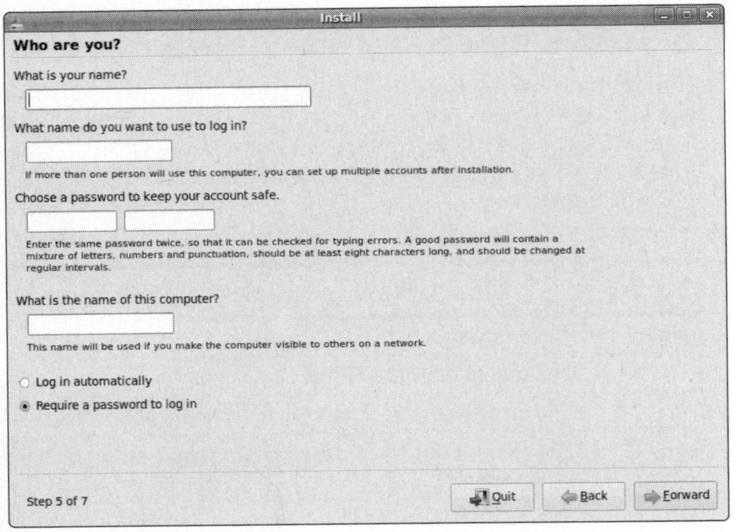

Figure 3-4:
The login ID
window.

11. **Create a login ID, then click Forward.**

The login user ID you create in this process is somewhat important.
Unlike some other Linux distributions, the Ubuntu distribution doesn't
use an administrator login account (usually called *root* in the UNIX/
Linux world). Instead, Ubuntu gives normal user accounts the option
of belonging to a group of administrator accounts. Members of such
groups can become temporary administrators on the system (see
Chapter 18).

Having an account with administrative privileges is important, as the
administrator account is the only account that's allowed to perform
most system functions, such as changing system features, adding new
devices, and installing new software. Without an administrative account,
you won't be able to do much of anything new on the system.

This window is also where you assign the computer name. Ubuntu uses
this name when advertising its presence on the network, as well as for
referencing the system in log files. You should select a computer name
that's unique on your network. If your network is on a domain, consult
with your network administrator.

The next step of the installation is for a relatively new feature in the
Ubuntu installer. It's the Migrate Documents and Settings window, which
may or may not appear next in your installation process, depending on
what your original system was before the Ubuntu installation.

The Migrate Documents and Settings window appears if you're making the transition from an existing Windows or Linux partition to an Ubuntu partition. The goal of the Ubuntu Migrate Documents and Settings feature is to enable a seamless transition from a Microsoft Windows or other Linux distribution workstation to an Ubuntu workstation. It's an aggressive feature in Ubuntu to allow current Windows users an easy path to migrate to Ubuntu.

12. Select Migrate Documents and Settings, then click Forward.

This step of the installer looks in the hard-drive partitions you're replacing; it checks for any existing Windows or Linux partitions. If it finds them, it offers to help migrate any user accounts to the Ubuntu environment.

The basic idea of the tool is that it looks for the Documents and Settings folder in an existing Microsoft Windows installation — or home folders in an existing Linux installation — and then attempts to duplicate that environment in Ubuntu. If any users are configured, the Migrate Documents and Settings window displays the individual users, along with folders containing data for each user. It allows you to select which users — and which folders — to migrate. Currently the Windows user features that Ubuntu attempts to migrate are

- Internet Explorer bookmarks
- Files in the My Documents folder
- Files in the My Pictures folder
- Files in the My Music folder
- Wallpaper saved by the user

Although this feature is useful, don't rely on it to work properly. If you're migrating a Windows workstation to an Ubuntu workstation, it's always a good idea to make a copy of your important data *before* starting the migration process.

13. Review your Options on the final screen.

The final step in the installation process produces a window that lists all the features you selected in the previous installation windows. At this point, you have the option to backtrack to a previous installation option window and modify your selections.

Pay close attention to the disk-partition settings; when you click the Install button, those become permanent.

14. Click the Advanced button to check other options.

The Advanced Options window opens, as shown in Figure 3-5.

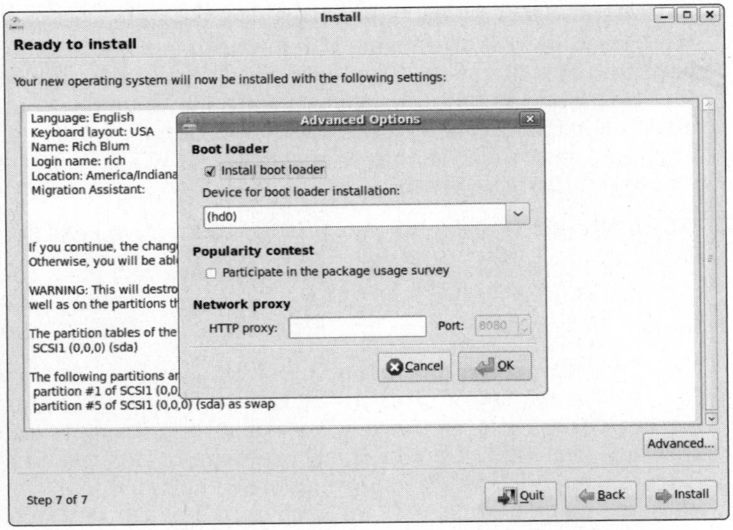

Figure 3-5:
The
Advanced
Options
window.

The Advanced Options window allows you to customize three additional features in Ubuntu:

- *The boot loader:* When Ubuntu installs on a workstation, it can provide its own *boot loader*. The boot loader is responsible for starting the operating system. When you have a Windows operating system installed, Windows provides its own boot loader.

  Ubuntu can replace the Windows boot loader with the Grand Unified Bootloader (GRUB) program. GRUB is the standard boot loader used in Linux systems; it can start not only Linux systems but also many other operating systems, including Windows.

  The GRUB bootloader can be loaded in the Master Boot Record (MBR) of the first hard drive (called hd0 in Ubuntu), or in a multiple hard-drive system, it can reside on the hard drive that contains the Linux partition.

  The Advanced Options window allows you to change the default setting for GRUB. By default, Ubuntu enables GRUB and installs it in the MBR of the first hard drive. This is recommended to boot Ubuntu; it is also recommended if you have a dual-boot Windows/ Ubuntu setup. If you keep the Windows boot loader, you won't be able to boot directly into Ubuntu.

- *The package survey:* The package usage survey retrieves some non-personal information about your setup (such as the CPU type, amount of memory, amount of hard-drive space, and what installation method you used) and sends it to a central repository for statistical purposes. You can view the current package usage survey results by going to http://popcon.ubuntu.com. Several different tables and graphs show the current survey totals.

- *The network proxy:* The final feature in the Advanced Options window is to set a network proxy server. Some local networks (especially those in businesses) must filter any outgoing network traffic to restrict the Web sites that employees can access. This is done using a network proxy. The firewall blocks all normal HTTP access from the network, but the network proxy can receive HTTP requests, then block the unacceptable ones, and forward the allowed ones. This gives a company total control over what their employees can and can't access on the Internet from the corporate network.

   If your Ubuntu workstation is on a network that uses a network proxy, you must configure that feature here for your Internet access to work properly.

   When you've finished setting any advanced options, you're ready to start the installation.

15. Click Install on the Options screen.

   After starting the installation, there's nothing more for you to do other than sit back and watch things happen. The Ubuntu installer takes over, creating the disk partitions you specified, and installing the entire Ubuntu operating system.

After the Ubuntu system is installed on the hard drive, the installation program prompts you to reboot. The next time your system boots, you'll be in Ubuntu-land! If you opted to keep your Windows partition, a nice menu appears when you boot, allowing you to select whether to boot using the Windows partition or to boot using the Ubuntu partition.

Ubuntu also provides a unique way to run the LiveCD system with the Windows Ubuntu Installer (Wubi). If you insert the Ubuntu LiveCD while in a Windows session, you're prompted to install Ubuntu as a Windows application. This creates a full Ubuntu installation within your Windows system, and allows you to dual-boot between Windows and Ubuntu. However, this method is not intended to be used as a full Ubuntu installation; it's not as reliable or as quick as a normal Ubuntu installation.

Installing Fedora

When you install from a full core Linux distribution, you're in for quite a surprise.

You have a lot of choices to control just what software the installation process installs.

This section walks you through the graphical Fedora installation process. If you can't use the graphical installer for some reason (if Linux doesn't support your video card, for example), follow the text-based installation instead. The steps are the same, it's just not as pretty, and you don't get all the options that are available in the point-and-click version.

The graphical interface is designed to work with a mouse to select options. If you don't have a mouse, you can use the keyboard to navigate around the screens. In most places, the Tab key or the arrow keys advance you to the next option, the spacebar toggles options off and on, and the Enter key accepts the choices and moves to the next screen. In most screens, if you want to change a previous setting, a Back button is available to navigate to earlier selection screens. If you want more information about the installation process, click the Release Notes button at any time.

If you're using the Fedora 11 full installation DVD image that came with this book, use an image-burning software package to create the installation DVD. The free `isorecorder` package can also burn DVD images. After you have the Fedora 11 installation DVD, follow these steps:

1. **Place the DVD in your DVD-ROM drive and reboot your system.**

   A number of boot options appear, as shown in Figure 3-6. Here's a run-down of each one:

   - *Install or Upgrade an Existing System:* The first (default) option in the graphical interface is for installing Fedora for the first time or for upgrading an existing version of Fedora Linux.

   - *Install System with Basic Video Driver:* This option allows you to use a generic video driver if Fedora can't properly detect the video card used in your system.

   - *Rescue Installed System:* This option is actually not used for installing Linux. Instead, you use it to boot into *rescue mode* if there's something wrong. (See Chapter 4 for more on rescue mode.)

   - *Boot from Local Drive:* This is also not an installation option. Selecting this menu item lets you boot from a hard drive in case your boot menu breaks after installation.

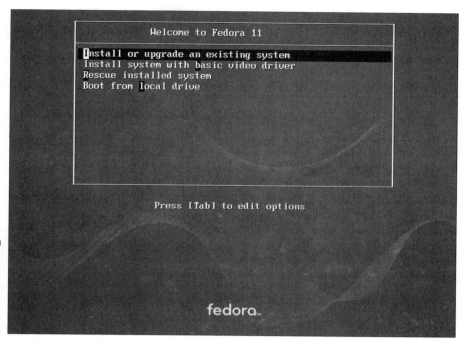

Figure 3-6:
The initial
Fedora
installation
screen.

2. **Select Install or Upgrade an Existing System and press Enter.**

   The Fedora graphical installation process starts, which causes many lines of information to scroll past as the installer launches.

   If you downloaded the full version of Fedora and burned it onto CDs or a DVD yourself, the CD Found (media-check) screen appears. This screen allows you to check the integrity of the media that you're using to install Linux. If this is the case, we recommend taking the time to perform this test personally on all the CDs or the DVD you downloaded. It's best to know now whether one of them is damaged or incomplete.

   Whether or not you check your media, the initial Fedora installer screen eventually appears.

3. **When you're ready to leave the initial Fedora installer screen, click Next.**

   The initial screen disappears and is replaced by the language-selection screen.

4. **Select your language and click Next.**

   The keyboard-configuration screen appears next.

5. **Choose your keyboard configuration and click Next.**

   Different languages arrange the keys differently on keyboards; you may want to choose the matching language for your keyboard. (The default is U.S. English.)

6. **Select the option to install Fedora, and click Next.**

   If the Fedora installer detects a previous version of Fedora on your hard drive, it gives you two options: You can just upgrade the existing version or do a clean installation of the new version.

7. **Select a hostname and domain name for your workstation, and click Next.**

   This is the name that other network devices will detect on the network if you share drives.

8. **Select your time zone, then click Next.**

   You can either select your time zone from the graphical map or select it from the drop-down list of cities.

   If your system uses local time instead of UTC time (which most computers in the United States do), deselect the System Clock Uses UTC check box.

9. **In the root password screen, type the root (administrator) account's password into the Root Password field, and then type the same password in the Confirm field.**

   You don't see the password when you type it — just a dot for each character. (The dots prevent unauthorized individuals from seeing the password.) If you mistype something in one of the boxes, you're warned when you try to move on to the next step of the installation and have a chance to reenter the values. You are also warned if you choose a password the installer considers weak — and therefore a danger to your system's security.

   Don't forget your root password! You need it to do any administrative tasks on your Linux box. If you do happen to forget your password, we show you, in Chapter 18, how to reset it.

   Now you've reached the tricky part of the installation for Fedora. The partitioning screen appears, as shown in Figure 3-7.

10. **Select a disk setup, and click Next.**

    You're given four initial options:

    - *Use Entire Drive:* Wipe everything off the hard drives you select in the check boxes that appear below this option.

    - *Replace Existing Linux System:* If you already installed a version of Linux on the hard drives marked with the check boxes shown below this option, the installer finds the previous instance and installs over it, wiping out the old one.

- *Shrink Current System:* Change an existing Windows or Linux partition to create space for your Fedora installation.
- *Use Free Space:* Find available free space and install Fedora there.
- *Create Custom Layout:* Manually define the partitions where Fedora should be installed.

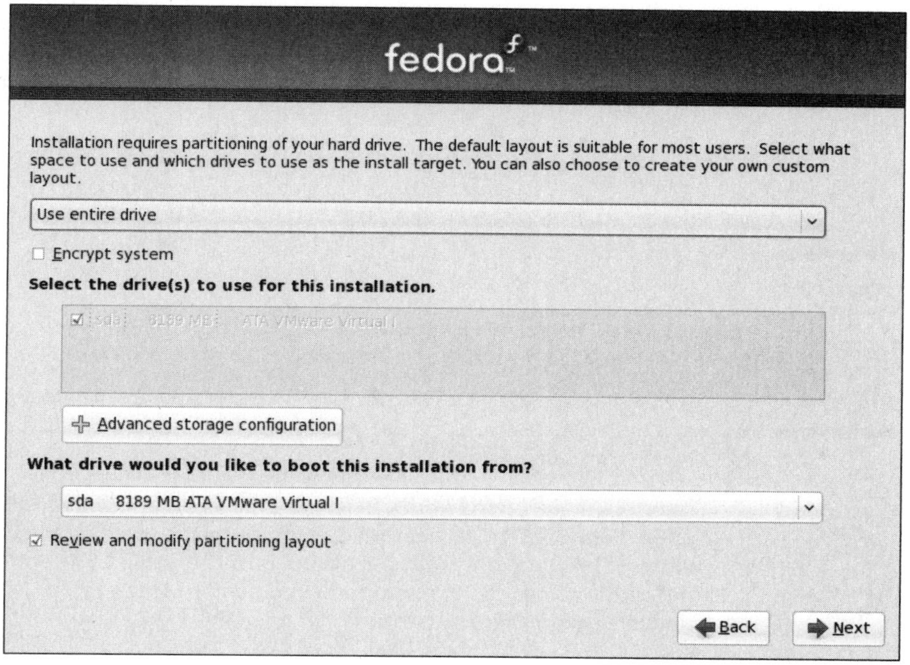

Figure 3-7:
The Fedora
partitioning
screen.

You can also select to encrypt the entire hard drive, making it more difficult for someone to break into your data, However, doing so slows down access to your files. If you want to use this option, select the Encrypt System check box.

If your system supports advanced disk options, such as access to remote network storage drives, click the Advanced Storage Configuration button to add advanced drives.

If you select to create a custom layout, the partition-editor screen, shown in Figure 3-8, appears.

You can add, delete, and modify any partition on the system from the editor. It even allows you to resize existing partitions to free up space for your Fedora Linux partition.

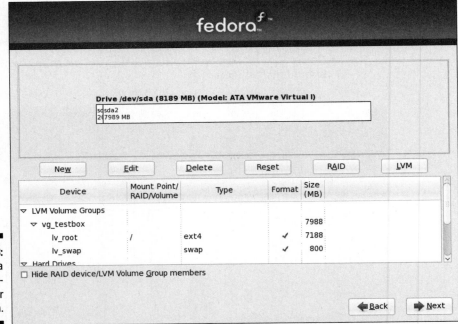

Figure 3-8:
The Fedora
partition-
editor
screen.

The default setup in Fedora is to create a Logical Volume Manager (LVM). The LVM controls the hard-drive partitions as a logical unit, allowing you to easily add partitions into the same LVM unit. With this method you can easily expand disk space on your system without having to reconfigure anything.

11. **Select the location for the boot loader, and click Next.**

    Fedora allows you to customize the Grand Unified Bootloader (GRUB) by selecting where to place it as well as by selecting which operating systems to include in the boot menu. This is what allows you to boot Fedora or Windows from your hard drive.

12. **Select the software to install.**

    Here's where the Fedora full installation shines. You can pick and choose just what application software to install in your system. Figure 3-9 shows the main application-selection screen.

    To add a software group, select its check box. To remove one, make sure the check box stays deselected.

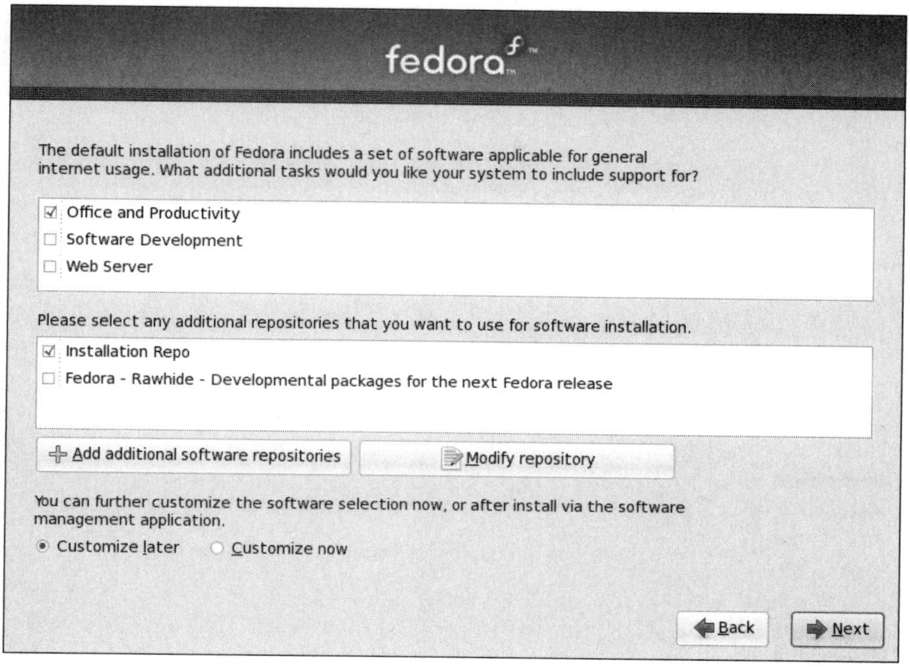

Figure 3-9:
The screen
where you
choose
Fedora
applications
to install.

The groups available are

- *Office and Productivity:* We're assuming you're setting up a desktop system (rather than a server), so you want to make sure this one is selected.

- *Software Development:* If you're a programmer, you want to add this group. Otherwise you can do without it.

- *Web Server:* If you want to run a Web server on this system or just experiment with the Apache Web-server software, add this one. Otherwise you don't need it.

Keep in mind that the last two options are beyond the scope of this book.

The Software Repositories section provides a listing of available Internet resources from which you can automatically load new updates and patches for your Fedora system (if your system is connected to the Internet). The Rawhide repository should only be selected if you want to experiment with developmental packages that aren't guaranteed to work!

13. At the bottom of the screen, select Customize Now, and then click Next to proceed.

The package-selection screen appears, as shown in Figure 3-10.

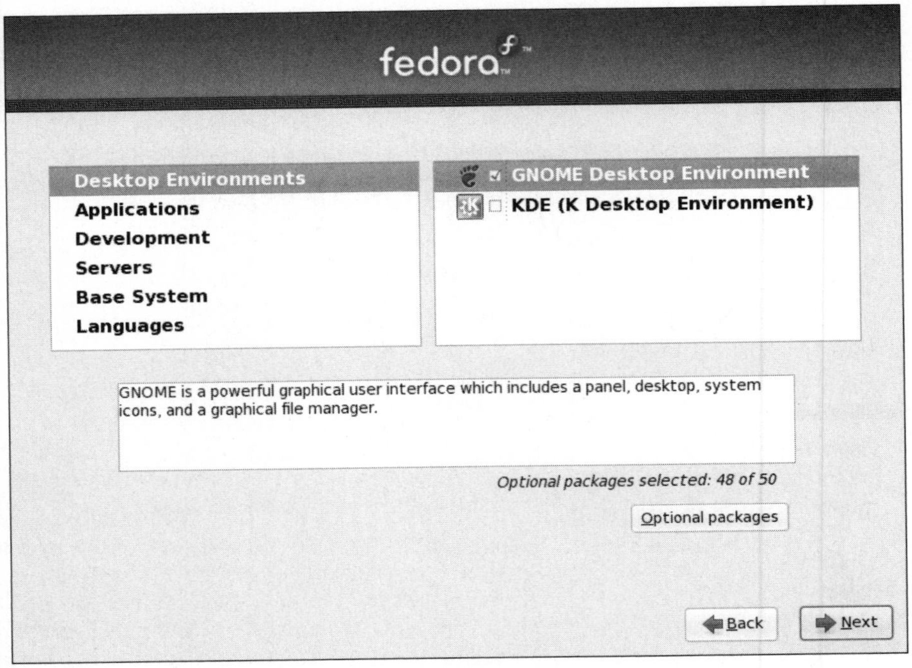

fedora f ™

Desktop Environments	☑ GNOME Desktop Environment
Applications	☐ **KDE (K Desktop Environment)**
Development	
Servers	
Base System	
Languages	

GNOME is a powerful graphical user interface which includes a panel, desktop, system icons, and a graphical file manager.

Optional packages selected: 48 of 50

Optional packages

⬅ Back   ➡ Next

Figure 3-10:
The
package-
selection
screen.

14. Click KDE (K Desktop Environment) if you want to have both major Fedora graphical interfaces installed on your system.

You'll want to have at least one graphical desktop installed on your system. We cover both the GNOME (see Chapter 4) and KDE (see Chapter 5) desktops in this book. The GNOME desktop is selected by default, if you want to follow along with everything in the book, select the KDE option as well.

15. Click Applications.

The types of packages available in this category appear on the right.

16. Scroll through the list on the right. Make sure the check boxes are checked for the groups you want, and make sure they aren't checked for the groups you don't want.

You can click the name of the group to see a description of it.

Quite a few packages are already selected by default. We cover all these packages throughout this book, so we recommend keeping the default packages selected to get the full Linux experience.

17. **(Optional) To look through the optional packages (programs) for this group, click the Optional Packages button. Select the optional packages in the Packages dialog box. Then click Close to return to the package-selection screen.**

    This button is not available if the group isn't already marked for installation. For each package group, some programs are installed by default and other programs are considered optional.

18. **Repeat Steps 15–17 for any remaining categories (for example, Development for Software Programming Tools).**

19. **When you've finished going through all the possibilities — you can change what is installed later — click Next.**

    A dialog box appears and tells you that the installer is looking over your list of selected software. If it discovers that you've left out programs that the software you chose depends on, it offers you the chance to add those too. (Say yes!) When all that's done, the install screen appears.

    If you want to stop your installation of Linux and/or stop short of the changes that the installation makes to your hard drive, the install screen is the *last* place where you can stop this process *without* changing anything on your hard drive(s). To stop the installation, press Ctrl+Alt+Del and your system reboots. If you do that, however, be sure to pull out the DVD or first CD as your system reboots if you don't intend to restart your installation.

20. **When you're ready to commit to the installation, click Next.**

    The Required Install Media dialog box may appear if you're installing from CDs, telling you exactly what CDs you need for the installation. If you're using CDs, you may not need all of them, depending on the software you requested.

    After this, the package-installation screen appears. The system first prepares for the installation and then starts installing. As the system is installing itself, you see the name of each individual package being installed along with a progress bar that tracks completion of the total installation.

    After the package installation has finished, you reach the final installation screen, which greets you with "Congratulations, the installation is complete." The CD or DVD is automatically ejected (if it isn't, eject it manually).

21. **Remove the installation media, click Reboot to restart your machine, and proceed to the next section of this chapter, "Your First Fedora Boot."**

    If you want to shut off the computer instead, it's safe to do so at this time. The next time you start the machine, you'll proceed to the process discussed in the next section, "Your First Fedora Boot."

Your First Fedora Boot

The first time your Fedora system boots, you still have to do some configuring.

When Fedora boots, you have your first chance to see your boot menu — the blue screen that gives you three seconds to make a choice before proceeding to the default choice — fly by:

✔ If you set Windows as your default, press a key (such as the spacebar) to enter the menu, select the Linux entry, and press Enter.

✔ If Linux is the default — or the only — operating system installed, just sit back and let the machine boot on its own.

If, for any reason, your computer fails to boot at this point, see Chapter 22.

The first time your computer boots, you see the first-boot Welcome screen. Do the following to complete your machine's initial setup:

1. **Click Forward to proceed to the setup routine.**

   The License Agreement screen appears.

2. **Read through this text, select Yes, I Agree to the License Agreement, and then click Forward.**

   The Create User screen appears.

3. **Enter a username, your full name, and your password, and then click Forward.**

   When you installed Fedora, you set a password for the root user account, but you only want to use that for administrative duties, such as adding new software. Most of the time, log in with your own user account to use the desktop applications.

   The Date and Time screen appears next.

4. **If you're on a computer network that is currently connected to the Internet and is usually connected to the Internet (or your network Administrator told you to use a time server), click the Network Time Protocol tab. Otherwise, skip to Step 7.**

   Letting a *time server* control your date and time makes sure that your computer gets regular input on what time and day it really is. Otherwise, over time, your computer's clock actually drifts from the correct time.

5. **Click the Enable Network Time Protocol check box to enable this feature.**

6. **If your network Administrator told you to add a specific time server, click Add and then enter the address for this server. Skip to Step 8.**

7. **If you intend to control the date and time on the machine manually, verify that the date and time are accurate; if they're not correct, fix those settings now.**

8. **After you've finished adjusting the date and/or network time server, click Forward to proceed.**

   If you told the system to use the Network Time Protocol (NTP), it may take a moment for the system to contact the server you selected. After a few seconds, the Hardware Profile screen appears.

9. **Select Send Profile so the Fedora Project will know what hardware Fedora is being used on, and then click Forward.**

   The data is sent anonymously — this ensures that the folks working on the project know what you're running (but not who you are). They keep in mind what's being used as they do further development of Fedora.

10. **Click Finish.**

    Fedora completes the boot process and greets you with a login screen.

    That's it! You've just survived the second Linux gauntlet! Your computer now brings you to a graphical login prompt. See Chapter 4 for instructions on what to do from here. Enjoy exploring Linux!

Chapter 4

Examining the GNOME Desktop

If a cluttered desk is the sign of a cluttered mind, what is the significance of a clean desk?

— Laurence J. Peter (1919–1988)

A lot of people like to characterize Linux as a DOS-like environment, where all you can do is operate from the command line in this antique-feeling world where you have to type a lot of cryptic stuff without any pretty pictures. However, the Linux desktop offers quite a nice working environment, as you find out throughout this chapter. The cool thing is that most of it is configurable. Those who like to customize their systems can have way too much fun changing things around.

The Linux world has two popular graphical desktop environments: GNOME and KDE. This chapter walks you through the GNOME desktop, which Fedora, Ubuntu, and gOS all use by default. (Chapter 5 walks through the KDE graphical desktop environment.)

Breaking Down the GNOME Desktop

GNOME stands for the GNU Network Object Model Environment — not that this expansion tells you much. Suffice it to say that GNOME is a full point-and-click environment — colors, little pictures, the works.

The GNOME desktop became popular in Red Hat Linux, the granddad of Fedora, so it's no surprise that it's the default desktop in Fedora. Many other Linux distributions also use the GNOME desktop as the default; Ubuntu is a typical example.

Figure 4-1 shows you what the GNOME desktop looks like after you log in to your Ubuntu system.

The menus   The menu-and-icon panel

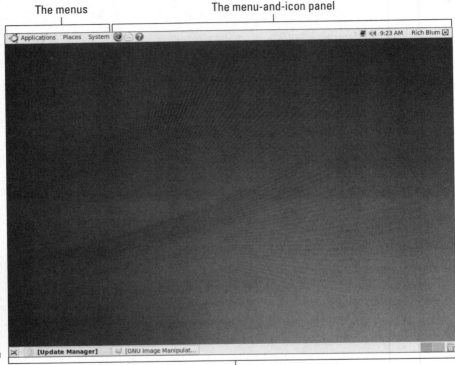

Figure 4-1:
The default
GNOME
desktop in
Ubuntu 9.04.

The desktop panel

To find out more about GNOME, visit the main GNOME Web site at www.gnome.org.

Keep in mind that the programs you have depend on the type of installation you chose and what system features you customized; if what you have is different from what you see in the descriptions or figures, don't panic!

The GNOME desktop environment is divided into four parts:

- ✔ The menus
- ✔ The menu-and-icon panel at the top of the screen
- ✔ The desktop panel on the bottom of the screen

✔ The icons on your desktop (Figure 4-1 doesn't show any icons on the desktop, because the default Ubuntu installation doesn't include icons. Find out how to add icons to your desktop in the "Configuring Your Desktop Appearance" section.)

The menus

GNOME has three primary menus, all of them visible on the upper panel. From left to right, they are

✔ **Applications:** Programs available through the graphical user interface (GUI).

✔ **Places:** Shortcuts to special locations on your hard drive. (Note that you don't *have* to use the special directories created for you in places such as Documents, Pictures, and so on.) Chapter 7 addresses how to view directories and files in far more detail.

✔ **System:** Personal and system settings, along with more general overall system commands.

Menu items that have an arrow to the right offer submenus, which you can open by holding your mouse pointer over that menu choice. Often the submenus have their own submenus within, offering even more programs.

In the following sections, we detail the more common submenus you'll find within these three menus.

Applications

Just as with everything else, each different Linux distribution likes to tweak the GNOME menus to provide its own style to the system — although a few menu items seem to stay consistent in the GNOME menu system regardless. Table 4-1 lists the common items on the Applications menu in most Linux distributions.

Table 4-1	Applications Menu Content
Menu Choice	*What You Find*
Accessories	Small, specific-function programs. Contains a calculator, character map, dictionary, screen-shot program, text editor, and more.
Games	A collection of games.
Graphics	A variety of graphics programs, including The GIMP (see Chapter 14).

(continued)

Table 4-1 *(continued)*

Menu Choice	What You Find
Internet	A few Internet tools you will find discussed in Chapters 9 and 10, such as Evolution (e-mail and calendar program), Pidgin (instant messenger), and Firefox (Web browser).
Office	The OpenOffice.org suite of applications (discussed in Chapter 12) and other useful productivity programs.
Sound & Video	Programs, such as a CD player and sound recorder, for working with your computer's multimedia hardware (see Chapters 13 and 14).
System Tools	Tools, such as a file browser and a software updater (not used in Ubuntu), for managing, monitoring, and updating your system.
Add/Remove Software	Opens the application installation and removal utility.

Places

The Places menu (described in Table 4-2) is a little more standard. The GNOME desktop provides several folders for storing specific types of data. The Places menu provides one-stop shopping for accessing all your folders.

Table 4-2 — Places Menu Contents

Menu Choice	What You Find
Home Folder	The contents of your user account's home directory, as discussed in Chapter 7.
Desktop	The contents of your user account's Desktop directory, which contains files and folders that should appear on your desktop.
Documents	The content of your user account's Documents directory, in which you can choose to place files you're working on.
Music	The content of your user account's Music directory, in which you can save your music files.
Pictures	The content of your user account's Pictures directory, where you can save your images.
Videos	The content of your user account's Videos directory, where you can save videos.
Download	Your user account's Download directory (not used in Ubuntu), where your online downloads end up.

Menu Choice	What You Find
Computer	The hard drives and temporary media available on your system.
CD/DVD Creator	A special folder for pulling together files that you want to burn onto a CD or DVD.
Network	The computers and hard drives available on your network.
Connect To Server	A tool for connecting to many different types of servers.
Search	A filesystem search tool that looks inside files as well as at their names.
Recent Documents	Documents you have opened lately.

System

The System menu provides access to your system configurations. As a general rule, GNOME provides two types of configuration settings:

✔ **User-specific settings:** Items that only affect the way your user account operates on the system, such as screen resolution, background colors, and keyboard preferences.

✔ **System-specific settings:** Items that affect the entire Linux system, such as network settings, sound settings, and user accounts.

Table 4-3 details how these settings appear on the System menu.

Table 4-3	System Menu Contents
Menu Choice	**What You Find**
Preferences	Your individual user settings.
Administration	System-wide settings.
Help	The GNOME help tool.
About GNOME	Information about GNOME.
Lock Screen	The capability to set your machine so no one can use your GNOME login without entering your password (not used in Ubuntu).
Log Out *user*	Enables you to leave your current login session (not used in Ubuntu).
Shut Down	Hibernate (put into sleep/hibernation mode), Restart (reboot), or Shut Down (shut off) the machine (not used in Ubuntu).

Ubuntu chose to move the last three menu items (Lock screen, Log Out, and Shut Down) out of the System menu and into a special panel applet (discussed in the "Applet area" section of this chapter). The Shut Down applet icon provides these options for you.

If you have your screensaver turned on and choose the Lock Screen option from the System menu, your screensaver appears or fades to black. Then if anyone moves the mouse or uses your keyboard, a dialog box appears with your login name in it and a password field. You can get back to work by entering your password. Until then, you're safe in knowing that no one else can mosey up to your computer and send off a joke e-mail to your boss while pretending to be you.

If you're logged in as the root user, the Lock Screen option doesn't work.

The Screensaver feature is on by default in both Fedora and Ubuntu. To change the setting, do the following:

1. **Choose System⇨Preferences⇨Screensaver (in Ubuntu) or Look and Feel⇨Screensaver (in Fedora).**

   The Screensaver Preferences dialog box appears, as shown in Figure 4-2.

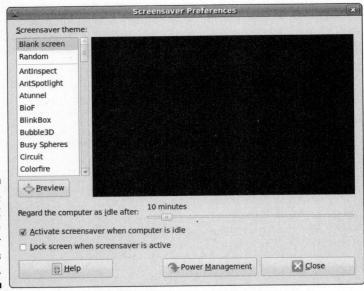

Figure 4-2:
The GNOME Screensaver Preferences dialog box.

2. **Click the Lock Screen When Screensaver Is Active check box to select or deselect it.**

3. **When you're finished making changes, click Close.**

The dialog box closes. (Note that in this dialog box, you can also change whether the screensaver turns on, how long it takes to turn on, and which screensaver to use.)

The panels

A pair of panels lives on your GNOME desktop — one along the top and one along the bottom. Because these bars are neatly divided into sections, take a look at what's in each section from left to right, starting with the top panel. On the far left side of the top panel are the three menus discussed in "The menus" section, earlier in this chapter.

There are three different areas to the panels: the quick-launch icons, the applets, and the bottom panel.

Quick-launch icons

After the menu section of the top panel, you run into a group of *quick-launch icons* (refer to Figure 4-1) that launch specific applications automatically. You can reach all these items through the menus, but they're on the panel to make them easy to find. In both Fedora and Ubuntu, these icons are

✔ **Firefox:** The planet-with-a-fox icon opens the Firefox Web browser. (See Chapter 9 for more.)

✔ **Evolution:** Just to the right of the Web-browser button; launches an e-mail and calendar program. (See Chapter 10 for more.)

Ubuntu also includes a Help icon to provide easy access to the Ubuntu Help manual.

Applet area

Next to the quick-launch icons is a large blank space where you can add new icons. To the right of the blank space is the *applet area* of the top panel.

GNOME applets are small programs that you access directly from the panel. They're powerful in that applets interact with the panel, often showing information directly on the panel, which saves you from having to launch a huge window to see the information.

Most Linux distributions that use the GNOME desktop place several applets on the top panel by default. In Fedora, here's what you find from left to right — though your particular installation may have extra options displayed:

✔ **Shut Down:** This applet provides a quick and easy location for you to terminate your desktop session. There are several options including restarting the computer, logging out the user and returning to the login screen, and powering down the system.

✔ **NetworkManager:** If you have a wired or wireless network card in your workstation, Ubuntu, Fedora, and gOS all start the NetworkManager applet by default. The NetworkManager provides easy access for you to configure your wireless card settings and control the network connection. It also indicates network traffic for wired connections and signal strength for wireless connections.

✔ **User Switcher:** If you've created more than one user account (root doesn't count here), click your name in the upper panel; a list of the other users on the system appears. You can use this applet to switch temporarily over to another user account. If you haven't created other accounts, then clicking your name just shows your name.

✔ **Date and Time:** Here you can see the day and time, depending on how this applet is configured.

✔ **Master Volume Control:** Click this to open the master volume control.

The bottom panel

Now for the bottom panel. From left to right, you find the following items on this panel:

✔ **Hide/Restore Desktop Applications:** This button lets you minimize all running programs immediately and then reopen them again with just one click.

✔ **Taskbar:** In this large space, you find entries for each program running on your desktop. You can change a program's status by using the boxes as indicated:

- If a program is minimized, you can open its window by clicking its panel task box.

- If a program is maximized but buried under another program, click its task box on the panel to bring it to the front.

- If a program is maximized and on top, you can minimize it by clicking its panel task box.

✔ **Workspace Switcher:** Allows you to work in four different desktop environments during a single login session. Each desktop environment has the same menus, panels, and background, but you can run different programs in each of the environments. It's an easy way to remain organized while you're working in multiple programs. Try it. It's like having four monitors in one!

✔ **Trash Can:** A shortcut to your desktop's Trash Can.

Want to move a program from one workspace window to another? Click the icon in the program's upper-left corner and select one of the following options:

✔ **Always on Visible Workspace:** Makes the window show up on all four workspaces.

✔ **Only on this Workspace:** Keeps the window from appearing in the other workspaces (on by default).

✔ **Move to Workspace Right:** Slides the window horizontally to the right, into the "next door" workspace.

✔ **Move to Another Workspace:** Gives you the option of specifying Workspace 1 (far left), 2 (second in from the left), 3 (third in from the left), or 4 (far right) (only seen if you have more than two desktops configured).

To see which workspace an open window is in, look at the Workspace Switcher; that's where you can spot the little windows that match the way your desktop is laid out.

Playing with GNOME desktop icons

The area on your screen between the top and the bottom panels is called the *desktop*. The desktop is actually a separate folder in your home folder, but the contents appear graphically on your screen as icons. This provides a place to store files, additional folders, and quick-launch icons for applications, all easily accessible from your desktop.

Your initial desktop icons may vary, depending on which Linux distribution you installed. The Ubuntu distribution prefers not to use any desktop icons by default. The Fedora default desktop icons form a vertical line along the top left of your screen. In order, here's what you see from top to bottom:

✔ **Computer:** Opens the Nautilus file manager (see Chapter 7) with a list of your CD-ROM drive(s), hard drive(s), and more.

✔ **Home:** Opens the Nautilus browser (Chapter 7) with your home directory's contents displayed.

✔ **Trash:** A GNOME shortcut that opens the Nautilus file manager to the Trash folder, which contains files that you dragged into it.

To use the Trash Can, drag into it any files you want to delete. Later, if you're sure you want to be rid of them, you can empty the trash in one of three ways:

✔ Right-click the Trash Can icon and choose Empty Trash from the context menu to empty the entire Trash Can. When you're asked for confirmation, click Empty.

✔ Open the Trash Can by double-clicking the icon. Then delete the entire contents of the Trash Can by choosing File⇨Empty Trash.

✔ Open the Trash Can by double-clicking the icon. To delete an individual item from the Trash Can, right-click it and choose Delete from Trash. When asked whether you're sure, click the Delete button to finish the job.

You can select more than one item by holding the Ctrl key to individually select them even if they're not next to each other; by holding the Shift key to select a range of items; or by left-clicking and then dragging to collect all the items that are in a box together.

You can also delete files manually from the Trash folder in your home-folder area (see how to do that in Chapter 7).

Customizing Your Panels

You can customize your upper and lower panels individually through the Panel menu. To do so, find free space on the panel you want to work with, right-click, and choose the appropriate item from the context menu. (For a list of what this menu offers, see Table 4-4.)

If you have so many programs open that you're using the whole width of the lower panel, you may not have any free space to right-click. Close a program or two to clear space.

Table 4-4	GNOME Panel Menu Content
Menu Choice	*What You Find*
Add to Panel	The dialog box that lets you add applets, menus, and other objects to your main panel.
Properties	The options for setting this panel's behavior.
Delete This Panel	The capability to delete a secondary panel but not the main icon panel.
New Panel	The options for creating new panels that sit on different parts of the screen.
Help	The Help browser for GNOME.
About Panels	A dialog box with some basic panel information.

Adding an applet to the panel

The Add to Panel dialog box (see Figure 4-3) is accessible from the Panel menu (see the previous section). This dialog box contains a list of *applets* — small, specialized programs you can use to add particular functionality to a panel. To add one of these applets to your panel, open the dialog box, select the applet you want to use, and then click Add. The applet now appears on your panel. If you right-click the applet and choose Move, you can then slide the applet along your panel until you have it where you want it, and then click to release it.

Figure 4-3:
The GNOME
Add to
Panel dialog
box.

 You may have noticed that the first applet item is Custom Application Launcher. Using this feature, you can create a panel icon that launches your own program or script.

Configuring an applet

After you have an applet placed and running, you may be able to play with configuration options. Some of these options enable you to change what information is displayed. Others have a variety of look-and-feel settings.

To determine which configuration and other options are available for your applet, follow these steps:

1. **Right-click the applet and examine the shortcut menu that appears.**

   This shortcut menu is different from applet to applet. The bottom portion is always the same: Remove from Panel, Move, and Lock to Panel (prevent the icon from moving). Common entries for the top portion are Help and About. The rest of the items are either configuration options (see Step 2) or special applet features, such as the ability to copy the date from the Clock applet.

2. **Choose Preferences from the shortcut menu.**

   Not every applet has a Preferences dialog box. If the one you've chosen does, then the dialog box opens when you choose this option, displaying the applet's configuration features.

3. **Alter the selections in the Preferences dialog box to customize this applet's behavior.**

   Now you get to have some fun. Make changes so you can see what this applet can do: As you make your changes, they appear in the applet on your panel. (Each applet has its own set of features, so we can't give you any specifics that would necessarily match what you have.)

   Experiment with the settings because you can always go back and change the settings later if you don't like 'em.

4. **Click Close to save your changes and close the dialog box.**

Ditching an applet

You have room for only so many applets. And, if you're like us, you probably don't want to have every bit of free space cluttered with icons. To remove an applet from the panel, simply right-click the applet you want to remove, and when the context menu appears, choose Remove from Panel. With nary a whimper, the applet vanishes from the panel. And of course, you can go back to the Add to Panel menu option to bring it back to life!

Adding a program to the panel or the desktop

If you have a program you use often, you can add it to your panel by following these steps:

1. **Choose Applications and browse to the program you want to add to the panel.**

   Don't open the program. Just point to the menu item with your mouse pointer.

2. **Right-click the program and choose Add This Launcher to Panel to add it to the panel, or choose Add This Launcher to Desktop to add it to the desktop.**

   An icon for this program appears on your panel or desktop.

After you have your program on the panel, you can run the program just by clicking its icon. If you added it to your desktop, double-click the icon.

If you're not happy with where a desktop icon is placed, click it and then drag it to a new location. For a panel entry, right-click it, choose Move, drag the icon to where you want it, and then click to fix it into place.

You can also add a *drawer* (menu button) to your panel for an entire menu. To do so, follow these steps:

1. **Click Applications and browse to the submenu you want to add.**

2. **Enter that submenu.**

   For example, if you want to add a button for the Graphics menu to your panel, open the Applications menu, move your mouse to the Graphics menu, and then move your mouse to the right into the contents of the Graphics menu.

3. **Right-click to open the context menu.**

4. **Choose Entire Menu, and then choose either Add This As Drawer to Panel or Add This As Menu to Panel.**

   Easy to see which is which: A drawer shows you its contents in icons only; a menu looks more like a submenu from the Applications menu.

Removing a program from the desktop or the panel

To get rid of an icon you have on your desktop, right-click the icon and choose Move to Trash from the shortcut menu that appears.

If you want to remove one of the programs on the panel, just right-click the icon you want to remove, and when the shortcut menu appears, choose Remove from Panel. The icon vanishes from the panel. That's it!

Configuring Your Desktop Appearance

Besides the objects on the desktop, GNOME also allows you to configure the way the desktop appears.

The main controller over the look and feel of your desktop is the Appearance Preferences dialog box. Choose System⇨Preferences⇨Appearance, and the Appearance Preferences dialog box opens, as shown in Figure 4-4.

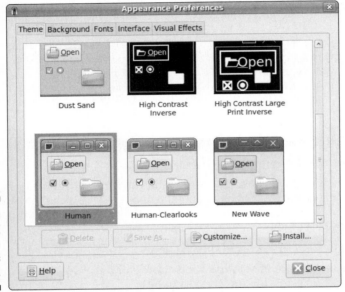

Figure 4-4:
The GNOME Appearance Preferences dialog box.

The Appearance Preferences dialog box provides five tabs for controlling the look and feel of your desktop:

- ✔ Theme
- ✔ Background
- ✔ Fonts
- ✔ Interface
- ✔ Visual Effects (in Fedora this is a separate menu item)

This section walks through how to customize your desktop to your liking using this tool.

The desktop theme

A *theme* is a named group of settings that controls the overall way objects appear on your desktop — for example, check boxes, radio buttons, folder icons, and color schemes for the windows. Ubuntu includes nine themes — some of them high-contrast for people with visual impairments.

The default theme set by Ubuntu is called Human. It produces the relaxing orange window theme on the desktop. Select any theme to test it out.

If you don't like the theme you've selected, you can easily change it by selecting a different theme from the Appearance Preferences dialog box.

After you select a theme, you can make additional changes to the look and feel of it. Click the Customize button to open the Customize Theme dialog box, as shown in Figure 4-5.

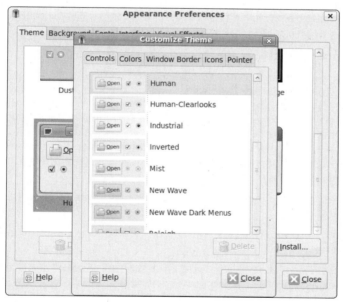

Figure 4-5: Customize a desktop theme.

The Customize Theme dialog box allows you to change the appearance of individual items such as check boxes and radio buttons, windows, windows borders, icons used for folders and documents, and the mouse pointer.

Many themes are available on the Internet for GNOME; however, you may have to hunt for a while and put up with some frustration until you find a theme you like that's *also* compatible with your installation. To find and grab themes for your own use, follow these steps:

1. **Point your Web browser to** `http://themes.freshmeat.net`.

   You're taken to the Themes Web site, which offers a boatload of items for customizing GUIs.

   If you're heavily into playing with customizing your GUI, you can also check out `http://art.gnome.org`. In particular, check out `http://live.gnome.org/GnomeArt/Tutorials`.

2. **On Freshmeat, enter** GTK themes **in the search box, and click the Search button.**

   You go to a section of the site where you can ensure that the themes you choose actually work with your system. (GTK is geek-speak for part of the GNOME desktop environment.)

3. **Select the GTK 2.X Themes area.**

   Now you're in the section for the latest version of GNOME.

4. **Browse and choose the theme you want to try.**

   If you create an account and log in, you can use the Sort Order drop-down list to change the order in which the items are displayed. When looking over a theme's information, keep your eye out for the require-ments (sometimes called *dependencies*) that go with the theme. Some themes require additional *engines* (software that runs behind the scenes); you want to avoid those if you're uncomfortable with finding and adding software at this point. You're safe from the additional hassle if you're looking for GTK themes.

5. **After you've chosen your theme, click its name to go to the theme-specific page.**

   There, you can find any comments someone has posted about the theme.

6. **Scroll down if necessary and click the link under Tar/GZ or Tar/BZ2. Click Save to Disk when you're asked what to do with the file, and, finally, click OK to download the file.**

   By default, the Firefox browser stores the file on your desktop (see Chapter 9).

7. **Open the Appearance Preferences dialog box, select the Theme tab, then click the Install button.**

   The Select Theme dialog box opens, as shown in Figure 4-6.

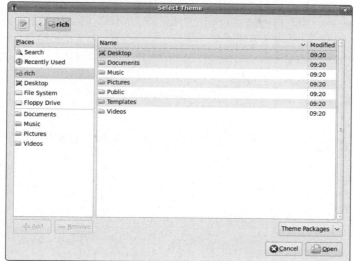

Figure 4-6:
The GNOME
Select
Theme
dialog box.

8. **Browse to where you stored the theme.**

   If you haven't changed the Firefox defaults, it will be in your Desktop directory.

9. **Make sure that the theme file is a** `.tar.gz` **file.**

   If it isn't, turn to Chapter 16 to find out how to convert this file to this format.

10. **Select the theme file and click the Open button.**

    When the theme is installed, you see a confirmation dialog box.

    If you're told that the theme is invalid — but the theme is in the specified format — then you've grabbed a theme that wasn't meant for your setup. If you look on the theme's page, it probably has something in its Environment or Dependencies section that tried to tell you that, but it's written for geeks, so don't beat yourself up if the explanation looks like gibberish. Just go back and try another theme.

11. **Choose Apply New Theme if you want to change your theme right now. Otherwise, choose Keep Current Theme.**

    You may or may not actually see this option. Don't panic if you don't: There are different kinds of themes — and some don't display the option. If you do see it crop up and you choose Apply New Theme, your desktop changes to match that theme.

Depending on the theme, your new theme may be added to the themes list. If you don't see it there, click the Customize button. In the Customize Theme dialog box, you see three different types of themes:

- *Controls* for themes affect how the controls on your desktop look.
- *Window Borders* for the themes change how your window borders look.
- *Icons* for themes change how your icons look.

Your new theme may be listed in one or more of these locations.

12. **If you haven't already, select your new theme from the list.**

    Whether you choose the theme in the main list or in the Theme Details dialog box, your desktop changes to match your choice. If the theme is not in the main list, you'll see Custom Theme at the top of the choices. Click Save Theme and assign a new name to your desktop's new look.

13. **Click Close when you're happy with your desktop's look.**

    The Appearance Preferences dialog box closes.

The background

The background on the desktop is an important feature because it's what you end up staring at the most. Both Ubuntu and Fedora allow you to use an image as the background (called *wallpaper*) or use a color background.

The Background tab controls what's on the background of your desktop. You can use the images that are loaded by default, select a color for the background, or load your own wallpaper image. To set your background, open the Appearance Preferences dialog box, click the Background tab, and then follow these steps:

1. **Click the Add button.**

2. **Use the browser to find your image file.**

   GNOME supports using any image file type as the background image.

3. **Click the Open button.**

   The image is imported into the backgrounds list, and it is automatically selected as the background wallpaper.

The No Wallpaper option allows you to select either a single color for the background or a gradual shading from one selected color to another color (either horizontally or vertically). GNOME uses a cool color wheel from which to select the color, as shown in Figure 4-7.

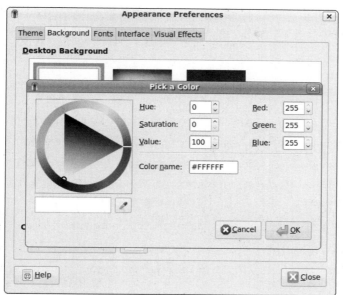

Just click the base color from the outside wheel, and then select the shading from the inner triangle.

Fonts

The Fonts tab allows you to customize which fonts Ubuntu uses for various functions within the desktop. As expected, Ubuntu provides lots of different fonts to choose from. Another nice feature is that you can customize how the fonts are rendered on your screen.

Clicking the Details button at the bottom of the Fonts tab page opens the Font Rendering Details dialog box, shown in Figure 4-8.

Here you can really get down to the basics of rendering fonts on your screen.

The more detailed you make the fonts, the nicer they appear — *but* the more processing time and power are required to display your text.

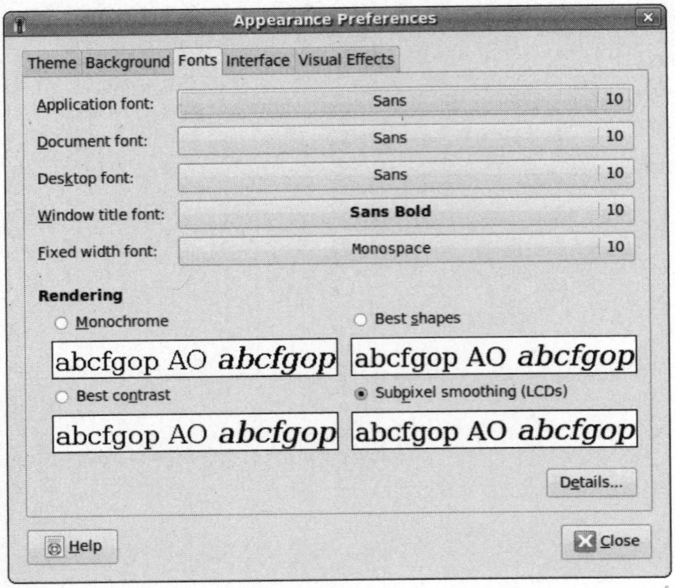

Figure 4-8:
The Font
Rendering
Details dia-
log box.

Interface

The Interface tab provides a few settings for customizing the way menus and toolbars appear in windows:

- ✔ **Show icons in menus:** Displays icons in the menu alongside the text menu item.

- ✔ **Editable menu shortcut keys:** Enables using shortcut keystrokes to select menu options.

- ✔ **Toolbar button labels:** Sets how toolbar items appear: text only, icon only, icon with next below, or icon with text next to it.

These window settings apply to any window that uses the GNOME interface. They don't apply to applications that don't use the GNOME library, such as applications built on the KDE desktop library.

Visual Effects

The Visual Effects tab allows you to select how fancy your desktop handles windows. There are three levels of effects:

> ✔ **None:** Windows just appear and disappear without any special effects.
>
> ✔ **Normal:** Windows fade in when started, and fade out when closed or minimized.
>
> ✔ **Extra:** This level offers fancier effects such as melting windows when they're minimizing.

The Extra level of effects requires an advanced graphics card in your PC.

Enabling Accessibility Features

The GNOME desktop includes several features that enable people with disabilities to operate applications on the desktop using alternative methods. These features include screen magnifiers (which enlarge areas of the screen), screen readers (which read text on the screen), and keyboard and mouse assistive features (such as sticky keys and slow mouse clicks). You can enable individual features as necessary.

Before you can use the individual accessibility features, you need to enable the accessibility features in GNOME. Follow these steps to enable the assistive technologies packages:

1. **Choose System⇨Preferences⇨Assistive Technologies.**

   The Assistive Technologies Preferences dialog box opens, as shown in Figure 4-9.

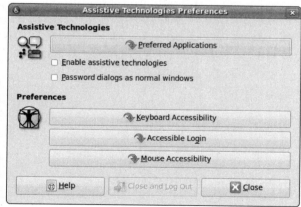

Figure 4-9:
The
Assistive
Tech-
nologies
Preferences
dialog box.

2. **Select the Enable Assistive Technologies check box.**

3. **Click the Close and Log Out button.**

GNOME enables the assistive technologies features when you log back in to the system. After you've enabled the assistive technologies features, you can configure the functions you require. There are three main categories:

✔ **Preferred Applications:** Allows you to define assistive applications, such as screen readers, that should start automatically at startup

✔ **Keyboard Accessibility:** Defines keyboard features, such as *sticky keys* to simulate multiple key presses and *slow keys* to ignore random key presses.

✔ **Mouse Accessibility:** Defines mouse features, such as simulating double clicks and mouse *dwells* (hovering the mouse over an item without clicking it).

Chapter 5

Examining the KDE Desktop

A bus station is where a bus stops.

A train station is where a train stops.

On my desk, I have a workstation . . .

— Steven Wright

*I*n Chapter 4 you get to see how the GNOME desktop works; this chapter
discusses the other popular desktop in the Linux world — KDE. The KDE
desktop environment provides a graphical interface to your Linux distribution using features commonly found in Microsoft Windows systems. It's available as a software package in Fedora and Ubuntu, and is the main desktop
used in Kubuntu, a Linux distribution based on Ubuntu, but focused on the
KDE desktop. This chapter walks through the KDE desktop features, showing
you how to work your way around the KDE desktop and get the most from
your workspace.

If you installed both the KDE and GNOME desktops in Fedora (see Chapter 3),
you can switch between the two when you log in. Select the arrow button in
the bottom panel next to the GNOME or KDE text. Whichever text displays is
the desktop you log into.

The KDE Desktop Basics

KDE desktop was first released in 1996 as the Kool Desktop Environment, but
these days it tries to be a little more sophisticated and prefers to be called
just the K Desktop Environment (but it's still pretty cool). It quickly became
popular among Linux beginners because it provides a Windows-like interface
for your Linux desktop. Figure 5-1 shows the KDE desktop used in Fedora.

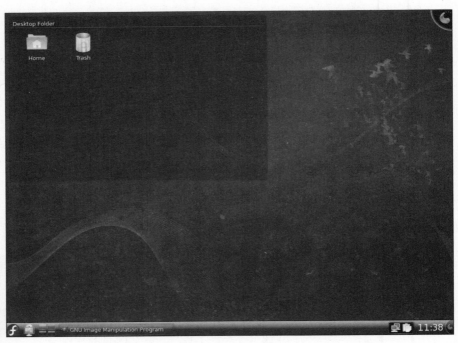

Figure 5-1:
The Fedora
11 KDE
desktop.

To find out more about KDE, take a look at the KDE Web site, which can be found at www.kde.org.

As with everything else in Linux, the KDE desktop layout is highly customiz-able, so what you have on your system may vary from what you see in the fig-ures in this chapter. Don't panic, all these features are there, and we show you just how to customize your desktop to suit your needs!

Similar to the GNOME desktop, the KDE desktop contains three main compo-nents that you should become familiar with:

- The KDE menu
- The panel
- The desktop

In the following sections, we walk you through each of these components and show you what they look like.

Menu, please!

You access the KDE menu (called *KickOff*) from a single icon on the far left side of the panel. Clicking the icon produces the entire KickOff layout, as shown in Figure 5-2.

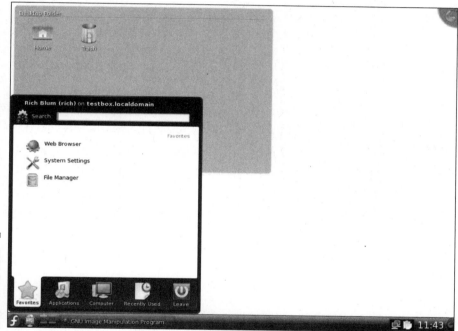

Figure 5-2:
The KDE KickOff menu layout.

Five tabs at the bottom of the menu contain a selection of menu items:

- ✔ **Favorites:** Icons for easy access to applications you use frequently.
- ✔ **Applications:** Submenus of program icons to launch programs on your system.
- ✔ **Computer:** Shortcuts to special locations on your computer.
- ✔ **Recently Used:** A list of the applications you recently ran, and the documents you opened recently.
- ✔ **Leave:** Options for exiting the current desktop session.

Menu items that have an arrow to the right offer submenus, which you can open by clicking your mouse on that menu choice. Often the submenus have their own submenus within, offering even more programs.

With all these different menu options, it can be cumbersome to find what you're looking for. To help out, the KDE menu also provides a quick-search tool at the top of the menu (refer to Figure 5-2). Enter text, and KDE returns the search results; then you can select the one you want. If your workstation is connected to the Internet, KDE also provides a link to launch the Konqueror Web browser quickly and search the Web for the term.

Favorites

The Fedora KDE desktop provides three entries for you on the Favorites tab:

- **Web Browser:** The KDE Konqueror desktop browser and file manager (see Chapter 7).
- **System Settings:** The KDE desktop's configuration tool.
- **File Manager:** The Dolphin file-manager program (see Chapter 7).

The Favorites tab also provides an area where you can collect icons for applications you use frequently. Navigate to a program in the menu, right-click it, and then select the Add to Favorites option.

You can remove entries from the Favorites tab by simply right-clicking the entry and selecting Remove from Favorites.

Applications

The Applications menu tab provides quick access to all the installed programs on your system. Obviously, the choices available here depend on what you've installed, but KDE uses some standard first-level menu items you may run into on your system. These are described in Table 5-1.

Table 5-1	The Applications Menu
Menu Choice	*What You Find*
Administration	Applications and utilities for modifying system settings and features.
Development	Applications for developing programs.
Education	Educational applications.
Games	Programs to kill some time.

Menu Choice	What You Find
Graphics	Image-manipulation programs.
Internet	Programs for interacting on the Internet.
Multimedia	Applications for handling audio and video files.
Office	Programs for office-related tasks, such as Word Processing for wordmongering, Spreadsheets for number-crunching, and Presentation for graphics.
Settings	Utilities for configuring user-specific settings.
System	Utilities for monitoring and setting system-wide features.
Utilities	Various programs and utilities for handling small functions on your desktop and system.
Help	The KDE Help Center documentation.
Personal Files	Access to your home folder (see Chapter 7).

You may notice some duplication of effort in the first-level menu items. Not all KDE systems use all these menu options. Different distributions offer different combinations of the menu items to provide a custom look and feel for their menu.

Computer

The Computer menu tab (described in Table 5-2) provides a quick way to jump to a specific location on your system to view files, plus quick access to the KDE settings.

Table 5-2	The Computer Menu
Menu Choice	What You Find
System Settings	This allows you access to the KDE desktop settings utility.
System Information	Provides quick access to information about your workstation — the hard drive size and usage, network status, OS version, and links to your important folders.
Home	View the contents of the user's home folder.
Network	View any file servers available on the local network.
Root	View the contents of the virtual directory structure.
Trash	View the items stored in the special Trash folder, and empty the trash.
PC Floppy Drive	View the contents of the floppy disk inserted into the floppy drive in the workstation.

The Computer menu items also expand to include any removable media you insert into your workstation, such as a CD, DVD, or USB memory stick. Just select that menu item to access files and folders on the removable media.

Recently Used

As you use applications, KDE adds them to this section of the menu. The more you use an application, the higher in the listing it appears.

Leave

There may be 50 ways to leave your lover, but there are only six ways to leave your desktop (at least without crashing your system)! The Leave tab provides six options, itemized in Table 5-3, for exiting the desktop session.

Table 5-3	The Leave Menu
Menu Choice	*What It Does*
Logout	Ends the current desktop session and returns to the login screen.
Lock	Locks the desktop and displays a screensaver. To re-enter the desktop, you must enter the password for the logged-in user.
Switch User	Suspends the current user's session, and allows another user to log in.
Suspend to Disk	Writes the current session state to a disk file and puts the system in a low-power mode.
Shutdown	Ends the current desktop session, halts all processes on the system, and powers-off the system.
Restart	Ends the current desktop session and reboots the system.

When you select an option from the Leave menu, a dialog box appears to prompt you for a confirmation. That helps prevent "oops" moments.

The panel

At the bottom of your KDE desktop, you see a line with a bunch of icons. This is called the *panel.* The panel contains *widgets,* or small programs that run on the panel to provide functions directly on the panel.

The layout of the KDE panel is another feature in KDE that is often different in the different Linux distributions. Most distributions place the KDE KickOff menu on the far left side of the panel — which just happens to be the same place that Microsoft Windows places its Start icon. (We told you KDE was kind to ex-Microsoft Windows users!)

On the Fedora KDE desktop (refer to Figure 5-1), next to the KDE KickOff menu's icon, you see the following widgets on the panel:

- ✔ **New Device Monitor:** Alerts you when a USB device is plugged into your workstation, and provides a list of installed devices. This is the box icon with the USB symbol inside it.

- ✔ **Pager:** Allows you to switch between different virtual desktop workspaces. This is the group of four boxes gathered together.

- ✔ **Task Manager:** Displays thumbnail images for running applications. If you don't have any applications running, it just appears as a blank area in the panel.

- ✔ **System Tray:** Contains icons for utilities and system applications, such as the sound system, the Network Manager, and the Clipboard, that run in background mode. The System Tray appears as a black area on the panel, with the icons inside.

- ✔ **Digital Clock:** Displays the current time.

- ✔ **Panel Editor:** Allows you to modify the panel layout and widgets. This is the half-circle icon at the far right of the panel.

You can easily modify the panel layout to suit your likes. Just click the Panel Editor icon on the far-right side of the panel to put the panel in edit mode, as shown in Figure 5-3.

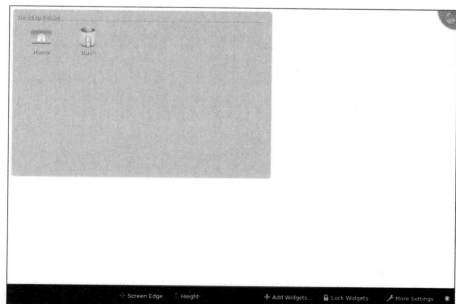

Figure 5-3:
The KDE panel in edit mode.

The Panel Editor contains icons for working with your panel. Table 5-4 shows what each of these icons do.

Table 5-4	The Panel Editor
Feature	**What It Does**
Screen Edge button	Selects which side of the desktop the panel appears on.
Height button	Selects the height of the panel.
Add Widgets button	Adds new widgets to the panel.
Lock Widgets button	Prevents widgets from getting moved or removed accidentally.
More Settings button	Accesses buttons you can use to align the panel widgets, autohide the panel, or specify whether windows can cover the panel.
Exit button	Exits the panel editor.
Left-side pointer	Sets the location of the left side of the panel.
Right-side top pointer	Sets the maximum location of the right side of the panel.
Right-side bottom pointer	Sets the minimum location of the right side of the panel.

In edit mode, you can also move existing widgets around the panel by dragging and dropping them, or you can remove existing widgets by right-clicking the widget icon and selecting the removal option. Using all these features, you can select just how your panel looks on your desktop.

The desktop

The desktop is possibly the most controversial feature in the latest version (Version 4) of KDE. Its behavior has significant differences from what you'd get in older versions of KDE — and from the desktop in GNOME as well. The desktop in KDE works more like an extension of the panel than a desktop. You can't place files, folders, or application icons in the desktop in KDE. Instead, you just place additional widgets.

That said, however, you can use a trick to make the KDE desktop behave similarly to the GNOME desktop. One of the widgets you can use is the *Folder View* widget, which provides a GNOME desktop-like area on your KDE desktop. The default Fedora KDE desktop uses the Folder View widget (refer to Figure 5-1), but if you install the KDE desktop in Ubuntu, that won't work; by default, Ubuntu doesn't include a Folder View widget (but you can add it using a software-package manager, as described in Chapter 16).

The Folder View area allows you to place files, folders, and application icons on your desktop within the defined Folder View area. Actually, you can create a folder view area for any folder on your system, but it's most common to create it for the Desktop folder in your Home folder (see Chapter 7). This is the default Folder View provided in the Fedora KDE desktop. Thus, items placed in the Desktop Folder View appear in the Desktop folder of your home area, just like the desktop in GNOME.

Aside from the Folder View, the default Fedora desktop includes only one other icon (in the upper-right corner of your desktop): the one that launches the *desktop editor,* the program you use to add more widgets to your desktop, just the way you would on the panel.

The KDE desktop and panel both use the same widgets, so we take a closer look at the widgets next.

Using Widgets

The keys to the KDE desktop environment are the *widgets* — handy little utilities or other small programs you can use directly from your desktop. This section walks through how to add, remove, and get new widgets in your KDE environment.

Adding widgets

The KDE package provides lots of different widgets for you to use in both your panel and your desktop. Selecting the Add Widgets option from the panel or the Desktop Editor produces a list of the widgets currently installed on your workstation. Figure 5-4 shows what this looks like.

Widgets that are already installed on your desktop or panel have a mark next to them. Adding a new widget is as easy as selecting the desired widget and clicking the Add Widget button. Table 5-5 lists the widgets that are available by default in Fedora.

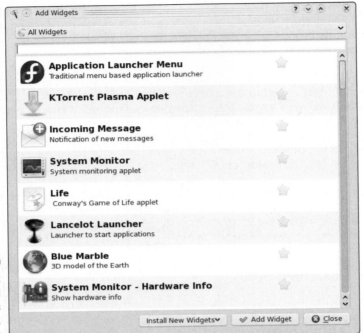

Figure 5-4:
The Add
Widgets
menu.

Table 5-5	Fedora KDE Widgets
Widget Name	*What It Does*
Analog Clock	Displays a good ol' round clock with hands!
Application Launcher	Starts a preset application.
Application Launcher menu	Provides a menu of applications.
Battery Monitor	Displays the charge status of your laptop battery.
Binary Clock	The geek's time tool!
Calculator	Provides quick access to the KDE calculator.
Color Picker	Allows you to capture the color values of any color on the desktop.
Comic Strip	Displays a daily comic strip.
Dictionary	For those times when you just can't figure out how to spell a word.
Digital Clock	Displays the time in digital format.

Widget Name	What It Does
Fifteen Puzzle	Quick entertainment for puzzle freaks.
File Watcher	Displays the real-time contents of a text file in scrolling fashion (ideal for watching log files).
Folder View	Provides a graphical display of a specific folder's contents.
Fuzzy Clock	Displays the time in everyday English, such as "ten to six" for 5:50.
Incoming Messages	Notifies you of new e-mail messages.
KGet	Graphically shows the download status of a KGet file download in progress.
Konq Profiles Applet	A menu providing quick access to all the different Konqueror file and Web browsing features.
Lock/Logout	Easy access to log out or lock your workstation.
Luna	Displays lunar phases.
New Device Monitor	Provides information on USB devices plugged into the workstation.
News Ticker	Offers up-to-the-minute news on your desktop!
Notes	Gives you a place to jot things down. (Just like real life — you can leave sticky notes for yourself all over your desktop!)
Now Playing	Displays the name of a music-video file currently playing.
Pager	Allows you to jump quickly between workspaces.
Picture Frame	Creates an area for displaying your favorite pictures in a slideshow.
Show Dashboard	Brings all the desktop widgets in front of any open application windows.
Show Desktop	Provides quick access to the desktop by minimizing all open applications at once.
System Monitor	Displays vital system statistics.
System Monitor - Network	Displays network statistics.
System Tray	Displays icons for system programs running in the background.
Task Manager	Displays icons for applications currently running on the desktop.
Trashcan	Provides a temporary place to put files you might want to delete.
Twitter Microblogging	Offers quick access to the popular Twitter social-networking site.

That's quite a collection of widgets available to play with! You can experiment with widgets by adding them to your panel or desktop, and then easily remove them if you don't find them useful.

To add the widget, just select the one you want, and then click the Add Widget button. Most widgets provide a simple control menu to modify the layout and behavior of the widget by either right-clicking the widget in the panel or hovering your mouse pointer over the widget on the desktop. From this menu you can move the widget, remove the widget, or (for some widgets) access a Properties dialog box to configure the widget.

Getting more widgets

Besides all of the standard widgets, you can download even more. Click the Install New Widgets button in the Add Widgets dialog box to find these two options:

- **Download New Plasma Widgets:** Browse the online repositories for new widget packages.

- **Install Widget from Local File:** Browse to a location on your workstation to install a new widget package from a file already on your workstation.

If your workstation is connected to the Internet (see Chapter 8), follow these steps to install new widgets from the Internet:

1. **Select the Download New Plasma Widgets option from the Install New Widgets button.**

   The Plasma Workspace Add-On Installer opens, as shown in Figure 5-5.

Figure 5-5:
The Plasma
Workspace
Add-On
Installer —
portal to
widgets
galore.

The installer dialog box contacts the configured widget repositories (which are approved by KDE) and provides a list of available widgets.

2. **Click the Install button for the widget you want to use.**

   The Add-On Installer automatically downloads the widget from the repository and installs it on your workstation.

3. **Click the Close button to close the Add-On Installer.**

   The newly installed widget appears in the Add Widgets dialog box.

4. **Select the new widget from the Add Widgets dialog box.**

5. **Click the Add Widget button to add the new widget to your desktop or panel.**

After you've installed the new widget on your desktop or panel, you can access and manage the widget from the control menu.

Adjusting the Desktop Settings

With KDE, you can configure just about every feature in your desktop environment to your liking. The KDE System Settings utility provides quick access to all your configuration needs.

You start the KDE System Settings utility from the KDE KickOff menu. In Ubuntu, choose Computer⇨System Settings. In Fedora, choose Favorites⇨System Settings. The main System Settings dialog box (shown in Figure 5-6) appears.

The dialog box contains two tabs:

- **General:** Access to most of the common features of the desktop.

- **Advanced:** Access to some additional features for more advanced users, such as setting programs to file extensions, managing services, and managing sessions.

The General tab contains the features you'll most want to mess with. It consists of four sections (or groups) of settings:

- Look & Feel
- Personal
- Network & Connectivity
- Computer Administration

In the next sections, we take a look at what's in these areas.

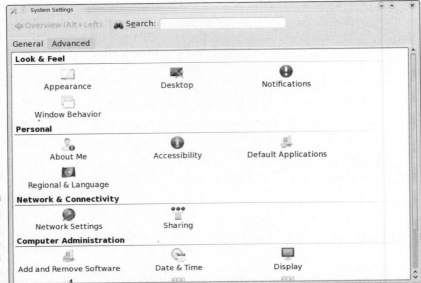

Figure 5-6:
The KDE
System
Settings
dialog box.

Look & Feel

The Look & Feel section contains utilities for defining how your KDE desktop appears and how it behaves. The Look & Feel utilities are

✔ **Appearance:** This utility controls the overall appearance of your desktop and the elements in it. It consists of seven different features you can customize:

- *Style:* The overall style of windows and window elements. This consists of several predefined styles to choose from.

- *Colors:* Define the color scheme used in your windows.

- *Icons:* Define the icon types used on the desktop.

- *Fonts:* Select the fonts used for text that appears in window elements.

- *Windows:* Select from a set of predefined window styles.

- *Splash Screen:* Select the screen that appears as KDE starts up.

- *Emoticons:* KDE allows you to define text key sequences to produce funny icons (such as smiley faces and frowny faces) that you can use in your documents.

✔ **Desktop:** This utility controls the desktop environment on your workstation. It consists of four different features to customize:

- *Desktop Effects:* If your workstation includes an advanced video cart, you can enable fancy desktop effects such as melting windows, shadows, magnifiers, and even snow on your desktop!

- *Multiple Desktops:* Define multiple desktops, or create virtual desktops to manage your applications more easily.

- *Screen Saver:* Select a screensaver to use if your workstation is inactive for a preset amount of time.

- *Launch Feedback:* Set special effects to tell you that KDE is working on a request to start an application, such as a bouncing cursor.

✔ **Notifications:** This utility lets you set how KDE notifies you of system events, such as errors, bad keystrokes, or bad mouse clicks. It consists of two features you can customize:

- *System Notifications:* Set different sound effects for specific actions in KDE applications.

- *System Bell:* Select to customize and play a bell noise instead of a specific notification sound.

✔ **Window Behavior:** This utility defines how application windows interact on your desktop. It has two configurable features:

- *Window Behavior:* Use this one to set the window actions for all windows on the desktop. For example, you can specify how to focus on an active application window, what the right, middle, and left mouse buttons do in your windows, and how to move a window on the desktop.

- *Window-Specific:* Use this one to define window actions for specific applications.

The Look & Feel settings provide a wide assortment of features for you to customize your desktop environment. If you're not into spending hours getting your desktop "just right," don't worry, the default settings used by most Linux distributions work just fine.

Personal

The Personal section allows you to personalize the desktop with features that you prefer to use or with features that give individuals with special requirements some useful ways to interact with files, folders, and applications on the desktop:

- ✔ **About Me:** Set features for your user account, such as your name, e-mail address, and Home folder locations. This also provides a quick way to change your password.

- ✔ **Accessibility:** Provide settings for keyboard and sound features to accommodate special needs.

- ✔ **Default Applications:** Set the default applications to use for e-mail, text editor, instant messaging, terminal emulator, and Web browsing.

- ✔ **Regional & Language:** Set the default language and keyboard layout you prefer to use in your desktop sessions.

With the Personal settings you can customize your desktop environment to feel just like home!

Network & Connectivity

The Network & Connectivity section contains only two utilities:

- ✔ **Network Settings:** This is a little misleading, because the utility doesn't really control how your network connection is configured (see Chapter 8 for that). Instead, it provides a place for you to define any default network proxy servers (such as Web proxy hosts — more about those in Chapter 8) on your network, and it allows you to play with the connection-timeout values for your specific network environment.

- ✔ **Sharing:** Set a Microsoft Windows username and password to use when connecting with remote Windows shares on the network (more on this in Chapter 7).

If your workstation is on a corporate network, you'll want to consult with your network administrator before messing with either of these utilities.

Computer Administration

The Computer Administration section provides utilities that you can use to configure settings for your system. Table 5-6 outlines the utilities available here.

Table 5-6	The Computer Administration Utilities
Utility	*What It's Used For*
Add and Remove Software	In Fedora, provides an interface for adding new software packages, selecting software-update repositories, and configuring settings used in the PackageKit package manager (see Chapter 16).
Date & Time	Sets the date and time on your workstation.
Display	Sets the display resolution; here you can also implement any power-saving features such as shutting down the display after a timeout.
Font Installer	Installs new fonts for your KDE applications.
Input Actions	Defines key combinations (called *hotkeys*) for specific functions.
Keyboard & Mouse	Sets basic keyboard and mouse features.
Multimedia	Sets the sound and video programs used for various desktop applications.

Part II
Getting Up to
Speed with Linux

The 5th Wave — By Rich Tennant

Linux really made the job a lot less complicated. Oh jeez, now what?

In this part . . .

In this part, you find out lots of Linux basics. You take a tour of the dusty nooks and crannies of the Linux filesystem to find out what is stored where. You then learn how to use the graphical tools provided on your desktop to move around in it and manage your files. Finally, you go through all of the fun of getting yourself connected to the Internet, if you don't have it working already.

Chapter 6

Getting to Know the Linux Filesystem

I have an existential map. It has "You are here" written all over it.

— Steven Wright

One of the most frustrating things about mastering a new operating system can be figuring out where it keeps files. Instead of keeping all the important system files in a single directory (such as the `C:\Windows` directory in Microsoft Windows), Linux follows the lead of its UNIX cousins and spreads things out a bit more. Although the Linux and Windows setups involve different methods, they are both logical, although it may not feel that way until you get a handle on where to look.

Putting Together the Pieces of the Puzzle

It helps to understand the lingo before getting started. A lot of this may be familiar to you from other operating systems such as Microsoft Windows, but you need to get used to some differences. To start, the word *filesystem* is actually used in more than one way. The general use (and what we typically refer to throughout the book) means "the files and directories (or folders) you have access to right now," instead of referring to the method used to store data on the hard drive (such as the `ext3` filesystem discussed in Chapter 3).

Here's what you need to know about filesystems:

- ✔ **Linux uses a forward slash (/) between directories, not the backslash (\) that Windows uses.** So, the file `yum.conf` in the directory `etc` is `etc/yum.conf`.

- ✔ **Files and directories can have names up to 256 characters long, and these names can contain underscores (_), dashes (-), and dots (.) anywhere within.** So `my.big.file` or `my.big_file` or `my-big-file` are all valid filenames.

- ✔ **Upper- and lowercase matter.** They have to match exactly. The files `yum.conf` and `Yum.conf` are not the same as far as Linux is concerned. Linux is case-sensitive — it pays attention to the case of each character. Windows, on the other hand, is case-insensitive.

- ✔ **The same filesystem can span multiple partitions, hard drives, and media (such as CD-ROM drives).** You just keep going down through subdirectories, not having to care whether something is on disk A, B, or whatever.

Touring the Linux Filesystem

In this section, we look at the contents of the typical Linux filesystem. Being at least a bit familiar with it helps you track things down later, and familiarity will help you to know where it's safe to mess with things and where you need to be very careful.

The root of the tree

Everything in the Linux filesystem is relative to the *root directory* — not to be confused with the system Administrator, who is the root *user*. The root directory is referred to as /, and it is the filesystem's home base — a doorway into all your files. As such, it contains a relatively predictable set of subdirectories. Each distribution varies slightly in terms of what it puts in the root directory, but certain standards exist to which all varieties of Linux conform. The standards keep the Linux world somewhat sane.

If you're interested in these standards, go to `www.pathname.com/fhs` and look at the latest version of the rules.

Table 6-1 lists what you might find in the base directory (that is, in /) in Linux. This list can vary depending on what you installed. An asterisk (*) at the end of a description indicates that you shouldn't mess with this directory unless you have a *really good reason* because it contains files that are *very important* to the functioning of your system. Really, most of the base directories should be left alone. There are sections inside them that are safe to change, but you have to know exactly what you're looking for before rummaging around in there.

Table 6-1	Standard / Contents in Linux
Directory	*Contains*
/bin	Essential commands that everyone needs to use at any time.*
/boot	The information that boots the machine, including your kernel.*
/dev	The device drivers for all the hardware that your system needs to interface with.*
/etc	The configuration files for your system.*
/home	The home directories for each of your users.
/lib	The *libraries,* or the code that many programs (and the kernel) use.*
/media	A spot where you add temporary media, such as floppy disks and CD-ROMs; not all distributions have this directory.
/mnt	A spot where you add extra filesystem components such as networked drives and items you aren't permanently adding to your filesystem but that aren't as temporary as CD-ROMs and floppies.
/opt	The location that some people decide to use (and some programs want to use) for installing new software packages, such as word processors and office suites.
/proc	Current settings for your kernel (operating system).*
/root	The superuser's (root user's) home directory.
/sbin	The commands the system Administrator needs access to.*
/srv	Data for your system's *services* (the programs that run in the background).*
/sys	Kernel information about your hardware.*
/tmp	The place where everyone and everything stores temporary files.
/usr	A complex hierarchy of additional programs and files.
/var	The data that changes frequently, such as log files and your mail.

*Some of these directories have some equally important subdirectories, which we cover in the upcoming sections.

The importance of being /etc

The /etc base directory contains primarily configuration files. It is best not to mess with these unless you know what you're doing. Some important directories (which will vary depending on what you have installed) include the following:

- The directories beginning with /etc/cron contain instructions for various programs that run at automated times.

- The /etc/cups directory contains configuration information for your printer.

- The directories beginning with /etc/rc all contain data about what starts and what doesn't at boot time and shutdown. These directories store the scripts the services run.

- The /etc/sysconfig directory has network-configuration information.

- The /etc/samba directory contains configuration files for the Samba software for communicating with Microsoft Windows servers (see Chapter 20).

- The /etc/X11 directory contains configuration details for the X Window System (X), which runs your graphical user interface (GUI). See Chapters 4 and 5 for more on the GUI.

- The /etc/opt directory contains configuration files for the programs in the /opt directory, if you decide to use it.

Where temporary media lives

You may or may not have any subdirectories in /media or /mnt by default. Typically, however, you can look for the following:

- The /media/floppy directory is used for adding a floppy disk to your filesystem — rather than seeing the word floppy, you might see fd0 or floppy0.

- The /media/sdb (or /media/sdc, /media/sdd, and so on) directory is used when you plug a USB flash drive into your workstation.

- The /media/cdrom (or /media/dvd, /media/cdrecorder, and so on, depending on what type of hardware you have) directory is used for adding a CD-ROM, DVD-ROM, CD-Writer, and so on to your system.

In Chapter 7, you find out how to do it in the handier point-and-click manner.

Where the computer is the /usr

The /usr directory is often referred to as its own miniature filesystem tree. This directory has lots of important or interesting subdirectories, as shown in Table 6-2. An asterisk (*) at the end of a description indicates that you need to leave that directory alone unless you have good reason to mess with it — *after* you gain lots of experience with Linux and know exactly what changes you need to make — so that you don't accidentally alter something your system needs in order to function correctly. An interesting thing to remember about this section of the filesystem is that many advanced Linux users often use /usr to store programs that can be shared with other Linux machines.

Table 6-2	Standard /usr Subdirectories
Subdirectory	*Contents*
/usr/X11R6	The files that manage the X Window System (the wireframe underneath your GUI).*
/usr/bin	The commands that aren't essential for users but are useful.*
/usr/games	The games that you install on your system, except for those that you can choose to place in /opt.
/usr/include	The files that the C programming language needs for the system and its programs.*
/usr/lib	The shared code used by many of the programs in this /usr subhierarchy.*
/usr/local	The programs and other items that you want to keep locally, even if you're sharing everything else in /usr.
/usr/sbin	The commands that aren't essential for Administrators but are useful.*
/usr/share	The information that you can use on any Linux machine, even if it's running incredibly different hardware.*

Managing Your Filesystem without a Net (Or Mouse)

Chapter 7 covers how to use the point-and-click file managers. In this section, we look at how to use the command-line tools to find your way around the filesystem. It isn't vital for you to know how to use the command line, but it could certainly prove useful someday!

In Chapter 17 we walk through the details of using the Terminal program (in the GNOME desktop) and the Konsole program (in the KDE desktop) to access the command line from your desktop. You'll find these programs in your desktop menus.

Viewing information about files on the command line

As you'll see in Chapter 17, the ls command lets you view files and directories. Just by itself it shows you the names of the non-hidden files and directories that you ask for. For example, if you were in the /etc directory and typed **ls**, you might see what is shown in Figure 6-1.

```
                              rich@testbox: /etc
 File  Edit  View  Terminal  Help
doc-base              mke2fs.conf       syslog.conf
dpkg                  modprobe.d        terminfo
e2fsck.conf           modules           timezone
emacs                 mono              ts.conf
environment           motd              ucf.conf
esound                motd.tail         udev
event.d               mtab              ufw
firefox-3.0           mtools.conf       updatedb.conf
fonts                 nanorc            update-manager
foomatic              netscsid.conf     update-motd.d
fstab                 network           update-notifier
fuse.conf             NetworkManager    usplash.conf
gai.conf              networks          vim
gamin                 nsswitch.conf     w3m
gconf                 obex-data-server  wgetrc
gdm                   openoffice        wodim.conf
gimp                  opt               wpa_supplicant
gnome                 pam.conf          X11
gnome-app-install     pam.d             xdg
gnome-system-tools    pango             xml
gnome-vfs-2.0         papersize         xulrunner-1.9
gnome-vfs-mime-magic  passwd            zsh_command_not_found
gre.d                 passwd-
rich@testbox:/etc$
```

Figure 6-1: The output of the ls command within /etc.

The colors displayed when you use this version of the command tell you something about the type of item you're looking at:

Text Color	Usually Means
Black	A regular file that doesn't match any of the special types that need a color.
Red	An *archive* or *package* (see Chapter 16).
Pink	An image file (if it recognizes the file extension, such as .jpg, .tif, and .gif). Sometimes pink is also used for another type of special file, but it's heavily specialized and not something you need to worry about. If you don't see an image extension on the filename but you see a pink file, just ignore it.

Text Color	Usually Means
Dark Blue	A directory.
Light Blue	A *soft link*.
Green	A program (called an *executable*) in Linux.
Gray text with a red background	A *SetUID* (*SUID*) executable file, which uses a different user account when you run it.
Dark text with an orange background	A SetGID (SGID) executable file, which uses a different group account when you run it.
White text with a red background	A *broken link* file.
Yellow text with a black background	A *device* file (basically, the file that is used to talk to a piece of hardware, like your monitor).
Black text with a green background	A directory where you can only delete or change the files that you own or have *write permissions* for (see the section "Understanding file listing information" later in this chapter for more).

The ls command shows everything in the requested location except for *hidden files*, which start with a dot. To see the hidden files too, type **ls -a**, and you get results as shown in Figure 6-2.

Figure 6-2:
A brand-new home directory with just ls, and then again with ls -a to see the hidden files as well.

```
                           rich@testbox: ~
File  Edit  View  Terminal  Help
rich@testbox:~$ ls
Desktop     examples.desktop  Pictures   Templates  Videos
Documents   Music             Public     tmp
rich@testbox:~$ ls -a
.                 examples.desktop   .gtk-bookmarks     .recently-used.xbel
..                .fontconfig        .gvfs              .sudo_as_admin_successful
.bash_logout      .gconf             .ICEauthority      Templates
.bashrc           .gconfd            .icons             .themes
.cache            .gegl-0.0          Music              .thumbnails
.config           .gimp-2.6          .nautilus          tmp
.dbus             .gksu.lock         Pictures           .update-manager-core
.dmrc             .gnome2            .profile           .update-notifier
Documents         .gnome2_private    Public             Videos
.esd_auth         .gnupg             .pulse             .Xauthority
Desktop           .gstreamer-0.10    .pulse-cookie      .xsession-errors
rich@testbox:~$
```

A lot of files begin with the dot in your home directory. Applications that allow you to customize features store those settings in hidden files in your home directory.

So far all we've done is look at files and find out a little about them from the colors. The next section shows you how to discover more.

Understanding file listing information

To see more information than just names and vague types, you'll want a long-format file listing.

To see just non-hidden files, type **ls -l**. To see both hidden and non-hidden files, type **ls -la**. Figure 6-3 shows a sample.

Figure 6-3:
The beginning of the brand-new home directory with both hidden and non-hidden files displayed in long format.

```
                              rich@testbox: ~
File  Edit  View  Terminal  Help
rich@testbox:~$ ls -al
total 2480
drwxr-xr-x 30 rich rich    4096 2009-05-16 13:58 .
drwxr-xr-x  3 root root    4096 2009-05-16 09:04 ..
-rw-r--r--  1 rich rich     220 2009-05-16 09:04 .bash_logout
-rw-r--r--  1 rich rich    3115 2009-05-16 09:04 .bashrc
drwxr-xr-x  2 rich rich    4096 2009-05-16 09:20 .cache
drwxr-xr-x  4 rich rich    4096 2009-05-16 09:23 .config
drwx------  3 rich rich    4096 2009-05-16 09:20 .dbus
drwxr-xr-x  2 rich rich    4096 2009-05-16 09:20 Desktop
-rw-------  1 rich rich      28 2009-05-16 13:49 .dmrc
drwxr-xr-x  2 rich rich    4096 2009-05-16 09:20 Documents
-rw-------  1 rich rich      16 2009-05-16 09:20 .esd_auth
-rw-r--r--  1 rich rich     357 2009-05-16 09:04 examples.desktop
-rw-r--r--  1 rich rich 2359676 2009-05-16 13:58 fg0602AR.tiff
drwxr-xr-x  2 rich rich    4096 2009-05-16 09:22 .fontconfig
drwx------  5 rich rich    4096 2009-05-16 13:49 .gconf
drwx------  2 rich rich    4096 2009-05-16 13:51 .gconfd
drwx------  4 rich rich    4096 2009-05-16 09:22 .gegl-0.0
drwxr-xr-x 22 rich rich    4096 2009-05-16 13:50 .gimp-2.6
-rw-r-----  1 rich rich       0 2009-05-16 10:38 .gksu.lock
drwx------  6 rich rich    4096 2009-05-16 11:35 .gnome2
drwx------  2 rich rich    4096 2009-05-16 09:20 .gnome2_private
drwx------  2 rich rich    4096 2009-05-16 09:20 .gnupg
```

You may find some parts of this format easier to understand at a glance than others:

✔ The first item in each listing (the part with the letters and dashes — for example, the drwx------ in the first line) is the *permission set* assigned to the item. Permissions define who can read the file, change it, or run it if it's a program. (You can read more about permissions in "A permissions primer," later in this chapter.)

✔ The second item in the first line (in this case, 30) is the number of hard links to the item.

✔ The third item (rich) is the file's *owner*.

✔ The fourth (rich) is the *group* the file belongs to.

Depending on which version of Linux you're using, both the third and fourth items may be identical. You can find out more about both of these in "A permissions primer," later in this chapter.

✔ The fifth item is the file's size in bytes. All directories show up as 4,096 bytes. Everything else has its own size. You can tell an empty file because its size will be 0 bytes.

✔ The sixth and seventh entries are all related to the date and time the file was last changed: the date in YYYY-MM-DD format, and the time in 24-hour format (17:22).

✔ The ninth item is the filename (for example, bash history, in the third row).

Linux uses two special files that you see in your file listings. The single dot (.) file represents the current directory, while the double-dot (..) file represents the parent directory. You can use these directory aliases when maneuvering around the system from the command line.

A permissions primer

If you find yourself scratching your head when looking at parts of that long-format file listing, don't worry. The group of nine after the first letter is the set of *permissions* (also called a *permission set*) for the file or directory. Linux, UNIX, and even Mac OS X use permissions as a way of providing file and directory security by giving you the means to specify exactly who can look at your files, who can change them, and even who can run your programs. You need this capability when you have a bunch of different users on the same machine, networked to the world.

Checking out the triplets

Each permission set consists of three triplets. Each of the triplets has the same basic structure but controls a different aspect of who can use what. Consider the long-format listing for /home/dee in the following code:

```
rich@testbox:~$ ls -al
total 2480
drwxr-xr-x 30 rich rich 4096 2009-05-16 13:58 .
drwxr-xr-x  3 root root 4096 2009-05-16 09:04 ..
-rw-r--r--  1 rich rich  220 2009-05-16 09:04 .bash_logout
-rw-r--r--  1 rich rich 3115 2009-05-16 09:04 .bashrc
drwxr-xr-x  2 rich rich 4096 2009-05-16 09:20 .cache
drwxr-xr-x  4 rich rich 4096 2009-05-16 09:23 .config
drwx------  3 rich rich 4096 2009-05-16 09:20 .dbus
drwxr-xr-x  2 rich rich 4096 2009-05-16 09:20 Desktop
```

The first character in the permission set refers to the type of file. For a directory, the character is shown as a d, as shown in the first two items in the preceding list; files are designated with a dash (–). Each file or directory's permission set is a group of nine characters — that is, the nine characters that follow the first character (for a total of ten). But this group of nine is really three groups of three, as shown in Figure 6-4.

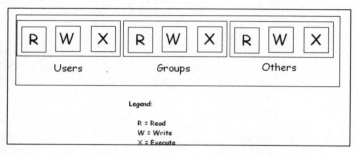

Figure 6-4:
Breakdown
of the nine
permission
characters.

The three triplets are read as follows:

✔ The first triplet consists of the second, third, and fourth characters in the long-format file listing. This triplet sets the permissions for the *user,* or *owner,* of the file. (Owners are discussed in the "Beware of owners" section, later in this chapter.)

✔ The second triplet consists of the fifth, sixth, and seventh characters in the long-format file listing. This triplet sets the permissions for the *group* that is assigned to the file. (Groups are discussed in the "Hanging out in groups" section, later in this chapter.)

✔ The third triplet consists of the eighth, ninth, and tenth characters in the long-format file listing. This triplet sets the permissions for *other,* or everyone who isn't the file's owner or a member of the owning group.

Although each triplet is often different from the others, the internal structure of each one is made up in the same way. Focus specifically on how to read one triplet before looking at the set of them together. Each triplet includes three characters:

✔ **The first character is either an** r **or a dash.** The r stands for *read* permission. If r is set, the triplet allows the entity it stands for (user, group, or other) to view the directory's or file's contents.

✔ **The second character is either a** w **or a dash.** The w stands for *write* permission. If w is set, the triplet allows the entity it stands for to add, delete, or edit items in this directory or file.

✓ **The third character is either an** x **or a dash.** The x stands for *execute* permission. If x is set, the triplet allows the entity it stands for to access the files contained in this directory or to run the particular program in this file.

In all cases, if the dash sits in place of r, w, or x, the triplet doesn't allow the entity the read, write, or execute permission.

The following sections describe owners and groups in more detail.

Beware of owners

You may have noticed by now that we talk a great deal about owners (users) and groups in Linux. Every file and directory has both of these components: a user from the /etc/passwd file that's assigned as its owner and a group from the /etc/group that's assigned as the group.

Although an everyday user probably doesn't need to change file ownerships often, the root user does so regularly. If you add the file comments, for example, to /home/tom while you're logged on as the *superuser* (another term for the Administrator, who is the person who owns the root account), the root user owns that file. The user tom can't do anything with it unless the file's owner (root) sets the last triplet's permissions to allow the *other* folks (those who aren't the file's owner or in the specified group) to read and write to the file. But this method is a pretty sloppy way of doing things because the whole idea of permissions is to *reduce* access, not to give everyone access. Instead, remember to change the file's owner to the user tom. You do this with the chown (*change own*er) command. For example, by typing chown mike comments, rich changes the ownership over to mike. Then mike can work with this file and even change its permissions to something he prefers:

```
rich@testbox:~$ ls -al comments
-rw-r--r-- 1 rich rich 5 2009-05-16 14:25 comments
rich@testbox:~$ sudo chown mike comments
[sudo] password for rich:
rich@testbox:~$ ls -al comments
-rw-r--r-- 1 mike rich 5 2009-05-16 14:25 comments
rich@testbox:~$
```

Hanging out in groups

Groups are more interesting to work with than owners. You use groups to allow the root user to assign multiple users the ability to share certain filesystem areas. For example, in many versions of Linux, all users are added to a group named *users* (openSuSE does this, for example). Then rather than a long-format file listing such as the one shown earlier in this chapter, you may see the following:

```
rich@testbox:~$ ls -al
total 2480
drwxr-xr-x 30 rich users 4096 2009-05-16 13:58 .
drwxr-xr-x  3 root root  4096 2009-05-16 09:04 ..
-rw-r--r--  1 rich users  220 2009-05-16 09:04 .bash_logout
-rw-r--r--  1 rich users 3115 2009-05-16 09:04 .bashrc
drwxr-xr-x  2 rich users 4096 2009-05-16 09:20 .cache
drwxr-xr-x  4 rich users 4096 2009-05-16 09:23 .config
drwx------  3 rich users 4096 2009-05-16 09:20 .dbus
drwxr-xr-x  2 rich users 4096 2009-05-16 09:20 Desktop
```

If all users are members of the same group, and each file belongs to the group, then each user has the group permissions for the files.

In other distributions (such as Fedora and Ubuntu), a unique group is created for every user, which is why the earlier listings showed the owner and group items as identical (rich rich).

Chapter 7

Using the Filesystem

There is no need to do any housework at all. After the first four years, the dirt doesn't get any worse.

— Quentin Crisp

In Chapters 4 and 5, we took a look at the GNOME and KDE desktops, and saw how to use them, but one skill was deliberately skipped: handling files. Chapter 6 addresses how to work with the filesystem on the command line and where to find things. This chapter focuses on pointing and clicking your way through your directories and manipulating your files with ease.

Choosing a File Manager

The key to managing files and folders from your graphical desktop is the *file manager* program — a nice graphical interface that offers neat access to the mess of files and folders present on your system. Instead of having to dig through the welter from the command line, you just point and click your way to a managed filesystem!

However, as with just about everything else in the Linux world, you can choose from several different file manager programs. The one you use in your desktop mostly depends on which desktop you're using. The main players are

- ✔ **Nautilus:** The default file manager used in the GNOME desktop.

- ✔ **Dolphin:** The new file manager used in the KDE desktop.

- ✔ **Konqueror:** The old file manager used in the KDE desktop, still popular today because of its versatility.

Of course, just because a file manager is the default for a desktop doesn't mean you *have* to use it! Any of the file-manager programs available in one Linux desktop work just fine in another Linux desktop. In fact, if you install the KDE desktop in Ubuntu, the Nautilus file manager still stays as the default — but you can use whichever one you want.

Sailin' through Folders with Nautilus

In the GNOME desktop environment, the default file manager is *Nautilus*. Moving through the filesystem in Nautilus involves a couple of different skills than using the command line. You may know exactly where in the filesystem you want to go, but not what to click to get there. In the first place, you need to know where you want to begin. This decision isn't as difficult as it sounds.

You have two options for navigating your filesystem with Nautilus:

- ✔ **Spatial mode:** Displays the contents of a single folder in a window. If you double-click a folder, it opens a new window with the contents of that folder, keeping the original window still open. Figure 7-1 shows spatial mode in use.

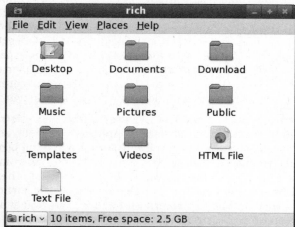

Figure 7-1:
The user rich's Home folder in Nautilus, using the spatial mode.

- ✔ **Browser mode:** Displays the contents of a folder in a window, along with a navigation bar to the left (as shown in Figure 7-2). If you double-click a folder in the window, that folder opens in the same window; it's much like going to a new page in a Web browser. You can navigate forward and backward through your filesystem, all within the same window.

Ubuntu configured Nautilus to always open in browser mode. Fedora opens Nautilus in spatial mode for some items and in browser mode for others. If you prefer one mode over the other, this chapter helps you out by showing how to control which mode opens.

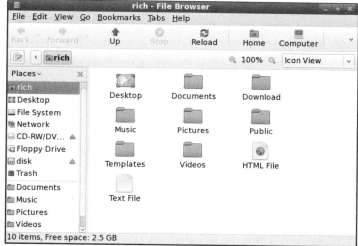

Figure 7-2:
The user rich's Home folder in Nautilus, using the browser mode.

There are usually a few different ways to start Nautilus from the GNOME desktop:

- ✔ **Double-click your desktop's Home icon:** Fedora (and many other GNOME-based distributions) includes the Home icon on the default desktop. Nautilus opens to the Home folder for the current user using spatial mode. Along the top is a menu bar, and at the lower left is a navigation drop-down list box that lets you move quickly to parent and "parent of parent" folders. Notice from Figure 7-1 that this window includes a Places menu.

- ✔ **Select Applications⇨System⇨File Browser:** Some Linux distributions (such as Fedora) include Nautilus in the Applications menu as a file browser. Choosing this option displays Nautilus using the browser mode, with a two-paned window with navigation options from Places on the left. (Click the Places drop-down list box to see what other options are available in the left pane, or click the X in the upper portion of the left pane to close it.) You can return to the Places section at any time by using the drop-down list again.

- ✔ **Select Places:** This panel menu item gives you the options discussed in Chapter 4, letting you open Nautilus immediately to a predefined location. Ubuntu uses browser mode by default, but Fedora uses spatial mode (as shown in Figure 7-1).

Regardless of how you open the window, much of the navigation is the same:

- ✔ To use a file, double-click it. If you're asked for instructions, proceed to the section "Opening files and running programs," later in this chapter.

- ✔ To open a folder in the spatial mode, double-click it. A separate window opens and displays the folder's contents, leaving the parent folder's window open as well.

    If you find that you have way too many folders open, choose one of the following commands:

    - • *File⇨Close Parent Folders:* Closes all the folders used to get to this directory.

    - • *File⇨Close All Folders:* Closes all the file-browser folders you have open.

    - • *File⇨Close:* Closes just this folder.

- ✔ To close a window, choose File⇨Close or click the X in the window's upper-right corner.

- ✔ If you are in the browser mode, you can navigate the filesystem in this way:

    - • Click Places in the left pane and select Tree from the drop-down list box.

    - • Click the right arrows to expand folders and see what other folders are inside. (Home Folder refers to your account's files, and File System refers to the root folder discussed in Chapter 6.)

    - • Click down-facing arrows to collapse sections of the tree and clean up the view.

    - • Click the folder itself on the left to see its contents on the right.

    - • Double-click folders on the right to see their contents replace the current view's contents. Notice that there is no Places menu along the top; instead, it's an option in the left pane.

Setting how much detail you see in a folder

Are you getting too much information about each file or not enough? Experiment with the View menu. The major listing options under the View menu include the following commands:

- ✔ **View As Icons:** This default option shows all files as icons with names beneath them; refer to Figure 7-1.

✔ **View As List:** This command gives you a list of information about the file, as well as its icon and name (see Figure 7-3). Note that there are still small icons available along the left of the listing.

For more advanced settings for the View As List mode, choose View➪Visible Columns.

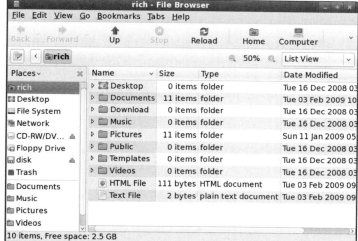

Figure 7-3:
Nautilus
with the
View As List
option in
rich's home
directory.

Along with these View menu commands, you can also use

✔ **Reload:** If you just created a file and don't see it in the folder, select this option.

✔ **Show Hidden Files:** All files in Linux whose names start with a dot (for example, .profile) are *hidden files* — you have to tell Linux explicitly that you want to see them.

✔ **Zoom In, Zoom Out, and Normal Size:** Change the visual size of the folder's contents.

✔ **Reset View to Defaults:** Start over from scratch.

Creating files and folders

To create a new file or folder in Nautilus, follow these steps:

1. **Browse to the folder you want to create the item in.**

   You need to have the folder open and be inside its window before proceeding.

2. **Right-click an empty spot inside that folder.**

   Make sure that you didn't highlight anything in the folder before you click.

   A context menu appears.

3. **Depending on what you want to accomplish, choose either Create Folder or Create Document.**

   • The *Create Folder* command creates a new, empty folder in this directory.

   • The *Create Document* command opens the submenu that lets you choose to create a document either from a Template (top section, if you already have templates created) or from an Empty File.

   The folder or file appears, highlighted and with its name open for editing.

4. **Type the name you want to assign to this folder or file and then press Enter.**

   The name is assigned to the folder or file.

Opening files and running programs

To open a file or run a program in Nautilus, double-click it. That's it! Well, not entirely. You can also right-click a file to open the context menu; when it opens, choose one of the following options:

✔ **Open with *program*:** If the file is associated with a particular program already, choosing this option is the same as double-clicking the file. If your system knows you have more than one program installed that can do the job, more than one option may be listed; the top item with the folder icon next to it is the default. Choose whichever option you prefer.

✔ **Open with Other Application:** Choosing this option opens a submenu that contains a list of installed programs that the system is aware of. If you find what you need in there, you can select one of these programs by clicking Use a Custom Command. From here, you can

   • Type the full path to the application (the full directory path, such as /usr/bin/konqueror).

   • Click the Browse button to open a file browser and surf to the program you want to use.

After you select the program to open the file with, click Open to proceed.

Copying and moving files

You can use different methods to copy and move items in Nautilus. The first is the usual method you're probably familiar with from Windows or the Mac OS — click and grab a file or folder and then drag it where you want it to go. You can click and drag between folder windows and into folder icons. Here are some handy tips:

✔ Hold down the Ctrl key while you drag if you want to make a copy rather than just move the file.

✔ If you want to drag the file into a folder icon, make sure that the folder icon is highlighted before you release the mouse button.

✔ If you want to drag the file into a folder window but not into one of the folder icons, make sure that the folder icons are *not* highlighted before you release the mouse button.

The other method for copying and moving files and directories involves following these steps:

1. **Right-click the file or directory you want to copy or move.**

2. **From the context menu that appears, choose Cut if you want to move the file, or choose Copy if you want to copy it.**

   The file doesn't disappear after you make your selection if you're trying to move it.

3. **Navigate to the folder you want to move the file into.**

   You're ready when you have that folder's window open.

4. **Do one of the following:**

   • If you want to move or copy the file into a folder window, right-click inside that window (just make sure that nothing is already highlighted) and then choose Paste.

   • If you want to move or copy the file into a folder icon rather than an open folder window, right-click the icon and then choose Paste Into Folder.

If you're used to the standard text-editor shortcut keys (Ctrl+C to copy, Ctrl+X to cut, and Ctrl+V to paste), those work just fine in Nautilus as well.

Deleting files and folders

To use Nautilus to delete either a file or a directory from the filesystem, follow these steps:

1. **Browse to the file or directory's location.**

2. **Select the file(s) or folder(s).**

   You can select the file or folder by doing one of the following:

   - Clicking the file or folder to highlight it.

   - Clicking the first item, holding down the Shift key, and then clicking the last item in the group to choose them all. (All these items must be lined up next to each other.)

   - Clicking the first item, holding down the Ctrl key, and then clicking each individual item you want to select.

   - Clicking and dragging your mouse pointer so you make a box that contains all the items you want to select.

3. **Press the Delete key or right-click and select Move To Trash.**

   The file or folder vanishes from view. Keep in mind that if you're deleting a folder and the folder contains other files or folders, everything in the folder goes into the Trash right along with it.

These deleted items are in fact sitting in the Trash folder; they aren't really deleted from your hard drive. If you haven't emptied the trash yet, you can move these files out of the Trash folder and back into your filesystem if you want to.

Taking out the trash

You can permanently delete the contents of your Trash folder by following these steps:

1. **Right-click the Trash icon.**

   This action opens a shortcut menu with options listed.

2. **Choose Empty Trash from the shortcut menu.**

   A confirmation dialog box opens.

3. **Click Empty in the confirmation dialog box to delete the contents of the Trash folder.**

Linux permanently removes the items in the Trash folder. You can tell whether the Trash folder is empty by looking at the Trash waste can. If it's empty, it contains no files. If you see papers in it, it contains trash.

Files and folders in the Trash folder are not automatically cleaned out by Linux. It's up to you to clean out your Trash folder to permanently delete files and folders from your workstation.

Viewing and changing permissions

In Chapter 6, you see that every file in Linux (and other forms of UNIX) has a set of *permissions* that govern who is allowed to view it, run it, delete it, and so on. Permissions are pretty important; they're assigned to make sure that people can't mess with the system's or each other's files. In this section, we focus on how to manage file permissions in the GUI.

To view and change a file or directory's permissions in Nautilus, follow these steps:

1. **Browse to the file or directory's location.**

   Opening the folder window that contains this item is sufficient.

2. **Right-click the file or directory.**

   A context menu appears.

3. **Choose Properties from the context menu.**

   The Properties dialog box appears with the Basic tab open.

4. **Click the Permissions tab.**

   The Permissions portion of the Properties dialog box appears, as shown in Figure 7-4.

5. **Set the new permissions and ownerships.**

   See Chapter 6 for a breakdown of what all this stuff means. Notice that the GUI divides Owner, Group, and Others into separate drop-down list boxes. Unless you're familiar with SELinux, leave the SELinux Context option alone.

6. **Click Close to close the dialog box.**

   The file's permissions are now changed.

That pretty much covers everything you'd want to do with the filesystem in Nautilus.

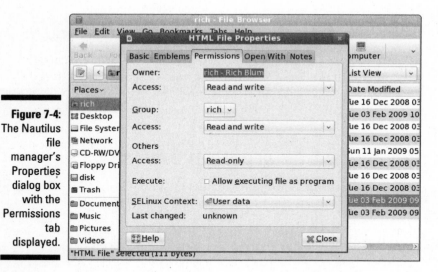

Figure 7-4:
The Nautilus
file
manager's
Properties
dialog box
with the
Permissions
tab
displayed.

Swimming with Dolphin

If you're using a new Linux distribution with the KDE desktop, most likely you're using the newer *Dolphin* file manager program. Dolphin works very much like the Nautilus browser mode, allowing you to easily browse through folders in the filesystem from a single window.

To open a Dolphin window, the KDE menu system (see Chapter 5) provides links, under the Computer tab, to specific locations on your workstation. You can view your Home folder, remote shared folders found on the network, the entire filesystem starting at the root folder (see Chapter 6), or the special Trash folder. Figure 7-5 shows the main Dolphin window layout.

Taking a look at the default Dolphin window, you'll see it has many of the same features as Nautilus:

✔ **The menu bar:** Allows you to access the settings used to display files and folders in your Dolphin window, along with options for creating new files and folders in the current window.

✔ **The toolbar:** Provides buttons for quick access to commonly used menu features:

 • *Back:* Navigate to the previously viewed folder.

 • *Forward:* Navigate to the folder viewed next if you've navigated backward.

- *Icons:* Display files and folders as icons.
- *Details:* Display detailed information for each file and folder.
- *Columns:* Display two columns of information, with the current folder shown in the left-side column, and files and folders in the selected folder appearing in the right-side column.
- *Preview:* Display a thumbnail image of the contents of text and image files.
- *Split:* Display two windows you can use to drag and drop files and folders easily from one location to another.

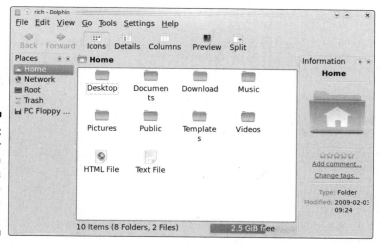

Figure 7-5:
The user rich's Home folder as seen in the Dolphin file manager.

- ✔ **The navigation bar:** The area on the left side of the window that displays location icons.
- ✔ **The view window:** Area to display file and folders contained in the current folder.
- ✔ **The information area:** This area, on the right side of the window, displays a thumbnail preview of the file, if possible (such as text and image files), along with file details.
- ✔ **The status bar:** Displays the number of files and folders in the currently viewed folder — along with the current amount of free space available on the disk.

When you single-click a folder in the view window, the folder opens in the same window, and the path (a *breadcrumb*) to the folder appears above the view window. Just like leaving breadcrumbs in the forest to find your way back, you can click anywhere along the breadcrumb path (also known as the *pathname*) to find your way back to the folder you started in.

Creating, copying, and renaming files and folders in Dolphin work exactly the same as in Nautilus. Right-clicking a file or folder produces a menu, which allows you to cut, copy, or move a file to the Trash folder.

Be careful when you're working in Dolphin; by default, it uses the KDE single-click method of activating an icon; if you select an icon, Dolphin attempts to display the file, using the default application for the file. That's somewhat annoying for those coming from a Microsoft Windows environment that uses double-clicks to open files. You can change that situation by using the System Settings feature (see Chapter 5).

Dolphin also allows you to produce side-by-side windows of your filesystem in the Split display mode, as shown in Figure 7-6. Just click the Split button on the toolbar.

Using Split display mode, you can easily drag and drop files from one folder to another — anywhere on the system!

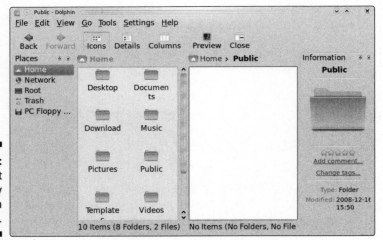

Figure 7-6:
The Split display mode in Dolphin.

All Hail the Konqueror

In the older versions of KDE (which are still popular in some Linux distributions), the default file-manager program was Konqueror. The Konqueror application is the Swiss Army Knife of the KDE project; it includes a file manager and a browser in one package.

Because of its versatility, many newer versions of KDE keep Konqueror around, even if Dolphin is loaded as the default file manager. To start Konqueror in Fedora, choose Favorites⇨Web Browser. The default Konqueror window opens, but points to the Fedora home page. You can easily enter a file path in the URL to view your local files. Figure 7-7 shows the URL /home/rich, which is a Home folder.

The beauty of Konqueror is that you can jump seamlessly between Web pages and local folders, all within the same window! Konqueror uses *tabbed browsing* to display multiple locations within the main window. Press Ctrl+T to open a new tabbed area. You can then easily switch back and forth between the Web and your local workstation filesystem by clicking the tabs.

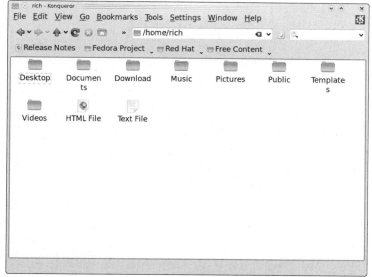

Figure 7-7:
A home folder using Konqueror in Fedora's KDE desktop.

But wait, there's more! Click the Settings menu bar item, and notice that you can also activate a Terminal window or a navigation bar. The navigation bar appears on the left side; it displays links for the home and root folders, the network, and the menu system, as shown in Figure 7-8. Click one of the local folders to access your filesystem.

Getting back to the file-manager world, Konqueror behaves like Dolphin in another important way: You can create, move, and delete files and folders by using standard drag-and-drop or right-click methods.

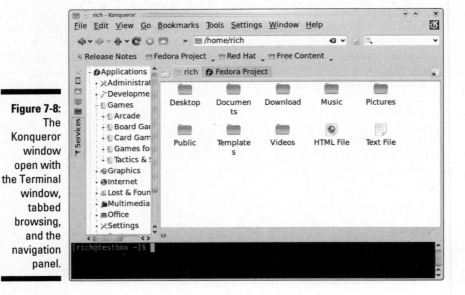

Figure 7-8:
The
Konqueror
window
open with
the Terminal
window,
tabbed
browsing,
and the
navigation
panel.

Using CDs and Other Removable Media

As discussed in Chapter 6, when it comes to removable media — CD-ROMs, DVD-ROMs, USB flash drives, floppy disks (if you have a retro system), and so on — if you're working from the command line, you have to look around for those media one drive at a time. Having a GUI file-manager program available makes your removable media much easier to find.

CDs, DVDs, and USB flash drives

Typically, when you insert a new removable item (say a data CD-ROM) in the GNOME desktop, an icon appears at the left on your desktop, showing the name of the device assigned to it. You can double-click the icon to see the medium's contents. Here's how you eject it:

✔ If an Eject option is available (for example, for a CD-ROM), you can right-click the icon and choose Eject from the context menu.

✔ Where Eject is not available, choose Unmount before removing the item (such as a USB flash drive) from the computer. This action ensures that all the data you saved actually is written to the removable medium; Linux doesn't always put the data on the drive right away.

In the GNOME desktop, when you insert a music CD or DVD, a music player (see Chapter 13) opens to play the music (for KDE you have to select it from the New Device Notifier widget). See Chapter 13 for how to add support for even more types of music files. When it comes to video CDs and DVDs, especially video DVDs, you often have to install extra software (that's due to a number of issues discussed in Chapter 14).

The KDE desktop doesn't automatically produce a desktop icon for removable media. The moment you insert a CD-ROM, USB flash drive, or floppy disk, however, the removable medium appears in the New Device Notifier panel widget (see Chapter 5). Accessing the removable medium is as easy as clicking the link in the pop-up window.

GNOME currently does a better job than its brethren of handling writable or rewritable blank CDs or DVDs. Inserting these discs into their drives causes a Nautilus window to open to its CD/DVD Creator window (discussed in a moment). The KDE desktop currently doesn't contain a CD/DVD-burning software package by default, but we'll remedy that a little later in this chapter.

Floppy drives

Floppy drives sometimes cause problems. For example, Linux computers can't reliably detect that a floppy disk was put into the drive; after you insert the disk, you have to tell Linux to look for it. So put the floppy into the drive, choose Places➪Computer in the GNOME desktop, and then double-click Floppy Drive to access the disk's contents and add a floppy icon on your desktop. For the KDE desktop, you'll have to open the Dolphin file manager and select the PC Floppy Disk entry from the navigation area.

When you're finished working with the floppy disk, you can remove it by right-clicking the floppy icon on your desktop and then choosing Unmount Volume (for GNOME) or clicking the Eject button in Dolphin (for KDE). Wait until the floppy drive's light turns off before you remove the disk. As long as the lights are on, Linux may still be writing to the disk.

Accessing Windows Drives on This Computer

If you're dual-booting between Windows and Linux, sometimes you want to access information on your Windows drive *from* Linux — and you can; unfortunately, Windows can't access information on Linux drives.

Here's how to access your Windows files from each Linux file manager:

- ✔ **Nautilus:** Select the Places menu. The Windows drive is listed along with all the other locations you can access (the name of the drive will match the long name used in Windows but not the drive letter).

- ✔ **Dolphin:** The Windows drive appears in the list of locations in the navigation bar area — again, using the same long drive name as in Windows.

Some Windows PCs use a hidden partition on the hard drive to hold emergency restore files. These partitions won't be hidden in Linux, so be careful that you don't ruin anything important to your Windows system (unless, of course, you're planning on removing Windows)!

Accessing Network Drives

Sometimes the drive you want to access is on another computer. If the drive on the other computer is set up to be accessible through your network, you can access it via the Nautilus, Dolphin, or Konqueror file managers:

- ✔ In the GNOME desktop, choose Places➪Network to walk through a list of shared folders found on your network. If you want to access a Windows computer, double-click Windows Network. The Windows computers on your network that have drives available for browsing are displayed. From there, you can browse to where you want to go!

- ✔ In the KDE world, choose KDE➪Computer➪Network (see Chapter 5). The Dolphin file manager opens in network mode, as shown in Figure 7-9.

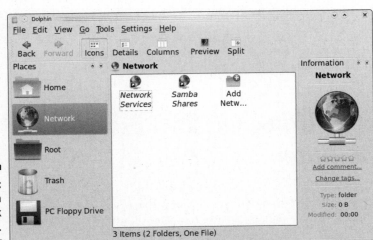

Figure 7-9: Dolphin in network mode.

✔ Your Windows network shares should appear under the Samba Shares folder (Samba isn't just a dance; it's the software Linux uses to talk to Windows networks — see Chapter 21).

If you can't see the Windows shared folders on your network, check whether your Linux distribution has a firewall enabled. By default, Fedora enables a firewall to block Samba connections; Ubuntu doesn't. (See Chapter 8 for more about these idiosyncrasies.)

Burning Data CDs and DVDs

A CD and DVD burner is a great way to make data backups (especially if the disc is rewritable), save and share your digital photos, put together multimedia mementos or scrapbooks, and more. Many tools are available that allow you to burn CDs under Linux; here's a quick look at a few of them.

The K3b package

By far the most popular CD and DVD burner used in the KDE environment is K3b. Unfortunately, it's not installed by default in Fedora. If you don't have it installed yet, see Chapter 16 for how to do so — the specific packages you want are k3b and k3b-extras. To open the K3b file, choose Applications⇨Multimedia⇨CD and DVD Burning. The window shown in Figure 7-10 opens.

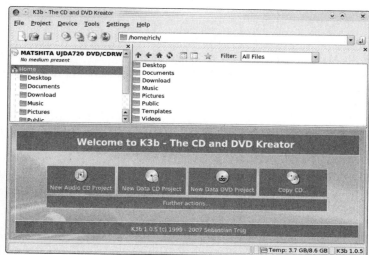

Figure 7-10: The K3b CD and DVD Kreator.

If all you want to do is create a CD or DVD out of an ISO file that you down-loaded, do the following:

1. **Choose Tools⇨Burn CD Image (if this is an ISO file for a CD-ROM) or choose Tools⇨Burn DVD ISO Image (if this is a file for a DVD-ROM).**

   Both actions open the Burn CD Image dialog box (see Figure 7-11).

Figure 7-11:
The K3b
Burn CD
Image
dialog box.

2. **In the Image to Burn section, click the folder button, navigate to the file you want to burn onto a CD or DVD, select the file, and click OK.**

   The filename and information now appear in the dialog box.

3. **If you have more than one burner for some reason, make sure that the proper one appears in the Burn Medium section, and change the selection if necessary.**

4. **In the Speed text box, if you're burning a CD or DVD of a Linux distri-bution, lower it to at least 4x. Otherwise you're usually safe to leave it as is.**

   If you find that when you burn CDs or DVDs, they often seem to end up as "coasters" (burns that didn't work), lower the speed you normally use.

5. **Click Save User Defaults if you want to use most of these settings for every burn.**

6. **Click Start to begin your burn.**

A dialog box appears, showing two progress bars. The first shows you write-preparation progress; the second shows you total progress, including burn time.

7. **If this is a rewritable medium, you'll be asked whether you want to erase its contents so it can be written over. Answer appropriately.**

If you tell K3b to erase the disc, the Erasing dialog box appears during that part of the process. When the erasure is finished, the tray opens, ejects the disc, and then closes automatically. This moment is when the actual burning session starts. The next time the disc ejects, the process is complete.

8. **Remove your new CD or DVD from the drive, click Close to close the Burn Information dialog box, and then click Close again to close the main Burn dialog box.**

9. **Choose File⇨Quit to close K3b.**

Notice that this program has some other interesting features listed in the bottom portion of the main window. Click one of the Project buttons to create a music (audio) CD, a data DVD, or a data CD from scratch. (Making audio CDs is covered in Chapter 13.)

Our friend, Nautilus

The Nautilus file manager for the GNOME desktop includes a built-in CD and DVD burner. To start it, choose Places⇨CD/DVD Creator. The CD/DVD Creator window opens, as shown in Figure 7-12.

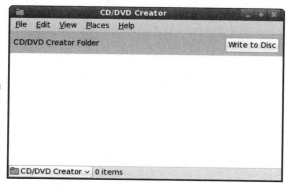

Figure 7-12: The Nautilus CD/DVD Creator window.

To burn files onto a CD or DVD, just follow these steps:

1. **Open another Nautilus window to browse for your files.**

2. **Copy the files and folders you want to burn into the CD/DVD Creator window.**

3. **Click the Write to Disc button to start burning the CD or DVD.**

And that's all there is to do! This is a great way to make quick backups of files on your system.

Brasero

The Ubuntu GNOME desktop also includes the Brasero CD-burning utility to help with your CD burning. Brasero is a full-featured CD-burning tool for creating data, audio, and video CDs and DVDs.

Choose Applications⇨Sound & Video⇨Brasero Disc Burning to open Brasero. There you can select what type of project to start, as shown in Figure 7-13.

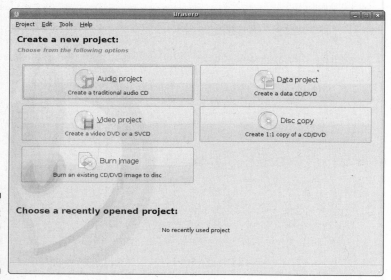

Figure 7-13:
The Brasero
main
window.

The layout of Brasero is very similar to the K3b package. Click the Data project button to burn files and folders onto a CD or DVD.

Finding Things

Both the GNOME and KDE desktops provide easy ways for you to search for items in the filesystem. For the KDE desktop, the KFind utility is the way to go. GNOME includes File Searcher.

KFind

Start KFind by choosing KDE⇨Applications⇨Find Files/Folders. The KFind main window, as shown in Figure 7-14, appears.

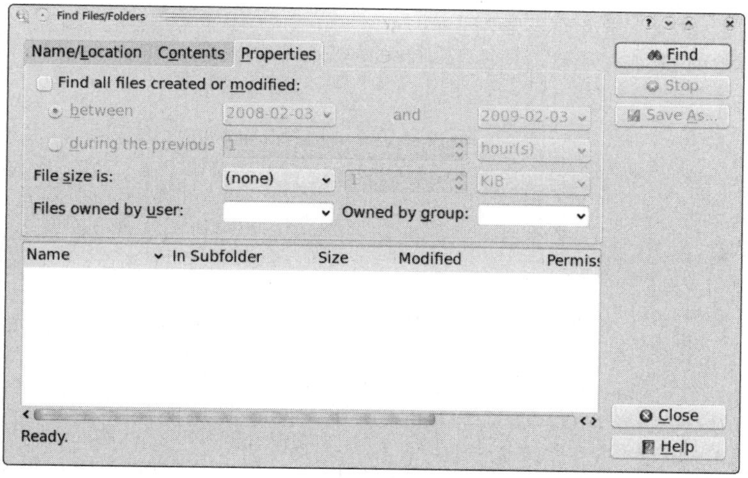

Figure 7-14: The KFind search window's Properties tab.

Here's how to find what you're looking for:

- ✔ In the main KFind tab, look for files or folders by their names or locations.
- ✔ The Contents tab provides a form you can fill out if you're interested in looking for specific contents within a text file (be careful, though; this search method can take awhile to complete).
- ✔ The Properties tab lets you search for files and folders according to a specific property of the file — such as when it was created, how large it is, or whether it's owned by a specific user.

File Searcher

As you might expect, the GNOME desktop also has its own file-searching utility, simply called File Searcher.

You can start the GNOME File Searcher by choosing Places⇨Search for Files.
The Search for Files dialog box opens, as shown in Figure 7-15.

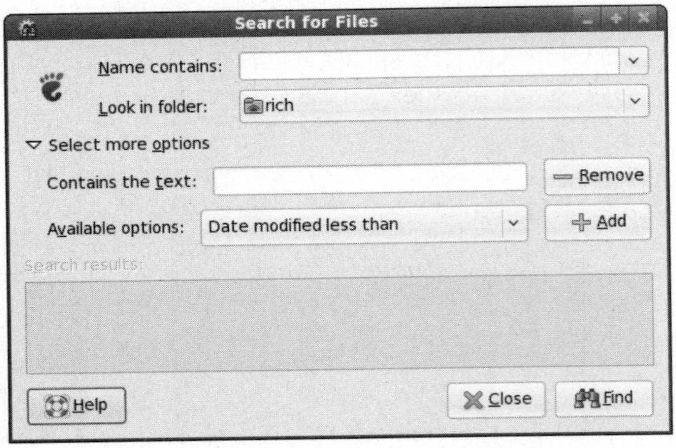

Figure 7-15:
The GNOME
Search for
Files dialog
box.

File Searcher has a feature that can really help narrow down your search —
it allows you to combine multiple search criteria. Just click the Add button
to add a new search option to the drop-down box. You can combine any
number of search criteria for File Searcher to use in your searches. That file
won't stay obscure for long!

Chapter 8

Connecting to the Internet

Every improvement in communication makes the bore more terrible.

— Frank Moore Colby

You may already be connected to the Internet if you're on a machine that's connected to a LAN and you've configured the networking during installation. To test whether you have a connection, open a Web browser and try to go to an outside Web site (such as `www.gnu.org`). If it works, you're up! No need for this chapter. Otherwise, read on.

Getting Information You Need from Your ISP

Most reputable ISPs provide you with a customer information sheet after you sign up for their services. This sheet should include the following information (at minimum):

- ✔ Local telephone dial-in numbers for modem users
- ✔ User login name
- ✔ User login password
- ✔ E-mail address

✔ E-mail outbound host or Simple Mail Transport Protocol (SMTP) server for routing outbound e-mail messages

✔ E-mail inbound host or Post Office Protocol (POP) server for receiving incoming e-mail messages

✔ News host

✔ Whether your computer address will be one of these two types:

- *Static:* You always have the same IP address. Static addresses are more common for servers than for desktops. If you're using static, your ISP needs to give you a few more pieces of information. You must define a *nameserver* IP address (which resolves hostnames into IP addresses), a *gateway* address (which routes your connection through the ISP to the Internet), and a *network* address and *netmask* combination (which define what addresses are local to your workstation). All this information should be on the customer information sheet.

- *Dynamic:* Your IP address changes each time you connect, or at regular intervals. On most desktops, you just don't always need to have the same address, and it makes life easier on ISPs. It also makes life easier for computers like laptops, which get moved around often from network to network. If you're using dynamic addressing, you're told that you need to connect using DHCP.

With this information, you can establish an Internet connection using your Linux system.

Configuring Your Connection

Okay, so you have your network hardware and your ISP information — now what? The answer is to configure your Fedora system to jump on the Internet!

The configuration process varies slightly, depending on the hardware you're using. This section covers the big three methods for accessing the Internet:

✔ Using a modem to dial your ISP

✔ Using an Ethernet card to connect to a DSL or cable modem

✔ Using a wireless card to connect to a wireless access point

Each situation requires a few slightly different items to configure, but you can perform all of them by using the Fedora Network Configuration tool.

Dialin' out

Using a modem to dial a connection to your ISP is a two-step process. First, you must configure your modem with the settings from your ISP. After that, you must manually start and stop the Internet connection (you probably don't want your modem tying up your phone line all day long).

The GNOME and KDE desktops each have distinct packages for configuring the modem and connecting to an ISP:

- ✓ **GNOME-PPP:** This one works for the GNOME desktop.
- ✓ **KPPP:** This one works for the KDE desktop.

If your Linux distribution doesn't include these programs (Fedora includes KPPP but not GNOME-PPP), both packages can be installed from the standard installation CD of most Linux distributions (see Chapter 16). After they're installed, you can walk through the upcoming sections that show how to configure them to work with your modem.

Setting up GNOME-PPP

After installing the GNOME-PPP package, you can follow these steps to configure a PPP session to connect with your ISP:

1. Choose Applications⇨Internet⇨GNOME PPP from the top edge panel menu.

The main GNOME PPP dialog box, shown in Figure 8-1, appears.

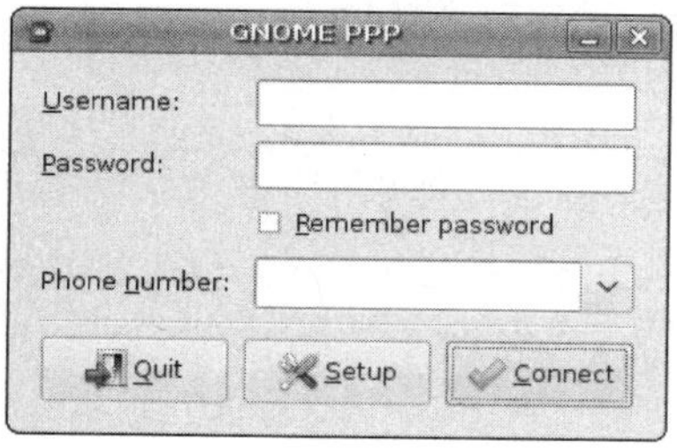

Figure 8-1:
The GNOME PPP dialog box.

2. Click the Setup button at the bottom of the dialog box.

The Setup dialog box opens, shown in Figure 8-2, where you can configure you modem settings.

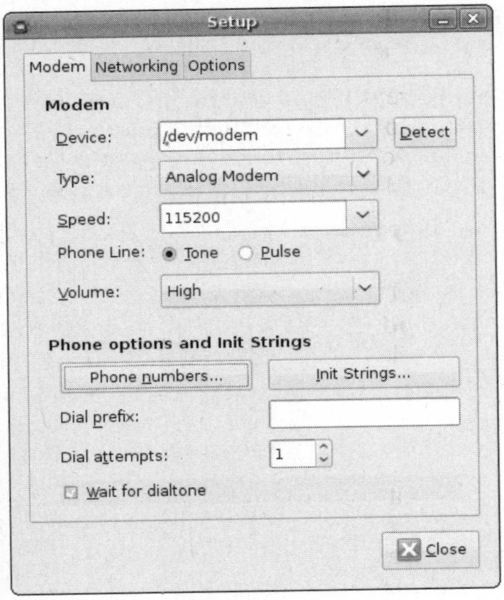

Figure 8-2:
The GNOME
PPP Setup
dialog box.

3. **Configure your modem settings in the Modem tab.**

   You must select which port your modem uses to communicate. If Linux automatically detects your modem, it assigns it to the special port /dev/modem. Use that first; if it doesn't work, Linux uses /dev/ttyS0 for COM1, /dev/ttyS1 for COM2, and so on. These ports are often labeled on the workstation using the Windows COM1 and COM2 names.

4. **Click the Networking tab and set your IP address information.**

   - If your ISP dynamically assigns an IP address to your workstation, select the Dynamic IP address radio button.

   - If you must specify a static IP address, select the Static IP address radio button and enter your address information in the text boxes.

   - If your ISP uses a static address, you'll also need to configure the nameserver server (called Domain Name Server [DNS] in the configuration window) to use for the network.

5. **Click the Options tab and set additional features for the modem connection.**

   You can set the modem connection icon either to minimize when the connection is established or to dock itself on the panel. You can also check advanced connection features from this page, such as having the modem reconnect if the connection drops.

6. **Click the OK button to save the settings.**

7. **Back in the main GNOME-PPP dialog box, enter the information needed to contact your ISP account.**

You must provide the phone number of your ISP, plus any special prefixes required (such as a 9 to get an outside line from some offices). Enter the user ID and password provided by your ISP, and select the check box if you want GNOME PPP to remember your password.

8. **Click the Connect button to initiate the connection to the ISP.**

You should now be able to go out and about roaming the Internet. When you're finished, it's usually a good idea to disconnect the session. Just right-click the icon in the panel and select the Disconnect option to shut things down and hang up the phone.

Setting up KPPP

The KPPP package requires about the same amount of work as the GNOME-PPP package for connecting to the Internet. After installing the KPPP package, choose Applications⇨Internet (Fedora labels it as Internet Dial-Up Tool) to open it. The main KPPP dialog box is shown in Figure 8-3.

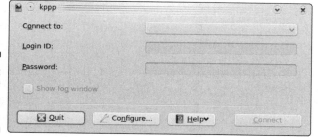

Figure 8-3:
The KPPP
main dialog
box.

Here's how to set up KPPP for your ISP account:

1. **Click the Configure button to change the default settings.**

The KPPP Configuration dialog box has four tabs for configuring your dialup connection:

- *Accounts:* Defines the logon information for your ISP
- *Modems:* Defines your modem properties
- *Graph:* Defines how to display connection statistics
- *Misc:* Defines various behaviors for the KPPP application

2. **Click the Modems tab to set up your modem.**

3. **Click the Add button to add a new modem.**

   The New Modem dialog box appears, as shown in Figure 8-4.

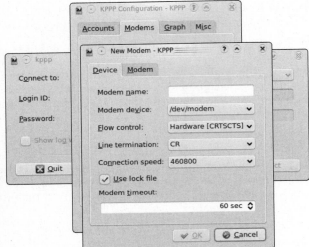

The modem device should already point to your /dev/modem entry. This is the device name that most Linux distributions assign to the modem. You can test the modem configuration by clicking the Query Modem button.

4. **Select the Accounts tab.**

   The Accounts tab allows you to define multiple ISP accounts to use.

5. **Click the New button to add a new account.**

   The New Account dialog box appears, asking whether you want to use the wizard process or enter your ISP information manually. Presently the wizard only supports a few ISPs in a few countries (and none in the United States). Most likely you'll need to use the manual setup method, shown in Figure 8-5.

6. **Enter your ISP account information as provided by your ISP.**

   Type the phone number provided by your ISP, and then click OK. The number will appear in the list. If your ISP provides other numbers, you can add them to the list as well. Consult your ISP to determine the authentication setting for the connection and any of the other configuration settings required.

7. **Click OK to return to the main configuration window.**

   You're now ready to connect.

8. **Type your ISP username and password, and click Connect.**

   KPPP dials the number, connects to the ISP, and logs in with your username and password.

When KPPP establishes a connection with the ISP, it places an icon in the KDE panel, showing the active connection. To stop the Internet connection, right-click the Panel icon, and select Disconnect.

Network Manager

The *Network Manager* application provides one-stop shopping for all of your network configuration needs. Just about every popular Linux distribution uses the Network Manager application these days, including Fedora and Ubuntu.

You start the Network Manager by right-clicking the Network Manager applet in your panel in either GNOME or KDE (it's either a picture of two monitors or a series of bars, depending on your network connection type). Select Edit configuration from the context menu to see your network configuration. The Network Connections dialog box, shown in Figure 8-6, appears.

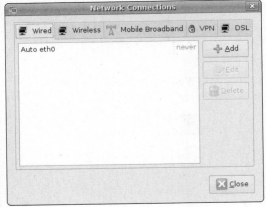

Figure 8-6:
The
Network
Connections
dialog box.

From this interface, you can configure

- ✔ Wired Ethernet card connections
- ✔ Wireless Ethernet card connections
- ✔ Mobile Broadband (wireless modem) connections
- ✔ Virtual Private Network (VPN) connections
- ✔ DSL connections

Most likely you're working on a network in your home, whether wired or wireless. The following sections walk through the basics of working on these two types of networks.

Playing with cards

With the increase of broadband connections, more Linux users are directly connected to the Internet these days. With most cable and DSL modems, you'll need a network interface card (NIC) to connect to the modem.

If you use a wired network card to access a broadband connection, most likely the Network Manager software automatically detected and configured it for you during the installation process. You can tell by looking for the Network Manager applet icon on the desktop panel.

If, for some reason, Network Manager didn't detect your network settings correctly (or if you have to manually set a static IP address), you can do that using the Network Manager interface.

Open the Network Connections dialog box and follow these steps to configure you wired network connection:

1. **Click the wired network card in the listing, then click the Edit button.**

   If the workstation has more than one wired network card, Ubuntu names the cards in numerical order, starting at `eth0` for the first card, `eth1` for the second card, and so on.

   The Editing dialog box, shown in Figure 8-7, appears.

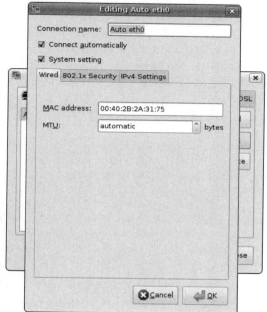

Figure 8-7:
The
Network
Connections
Editing
dialog box.

2. **Configure the wired network card settings.**

   The Editing dialog box contains three tabs of information for the network card:

   - *Wired:* Sets the Media Access Control (MAC) address for the card (which Ubuntu automatically detects) and the Media Transfer Unit (MTU) size, set for automatic.

   - *802.1x Security:* Sets login details for connecting to a protected wired network. Some network switches use this feature to restrict access to a wired network. If your network uses 802.1x security, consult your network administrator for the proper settings to use.

   - *IPv4 Settings:* Determines how the IP address for the network card is set. This can be either dynamically from a DHCP server, using the `zeroconf` protocol to negotiate an address with other devices on the network, or statically using a configured IP address.

   3. Click OK to save the new settings.

After you configure Network Manager for your wired Ethernet card, it attempts to start the card at the same time you start your workstation. If the Network Manager applet appears on the panel but shows no connection (a red X on the icon), check the cabling to make sure you plugged in things correctly. Also, check the network hub you're connecting to.

Look Ma, no cables!

The wireless phenomenon has taken home networking by storm. Nowadays a wireless router is just as easy to purchase and install as a wired switch. If you've jumped on the wireless bandwagon, you need to know how to connect your Fedora system to your wireless access point.

You first hurdle may be the wireless network card itself. Unfortunately, wireless network support is still in its infancy in the Linux world. Although each new version of Fedora includes support for more wireless network cards, it's still quite possible that your wireless network card is not supported.

If your wireless network card is not supported, you have a last-ditch measure you can resort to: the `ndiswrapper` project. The `ndiswrapper` project is an open-source project that uses Windows network drivers supplied for wireless network cards to create a pseudo-Linux driver. Unfortunately, neither Fedora nor Ubuntu provide the `ndiswrapper` software in the default configuration, but you can find it in other areas. You can find out more about `ndiswrapper` by visiting `http://sourceforge.net/projects/ndiswrapper/`.

If you're lucky enough to have a wireless network card that is supported by your Linux installation, you can use the Network Manager tool to configure it for your wireless access point:

1. **Left-click the Network Manager Applet icon to display a list of wireless access points detected, as shown in Figure 8-8.**

   The signal strength of each network is depicted by the orange bar. Networks protected by security passwords show an additional icon.

2. **Select the network you want to connect with, and then enter the network security password (if required). Skip to Step 4.**

   If the network is security protected, Network Manager prompts you to enter the password required to connect with the network.

3. **If you don't see the name of the network you want to connect with, (such as if the network uses a hidden SSID), select Connect to Hidden Wireless Network.**

   The Hidden Wireless Network dialog box opens, as shown in Figure 8-9.

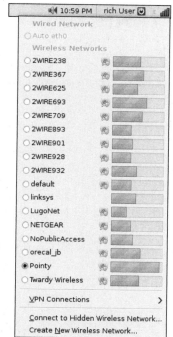

Figure 8-8:
The
Wireless
Networks
list.

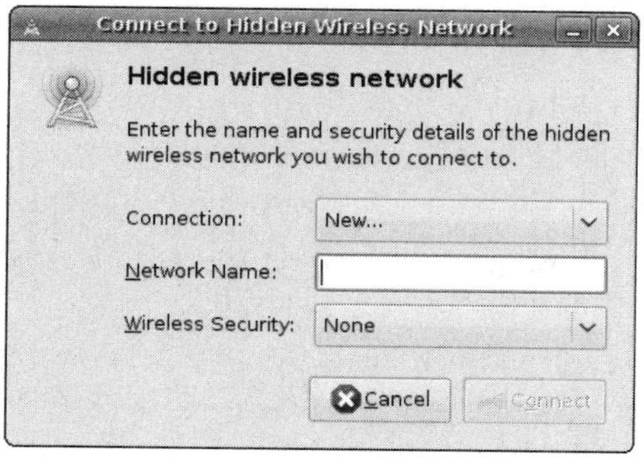

Figure 8-9:
Specifying
a hidden
wireless
network.

Enter the name of the wireless network, and then enter the security
scheme (if any) that it uses. If you select a security scheme that requires
a password, a new text box appears for you to enter the password.

4. Save the settings by clicking Connect.

The Network Manager Applet displays an animated icon in the panel indicating that it's trying to connect to the wireless network. If the connection is
successful, you see the signal strength meter icon.

It's All Fun and Games Until Something Doesn't Work

In a perfect world, the network configuration steps in the preceding section would work 100 percent of the time — because the Linux vendors have truly hidden all the mystery that has traditionally surrounded networking. Unfortunately, in many situations (mostly related to modems and hardware), a simplified configuration doesn't work. If you can't connect to the Internet after following these steps, an excellent site to find help is LinuxQuestions. org (www.linuxquestions.org). And yeah, we know — you'll have to use a computer that already has Internet access to get that help. (Catch-22, anyone?) It's simply impossible to anticipate the wide range of problems people can run into, and the Linux community is your best bet; this site is well known for its helpful community members.

Also, go to your favorite Web-search site and search on the error message you're getting from the system — it doesn't hurt to add the network hardware's make and model and the name of your distribution as well if just the error message isn't working. When you're trying to figure out what's wrong with your network connection — or trying to gather information that can help someone else figure out what's wrong — you can use a cool tool: the handy ping command-line program.

Some firewalls block the kind of traffic sent with pings, so these commands don't always work as expected, even with a good connection.

The ping command works somewhat like a submarine using sonar to detect other objects in the ocean. Sonar sends out a *ping* signal, which reflects off a hard surface. By measuring the amount of time between sending the ping and the ping's return, the submarine's engineer can determine whether an object is out there and how far from the submarine the object is.

The ping command in Linux provides information similar to what sonar provides — and it's so useful that you see it here as both a Linux command and a time-honored word. If you consider the Internet to be your ocean, you can determine, by *pinging,* what other network computers exist — and also how long it takes for your ping command to return. You use this command in the format ping *hostname* or ping *ipaddress,* such as ping bob. example.com or ping 192.168.1.5. If you can't ping another computer in your house or office (assuming that you have them all connected with Ethernet and not on separate dialup connections), something is wrong with the machine you're pinging from. On the other hand, if you can ping another machine in your house or office but you can't ping a machine elsewhere on the Internet, something may be wrong with your connection to your ISP.

Latency, or the amount of time it takes for a signal to travel on the Internet, has little to do with physical distance. Rather, factors such as network traffic, bandwidth, and network hardware all contribute to slow latency. These factors determine whether a `ping` command to your neighbor's computer takes longer than pinging a host at (say) the South Pole.

For example, try pinging Yahoo! by opening a command prompt (see Chapter 17) and typing the following command:

```
ping www.yahoo.com
```

Press Ctrl+C to stop the `ping` command; otherwise your computer continues to ping the target.

The output, shown in Figure 8-10, provides information about what `ping` is doing. If the `ping` command you've sent can't reach the host, you receive a message that the host is unreachable. If the `ping` command can reach the host, you receive feedback that tells you how long it takes — in milliseconds (ms) — for the signal from your computer to get to the destination computer and back again. (The lower the numbers, the better.) For computers connected through Ethernet, a `ping` time of 1 millisecond (ms) to 3 ms is an acceptable response time. For dialup connections, expect somewhere around 150 ms. When you start seeing `ping` times climbing to 900 ms or higher, the network is likely under heavy use (or you have something wrong with your cables).

Figure 8-10:
Sample
results of
the `ping`
command.

```
rich@testbox: ~
File  Edit  View  Terminal  Tabs  Help
rich@testbox:~$ ping www.yahoo.com
PING www.yahoo-ht3.akadns.net (69.147.76.15) 56(84) bytes of data.
64 bytes from f1.www.vip.re1.yahoo.com (69.147.76.15): icmp_seq=1 ttl=55 time=45
.7 ms
64 bytes from f1.www.vip.re1.yahoo.com (69.147.76.15): icmp_seq=2 ttl=55 time=43
.9 ms
64 bytes from f1.www.vip.re1.yahoo.com (69.147.76.15): icmp_seq=3 ttl=55 time=43
.0 ms
64 bytes from f1.www.vip.re1.yahoo.com (69.147.76.15): icmp_seq=4 ttl=55 time=42
.2 ms
64 bytes from f1.www.vip.re1.yahoo.com (69.147.76.15): icmp_seq=5 ttl=55 time=43
.3 ms
64 bytes from f1.www.vip.re1.yahoo.com (69.147.76.15): icmp_seq=6 ttl=55 time=42
.5 ms
64 bytes from f1.www.vip.re1.yahoo.com (69.147.76.15): icmp_seq=7 ttl=55 time=43
.8 ms
^C
--- www.yahoo-ht3.akadns.net ping statistics ---
7 packets transmitted, 7 received, 0% packet loss, time 6021ms
rtt min/avg/max/mdev = 42.204/43.525/45.750/1.090 ms
rich@testbox:~$
```

Part III
Getting Things Done

In this part . . .

In this part of the book, the real fun starts. Here's where you discover how to use all the fun software that comes with your Linux system! You start out with the Internet tools you need to survive, you know, the ones that you want to gnaw your leg off if you don't have access to these days: the Web, e-mail, instant messaging, and more. You'll also find out how to edit files, both plain old text ones and those that require an office suite — yes, you'll see how you can work with Windows documents in your Linux environment! Then you get to what we think are the best parts: the audio and video! Finally, this part closes with coverage of Google Gadgets, a desktop tool that's becoming quite popular these days.

Chapter 9

Using the Internet

• •

In This Chapter

▶ Browsing the Web

▶ Sending instant messages

▶ Grabbing files

▶ Talking across the Internet

• •

Give a man a fish and you feed him for a day; teach him to use the Net, and he won't bother you for weeks.

— Anonymous

The *Internet* is a vast network of computers that spans the globe. Many different types of computers and operating systems work together to allow you access to information across this network. Linux, along with the other related UNIX operating systems, has long supported and worked with the Internet. Practically all the different services available on the Internet are available from your Linux desktop.

When you install Linux (see Chapter 3), you get one or more Web browsers, e-mail programs, and instant-messaging tools placed on your new system. In this chapter, we introduce you to some of those tools; you can use them to access different services on the Internet — such as Web sites, e-mail, newsgroups, and FTP — after your Internet connection is configured (see Chapter 8).

Browsing the Web with Firefox

Many people attribute the explosive growth of the Internet to the graphical Web browser. The Internet has been around for much longer than the invention of the browser. It's just that most of the work done on the Internet was in plain old text, which held little attraction for those people who like pretty pictures. In the world of Linux, the most popular browser is arguably Firefox (`www.mozilla.org/products/firefox`), the Web-browser portion of Mozilla (a communications program that can also handle e-mail and news browsing). Another popular option is Konqueror (`www.konqueror.org`), which besides being a good Web browser, also includes file-browsing features similar to the Nautilus and Dolphin programs (see Chapter 7).

Currently the developers of some major Linux distributions have a bit of an issue with the Firefox developers. The Firefox developers have copyrighted the Firefox name and logo, which is considered a no-no in the open-source software world. Because of that, some Linux distributions refuse to include Firefox. Instead, they include the IceWeasel browser (you gotta love open-source humor), which uses the same source code as Firefox (because the source code is still open, even if the logo and name aren't). If your distribution uses IceWeasel, you can follow the same steps in this chapter.

Configuring Firefox

You can start surfing right now, if you want. You don't need to customize your browser. However, you may want to take a moment to tell Firefox your preferences, such as the default Web site to show when it starts up, what font sizes to use by default, what colors to use, and many other options.

Follow these steps to configure your Firefox settings in the Preferences window:

1. **Start Firefox.**

   There's usually more than one way to start Firefox. Linux distributions that use the GNOME desktop often put an application-launcher icon in the top edge panel (see Chapter 4). Distributions that use the KDE desktop sometimes include Firefox as an application launcher, and they put that icon in the panel (see Chapter 5).

   In both desktop environments, you can always choose Applications⇨Internet⇨Firefox (in GNOME), or KDE⇨Applications⇨Internet⇨Firefox (in KDE).

2. **Choose Edit⇨Preferences.**

   The Preferences window appears, as shown in Figure 9-1. This dialog box contains all the settings you need to play with for your Web-browsing experience.

3. **Click the icons along the top of the Preferences window to access the various preferences categories.**

   The Advanced category is complex enough to offer tabs for various sub-categories. These tabs can be worth exploring as well.

   We discuss the more important categories in the upcoming sections.

Figure 9-1:
The Firefox
Preferences
window.

4. **If you get tired of reading through menus, just click Close to close the Preferences dialog box and get back to surfing.**

General preferences

Click the Main icon to determine how you want Firefox to look and act when it runs. Two separate sections govern this dialog box:

✔ **Startup:** This section allows you to choose what Firefox shows you immediately upon starting. You can type a URL directly into the Home Page text box, or click one of the following buttons:

   • *Use Current Pages:* Navigate to the page you want to use for your default Web page, and then click this button. The URL for this page appears in the Location(s) text box.

- *Use Bookmark:* Click this button to open the Set Home Page dialog box, which contains all your bookmarks. Select the bookmark you want to use and then click OK to add the URL for this page into the Location(s) text box.

- *Restore to Default:* Click this button to have Firefox open to just an empty window.

✔ **Downloads:** This section allows you to set how Firefox performs file downloads. You can set where you want Firefox to download files to, as well as whether the Downloads window appears while a file is downloading.

✔ **Add-ons:** The Manage Add-ons button takes you to the Add-ons Configuration dialog box. We talk about that in the "Expanding your universe with add-ons" section.

Privacy preferences

Every time you send an e-mail or click a Web site, you're exchanging information across a network. Although you don't need to lose sleep over it, you should be conscious of every request you make on the Internet. Click the Privacy icon in the Preferences window to see the Privacy settings (see Figure 9-2).

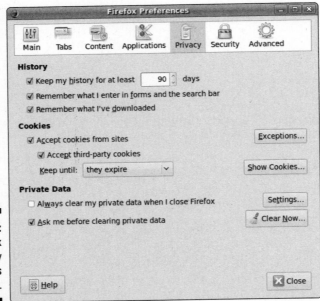

Figure 9-2:
The Firefox Privacy Preferences window.

Here's what you find:

- ✔ **History:** The History section lets you designate how many days you want your browser to remember where you've been. You can also choose to let Firefox remember text you've entered into forms and into the search bar. If you use this feature, Firefox will attempt to autocomplete words you've already typed before in those forms. You can also set Firefox to remember the files you've downloaded so you can easily review them instead of downloading a 500MB file a second time.

- ✔ **Cookies:** *Cookies* are bits of information a Web site stores on your machine so data can be accessed again quickly. Some people don't care how many cookies are created; some folks don't want any on their systems so Web sites can't track them. To prevent cookies from being stored, click the Accept Cookies from Sites check box to deselect it. To allow only certain sites to set cookies, click the Exceptions button and add those sites to the list of sites whose cookies you've decided to accept.

  You can view every cookie you have by clicking the Show Cookies button, and you can either remove them individually (select the cookie you want to remove and then click Remove Cookie) or remove them all (click the Remove All Cookies button to toss out all of your cookies immediately). You can specify how you want Firefox to keep or dump cookies by choosing an option from the Keep Until drop-down list:

  - • *They Expire:* Most cookies have an automatic expiration date. If you want to let the cookies dictate when they'll be deleted, choose this option.

  - • *I Close Firefox:* If you are using a library computer or another machine that is shared, or just don't want the computer storing cookies past when you're done using the browser, choose this option.

  - • *Ask Me Every Time:* If you want to be ultra-paranoid about cookies or to find how often they are actually used, choose this option.

- ✔ **Private Data:** This section allows you to set what and how stored items (such as cookies, temporary files, history items, and stored form data) are cleared. Select the Always Clear My Private Data When I Close Firefox check box if you want to clear all your stored files every time you exit Firefox. You can select exactly what items are cleared by clicking the Settings button and choosing individual items. As a safety feature, the Ask Me Before Clearing Private Data check box is selected by default to prevent accidentally clearing your data.

Content preferences

Click the Content icon to go to the Content portion of the Firefox Preferences dialog box (see Figure 9-3).

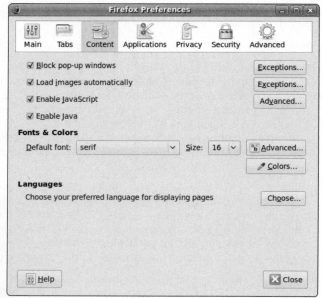

Figure 9-3:
The Firefox
Content
Preferences
window.

This section lets you control how Firefox reacts to various types of content. The top portion refers to items you can either block or allow; each has a button to its right that offers additional control:

✔ **Block pop-up windows:** Tells Firefox to block new windows that you didn't ask for — pop-up windows are a favorite way for some site owners to throw advertisements in your face as you try to read their sites. Some sites, however, have functionality that requires the opening of certain unasked-for windows (say, for login); click the Exceptions button to add those sites to the Allowed Sites list. Whenever a pop-up window tries to open, a yellow bar appears in the browser window, allowing you to open the pop-up window or delete it.

✔ **Load images automatically:** Lets you block all images. Useful for those who are sight-impaired or who are trying to speed up browsing by ignoring pictures. If you select For the Originating Web Site Only, you block many of the ads that are often loaded from other sites to appear on the one you're viewing. Choosing this option, however, can also block legitimate graphics. Click the Exceptions button to manage what you do and don't want to see.

✔ **Enable JavaScript:** Some people shut off this feature for security reasons. Many don't. Clicking the Advanced button opens the Advanced JavaScript Settings dialog box, where you can choose what you'll allow JavaScript to do. If you find a site that does annoying things such as resizing your windows, go to this dialog box to disable that capability.

✔ **Enable Java:** If you have Java installed and this option enabled, Firefox runs whatever Java code it finds.

The middle section is Fonts & Colors. These features include

✔ **Default Font:** Click this drop-down list box to select a font.

✔ **Size:** Click this drop-down list box to choose a font size.

✔ **Advanced:** Click this button to open the Fonts dialog box, which lets you choose the default fonts and sizes to use for various font classes, along with other visual settings. Here you can also specify that pages can use their own fonts rather than your overrides.

✔ **Colors:** Click this button to open the Colors dialog box and change the default colors assigned to text, the background, and links.

The lower section is Languages. This allows you to set the language you prefer your Web sites to appear in when there's a choice. Click the Choose button to set up what languages you prefer, along with the order of your preferences.

When browsing, if you are unhappy with a font's size, press Ctrl++ (plus) to make the fonts bigger and Ctrl+– (minus) to make the fonts smaller. The + and – are the versions on your number keypad, not on the main keyboard.

Advanced preferences

This section provides four tabbed sections of settings for more advanced features that most users probably won't need to mess with:

✔ **General:** The General tab lets you set up features for the movement-impaired, set up extra browser-control features, and specify whether you want Firefox to check if it's the default browser configured for your system.

✔ **Network:** Click the Settings button in the Connections section if your network administrator told you to use proxy servers to access online content. The proxy server provides a gateway to the Internet, where the network administrator can control access to sites you shouldn't be visiting. The Offline Storage section allows you to set how much disk space Firefox is allowed to set aside as a cache for storing content from visited Web pages. If you allow a large cache, then Firefox can display the pages faster the next time you visit them. You can clear the cache by clicking the Clear Now button. The cache data is also part of the private data that you can set to clear automatically when you exit Firefox.

✔ **Update:** The Update tab tells Firefox how to handle checking for updates — both for itself and for any plugins you've installed. Most Linux distributions install Firefox updates as part of their software-management system (see Chapter 16 for details); if yours has done so, you don't need Firefox to check for updates on its own.

✔ **Encryption:** The Encryption tab has settings for security protocols Firefox uses; it's also the place you can specify any special encryption certificates for visiting encrypted Web sites. Usually you can leave these settings alone.

Expanding your universe with add-ons

Firefox has a set of features that it supports in the basic setup. In the wide world of Web browsing, however, sooner or later you'll run into some things that the basic Firefox setup does not support.

But never fear — help is close by! Firefox allows you to add new features to the basic setup with just a few clicks of the mouse button. Firefox supports these new features through *add-ons* — small software programs that tack more features onto the basic browser. Three types of add-ons are in Firefox:

✔ **Extensions:** Add new features to the Firefox program, such as customized toolbars and utilities such as dictionaries.

✔ **Themes:** Allow you to change the look and feel of your entire Firefox browser interface.

✔ **Plugins:** Provide support for additional multimedia formats, such as video and audio types, directly in the browser window.

Do you ever get irritated at those Web sites that insist that you download special software just to view the site? The difference between a plugin and an external program is this: A plugin displays the results in the browser, and an external program runs *outside* the browser. Although plugins can be annoying if you're just looking for some basic information, they can provide some pretty cool stuff, such as streaming video and music through your Web browser. Chapter 14 explains how to add popular video plugins (such as the Adobe Flash plugin) to your system.

Firefox provides a separate interface for managing add-ons. Choose Tools⇨ Add-ons to open the Add-ons dialog box (see Figure 9-4).

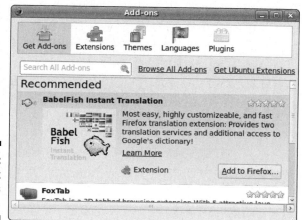

Figure 9-4:
The Firefox
Add-ons
dialog box.

The Extensions, Themes, and Plugins icons show what you have currently installed for each. Here's how to install add-ons:

1. **Click the Get Add-ons icon (if you are connected to the Internet) to see some recommended add-ons.**

2. **Click the Browse all Add-ons link to open a Web page that lets you surf to see what add-ons are available.**

3. **When you find an add-on you want to try, click the Install link underneath its description; if your version of Firefox is one of the versions in the list of supported versions, click Install Now.**

Choose Help⇨About Mozilla Firefox to find which version of Firefox you're using.

You may get an error message and the add-on may be uninstallable if you're not running a version of Firefox that supports the add-on.

Surfing the Web

Firefox is your viewing window into the wonderful World Wide Web. Firefox's primary purpose is to fetch Web pages on your command, download all their graphics and related files into your computer's memory, and (finally) render the page for your interactive viewing pleasure.

If you're used to using an Internet browser, using Firefox should be a snap. It has all the familiar navigation tools, such as an address bar; Back, Forward, Reload, and Stop buttons; and a feature that stores links to your favorite Web sites (bookmarks).

Firefox, like Netscape, has a History sidebar — press Ctrl+H to show or hide it (see Figure 9-5) — that you can use to access a Web page you recently visited.

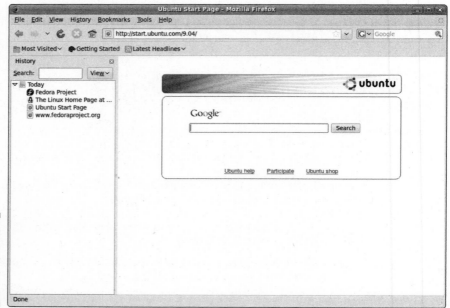

Figure 9-5:
Firefox with the History sidebar open.

Tabbed browsing — a feature of Firefox that may be new to you — enables you to open several Web sites in the same window. For many people coming from Internet Explorer 6 or Netscape, the tabbed-browsing feature of Firefox may seem odd at first, but you'll probably fall in love with it.

After you start the Firefox Web browser, the Web site defined as your home page appears in a tabbed page. You can keep that page open and open a new Web site in a new tabbed page by pressing Ctrl+T. The new Web page appears within the same Firefox window, but as a tabbed page. You can switch between the two tabbed pages by simply clicking the appropriate tab at the top of each page.

You can also open Web links as new tabbed pages by right-clicking the link and selecting Open Link in New Tab. This feature is great for navigating through complex Web sites where you need to refer back to previous pages.

If you have multiple tabs open when you try to close Firefox, you get a warning message asking if you want to save the open tabs. If you click the Save and Quit button, the next time you open Firefox, your tabs open to the sites you saved.

Taking Advantage of Instant Messaging

Instant messaging (IM) between people is like using a telephone — except you type your conversation rather than speak it. In addition, you can simultaneously hold multiple instant-messaging conversations without the need for additional connections to the Internet. America Online (AOL) provides one popular instant-messaging service — AOL Instant Messenger (AIM). Other IM services are available from ICQ, MSN, Yahoo!, and Google. A wide variety of computer operating systems, including Linux, support these various services.

In the Linux world, you'll probably run into two popular IM packages:

✔ **Pidgin:** Used in the GNOME desktop environment.

✔ **Kopete:** Used in the KDE desktop environment.

We take a look at how to set up each of these packages for your IM accounts.

The Pidgin software package used to be called GAIM. Unfortunately, the name of the package had to be changed due to copyright restrictions. If you've used GAIM in previous versions of Fedora or Ubuntu, Pidgin works exactly the same way.

Using the Pidgin Instant Messenger

To launch Pidgin IM software from the Fedora GNOME desktop, choose Applications➪Internet➪Internet Messenger. From Ubuntu, choose Internet➪Pidgin Instant Messenger.

When you open Pidgin for the first time (see Figure 9-6), an empty Accounts dialog box (for managing your account) appears.

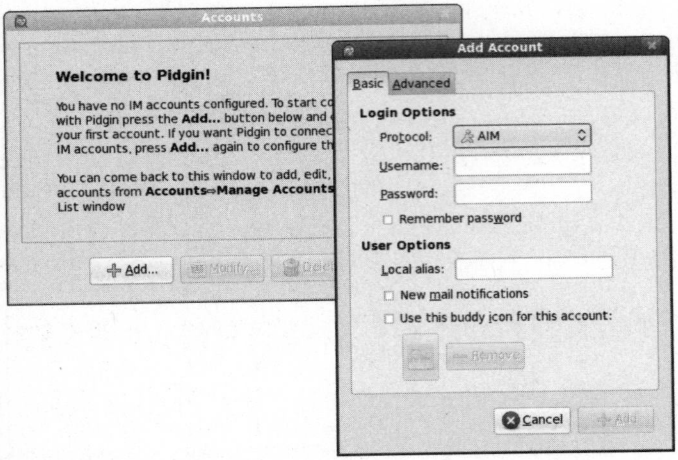

Figure 9-6:
The
Pidgin IM
Accounts
dialog box
(empty)
and Add
Account
dialog box.

To tell Pidgin about one of your IM accounts, follow these steps:

1. **Click the Add button in the Accounts dialog box.**

   The Add Account dialog box, shown in Figure 9-6, appears.

2. **In the Protocol drop-down list box, select the IM network you want to use.**

   There are quite a few options to choose from, including the popular AIM, Bonjour, Gadu-Gadu, Google Talk, GroupWise, ICQ, IRC, Jabber, MSN, MySpace IM, QQ, SILC, SIMPLE, Yahoo!, and Zephyr sites.

3. **Enter the login name and password for your IM account in the Username and Password boxes.**

   Different IM hosts use different login-name conventions, such as your e-mail address or a pre-assigned login ID.

4. **In the User Options section, enter a local alias to use; then select a buddy icon to represent that account.**

   The local alias appears instead of your login name, making it easier to identify which IM site you're interacting with if you interact with multiple sites.

5. **If you get e-mail through this service and want to know when new mail has arrived, select the New Mail Notifications check box.**

6. **If you want access to the more advanced options for this IM service, click the Advanced tab.**

Each IM service has its own set of advanced options you can configure. For example, the AIM IM service allows you to change the default AOL server you connect with, as well as the default TCP port number.

7. **When you finish entering your information, click Add to add this IM account to your accounts list.**

Go through this process for each account you want to use with Pidgin. As you create an account, it appears in the Accounts dialog box. Select the box in the Enabled column for those accounts you want to log in to automatically.

After you create the account, the Pidgin Buddy List dialog box (shown in Figure 9-7) appears.

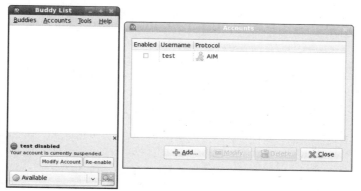

Figure 9-7:
The Pidgin
Buddy List.

You can modify the account settings by selecting the account in the Pidgin Buddy List dialog box and then clicking the Modify Account button.

When you start a session, the Buddy List window displays your active connections. If you close the Buddy List window, the Pidgin icon appears on your panel as the program runs in the background. You can open the Buddy List window by right-clicking this icon.

Again, Pidgin has more to it than this, so it's definitely worth your time to play around with this tool.

After you close the Accounts and Buddy List dialog boxes, you can reopen them by right-clicking the IM icon in your system tray and selecting the dialog box you want to open from the menu.

Checkin' out Kopete

If you're using a KDE desktop, you'll most likely have the Kopete instant-messaging application installed. To start Kopete, choose KDE⇨Internet⇨Kopete in KDE. In Fedora, choose KDE⇨Applications⇨Internet⇨Instant Messenger. After you start Kopete, its main window (shown in Figure 9-8) appears.

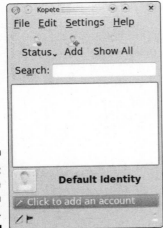

Figure 9-8:
The Kopete main window.

To get started in Kopete, you have to add your IM account. Just follow these steps:

1. **Click the Click to Add an Account button in the main window.**

   Kopete starts a wizard that guides you through the steps of creating a new account. The first page lists the networks Kopete can communicate with, shown in Figure 9-9.

2. **Select the IM network you want to use, then click the Next button.**

   The second page in the wizard contains one or more tabs of information for you to fill out, depending on the specific IM network you selected.

   Each network has a Basic Setup tab where you configure your login name and password. For some IM networks, Kopete provides a button that links you to the service so you can create a new account.

   Some networks have an Account Preferences tab, allowing you to set an alternative server, port, or proxy server to use. Some may also provide a Privacy tab, allowing you to determine which users are blocked and which users are allowed to communicate with your IM account.

Step One: Select Messaging Service

Welcome to Kopete

Which messaging service do you want to connect to?

Name	Description
AIM	An Instant Messenger
Gadu-...	Gadu-Gadu: the Polish IM service
Group...	Novell GroupWise Messenger
ICQ	Seek and Chat with ICQ
Jabber	XMPP, Jabber, Google Talk
MSN ...	Windows Live Messenger compatibility
QQ	A popular Chinese IM system
SMS	Send SMS messages to mobile phones
Testbed	Kopete test protocol

Help   Back   Next   Finish   Cancel

Figure 9-9:
Selecting an
IM network
in Kopete.

3. **Fill in your account information, then click the Next button.**

4. **Click the Finish button on the final page to create the account.**

If you want Kopete to connect to the IM server automatically, select the Connect Now check box before clicking the Finish button.

The wizard returns you to the main Kopete window (refer to Figure 9-8), but shows your IM account now as your default identity. The Buddy List window shows your active connections.

To add contacts to your IM account, click the Add button in the toolbar. To change your status, click the Status button in the toolbar and select your current status (such as online, away, or busy).

To modify your account settings, add new accounts, or change the behavior of Kopete, open the Configure window by choosing Settings➪Configure. The Configure window, shown in Figure 9-10, appears.

As you can see from the Configure window, you can customize Kopete in many ways to maximize your IM experience.

After you start Kopete, it creates an icon in the system tray area of the KDE panel. Just right-click the icon to bring up the buddy list and use Kopete.

Troubleshooting your IM connections

If you've been using most of these IM clients with other operating systems, after your Linux system has successfully connected to the IM service, your existing buddy lists are automatically imported. If you haven't ever used AIM or MSN, you can now set up buddy lists. Buddy lists contain the usernames of people you want to communicate with through the instant-messaging service. Your buddy list lets you know when your "buddies" are online and available to receive an instant message.

Sometimes, your Linux system can't connect properly to the IM service. When this problem happens, an error message pops up on your screen and indicates a failure to connect. You may be unable to connect to the IM service for several reasons:

✔ You may have entered the wrong password for your IM account or chosen the incorrect IM account name.

✔ Your computer may not be connected to the Internet. Try opening your Web browser to see whether you can get to a Web site, which tells you whether you're connected to the Internet.

✔ If you can open a Web site but can't get IM to work, the IM system may be unavailable. This problem occurs at times because of maintenance of the IM service or an excessive amount of traffic on the Internet or on the IM service.

- If you attempt to access the IM service from your computer at work, your company or organization may block the IM service for security or productivity reasons. If using IM at your workplace is permitted, check with your network administrator to see whether he or she can help.

- Often companies use firewalls between the company network and the Internet to keep unwanted traffic off the company's network. If the firewall is configured to block IM traffic, you cannot use IM across the Internet.

Downloading with BitTorrent

Say what you want about file sharing, it's popular. Networks such as BitTorrent (www.bittorrent.com) have actually found legitimate use among software companies and other content distributors. They use it as a way to offer larger files for download without having to take on the brunt of the bandwidth use themselves, so it's worth looking at how to use this software under Linux.

You probably have already guessed that there are a few different graphical BitTorrent client packages available in the Linux world:

- **BitTorrent:** The software package developed by the BitTorrent network and popular with both Windows and Linux users.

- **Transmission:** A BitTorrent package created by the GNOME desktop developers *for* the GNOME desktop, installed by default in both Fedora and Ubuntu.

- **KTorrent:** A BitTorrent package created by the KDE developers for the KDE desktop, installed by default in Fedora when you select the KDE desktop.

All BitTorrent client packages work pretty much the same way. Here's the rundown:

1. A BitTorrent download consists of a control file that you must download.

   The control file is identified by a `.torrent` extension in the filename. It tells the BitTorrent client software where to contact the server that controls the download information.

2. When the client connects to the server, the server directs the client to other clients that have parts of the download file.

3. A give-and-take begins, with clients downloading parts of the file from other clients, while at the same time sharing the parts they've already downloaded with other clients.

Here's how to start a BitTorrent session on your Linux desktop:

1. **Start your BitTorrent client.**

   The BitTorrent client is accessible from the Internet group within your desktop menu system. The Fedora Transmission client is shown in Figure 9-11. For most Linux distributions, the Firefox Web browser is configured to start the BitTorrent client whenever you select a `.torrent` file from a Web page.

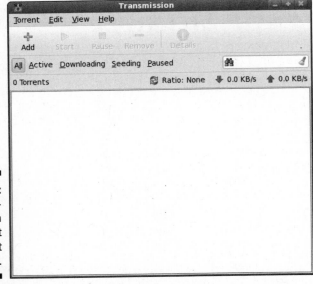

Figure 9-11:
The Trans-
mission
BitTorrent
client
window.

2. **Select the option to open a Torrent File.**

   For Transmission, click the Add button in the toolbar. For KTorrent, click the Open button. A file browser window appears.

3. **Navigate to and select the** `.torrent` **file for the document you want to download, and then click your selected torrent to add it to the list.**

   The file appears in what looks a lot like a music-player format, as shown in Figure 9-12 with KTorrent. You can often control the download by offering faster uploads to other BitTorrent users. If you have broadband (see Chapter 8), an upload speed of 40 Kbps works well.

   It can take a minute or so for the tool to fully synchronize, so expect the projected time to change drastically for a while until it settles on a consistent value.

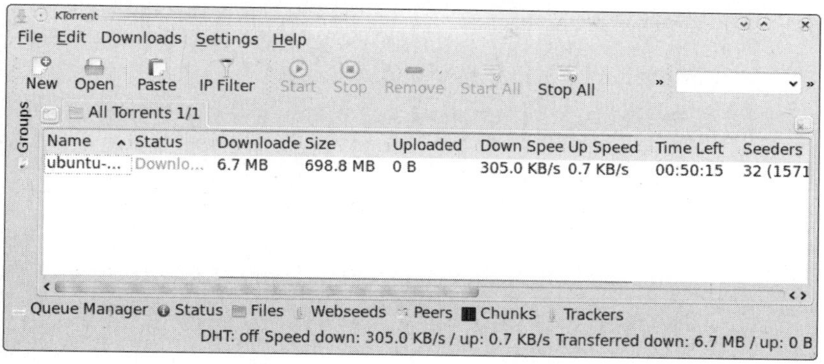

Figure 9-12:
The
KTorrent
window
with a
file down-
loading.

4. **When you're ready to exit, choose File⇨Quit to close the client.**

Even after the download finishes, the BitTorrent client continues to host the file for others to download. If you want to be a good Internet neighbor, keep the BitTorrent client running for a while after your download finishes to let others grab their pieces as well.

Dealing with Old-Fashioned File Transfers

While BitTorrent is the wave of the future, there are still plenty of Internet sites that require you to download files by using the old File Transfer Protocol (FTP) method. You will often find file repositories for applications, utilities, and other neat stuff on FTP sites.

Most Linux distributions include a command-line FTP client program (simply called `ftp`), but don't include a graphical FTP client in the default installation. However, it's no problem to add one using the software-package manager (see Chapter 16). The three most popular graphical FTP programs in the Linux world are

- ✔ **gFTP:** The GNOME project's graphical FTP client.
- ✔ **Kget:** The KDE project's graphical FTP client.
- ✔ **FileZilla:** A graphical FTP client program created to run on any desktop, including Windows and Mac.

The FileZilla package is available in most Linux distributions, and it works equally well in both the GNOME and KDE desktop environments. It also has support for secure FTP sessions, which are becoming more popular these days. If you're looking for a robust graphical FTP client program, try FileZilla by installing it (see Chapter 16).

When you have FileZilla installed, follow these steps to give it a whirl:

1. **Start FileZilla from the Internet group in your desktop menu system. From the GNOME menu, choose Applications⇨Internet⇨FileZilla.**

   The main FileZilla window appears, as shown in Figure 9-13. FileZilla provides a side-by-side look at your filesystem and the remote FTP server's filesystem. By default, FileZilla points to your home directory as the local directory (shown in the left-side list box).

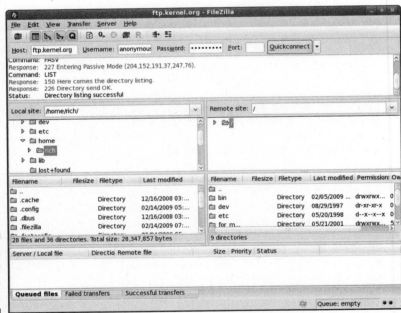

Figure 9-13: The FileZilla main window.

2. **Enter the hostname of the remote FTP server in the Host text box, enter the username in the Username text box, and enter the password in the Password text box.**

   If you've connected to a host previously, its hostname and user-login name appear in the text boxes.

3. When the remote FTP session starts, a list of available files and folders appears in the right-side list box.

4. Find and select the file(s) you want to download, select the folder to download them to in the left-side list box, and then drag and drop to transfer the file(s).

5. When you're finished, click the Disconnect icon in the toolbar (the icon with the big red X over it) to disconnect and end the session.

It's as simple as that. Using a graphical FTP client makes transferring lots of files almost painless.

Talkin' on the Phone

The craze these days is chatting on the phone over the Internet. Whether you just want to experiment or are a complete devotee, Linux offers the software you need if you want to take part. Think of the Internet phone networks such as Instant Messenger networks. One of the most popular networks for supporting Internet phones is Skype (www.skype.com), which uses SIP (Session Initiation Protocol), a popular default that you can use with a wider variety of programs. First, however, you need the proper hardware — whether it's a phone you can actually plug into your computer (a SIP phone, for example) or just a combination of a headset and a microphone — preferably *not* the lowest-end model so you'll get the best sound quality. When you have the hardware, it's time to get the software.

In Fedora and Ubuntu, the default client software is Ekiga (www.ekiga.org). Two other SIP clients are also included in the repositories, as discussed in Chapter 16: KPhone (http://sourceforge.net/projects/kphone) and Linphone (www.linphone.org). The popular Skype package isn't included, but you can download a Linux client for Skype from www.skype.com.

In the upcoming sections, we show you how to configure the default Ekiga package and the popular Skype package.

Using the default: Ekiga

The default Ekiga Internet Phone software is a redesign of the old GNOME GnomeMeeting package for Internet voice and videoconferencing applications. Ekiga was expanded to provide the same basic functions as the more popular Skype software, along with compatibility with Microsoft NetMeeting.

This compatibility allows you to join in conferences with your Microsoft friends (just don't brag too much that your software was free).

To start Ekiga, choose Applications⇨Internet, then look for either the Ekiga software by name (that's how Ubuntu lists it), or look for IP Telephony, VoIP and Video Conferencing (that's how Fedora lists it). The first time you start Ekiga, you get a series of configuration windows. Follow these steps to get your Ekiga software configured:

1. **Click Forward to start the wizard.**

   The Personal Information dialog box appears.

2. **Where prompted, type the name you want to be identified by on the network.**

   Other Ekiga users see you listed by the name you enter here.

3. **Click Forward.**

   The wizard proceeds to the Ekiga Account page.

4. **Type your Ekiga account username and password where prompted.**

   If you don't have an account yet, you can jump over to the Ekiga Web site (www.ekiga.net) and register for a free account.

5. **Click Forward to continue.**

   The configuration wizard is now set to go through a series of windows to determine your system's hardware and software specifics automatically.

   The series of windows includes the following:

   - *Connection Type:* Sets the speed of your Internet connection. For a dialup modem, that'll be the 56K entry. For a broadband connection, that'll be the xDSL/Cable entry.

   - *Audio Devices:* Detect the audio input and output devices on your system. The Ekiga software will most likely succeed in detecting these devices with no intervention on your part.

   - *Video Devices:* Determines whether a video-input device (webcam) is connected to your system.

6. **Select the type of Internet connection your system uses and then click Forward.**

7. **For each subsequent window, click Forward after Ekiga completes the relevant determination or detection.**

   When the configuration wizard is complete, a final configuration window appears, showing the choices you've made.

8. **Click the Apply button to finalize the configuration.**

   After you finish the configuration, the main Ekiga window (shown in Figure 9-14) appears, listening for new calls and waiting for you to place a call.

Figure 9-14:
The main
Ekiga
window.

Talking with Skype

Skype is by far the most popular IP phone network around. Many Linux distributions install Skype as the default IP phone software. Unfortunately, neither Fedora nor Ubuntu do. If you prefer to use Skype on your Fedora or Ubuntu system, you have to install it yourself.

To install Skype on your Linux system, do the following:

1. **Point your Web browser to** www.skype.com.

2. **On the Skype home page, click the Download link.**

   You are taken to the Download Skype page.

3. **Click the Skype for Linux link on the left side of the page.**

   You are taken to the Download Skype for Linux page. Here you see several links for various Linux distributions.

4. **Click the link for your specific Linux distribution.**

   If your specific distribution version isn't listed, you should be able to install an older version. An Opening Skype dialog box appears, with the full name of the file in the title.

5. **Either select the Open with Software Installer option and click OK, or click the option that downloads the Installer file to your workstation.**

If your distribution has the option to open the Software Installer immediately when the download is complete, then the Software Installer program will start (see Chapter 16). If you download the Installer file to your workstation, you'll need to find it on your workstation and *then* click it to start the Software Installer program.

6. **Start the installation from your Software Installer.**

   Depending on your distribution, the Software Installer may have to download additional files to support the Skype installation. The Software Installer handles this operation automatically; just sit back and watch the installation happen.

   When the installation finishes, Skype appears in the Internet menu group on your desktop.

7. **Choose Internet⇨Skype to start Skype.**

   When Skype starts, a wizard appears. Use it in one of two ways:

   - To enter your Skype account information.
   - To connect to a Skype server and create a new account (as shown in Figure 9-15).

   After you have an account set up, you can use the Skype interface to connect to the Skype server and start placing calls!

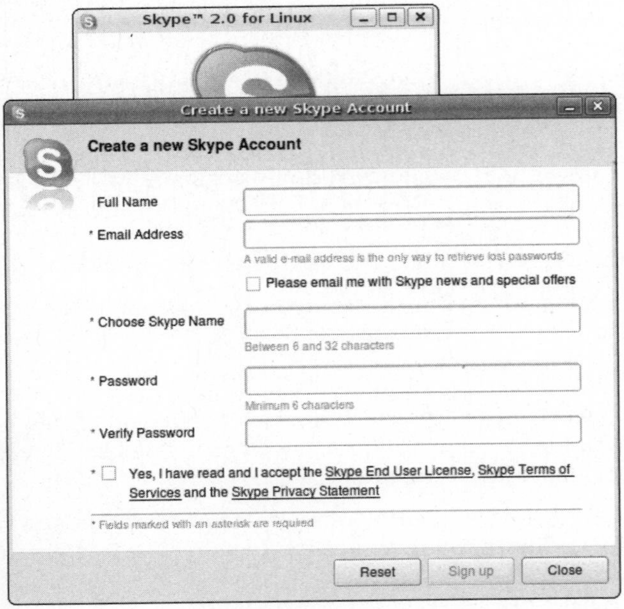

Figure 9-15:
Create a
new Skype
account.

The Skype network is a bandwidth-sharing application. After you connect to a Skype server, others can connect through your client program by using your bandwidth. If you are on a limited-bandwidth connection, this could be a problem.

Working with Other Internet Tools

You may want to explore a variety of other types of tools, depending on your needs. This section covers some pointers to get you started, so if you go to Chapter 16 and add the appropriate software (or find yourself digging through menus and wondering what the program may be called), you aren't completely lost. Here are some resources to help steer you right:

- ✔ **IRC programs:** Internet Relay Chat (IRC) is a protocol that provides connections to servers where people use messaging to discuss just about any topic imaginable. Although the IM clients support IRC these days, you may prefer a program that's used *only* for IRC. Common programs for this purpose are X-Chat and KIRC.

- ✔ **File sharing:** LimeWire is a popular file-sharing application if you want to use the Gnutella network.

- ✔ **RSS readers:** Many news-oriented sites use the Really Simply Syndication (RSS) protocol to stream news directly to RSS reader programs. Firefox has a number of RSS extensions designed for it. In addition, Straw is a popular RSS program.

If you're not sure what programs to use, do a Web search on the type of thing you want to do (such as RSS) and include the word *Linux*.

Chapter 10

E-Mailing the World

Your mailbox is your window to your heart! Make sure you leave that window open!

— *Takayuki Ikkaku, Arisa Hosaka, and Toshihiro Kawabata*

Although most people think of the Web when they think of the Internet, e-mail may, in fact, be the most used and beloved of all Internet applications. A multitude of e-mail programs are available for Linux users. Most Linux distributions install at least one e-mail application by default, and which one it is depends on the default desktop you're using (see Chapter 1). Of course, with Linux you're always free to install a different e-mail program to use if you find one you like better!

This chapter provides an overview of the three most popular e-mail packages used in Linux these days. Hopefully you'll find one that fits your needs.

Looking Before You Leap

Before you start hacking away at trying to set up your e-mail package, you'll need to grab some information about the Internet service provider (ISP) that supports your e-mail address. You should be able to obtain most of this information either from the information you received from your ISP with your e-mail account or by calling the Help Desk at your ISP and asking a few simple questions.

The items you'll need to have handy before you start are

✔ **Your e-mail address:** This should be assigned by your ISP, with a format such as me@myhost.com. You'll need to remember to enter this in your e-mail package exactly as it appears in your e-mail or people won't be able to respond to your messages!

✔ **The type of e-mail server your ISP uses for incoming mail:** There are several different methods used by ISP e-mail servers to communicate with e-mail clients. The two most popular are *POP* (also called POP3 to refer to the version) and *IMAP*.

  • The main difference between these two protocols is that POP usually requires you to download all your incoming messages from the ISP server to your local workstation. After they're downloaded to your PC, the ISP deletes them from the server.

  • IMAP allows you to create folders on the ISP server and store all your messages on the server. IMAP servers usually allow you a specific amount of storage space on the server, so keep an eye on how much mail you accumulate.

✔ **The hostname or IP address of your ISP incoming mail server:** Your ISP should provide a hostname or IP address, such as `pop.isp.com`, for you to connect to in order to receive your mail.

✔ **The type of e-mail server your ISP uses for outbound mail:** Sending outbound e-mail requires a different protocol from the one used to retrieve inbound e-mail. Most ISP e-mail servers use SMTP for sending e-mail from clients.

✔ **The hostname or IP address of your ISP outbound mail server:** Some ISPs use separate servers for outbound and inbound mail. Check with your ISP for the outbound server's hostname (such as `smtp.isp.com`).

✔ **Any special ports or passwords needed for authentication in an encrypted session:** Nowadays many ISPs require that you log in to establish an encrypted connection for both inbound and outbound e-mails. If this isn't a requirement on your ISP's server, you should still consider using it if your ISP supports it.

When you have all that information in hand, you're ready to configure your e-mail package.

Evolving into E-Mail: Evolution

If you're using the GNOME desktop, the default e-mail package is called *Evolution*. Evolution should remind you very much of Outlook. If you like being able to integrate your calendar, address book, task manager, and e-mail, you should feel right at home with Evolution.

This section walks you through the steps of getting Evolution talking with your ISP.

Setting up Evolution

You can start Evolution by either clicking the Evolution panel icon (the open envelope) or choosing Applications➪Internet➪Evolutions. After you start Evolution for the first time, the Evolution Setup Assistant launches.

Click Forward to proceed past the Welcome screen, after which the Restore from Backup screen appears. If you've previously saved a backup copy of your Evolution setup, you can restore it quickly from this screen. Click Next if this is the first time you've used Evolution.

The Identity screen (see Figure 10-1) opens next. To complete the Evolution Setup Assistant, follow these steps:

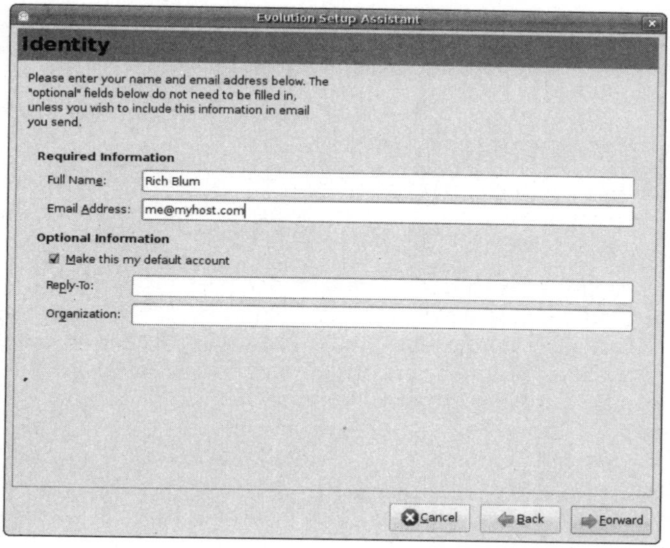

Figure 10-1:
The
Evolution
Identity
screen.

1. **(Optional) Change the Full Name field.**

   Some people don't want to use their real names online; many opt to use nicknames. There may or may not be default values assigned, depending on what other programs you've configured on your machine.

2. **Change the E-Mail Address field if it doesn't match the address your ISP gave you (it probably doesn't).**

3. **If you want this particular account to be your default mail account, be sure to select the Make This My Default Account check box.**

If you want people to respond to a different e-mail account than the one you're sending the message from, enter the e-mail address you want them to use in the Reply-To field. Otherwise you can keep this field blank. You can also choose to enter your organization in the Organization field.

4. **Click Forward to proceed.**

   The Receiving Email screen opens, as shown in Figure 10-2.

5. **In the Server Type list box, select the type of incoming e-mail server your ISP uses.**

   Leave it as None if you don't want to receive e-mail on this computer — this setting is useful if you only want to be able to send or only want to use the calendar and task management features in Evolution. Depending on which item you choose, the screen changes to ask for the appropriate information. We assume you're using a POP mail server to receive mail; those options are shown in Figure 10-2. If you're not using POP, complete the screen you do see and then proceed to Step 17.

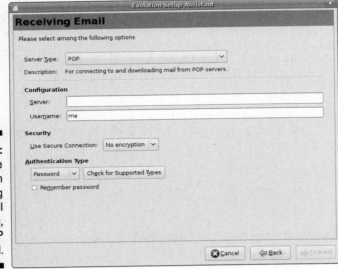

Figure 10-2:
The
Evolution
Receiving
E-Mail
screen,
with POP
selected.

The latest versions of Evolution have support for Microsoft Exchange servers available. If you need this feature, it may or may not already be installed in your distribution. Use the information in Chapter 16 to add the Evolution-connector package to your system, and then restart the Evolution setup process.

6. **Enter the full name for your POP mail server in the Server text box.**

   The name may be something like `pop.example.com`.

7. **Enter your login name for checking mail in the Username text box.**

   If (for example) your e-mail address is `jane@example.com`, your user-name is `jane`.

8. **If you were told to use SSL for security, in the Use Secure Connection (SSL) drop-down list box, select either Always or Whenever Possible, depending on what your ISP has specified.**

9. **Under Authentication Type, select the appropriate authentication option.**

   If you don't know what kinds of authentication your mail server uses, click the Check for Supported Types button. If your ISP server supports an encrypted authentication method, Evolution will automatically detect and use it. Typically, the authentication method is just a plain-text pass-word, so you can select the Password option.

10. **Select the Remember Password check box so that you don't have to enter your e-mail password every time you check mail.**

    If you're going to walk away from your computer and someone else may possibly access it, protect yourself from outgoing prank e-mails by going to the Main Menu and selecting Lock Screen. Doing so makes sure that no one can use your GUI until you type in your login password. (Note that you have to have your screen saver turned on for this feature to work. Screen savers are on by default.)

11. **Click Forward.**

    Which screen you get next is determined by which type of incoming mail server you're using. If you're using POP, the Receiving Options screen opens, as shown in Figure 10-3.

12. **If you want to check for new e-mail automatically, select the Check for New Messages Every check box.**

    If you don't have a permanent connection to the Internet, you may prefer to check mail manually. If so, leave the box unchecked and skip to Step 14.

13. **In the Minutes text box, set how often you want to check automatically for new e-mail.**

14. **If you check mail from multiple computers, select the Leave Messages on Server check box so you can access the same messages from all your machines.**

    If you select this option, you end up with copies of messages on multiple machines — but it also means that you have access to your e-mail no matter where you're checking it from. Keep in mind that occasionally you need to deselect this box, check your mail, and clear out all the space that your old e-mail is taking up on the server. You don't want to run out of space.

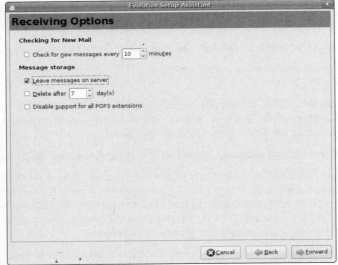

Figure 10-3:
The
Evolution
Receiving
Options
screen, for
POP mail
users.

You can also select the Delete After check box, and select the number of days to keep messages on your server. Any messages older than that are removed from your server automatically.

15. **If your ISP told you not to use POP3 extensions, select the Disable Support for All POP3 Extensions check box.**

16. **Click Forward to proceed.**

    The Sending E-Mail screen appears, as shown in Figure 10-4, which indicates that you've finished setting up incoming mail.

17. **Change the Server Type entry if yours isn't SMTP.**

    We assume that you're sending e-mail with SMTP.

18. **Enter the full name of the SMTP mail server in the Server text box.**

    The name may be something like `smtp.example.com`.

19. **If you were told to use additional authentication for sending mail, select the Server Requires Authentication check box.**

    These days, many ISPs require authentication before they allow you to forward e-mail messages. If you don't select this box, skip to Step 24. Otherwise proceed to the next step.

20. **If you were told to use SSL for security, in the Use Secure Connection (SSL) drop-down list, select either Always or Whenever Possible, depending on what your ISP has specified.**

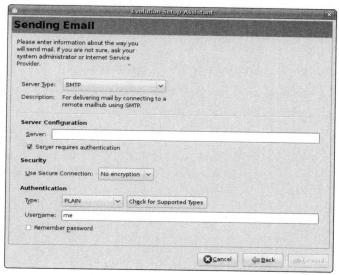

Figure 10-4:
The
Evolution
Sending
E-mail
screen.

21. **Under Authentication, select the appropriate Type as instructed by your ISP.**

    If you're not sure, click Check for Supported Types.

22. **Under Username, enter the login name you're supposed to use to authenticate your outgoing mail server.**

    This name may be different from the one you use for incoming mail.

23. **Select the Remember Password check box so you don't have to enter your password each time you send mail.**

    Just make sure (again) that you log out or use the Lock Screen option so no one can send joke e-mails at your expense!

24. **Click Forward to proceed.**

    You have now reached the wonderfully simple Account Management screen.

25. **Either leave the Name entry as it is (your e-mail address) or change it to something descriptive so you can tell which account you're looking at if you have a list of accounts you need to use.**

    It's common for your e-mail address to appear in this final box as something like jane@computer5.example.com. If this happens for you, you'll want to edit this entry so it matches your real e-mail address (which in Jane's case is jane@example.com).

26. **Click Forward to proceed to the Time Zone screen.**

    Select the city closest to yours on the time zone map, or use the Select drop-down list to choose your proper time zone.

27. **Click Forward to proceed to the Done screen.**

    Here you see just a quick message saying you've finished.

28. **Click Apply to save your settings.**

    The Evolution program opens, as shown in Figure 10-5.

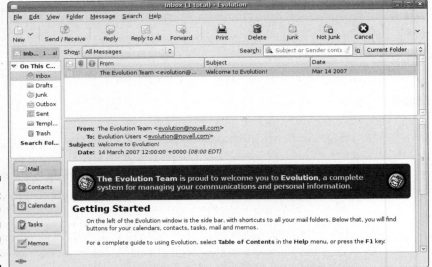

Figure 10-5:
The Evolution application window.

Sending and checking e-mail

The following steps outline how to create a new e-mail and send it:

1. **Click New.**

   A Compose Message window opens, as shown in Figure 10-6.

2. **Type the recipient's e-mail address (such as** bob@example.net**) or a list of addresses separated by commas (such as** bob@example.net, tom@example.org**) in the To text box.**

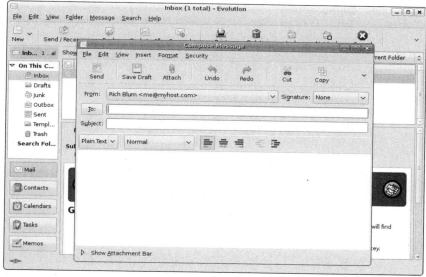

Figure 10-6:
An Evolution
Compose
Message
window.

3. **If you need to add a CC (Carbon Copy) or BCC (Blind Carbon Copy) to the list of recipients, choose View from the menu, select the appropriate field(s) to appear, and then enter the appropriate address(es) into those fields.**

   Mail addresses added to the CC field appear in the header of the mail message for everyone to see. Mail addresses added to the BCC field don't appear in the header of the mail message (but the message is still delivered to them). This is a sneaky (okay, maybe just *discreet*) way to send someone a copy of a message without others knowing it.

4. **Type the topic of your e-mail into the Subject text box.**

5. **In the lower window, type the body of your e-mail.**

   Use the handy formatting buttons and the Format menu if you want to "pretty up" your e-mail. If you want to use the formatting buttons, set your Format type to HTML first.

6. **If you want to add a signature to the bottom of your e-mail, click the drop-down list box next to Signature and select Autogenerated.**

   To create custom signatures, go to the main Evolution window and choose Edit➪Preferences to open the Evolution Preferences dialog box (see Figure 10-7). Select the account you want to create the signature(s) for and then click the Edit button to open the Evolution Account Editor. In this dialog box, in the Identity tab, click Add New Signature. Here, you can create and format your new signature, and after you click the Save and Close button, you can choose which signature should be the default in the Identity tab's Signature drop-down list box. Get rid of the extra dialog boxes by clicking OK or Close on each one.

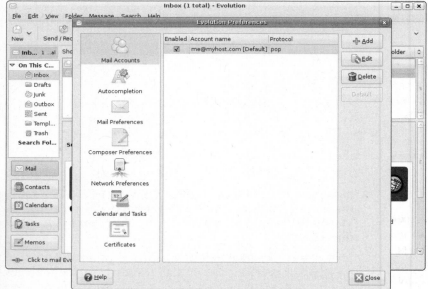

Figure 10-7:
The
Evolution
Preferences
dialog box.

7. **When you finish typing your message, click the Send button.**

   The e-mail is now added to your Outbox, where you can edit it if you want.

8. **Click the Send/Receive button.**

   Your e-mail goes out, and Evolution checks for new incoming mail.

Take some time to really explore Evolution. As you can see just from the figures in this chapter, this program has many features, including the capability to filter junk mail.

Working with KMail

Linux distributions that use the KDE desktop often provide the *KMail* application for e-mail access. KMail is another all-in-one package like Evolution — it provides an e-mail client, calendar, and task scheduler all in one window.

This section walks through the steps you'll need to take to get your KMail software working with your ISP, and then shows you how to send and receive e-mail.

Setting up KMail

You can usually find the KMail application by choosing Applications⇨ Internet⇨Kmail (see Chapter 5). The first time you start KMail you're greeted by the KMail Welcome Wizard, shown in Figure 10-8.

Figure 10-8:
The KMail
Welcome
Wizard to
set up your
mail.

Just click the Next button to get the configuration process started. Before you can start sending and receiving e-mail, however, you'll need to tell KMail how to interact with your ISP e-mail server. Unlike the monolithic Evolution Setup Wizard, KMail's wizard is a little more compact:

1. **Select your type of ISP e-mail server, and click Next.**

   The account type identifies the type of server you're connecting with to get your e-mail. Figure 10-9 shows the options you have available. The most common are POP3 and IMAP. KMail also allows you to connect to a mailbox on your workstation, which is somewhat silly unless you're sharing your workstation with others (or you just like sending yourself messages).

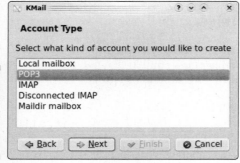

Figure 10-9:
The KMail
Account
Type
screen.

2. **Enter your account information, and click Next.**

   The Account Information screen appears and asks for your real name,
   your e-mail address, and an option organization name as they will
   appear in your outgoing e-mail messages (see Figure 10-10). Be careful
   entering your e-mail address, as that's what others will reply to.

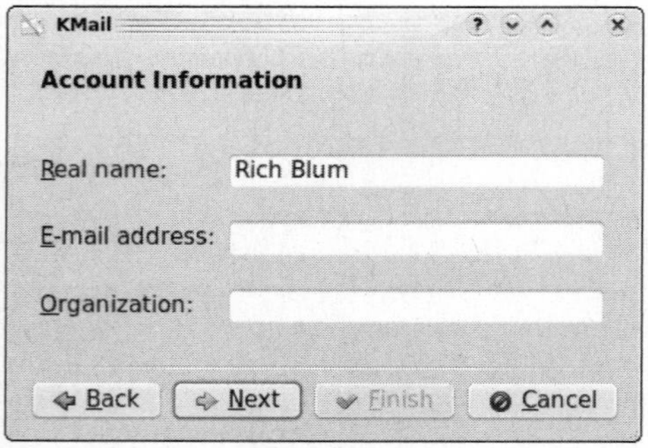

Figure 10-10:
The KMail
Account
Information
screen.

3. **Enter your ISP login information, and click Next.**

   Some ISPs assign separate user IDs and passwords for connecting to the
   e-mail server, while others just use your e-mail address. Enter whichever
   your ISP uses.

4. **Enter your ISP server information, and click Next.**

   The Server Information screen asks for both the incoming and outgoing
   server names for your ISP account (shown in Figure 10-11). The incoming server is the name of your POP3 or IMAP server. The outgoing server
   is the name of your SMTP server. (Unfortunately, you can't configure
   any advanced settings, such as SSL access, here. If your ISP server
   requires those, you'll need to set them up, as explained later.)

The KMail Welcome Wizard finishes, and the next wizard, KWallet, automatically starts.

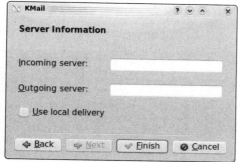

Figure 10-11:
The KMail
Server
Information
screen.

5. **Select the Basic setup in the KWallet Wizard and click Next.**

   Just like keeping little slips of paper in your wallet, the KWallet application stores all of your passwords in a single location that applications can access only with your approval. This makes storing passwords a lot easier; you only have to remember one password to allow applications to access your stored passwords.

6. **Select the check box to use KWallet, then enter and confirm a password. Click Finish when done.**

   The KWallet Wizard completes, and you see the main KMail window, shown in Figure 10-12.

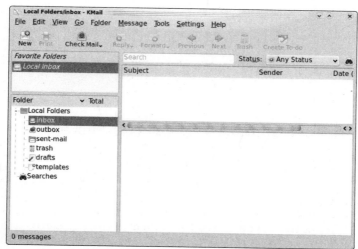

Figure 10-12:
The main
KMail
window.

Customizing KMail

The main KMail window is divided into four sections:

- ✓ **Favorite folders:** Gives you quick access to popular folders if you have more than one e-mail account configured.
- ✓ **Folder:** Displays all the folders used in KMail for the account. Each e-mail account has a separate group of folders.
- ✓ **Message list:** Displays your messages, sorted by any of the columns (just click a column to sort by it).
- ✓ **Preview pane:** Displays the currently selected e-mail message.

Before you can start using anything, you may have to customize the settings. To do that, choose Settings⇨Configure KMail. The Configure dialog box, shown in Figure 10-13, appears.

Figure 10-13: The KMail Configure dialog box.

To add additional settings to your e-mail setup, follow these steps:

1. **Click the Accounts icon in the left pane.**

   The Accounts window has two tabbed panes — one for receiving and one for sending. Make sure the Receiving tab is selected first.

2. **Select the account to configure, and click the Modify button.**

   The Modify Account dialog box appears, as shown in Figure 10-14.

3. **Modify the settings in the Modify Account dialog box and click OK.**

   The Modify Account dialog box contains three tabs:

   - *General:* Contains general account information, such as the ISP server hostname, TCP port used, and login information.

   - *Advanced:* Contains settings for how long to leave messages on the ISP server.

   - *Security:* Contains settings for the encryption and authentication methods used by the ISP server.

4. **Select the Sending tab in the Accounts page to view SMTP server settings; then select the e-mail account used for sending mail, and click the Modify button.**

   If your Linux distribution configures a local e-mail server program, you may see another option for local mail delivery here. Make sure you select the entry that corresponds to your ISP account. You see the Modify Transport dialog box, as shown in Figure 10-15.

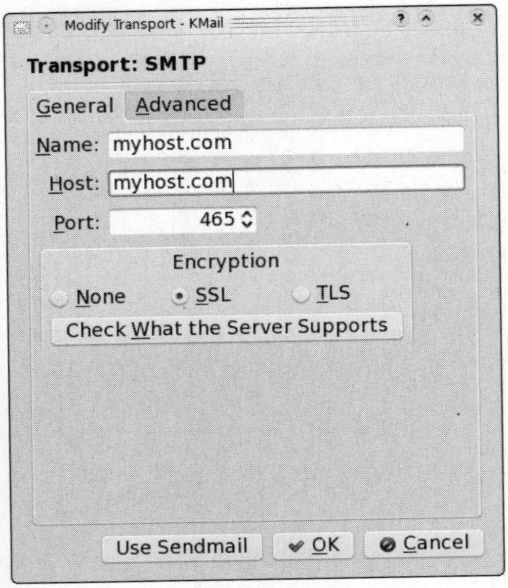

Figure 10-15:
The KMail
Modify
Transport
dialog box.

5. Modify the settings in the Modify Transport dialog box and click OK.

The Modify Transport dialog box contains two tabs:

- *General:* This tab contains settings for the SMTP server hostname and port number, and to specify whether it uses encryption in the connection.

- *Advanced:* This tab contains settings for authenticating the SMTP server to forward e-mail messages.

6. Click OK to exit the Configure dialog box.

Now that your KMail software is configured, you're ready to start using it. From the main KMail window (refer to Figure 10-12), you can view your inbox by simply selecting the inbox entry in the Folders section. To check your mailbox, click the Check Mail icon in the toolbar to connect manually with your ISP server.

Sending e-mail messages is as easy as clicking the New button in the toolbar. The Composer window, shown in Figure 10-16, appears with the standard e-mail layout, as we already discussed in the "Evolving into E-Mail: Evolution" section.

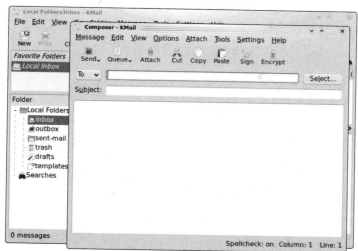

Figure 10-16:
The KMail
Composer
window.

Eating spam

One nice feature about KMail is its automatic spam- and virus-filtering capability. KMail can scan your incoming e-mail and filter out spam and viruses automatically. These days, *spam* (officially called *unsolicited commercial e-mail*) can overwhelm your inbox, and being able to catch and redirect that junk early comes in handy.

Both Fedora and Ubuntu include spam-filtering programs in their default setups, but you have to enable them in your KMail configuration. To do that, just follow these steps:

1. **Choose Tools⇨Anti-Spam Wizard to start the wizard, then click Next after your spam filter has been detected.**

   The wizard scans your computer for installed spam-filter programs — and your Linux distribution probably has one (Fedora installs SpamBayes; Ubuntu includes Bogofilter). After the wizard detects your installed program, it appears as shown in Figure 10-17.

2. **Select how you want KMail to handle spam, then click Next.**

   You can configure KMail to just mark spam as having been read so it doesn't count it in your total of unread messages, or you can have it move any messages it thinks are spam to a separate folder automatically.

3. **Review your selections, and click the Finish button.**

Figure 10-17:
The KMail
Anti-Spam
Wizard.

Spam detection is still something of a work in progress. There's no one solution that detects all possible spam messages, so you have to be on the watch constantly. Most spam filters learn as they go, so it may take a while for your spam filter to get used to spotting the spam messages you receive. Make sure you check your spam folder for any messages that might have been marked incorrectly as spam. You can then unmark them to help the spam filter learn what is and isn't okay to trash.

Chapter 11

Putting the X in Text

. . . .

In This Chapter

▶ Working with text files in `gedit`

▶ Editing in KWrite

. . . .

*F*rom text editors to word processors, Linux offers a wide variety of options for working with words. In this chapter, we take a look at different ways to view the contents of a text file, using some simple text editors in the GUI environments. In Chapter 12, we take a look at office suites for those who would rather do word processing.

Going with gedit

Lots of graphical options are available. In this section, we cover `gedit` (see Figure 11-1), which is the default GUI text editor for the GNOME desktop. To start gedit, choose Applications⇨Accessories⇨Text Editor from the panel menu in either Ubuntu or Fedora.

`gedit` is strictly a *text editor;* you use it to generate raw text, whereas a *word processor* creates marked-up text that can be opened only by programs that can read that word processor's file formatting. If you want to add bold, italics, underlines, or any other special features to your document, proceed to Chapter 12.

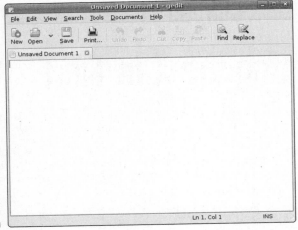

Figure 11-1:
The gedit
window
in Ubuntu,
showing a
blank file.

Entering and editing text in gedit

To enter text in gedit, just click in the big white space and start typing. You have access to the standard collection of editing tools, such as cut, paste, and copy. To use these, select the text you want to work with and then click the appropriate button on the gedit toolbar (or right-click and choose the appropriate command from the context menu).

The interesting thing about this particular text editor is its plugins. The gedit plugins provide advanced features that turn the simple gedit text editor into an almost full-featured word processor. Some of the more popular plugins available can spellcheck, automatically indent lines, add the current date and time, and even provide sentence, word, and character counts. (We talk about other plugins in the "Setting preferences" section.)

Saving your work

As with most programs, you have two choices for saving your work. You can save your work and keep going or save it and then close the program. To just save the file and keep going, follow these steps:

1. **Click the Save button.**

   This button looks like a floppy disk. If you've never saved this file, clicking it opens the Save As dialog box.

2. **Either choose one of the folders in the Save In Folder drop-down list box to save your file into, or click the right-facing arrow next to Browse for Other Folders to open the file-browsing section.**

   The dialog box expands to allow you to browse to the location you want to use.

3. **If necessary, browse through the directories in the left or right pane until you're in the directory in which you want to save the file. Double-click the name of a directory to enter it — or double-click the entry in the left pane to jump to its location.**

4. **Type the file's name in the Name text box.**

5. **Click Save to save the file.**

   The dialog box closes.

To close gedit, follow these steps:

1. **Choose File⇨Quit.**

   If you haven't saved this file since the last time you changed it, the Question dialog box appears.

2. **If you see the dialog box, click Save to save your work or click Close Without Saving to abandon it.**

   The program closes, unless you have more than one file open — in which case, you see the Question dialog box for each file you have altered but not saved.

Setting preferences

The gedit preferences are what you use to set the look and feel of gedit. The gedit Preferences dialog box, shown in Figure 11-2, contains a few different features. This is where you can customize the operation of the gedit editor. The Preferences dialog box contains four tabbed areas for setting the features and behavior of the editor.

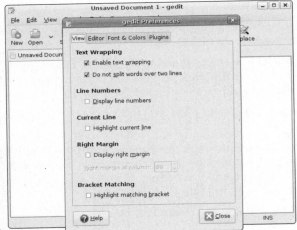

Figure 11-2:
The gedit
Preferences
dialog box.

View

The View tab provides options for how `gedit` displays the text in the editor window:

- **Text Wrapping:** Determines how to handle long lines of text in the editor. Selecting the Enable Text Wrapping check box wraps long lines to the next line of the editor. If you select the Do Not Split Words Over Two Lines check box, it prevents the auto-inserting of dashes between syllables in long words that occur at the ends of lines.

- **Line Numbers:** Displays line numbers in the left margin on the editor window.

- **Current Line:** Highlights the line of the current cursor position, enabling you to find the cursor's position easily.

- **Right Margin:** Enables the right-side margin, and allows you to set how many columns should be in the editor window. The default value is 80 columns.

- **Bracket Matching:** When enabled, highlights bracket pairs in programming code so you can easily match brackets in `if-then` statements, `for` and `while` loops, and other coding elements that use brackets.

The line-numbering and bracket-matching features help programmers troubleshoot code — these amenities are not found in some text editors.

If you're using `gedit` to edit program code, choose View➪Highlight Mode. You can select the programming language you're using from the list to customize `gedit`. Your code appears with the different elements (such as variable names, constants, and text) in different colors.

Editor

The Editor tab provides options for how the `gedit` editor handles tabs and indentation, along with how files are saved:

- ✔ **Tab Stops:** Sets the number of spaces skipped when you press the Tab key. The default value is eight. This feature also includes a check box that, when selected, inserts spaces instead of a tab skip.

- ✔ **Automatic Indentation:** When enabled, `gedit` indents text lines automatically for paragraphs and code elements (such as `if-then` statements and loops).

- ✔ **File Saving:** Provides two choices for saving files, whether to create a backup copy of the file when opened in the edit window, and whether to save the file automatically at a preselected interval.

Font & Colors

The Font & Colors tab allows you to configure (not surprisingly) two items:

- ✔ **Font:** Allows you to select the default font of Monospace 10 or to select a customized font and font size from a dialog box.

- ✔ **Color Scheme:** Allows you to select the default color scheme used for text, background, selected text, and selection colors, or to choose a custom color for each category.

The default colors for `gedit` match the standard GNOME desktop theme selected for the desktop. These colors change to match the scheme you select for the desktop.

Plugins

The Plugins tab provides control over the plugins used in `gedit`. Plugins are separate programs that can interface with `gedit` to provide additional functionality.

To install plugins, follow these steps:

1. **Click the PlugIns tab.**

   The PlugIns tab's contents appear, as shown in Figure 11-3.

2. **Click an item you're interested in within the PlugIns tab.**

   If you want more information about a certain plugin, click the About Plug-In button. Click Close to get rid of the About window.

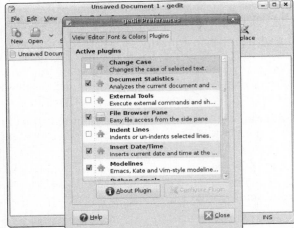

3. **When you find a plugin you want, select its check box to activate it.**

   The plugin is activated if a check appears in the check box.

4. **If the Configure PlugIn button becomes active for the plugin you selected, click the button to open the tool's PlugIn Configuration dialog box.**

   This dialog box differs depending on which plugin you're using.

5. **Configure your plugin and click OK to return to the Preferences dialog box.**

6. **If you want additional plugins, repeat Steps 3 and 4.**

7. **When you're finished selecting plugins, click Close to close the Preferences dialog box.**

You can now access the plugins from your gedit menus, as shown in Figure 11-4. Each one is placed in its appropriate location; for example, Change Case appears on the Edit menu, while the spellchecker appears on the Tools menu.

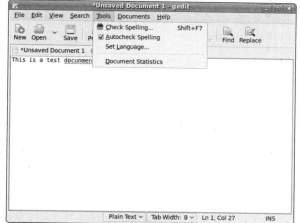

Figure 11-4:
Using the
spell-
checker in
gedit.

Editing Text in the KDE Desktop: KWrite

Not to be left out, the KDE environment also provides a way to graphically
edit text files. The basic editor for the KDE environment is KWrite. It provides
simple word-processing-style text editing, along with support for code-syntax
highlighting and editing.

To open KWrite, select KWrite from the KDE menu system on your desktop.
(In Fedora it's under the Utilities section. Some Linux distributions even
create a Panel icon for it.) The default KWrite editing window is shown in
Figure 11-5.

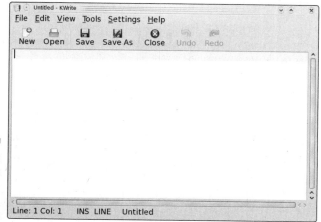

Figure 11-5:
The default
KWrite
window.

The KWrite editing window provides full cut-and-paste capabilities, using the mouse and the arrow keys. Just as in a word processor, cut (or copy) text anywhere in the buffer area and paste it at any other place.

The menu bar contains the following items:

- ✔ **File:** Load, save, print, and export text from files.

- ✔ **Edit:** Manipulate text in the buffer area.

- ✔ **View:** Manage how the text appears in the editor window.

- ✔ **Tools:** Manipulate the text, using specialized features.

- ✔ **Settings:** Configure the way the editor handles text.

- ✔ **Help:** Get information about the editor and commands.

The Edit menu provides all your text-editing needs. Instead of having to remember cryptic key commands (which by the way, KWrite also supports), you can select items from the Edit menu, as shown in Table 11-1.

Table 11-1	The KWrite Edit Menu
Item	*What It Does*
Undo	Reverses the last action or operation.
Redo	Reverses the last undo action.
Cut	Deletes the selected text and places it in the Clipboard.
Copy	Copies the selected text to the Clipboard.
Paste	Inserts the current contents of the Clipboard at the current cursor position.
Select All	Selects all text in the editor.
Deselect	Deselects any text that is currently selected.
Overwrite Mode	Toggles insert mode to overwrite mode, replacing text with new typed text instead of just inserting the new text.
Find	Produces the Find Text dialog box, which allows you to customize a text search.
Find Next	Repeats the last find operation farther forward in the buffer area.
Find Previous	Repeats the last find operation farther backward in the buffer area.

Item	What It Does
Replace	Produces the Replace With dialog box, which allows you to customize the text you want to search and replace.
Find Selected	Locates the next occurrence of the selected text in the document.
Find Selected Backwards	Locates the previous occurrence of the selected text in the document.
Go to Line	Produces the Goto dialog box, which allows you to enter a line number. The cursor moves to the specified line.

The Find Text dialog box, shown in Figure 11-6, is a powerful tool for searching for text in the text file.

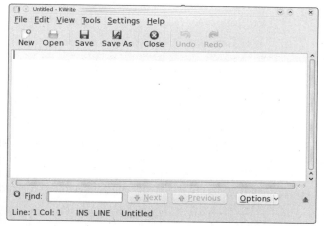

Figure 11-6:
The KWrite
Find Text
dialog box.

The Find Text dialog box uses the word at the current cursor location as the default text value to search for. Click the Options button to customize the search, such as whether to perform a case-sensitive search, or to only look for whole words instead of finding the text within a word.

The Tools menu provides several handy features for working with the text in the buffer area. Table 11-2 describes the tools available in KWrite.

Table 11-2	The KWrite Tools
Tool	*What It Does*
Read Only Mode	Locks the text so no changes can be made while it's in the editor.
Indentation	Automatically indents lines based on a selection.
Encoding	Specifies the character-set encoding used by the text. This defines what codes are used to represent what characters. KWrite supports lots of different character set codes to represent lots of different languages.
Spelling	Starts the spellcheck program at the start of the text.
Spelling (from cursor)	Starts the spellcheck program from the current cursor position.
Spellcheck Selection	Starts the spellcheck program only on the selected section of text.
Indent	Increases the paragraph indentation by one.
Unindent	Decreases the paragraph indentation by one.
Clean Indentation	Returns all paragraph indentation to the original settings.
Align	Forces the current line or the selected lines to return to the default indentation settings.
Uppercase	Sets the selected text, or the character at the current cursor position to uppercase.
Lowercase	Sets the selected text, or the character at the current cursor position to lowercase.
Capitalize	Uppercases the first letter of the selected text or the word at the current cursor position.
Join Lines	Combines the selected lines, or combines the line at the current cursor position with the next line.
Word Wrap Document	Enables word wrapping in the text. If a line of text extends past the editor window's edge, the text continues on the next line.

The Settings menu includes the Configure Editor dialog box (shown in Figure 11-7), where you tweak the editor window to fit your work. Choose Settings⇨Configure Editor to see what you can customize.

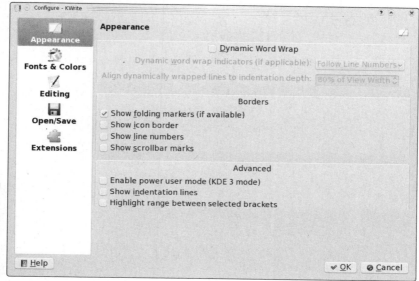

Figure 11-7:
The KWrite
Configure
Editor dialog
box.

Click the icons on the left side of the dialog box to configure features. The right side of the dialog box shows the configuration settings for each feature.

The Appearance setting allows you to set how the text appears in the text editor window. You can enable word wrap, line numbers (great for programmers), and folder markers. With the Fonts & Colors feature, you can customize the editor's color scheme, determining which colors to assign to each category of text in the program code.

The KWrite editor recognizes several programming languages, and uses color-coding to distinguish constants, functions, and comments. Also, notice that the for loop in the code has an icon that links the opening and closing braces. This is called a _folding marker_. By clicking the icon, you can collapse the function into a single line.

Chapter 12

Word Processing and More with OpenOffice.org

Words fly, writing remains.

— Spanish proverb, from Dictionary of Proverbs, by Delfín Carbonell Basset

*T*hese days, just about everyone who has a computer has at least one office suite at their fingertips. If they're Microsoft Windows users, this suite is probably Microsoft Office, although it may be another worthy contender, such as Corel WordPerfect Office. In Linux, typically the suite is OpenOffice.org. This suite comes with Base (database), Calc (a spreadsheet), Draw (diagrams and figures), Impress (for presentations), Math (a word processor for writing mathematical formulas), and Writer (for word processing).

After you figure out how to use one of the programs in this suite, you may be happy to find that the others are designed to look and work in very similar ways. You can even open and save files in Microsoft Office format, if you need to share them with people who are using that product — and you can edit the Office files people send you, too.

That's enough *about* OpenOffice.org. In this chapter, you can actually *use* it!

Other office suites available for Linux users are the commercial OpenOffice.org-relative StarOffice (`www.sun.com/staroffice`), Applixware Office (`www.vistasource.com/products`), KOffice (`www.koffice.org`), and GNOME Office (`www.gnome.org/gnome-office/`).

Installing the OpenOffice.org Suite

Before you can take off creating your masterpieces, you must make sure that OpenOffice.org is available. When you installed Fedora, one of the installation options was to install the Office productivity software. If you selected this option, you installed most of the OpenOffice.org suite of programs.

By default, Fedora includes these OpenOffice.org packages in the Office productivity installation:

- **Writer** for word processing
- **Calc** for spreadsheets
- **Impress** for presentation graphics
- **Draw** for drawing graphics
- **Math** for creating complex mathematical formulas

However, not all Linux distributions install all these pieces. For example, Ubuntu only installs the Writer, Calc, and Impress packages by default. There's one additional OpenOffice.org package available, but it's usually not installed by default: Base, which is used for creating personal databases.

If you chose not to install the Office productivity software at installation time, or you need to install one of the packages that wasn't installed by default in your Linux distribution, don't sweat it; you can do that now without having to completely reinstall your Linux distribution. Turn to Chapter 16 to find out how to add the OpenOffice.org packages from the software-package manager used in your distribution.

After you've installed the OpenOffice.org packages, you'll find most of them by choosing Applications➪Office in GNOME or KDE (even the additional Base package if you install it).

The two oddballs are the Draw and Math packages, which (unfortunately) often don't get listings of their own. To access either of these packages, you'll have to start one of the other OpenOffice.org packages (such as Writer), and then choose File➪New. You see the options for creating a new Drawing (which starts Draw) or a new Formula (which starts Math).

Word Processing with OpenOffice.Org Writer

Word processors are almost required equipment these days. Kids use them to write letters to their grandparents. Grandparents use them to write letters to their grandkids. Whether you're working on the great American novel or a book report, OpenOffice.org Writer has all the best features you expect to find these days in a word processor.

Taking a tour of OpenOffice.org Writer

Before you proceed, take a look at the GUI layout shown in Figure 12-1.

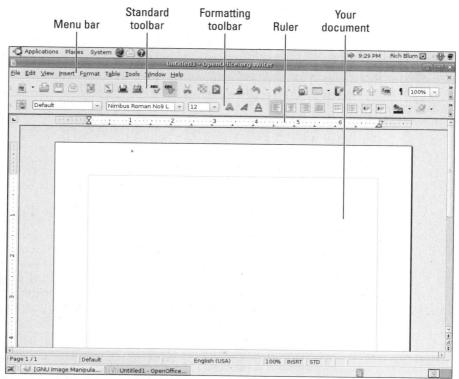

Figure 12-1: The Open Office.org Writer layout.

Along the top of the window is the menu bar, something you should be used to if you've worked with other word-processing software. OpenOffice.org Writer has all the features you expect from a modern word processor. It has too many menu options to cover in depth, so we give you instead a (non-exhaustive) summary of what you find on each major menu:

- **File:** The usual Open, Save, Save As, Print, and Print Preview (under the term Page Preview) commands, along with a set of wizards (under the term AutoPilot), plus capabilities to send documents through e-mail, to create templates, to create Web pages, and to access your database information

- **Edit:** The usual Select All and Find commands, along with change tracking, document merging, and document comparing

- **View:** The usual Zoom functions and toolbars, along with capabilities to show or hide formatting characters to see what the document would look like as a Web page

- **Insert:** The usual page breaks and special characters, along with indexes, tables, bookmarks, headers, footers, and cross-references

- **Format:** The usual character, paragraph, and page settings, along with styles, autoformatting capabilities, and columns

- **Table:** The usual table-control options, including capabilities to insert, delete, and select cells, as well as convert between tables and text

- **Tools:** The usual spellchecking and thesaurus entries, in addition to hyphenation, autocorrection, an image gallery, and a bibliography database

These menus have even more features than what's listed here. Go through and take a look; you may find a new favorite feature in there somewhere.

Beneath the menu bar is the Standard toolbar. Each icon on this toolbar represents a different functionality, which is detailed in Table 12-1.

Table 12-1	The OpenOffice.org Writer Standard Toolbar
Button or Item	**What You Can Do**
New	Create new documents of various types. Click the downward-pointing arrow to select a particular type of document to create from among any of the OpenOffice.org (OOo) types.
Open	Open an existing file for reading or editing.
Save	Save the current document. If you haven't saved this document before, the Save As dialog box opens.

Button or Item	What You Can Do
Document as E-mail	Open a Compose e-mail window in your preferred e-mail program and automatically attach this document.
Edit File	Edit the displayed Web page.
Export Directly as PDF	Open a Save As dialog box with PDF selected as the file type.
Print File Directly	Send a file to the default printer.
Page Preview	Show this page as it would look if you printed it. To return from preview mode, click Close Preview.
Spellcheck	Run the spellchecker on your entire document or the selected text.
AutoSpellcheck On/Off	Activate or turn off the automatic spellchecker feature.
Cut	Remove the selected text from the document and save it in memory.
Copy	Make a copy of the selected document text and save it in memory.
Paste	Place the text from memory in the document at the cursor's current location. Click the down arrow to see options for how your text can be pasted.
Format Paintbrush	Pick up the formatting of the first text you click and apply it to the second text you click.
Undo	Undo the last change you made to the document. Click the down arrow to choose how far you want to back up through changes you've made.
Redo	Reinstate the last change to the document after using Undo to cancel it. Click the down arrow to choose how many undone changes you want to redo.
Hyperlink	Open or close a dialog box that you can use to build complex hyperlinks.
Table	Insert a new table. Click the down arrow to choose how many rows and columns the table should have.
Show Draw Functions	Access the many OpenOffice.org drawing utilities.
Find and Replace	Open or close the Find and Replace dialog box.
Navigator	Open or close the Navigator window, which allows you to jump to specific features within your document.
Gallery	Open or close a pane along the top of the document that provides access to clip art. Click this button again to close the pane.

(continued)

Table 12-1 *(continued)*

Button or Item	What You Can Do
Nonprinting Characters On/Off	Show all spaces, returns at the ends of paragraphs, and other characters that you don't normally see in your documents.
Zoom	Alter how large the document appears on-screen.
Help	Open the OpenOffice.org Help dialog box.

The Formatting toolbar is directly below the standard toolbar in a default OpenOffice.org setup — though not on all distributions. You can remove the Formatting bar at any time by choosing View⇨Toolbars⇨Formatting.

This toolbar allows you to click buttons and expand drop-down lists that represent standard word-processing functions such as styles, fonts, font sizes, and formatting instructions. Most features on this bar are identical to what you see in most modern word processors. The button for paragraph background formatting is the only one that's particularly unusual. It allows you to change the background color of the paragraph, which can produce some interesting results.

This toolbar actually changes depending on what you're doing. If the cursor is within a table, for example, the Formatting bar contains useful buttons for working with tables.

Directly below the Formatting toolbar in a default OpenOffice.org setup is the ruler. All modern word processors offer this item, which marks (for example) the margins and tabs of your document in the measuring system of your choice. To change the units of measurement you're using, right-click the ruler to open the Measurements dialog box.

Oh, yeah — that big, blocked-off white space that takes up most of the window is the Document area. That's where you actually work on your documents! Just click in there and start typing. You can also access a Formatting shortcut menu by right-clicking in the document section.

Working with Writer files

OpenOffice.org Writer can work with lots of different file types. This allows you to create documents that can be used with many different types of word-processing systems.

Not only can you save new documents in various formats, but you can also read documents created on other word-processing programs. Here's a list of the different document types you can use with OpenOffice.org Writer:

- ✔ **OpenDocument (ODT) format:** A proposed open standard that may one day be supported by all word-processing programs. (What a concept.)

- ✔ **OpenOffice.org 1.0 (SXW) format:** The original OpenOffice document format.

- ✔ **Microsoft Word 97/2000/XP (DOC) format:** Yes, you can read and write Word documents with Writer.

  The current version of OpenOffice.org can't open Word 2007 (`.docx`) documents. However, if you have access to a copy of Word 2007, you can convert those documents to `.doc` format, then read them in OpenOffice.org. As with any type of document conversion, be careful that you don't lose any important features in your document during the conversion.

- ✔ **Microsoft Word 95 (DOC) format:** Even some of the older Word formats.

- ✔ **Microsoft Word 6.0 (DOC) format:** And even some of the _really_ old Word formats.

- ✔ **Rich Text (RTF) format:** A standard format for saving basic font and document information.

- ✔ **StarWriter 3.0 – 5.0 (SDW) format:** Sun's StarOffice word processor (a close cousin to OpenOffice.org).

- ✔ **Microsoft Word 2003 (XML) format:** An attempt by Microsoft to create a standard word-processing document format by using the XML standard markup language.

Although not available in the Save As dialog box, the OpenOffice.org Writer toolbar allows you to export any document format to the PDF document format. This feature alone can save you from having to purchase an expensive commercial product (from a commercial software company that shall remain nameless).

Spreadsheets with OpenOffice.Org Calc

Some people like to balance their checkbooks by hand. But a spreadsheet can make that task — and many other mathematical chores — much easier. The following sections take a look at OpenOffice.org Calc so you can get to work.

Taking a tour of OpenOffice.org Calc

Much of what you see in OpenOffice.org Calc should look familiar from looking through OpenOffice.org Writer and other spreadsheet programs you've used. Take a look at the GUI layout shown in Figure 12-2.

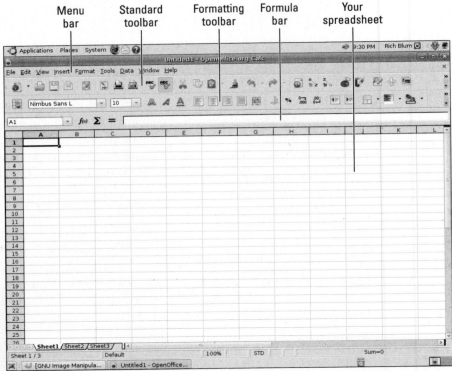

Menu bar   Standard toolbar   Formatting toolbar   Formula bar   Your spreadsheet

Figure 12-2:
The Open
Office.org
Calc layout.

Along the top of the window is the menu bar. OpenOffice.org Calc has all the features you expect from a modern spreadsheet system. It has too many menu options to cover in depth, so, instead, here's a (non-exhaustive) summary of what you find on each menu:

- ✔ **File:** The usual Open, Save, Save As, Print, and Print Preview (under the term Page Preview) commands; a set of wizards; plus the capabilities to send documents through e-mail, create templates, and create Web pages

- ✔ **Edit:** The usual Select All and Find commands, along with change tracking, headers and footers, and plugin loading

- ✔ **View:** The usual Zoom functions and toolbars, along with the options for showing or hiding column and row headers

✔ **Insert:** The usual page breaks and special characters, along with cells, rows, functions, and external data

✔ **Format:** The usual cell and row formatting, cell merging, and page settings, along with conditional formatting

✔ **Tools:** The usual spellchecking and thesaurus entries, in addition to hyphenation, autocorrection features, an image gallery, and a macro creator and editor

✔ **Data:** The usual data selection, sorting, and grouping routines in one easy place for quick access

These menus have more features than those listed here. Go through 'em and take a look; you may find a favorite feature to use.

Beneath the menu bar is the Standard toolbar. Each icon on this toolbar represents a different functionality, as shown in Table 12-2.

Table 12-2	The OpenOffice.org Calc Standard Toolbar
Button or Item	**What You Can Do**
New	Open new documents of various types. Click the downward-pointing arrow to select a particular type of document to create from among any of the OOo types.
Open	Open an existing file for reading or editing.
Save	Save the current document. If you haven't saved this document before, the Save As dialog box opens.
Document as E-mail	Open a Compose e-mail window in your preferred e-mail program, and attach this document automatically.
Edit File	Edit the displayed spreadsheet.
Export Directly as PDF	Open a Save As dialog box with PDF selected as the file type.
Print File Directly	Send a file to the default printer.
Page Preview	Show this page as it would look if you printed it. To return from preview mode, click Close Preview.
Spellcheck	Run the spellchecker on your entire document or the selected text.
AutoSpellcheck	Activate or turn off the automatic spellchecker feature.
Cut	Remove the selected text from the document and save it in memory.
Copy	Make a copy of the selected document text and save it in memory.

(continued)

Table 12-2 *(continued)*

Button or Item	What You Can Do
Paste	Place the text from memory into the document at the cursor's current location. Click the down arrow to see options for how to paste your text.
Format Paintbrush	Pick up the formatting of the first text you click and apply it to the second text you click.
Undo	Undo the last change you made to the document. Click the down arrow to choose how far you want to back up to.
Redo	Reinstate the last change to the document after using Undo to cancel it. Click the down arrow to choose how far you want to redo.
Hyperlink	Open or close a dialog box that you can use to build complex hyperlinks.
Sort Ascending	Re-order the selected data in ascending order.
Sort Descending	Re-order the selected data in descending order.
Insert Chart	Create a chart based on the selected data.
Show Draw Functions	Access the many OpenOffice.org drawing utilities.
Find and Replace	Open or close the Find and Replace dialog box.
Navigator	Open or close the Navigator window, which allows you to jump to specific features within your document.
Gallery	Open or close a dialog box that provides access to clip art.
Zoom	Alter how large the document appears on-screen.
Help	Open the OpenOffice.org Help dialog box.

The Formatting toolbar is directly below the Standard toolbar in a default OpenOffice.org setup. You can remove the Formatting toolbar at any time by choosing View⇨Toolbars⇨Formatting.

This toolbar allows you to click buttons and expand drop-down lists that represent standard spreadsheet functions such as styles, fonts, font sizes, and number-formatting instructions. Most features on this toolbar are identical to what you see in most modern spreadsheet software.

Directly below the Formatting bar in a default OpenOffice.org Calc setup is the Formula bar. Table 12-3 lays out what you find in this short collection of entries. This bar actually changes in response to what you're doing, offering you buttons for particular tasks — so don't panic if you look here and this table doesn't match what you see on your own Formula bar.

Table 12-3	The OpenOffice.org Calc Formula Bar
Button or Item	**What You Can Do**
Name Box	Displays the name of the current cell. You can also assign a name to a group of cells for future reference in your spreadsheet.
Function Wizard	Click to open the Function Wizard dialog box and browse to find the particular spreadsheet function you're looking for.
Sum	Click to start a SUM (addition) function in the Input Line.
Function	Click to place an equal sign (=) in the Input Line to signal that you're about to enter a function.
Input Line	Assign values or enter functions to fill a spreadsheet cell.

The spreadsheet area is where you work on your spreadsheet. Just pick a cell and start typing. You can also access a Formatting shortcut menu by right-clicking in the document section.

Working with Calc files

Like the Writer package, the Calc package allows you to read and write your document in many different formats:

- **OpenDocument Spreadsheet (ODS) format:** A proposed standard document format for spreadsheets.

- **OpenOffice.org 1.0 Spreadsheet (OTS) format:** The older OpenOffice 1.0 spreadsheet format.

- **Data Interchange Format (DIF):** A text-file format used to import and export spreadsheets between dissimilar spreadsheet programs.

- **dBase (DBF):** This option exports the spreadsheet data into a dBase database file.

- **Microsoft Excel 97/2000/XP (XLS) format:** The standard Microsoft Excel spreadsheet formats used by the most popular versions of Excel.

  The current version of OpenOffice.org doesn't support the Excel 2007 (.xlsx) format. However, if you have a copy of Excel 2007, you can convert a spreadsheet in that format into a standard .xls format, which you can read in OpenOffice.org.

- **Microsoft Excel 95 (XLS) format:** And the older Excel spreadsheet format.

- ✔ **Microsoft Excel 5.0 (XLS) format:** And even older Excel spreadsheet formats.

- ✔ **StarCalc 3.0 – 5.0 (SDC) format:** Sun's StarOffice spreadsheet format (a close cousin of the OpenOffice.org suite).

- ✔ **SYLK (SLK) format:** The Symbolic Link format, used to exchange data between spreadsheets and other applications, such as databases.

- ✔ **Text CSV (CSV) format:** The comma-separated text values, often used to export data to databases.

- ✔ **HTML (HTML) format:** Formats spreadsheet data as an HTML Web page.

- ✔ **Microsoft Excel 2003 (XML) format:** A standard proposed by Microsoft for using the Internet XML standard markup language for defining spreadsheet data.

Like Writer, the Calc standard toolbar also provides a button for you to export the spreadsheet directly as a PDF document.

Presentations with OpenOffice.Org Impress

Most people would rather eat glass than speak in front of a group. Still, if you have to, you may as well have some cool presentation software to back you up. Give OpenOffice.org Impress a chance to impress you.

Impress is listed in the Fedora and Ubuntu menus as OpenOffice.org Presentation. You can also open a new Impress presentation from any OpenOffice.org program by choosing File➪New➪Presentation from the menu bar.

Using the Presentation Wizard

When you open OpenOffice.org Impress, the first thing that launches is the Presentation Wizard (see Figure 12-3), which you can always open by choosing File➪Wizards➪Presentation. If you don't want this wizard to show up the next time you open OpenOffice.org Impress, select the Do Not Show This Wizard Again check box.

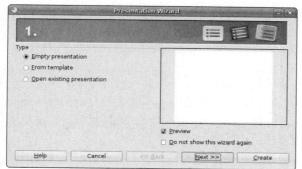

Figure 12-3:
The Open
Office.org
Presenta-
tion Wizard.

To use this wizard, follow these steps:

1. **Leave the Empty Presentation option selected (unless you have a template you need to work from), and click Next.**

   The next screen in the wizard appears.

2. **If you want to select one of the default slide backgrounds that come with OpenOffice.org Impress, choose Presentation Backgrounds from the Slide Design drop-down list, and then click the various options to see what they look like.**

   By default, there aren't many background templates. This is one area where Sun's StarOffice offers added value.

3. **If you want to select a presentation (content) layout template that was designed specifically for the template, choose Presentation(s) from the Select a Slide Design drop-down list, and then select the presentation type you want to use.**

   Again, you find limited options here by default.

4. **If you want your presentation ultimately to appear on something other than a computer screen, adjust the Select An Output medium to match its intended setting.**

   Your choices are Screen, Overhead Sheet, Slide, and Paper.

5. **Click Next to proceed.**

   The next screen of the wizard appears.

6. **Under Select a Slide Transition, experiment with the various options in the Effect and Speed drop-down lists to decide how you want to move from one slide to another.**

   OpenOffice.org Impress animates these transitions for you as long as the Preview check box is selected.

7. Choose how to navigate your presentation:

- If you want to navigate slides manually (the Default option) while you give your presentation, skip to Step 10.

- If you want to have your presentation advance automatically, click the Automatic option.

8. In Duration of Page, set how long you want each slide to stay up.

9. In Duration of Pause, set how long of a blank gap you want to have between slides.

If you have the Show Logo check box selected, the OpenOffice.org logo appears during the blank pauses.

10. After you have your settings selected, click Create to proceed.

OpenOffice.org Impress opens, as shown in Figure 12-4. You may find it useful to click the X in the upper-right corner of the Slides pane to clear up the window some.

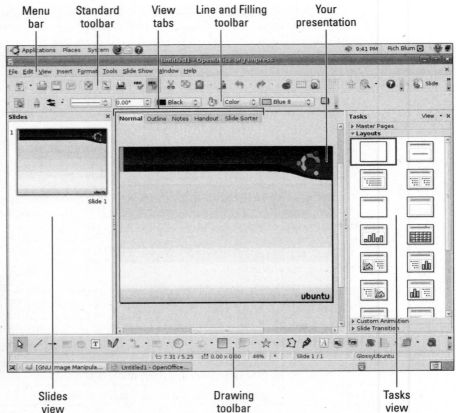

Figure 12-4:
The Open
Office.org
Impress
default look.

Taking a tour of OpenOffice.org Impress

Before you proceed, take a look at the GUI layout shown in Figure 12-4. The Slides view on the left and the Tasks view on the right might look like clutter to some; if you don't need them, just click the X in the upper-right corner of each pane. You can bring them back at any time by choosing View⇨Slide Pane and/or View⇨Task Pane.

Along the top of the window is the menu bar. OpenOffice.org Impress has the many features you expect from a modern presentation package. It has too many menu options to cover in depth, so here's a (non-exhaustive) summary of what you find on each menu:

- **File:** The usual Open, Save, Save As, and Print commands, a set of wizards, plus capabilities to send documents through e-mail and create templates

- **Edit:** The usual Select All and Find commands, along with the capability to duplicate a slide quickly

- **View:** The usual Zoom functions and toolbars, along with the capability to select whether you're looking at just slides, notes, or another section

- **Insert:** The usual new slide, along with charts, frames, graphics, and spreadsheets

- **Format:** The usual text-formatting features, along with layout, graphics, and style formatting

- **Tools:** The usual spellchecking feature, in addition to hyphenation, autocorrection, and an image gallery

- **Slide Show:** The usual slide-show controller menu

These menus have more features than those listed here. Don't forget to do some exploring on your own.

Along the top of the window is the Standard toolbar, which you can remove at any time by choosing View⇨Toolbars⇨Standard. Each icon represents a different functionality; all are described in Table 12-4.

Table 12-4	The OpenOffice.org Impress Standard Toolbar
Button or Item	**What You Can Do**
New	Open new documents of various types. Click the downward-pointing arrow to select a particular type of document to create from among any of the OOo types.
Open	Open an existing file for reading or editing.

(continued)

Table 12-4 *(continued)*

Button or Item	What You Can Do
Save	Save the current document. If you haven't saved this document before, the Save As dialog box opens.
Document as E-mail	Open a Compose e-mail window in your preferred e-mail program and automatically attach this document.
Edit File	Edit the displayed file.
Export Directly as PDF	Open a Save As dialog box with PDF selected as the file type.
Print File Directly	Send a file to the default printer.
Spellcheck	Run the spellchecker on your entire document or the selected text.
AutoSpellcheck	Activate or turn off the automatic spellchecker feature.
Cut	Remove the selected text from the document and save it in memory.
Copy	Make a copy of the selected document text and save it in memory.
Paste	Place the text from memory into the document at the cursor's current location. Click the down arrow to see options for how you can paste your text.
Format Paintbrush	Pick up the formatting of the first text you click and apply it to the next text you click.
Undo	Undo the last change you made to the document. Click the down arrow to choose how far you want to back up through the changes you've made.
Restore	Reinstate the last change to the document after using Undo to cancel it. Click the down arrow to choose how many of your changes you want to redo.
Chart	Insert a chart into the presentation by using the selected data.
Spreadsheet	Insert a spreadsheet into the presentation.
Hyperlink	Open or close a dialog box that you can use to build complex hyperlinks.
Display Grid	Display or remove the line-up grid from the slide.
Navigator	Open or close the Navigator window, which allows you to jump to specific features within your document.
Zoom	Alter how large the document appears on-screen.

Button or Item	What You Can Do
Help	Open the OpenOffice.org Help dialog box.
Slide	Insert a new slide after the current one.
Slide Design	Open the Slide Design dialog box.
Slide Show	Start a slide show.

The Line and Filling toolbar is directly below the Standard toolbar in a default OpenOffice.org setup. As usual, you can remove the toolbar at any time by choosing View⇨Toolbars⇨Line and Filling.

This toolbar allows you to click buttons and expand drop-down lists that represent standard presentation-software functions — for example, arrow styles, colors, line styles, and other formatting instructions. Most features on this bar are identical to what you see in most modern presentation programs.

Just above your document you see a series of tabs, each of which takes you to a particular way of viewing your slide(s). Table 12-5 outlines the available views and what you find in them.

Table 12-5	Available OpenOffice.org Impress Views
View	**What You Find**
Normal	Individual slide view in which you can add art to your slide.
Handout	Six slides per page, as you might print it for handouts.
Master	Individual slide view in which you can apply _master formatting_ that will apply to all slides. Access this view by choosing View⇨Master. On the Master submenu, you can choose Slide Master to view the master slide, Notes Master to view the master note page, or Master Elements to assign the information to be made available in the Master views.
Notes	Individual slide view in which you can see a small version of the slide plus your notes about that slide.
Outline	All-slides view with the slides listed in order for easy stepping through. Along the side, the slides are shown in thumbnail mode in a separate window as you navigate.
Slide Sorter	All-slides view with as many slides packed in as possible in columns and rows. Re-ordering slides is as simple as dragging them to where you want them to go and then dropping them.

The tabbed window contains your presentation. In Normal view, that presentation is your slide. You need to click one of the tools on the Drawing bar (discussed in the next section) in order to enter any content. To add more slides before or after this one, right-click the area and choose Slide⇨New Slide. For each slide, you can use the layouts in the Tasks pane on the right to change the setup.

Beneath your presentation is a drawing toolbar, which allows you to select lines, arrows, shapes, and more for your presentation-creation needs. Most of these buttons have downward-pointing arrows, which you can use to see the full range of features offered.

Working with Impress files

The OpenOffice.org Impress application doesn't support as many file types as its Writer and Calc siblings. Mostly this is due to a lack of universally accepted standards in the presentation-graphics industry.

The formats that Impress does support are

- **OpenDocument Presentation (ODP) format:** A standard presentation-graphics format proposed by OpenOffice.org.

- **OpenOffice.org 1.0 Presentation (OTP) format:** The original OpenOffice.org presentation-graphics file format.

- **Microsoft PowerPoint 97/2000/XP (PPT) format:** Possibly the most popular presentation-graphics tool used in business. You can use Impress to read and write most PowerPoint slide presentations.

   The current version of Impress doesn't support the newer PowerPoint 2007 .pptx format. You can, though, use PowerPoint 2007 to convert the presentation into a .ppt file, which OpenOffice.org can read and modify.

- **OpenOffice.org 1.0 Drawing (SXD) format:** An older rudimentary graphics-drawing format.

- **StarDraw 3.0 – 5.0 (SDA) format:** Files created in Draw's commercial cousin from Sun.

- **StarImpress 4.0 and 5.0 (SDD) format:** Files created in Impress's commercial cousin from Sun.

- **OpenOffice.org Drawing (ODG) format:** Rudimentary graphics-drawing format.

Although Impress can work with OpenOffice.org Draw files, the default file format for Impress files is the ODP format. As with the other packages in the OpenOffice.org suite, Impress also provides a toolbar icon you can use to save your slides as PDF files.

Fine Art with OpenOffice.Org Draw

Whether you're an aspiring graphic artist or just need a tool that lets you generate simple graphics for use on their own, in a presentation, or elsewhere, OpenOffice.org Draw provides a host of drawing functions. If nothing else, it's a whole lot of fun to play with! Not everything in life has to be practical.

Taking a tour of OpenOffice.org Draw

Before you proceed, take a look at the GUI layout shown in Figure 12-5. If you find the Pages pane on the left to be too much clutter, click the X in its upper-right corner to get rid of it. You can bring it back at any time by choosing View➪Page Pane.

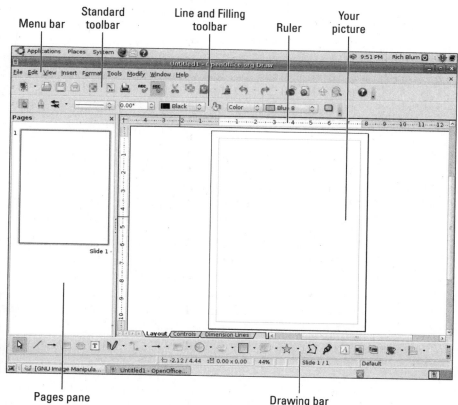

Figure 12-5:
The Open Office.org Draw layout.

Menu bar · Standard toolbar · Line and Filling toolbar · Ruler · Your picture

Pages pane · Drawing bar

Along the top of the window is the usual menu bar. OpenOffice.org Draw is a typical *vector graphics* program; it relies on calculated on-screen lines rather than on pixelated approximations or other techniques. (See Chapter 14 for discussion of the software used for editing photographs and other fine-detail work.)

OpenOffice.org Draw has too many menu options to cover in depth; here's a (non-exhaustive) summary of what you find on each menu:

- ✔ **File:** The usual Open, Save, Save As, Print, and Export commands, along with a set of wizards (under the term AutoPilot) plus the capability to send documents through e-mail and create templates

- ✔ **Edit:** The usual Find, Replace, and other commands, and the not so usual Image Map, which allows you to assign a URL to a clickable area in an image

- ✔ **View:** The usual Zoom functions and toolbars, along with the capability to select the display quality

- ✔ **Insert:** The usual charts, frames, graphics, and spreadsheets, along with scanning functions

- ✔ **Format:** The usual line and graphics formatting, along with layers and style formatting

- ✔ **Tools:** The usual spellchecker, as well as hyphenation, autocorrection, an image gallery, and an "eyedropper" for grabbing colors

- ✔ **Modify:** Various options for altering the appearance of an object

These menus have more features than those listed here. Try them out; you may find a new favorite.

Beneath the menu bar is the Standard toolbar, which you can remove at any time by choosing View➪Toolbars➪Standard. Each icon on this toolbar represents a different functionality, as described in Table 12-6. As you can see, this main toolbar is more similar to the one in OpenOffice.org Impress than to the one in OpenOffice.org Writer.

Table 12-6	The OpenOffice.org Draw Main Toolbar
Button or Item	**What You Can Do**
New	Open new documents of various types. Click the downward-pointing arrow to select a particular type of document to create from among any of the OOo types.
Open	Open an existing file for reading or editing.

Button or Item	What You Can Do
Save	Save the current document. If you haven't saved this document before, the Save As dialog box opens.
Document as E-mail	Open a Compose e-mail window in your preferred e-mail program, and attach this document automatically.
Edit File	Edit the document.
Export Directly as PDF	Open a Save As dialog box with PDF selected as the file type.
Print File Directly	Send a file to the default printer.
Spellcheck	Run the spellchecker on your entire document or the selected text.
AutoSpellcheck	Activate or turn off the automatic spellchecker feature.
Cut	Remove the selected text from the document and save it in memory.
Copy	Make a copy of the selected document text and save it in memory.
Paste	Place the text from memory into the document at the cursor's current location. Click the down arrow to see options for how to paste the text.
Format Paintbrush	Pick up the formatting of the first item you click and apply it to the second item you click.
Undo	Undo the last change you made to the document. Click the down arrow to choose how far you want to back up through changes you've made.
Restore	Reinstate the last change to the document after using Undo to cancel it. Click the down arrow to choose how far you want to redo changes you made before.
Chart	Insert a chart using the selected data.
Hyperlink	Open or close a dialog box that you can use to build complex hyperlinks.
Navigator	Open or close the Navigator window, which allows you to jump to specific features within your document.
Zoom	Alter how large the document appears on-screen.
Help	Open the OpenOffice.org Help dialog box.

The Line and Filling toolbar is directly below the Standard bar in a default OpenOffice.org setup. As usual, you can remove the Line and Filling toolbar at any time by choosing View⇨Toolbars⇨Line and Filling.

This toolbar allows you to click buttons and expand drop-down lists that represent standard presentation software functions, such as arrow styles, colors, line styles, and other formatting instructions.

Directly below the Line and Filling toolbar in a default OpenOffice.org setup are the rulers. These items mark out the margins and tabs, for example, of your picture in the measuring system of your choice. To change which system you want to use, right-click the ruler and change the measurements to your preferences.

Click in that big white space and start doodling. You can also access a formatting pop-up menu by right-clicking.

If you prefer to deface other pictures, you can choose File➪Open to select any standard graphics file format (such as BMP or JPG) to work with. When the file opens in Draw, you can use all the standard Draw tools to modify the picture.

Beneath the document window is a Drawing bar, which allows you to select lines, arrows, shapes, and more for your drawing-creation needs. Most of these buttons have downward-pointing arrows, which allow you to see the full range of features they offer.

Working with Draw files

At first glance, OpenOffice.org Draw appears to offer the most limited support of file types. When you use the Save As dialog box, the only file formats in which you can save a document are

- **OpenDocument Drawing (ODG) format:** The OpenOffice.org proposed standard for graphics files
- **OpenOffice.org 1.0 Drawing (SXD) format:** The older OpenOffice.org graphics format
- **StarDraw 3.0 (SDD) format:** The older Sun StarDraw format
- **StarDraw 5.0 (SDA) format:** The newer Sun StarDraw format

That's not much to work with, especially when you're dealing with picture files. Fortunately, Draw has a few tricks up its sleeve. You can save images to a format other than the standard formats by choosing File➪Export.

This produces a host of supported graphics formats: BMP, EMF, EPS, GIF, JPEG, MET, PBM, PCT, PGM, PNG, PPM, RAS, SVG, SWF (Flash), TIFF, WMF, and XPM. That should satisfy any computer artist.

Managing Data with OpenOffice.org Base

If you're accustomed to using Microsoft Access (or have to interact with a variety of database products), and often have been left scratching your head, wondering how to handle these needs under Linux, wonder no more! OpenOffice.org Base provides an interface both to Microsoft Access files and to other databases.

Getting help from the wizard

There are many different ways you can use this program. The essentials involve creating a database from scratch in a file on your system, working with Microsoft Access files, and working with databases created for use with major database-server programs — even over the network. Because approaches abound and space in this book is limited, we focus on two of the more common choices: creating new database files and opening existing files, including Microsoft Access files.

The first interface you encounter when you open a new database file is the Database Wizard (see Figure 12-6).

Figure 12-6: The Open Office.org Database Wizard, used to open existing databases and create new ones.

Creating a new database file in the Database Wizard

In the Database Wizard dialog box, do the following to create a brand-new database file:

1. **Select the Create a New Database radio button.**

2. **Click Next.**

   The Decide How to Proceed After Saving the Database screen appears, as shown in Figure 12-7.

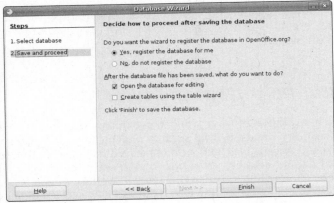

Figure 12-7:
The Decide How to Proceed After Saving the Database screen.

3. **If you want to register this database as a data source in OpenOffice. org, leave Yes, Register the Database for Me selected; otherwise, select the No, Do Not Register the Database radio button.**

   A registered database is accessible by all your OpenOffice.org applications, rather than just OpenOffice.org Base.

4. **If you immediately want to open this file for editing, leave the Open the Database for Editing check box selected; otherwise click this option to deselect the check box.**

5. **If you want to create a new table immediately in the database by using the Table Wizard (the recommended method), select the Create Tables Using the Table Wizard check box.**

   For now, it's best to leave the wizard off so you can explore one step at a time.

6. **Click Finish.**

   The Save dialog box opens.

7. **Enter the name for your document in the Name text box.**

8. **Either select the directory you want to save the document to in the Save In Folder drop-down list box, or click the right-facing arrow next to Browse for Other Folders to navigate to where you want to save the document.**

9. Click the Save button.

Whatever you specified should happen, happens. If you chose to immediately open the database, you see something equivalent to Figure 12-8.

Menu bar   Standard toolbar   Tasks pane

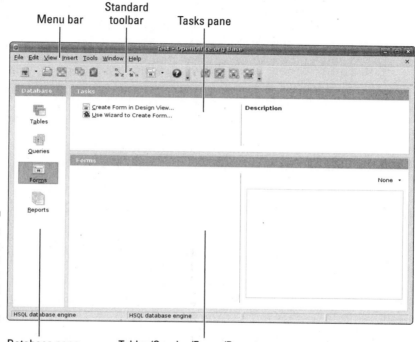

Database pane   Tables/Queries/Forms/Reports pane

Figure 12-8:
A database
open in
Open
Office.org
Base.

Opening an existing file in the Database Wizard

If you have an already existing Microsoft Access file that you want to open in
OpenOffice.org Base, do the following from the initial Database Wizard:

1. Select Open an Existing Database File.

2. Select a file.

You have these options:

- *Recently Used:* If the file is in the Recently Used drop-down list,
  select the file there. Click Finish, and you're done opening the file.

- *Open button:* If the file you want isn't in the Recently Used drop-
  down list, click the Open button and proceed to Step 3.

3. **Navigate to the file you want to open, and select the file.**

4. **Click Open.**

   The file opens in a window (refer to Figure 12-8).

Taking a tour of OpenOffice.org base

Before you proceed, refer to the layout shown in Figure 12-8. This is your main OpenOffice.org Base window after you have a database open to work with. Here's a look at what you'll find there.

Along the top of the window is the menu bar. OpenOffice.org Base gives you access to many of the features you may expect in a database interface:

- ✔ **File:** The usual Open, Save, and Save As commands, along with a set of wizards and the capability to send files through e-mail
- ✔ **Edit:** The usual Copy and Paste commands, along with access to database properties, advanced settings, and the Form and Report Wizards
- ✔ **View:** Access to toolbars and database objects, along with preview and sort features
- ✔ **Insert:** Use this capability to create forms, queries, and more
- ✔ **Tools:** Use these capabilities to assign relationships between tables, filter tables, run SQL queries, create macros, and more

Beneath the menu bar is the Standard toolbar, which you can remove at any time by choosing View➪Toolbars➪Standard. Each icon on this toolbar represents a different functionality, as described in Table 12-7. As you can see, this toolbar is more similar to the one in OpenOffice.org Impress than it is to the one in OpenOffice.org Writer.

Table 12-7	The OpenOffice.org Base Standard Toolbar
Button or Item	*What You Can Do*
New	Open new documents of various types. Click the downward-pointing arrow to select a particular type of document to create from among any of the OOo types.
Open	Open an existing file for reading or editing.
Save	Save the current document. If you haven't saved this document before, the Save As dialog box opens.

Button or Item	What You Can Do
Copy	Make a copy of the selected document text and save it in memory.
Paste	Place the text from memory into the document at the cursor's current location. Click the down arrow to see options for how the text can be pasted.
Sort Ascending	Sort the entries in the lower-right pane in alphabetical order.
Sort Descending	Sort the entries in the lower-right pane in reverse alphabetical order.
Form	Create a form.
Help	Open the OpenOffice.org Help dialog box.
Open Database Object	Open the selected item in the lower-right pane.
Edit	Open the design view for the selected item in the lower-right pane.
Delete	Delete the selected item in the lower-right pane.
Rename	Rename the selected item in the lower-right pane.

To the left of the main window is the Database pane. This pane has four icons: Tables, Queries, Forms, and Reports. Select these icons to determine what appears in the two rightmost panes — for example, to work with your tables, select the Tables icon.

A *query* allows you to ask complex questions regarding your database.

The upper-right pane is the Tasks pane. Here you see what you can do for (or to) a particular selection in the Database pane. Use the description to the right to decrypt any of the terms that make your eyes cross.

The lower-right pane shows the tables, queries, forms, or reports that already exist. You can open any of these you want to work in: Double-click them in this pane to open them.

Sitting down at the table

Tables are the core of the database system. They hold your data and give you quick access to information. It's a good idea to understand how tables are organized in Base, and how you can use them to hold and display your data.

To create a new table, you can use the Base Table Wizard if you think you have a standard table, or you can just create your own table in Design View; select the appropriate option from the list in the Tables page. Figure 12-9 shows a table being created in the Table Design View dialog box.

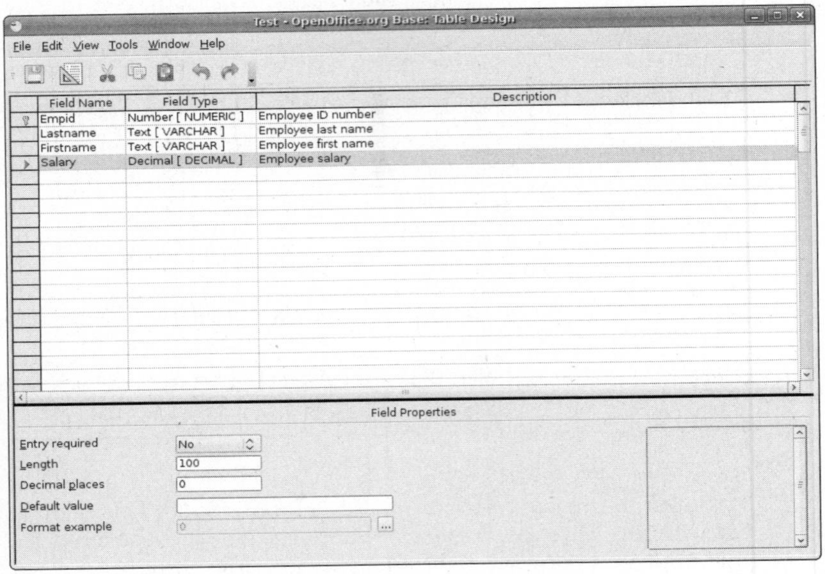

Figure 12-9:
The Table Design View dialog box in Base.

Each row in the Table Design represents a data field in the table. Each field must have a unique Field Name and be assigned a Field Type. The Field Type defines the type of data present in the field (characters, numbers, dates, and so on). Use the Description area to write a brief description of what the data field means.

Creating a new table is easy:

1. **Enter a text name for the Field Name describing the data.**

2. **Select a Field Type from the drop-down menu.**

3. **Enter a brief description in the Description text area.**

4. **If the field is a primary key, right-click the left of the row and choose Primary Key.**

    A table's *primary key* is a data field that can uniquely identify each record in the table. In the example in Figure 12-9, each employee is identified by a unique employee ID because more than one employee can have the same last name.

5. **Enter the remaining rows to complete the data elements in the table.**

6. **Choose File⇨Save As to save the table using a unique name.**

The new table now appears on the main Base window under the Tables area. Double-clicking the new table brings up the Data Viewing and Entry window, as shown in Figure 12-10.

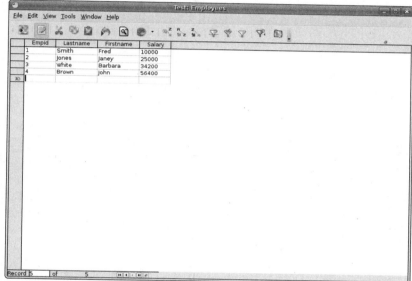

	Empid	Lastname	Firstname	Salary
	1	Smith	Fred	10000
	2	Jones	Janey	25000
	3	White	Barbara	34200
	4	Brown	John	56400

Figure 12-10:
The Data Viewing and Entry window in the Base application.

If you are familiar with Microsoft Access, you should feel right at home here. This window allows you to view the existing data records in the table and to easily add new data records.

Layout with OpenOffice.Org Math

There's nothing like trying to type a math or science report and having to either use multiple lines to show your equations (which never looks right!) or write them by hand. OpenOffice.org Math is a great solution to this problem. You can lay out your equations in this program and then insert them into any OpenOffice.org document. Whether you're a middle-school student or a professional engineer, OpenOffice.org Math just may thrill you.

Many OpenOffice.org Math functions are different from what you're used to if you've looked at all the other OpenOffice.org programs. In many ways, however, this program is less complex than some, thanks to its special-purpose nature.

Math is not a calculation program. It's for laying out complex formulas on paper or on-screen. It's great for adding complex formulas to research papers, but it's useless for balancing your checkbook.

Starting OpenOffice.org Math is a little tricky; often you can't find it in the panel menus (such as those in Ubuntu). If your Linux distribution doesn't have Math in the menus, you can still start a new Math document by opening Writer, and then choosing File➪New➪Formula.

Before you proceed, take a look at the GUI layout shown in Figure 12-11.

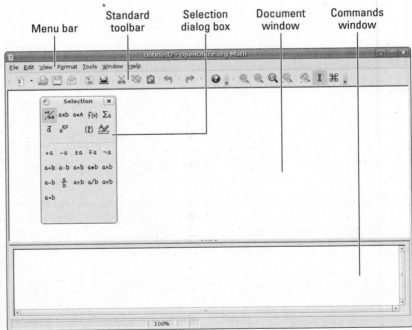

Figure 12-11:
The Open Office.org Math layout.

Close the Selection dialog box by clicking the small X in the upper-right corner of its window for now, to keep things as uncluttered as possible. You can get it back at any time by choosing View➪Selection.

Menu bar

Along the top of the window is the menu bar, a standard in the GUI world. Here is a (non-exhaustive) summary of what you find on each menu:

- **File:** The usual Open, Save, Save As, and Print commands that you find in most GUI programs, along with a set of wizards and the capability to send documents through e-mail

- **Edit:** The usual Select All, Copy, and Paste commands, along with specialized commands for moving within the formula

- **View:** The usual Zoom functions and toolbars, along with screen-update features and more

- **Format:** The usual font type, size, spacing, alignment, and other features

- **Tools:** The usual Customize and Options entries for customizing the program's setup and behaviors, in addition to formula importing and access to a catalog of symbols

Standard toolbar

Along the top of the window is the Standard toolbar, which you can remove at any time by choosing View⇨Toolbars⇨Standard. Each icon on this toolbar represents a different functionality. You're likely to find this main toolbar quite different from those in the other OpenOffice.org programs. Mostly, it's just smaller. Each icon is described in Table 12-8.

Table 12-8	The OpenOffice.org Math Standard Toolbar
Button or Item	**What You Can Do**
Zoom In	Enlarge the image.
Zoom Out	Shrink the image.
1	Show the image at its actual size.
Show All	Show the whole formula in the largest size that will fit on the screen.
New	Open new documents of various types. Click the downward arrow to select a particular type of document to create from among any of the OOo types.
Open	Open an existing file for reading or editing.
Save	Save the current document. If you haven't saved this document before, the Save As dialog box opens.

(continued)

Table 12-8 *(continued)*

Button or Item	What You Can Do
Document as E-mail	Open a Compose e-mail window in your preferred e-mail program, and automatically attach this document.
Export Directly as PDF	Open a Save As dialog box with PDF selected as the file type.
Print File Directly	Send a file to the default printer.
Cut	Remove the selected text from the document and save it in memory.
Copy	Make a copy of the selected document text and save it in memory.
Paste	Place the text from memory in the document at the cursor's current location.
Undo	Undo the last change you made to the document. Click the down arrow to choose how far you want to back up to.
Restore	Reinstate the last change to the document after using Undo to cancel it. Click the down arrow to choose how far you want to redo.
Help	Open the OpenOffice.org Help dialog box.
Update	Update the formula shown in the document window.
Formula Cursor	Turn on or shut off the formula cursor.
Catalog	Open the Symbols dialog box.

Commands window

Things get tricky in OpenOffice.org Math if you've never used formula-editing software. For instance, you can't type anything in the main (upper) document window; instead, you type in the Commands (lower) window. Right-clicking the Commands window opens a shortcut menu. To start working with formulas, follow these steps:

1. **Right-click the Commands window.**

   The main shortcut menu opens.

2. **Select a submenu to open.**

   For example, Formats.

3. Select a formula component within this submenu.

We chose matrix {. . .} as an example. Immediately, the code that's needed in order to add a matrix to a formula appears in the Commands window. A moment later, the matrix appears in the document window. The combination is shown in Figure 12-12.

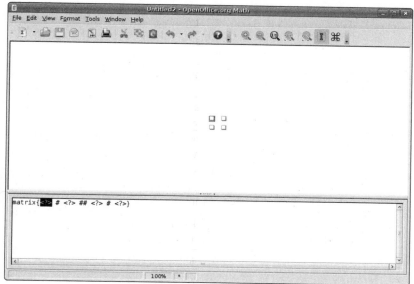

Figure 12-12:
Starting to add a matrix in Open Office.org Math.

4. Replace each of the `<?>` entries with the proper letters and numbers for your formula.

When we type the letters and change `matrix{<?> # <?> ## <?> # <?>}` to `matrix{A # B ## C # D}`, we get the result shown in Figure 12-13.

5. Continue adding components to the formula until you finish.

Suppose that you want to multiply the matrix by 3. To find out how, press Enter to go down to the next line in the Commands window, right-click to display the menu, and choose Unary/Binary Operators⇨a Times b. This choice adds the phrase `<?> times <?>` beneath the matrix code. Now that you know how to format a multiplication operation, erase this phrase from the screen and use it as a guideline to change your formula to:

```
3 times matrix{A # B ## C # D}
```

This line gives you the result shown in Figure 12-14.

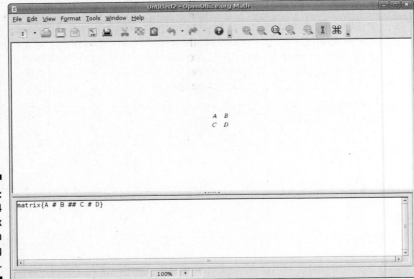

Figure 12-13:
A 4-x-4
matrix
in Open
Office.org
Math.

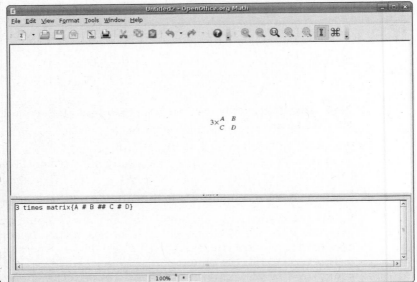

Figure 12-14:
A complete
formula
in Open
Office.org
Math.

OpenOffice.org Math supports (among others) its own OpenDocument format (ODF), the equivalent StarOffice format (SXM) and MathML 1.01 (MML), which isn't a program. *MathML* is a standard — similar to HTML for working on the Web — specifically it's version 1.01 of this standard. For this particular version of MathML, see www.w3.org/TR/REC-MathML. The main standard page is available at www.w3.org/Math/. If you need to add formulas to Web pages, this site can be quite an interesting read!

Chapter 13

Messing with Audio

> *The price of freedom is responsibility, but it's a bargain, because freedom is priceless.*
>
> — Hugh Downs

If you're like us, everything's better with music. If a computer can't take the place of a stereo wherever we are, then we just aren't interested. So we can assure you that Linux offers many ways to listen to music on your computer. Read on to find out what Linux can do!

Listening to MP3s on Linux used to be problematic; MP3 is a patented format and was unavailable to Linux users. But now RealPlayer is available for Linux and *has* a license to play MP3s, so you're all set. See Chapter 16 for how to install RealPlayer.

What Sound? I Don't Hear a Thing!

These days, most Linux distributions detect sound cards automatically during the installation process — and they do a great job of it. However, if your sound card failed the test — or you try to play sound using one of the software options in this chapter and it doesn't work — use this section to diagnose and fix your problem.

Suppose your sound card passed the test, but for some reason you can't hear anything. Here's what to do:

1. Check that your speakers or headphones are hooked up correctly.

You wouldn't be the first person to discover that the cat pulled the connectors out of their sockets.

2. **Click the speaker icon on your panel to make sure your audio settings didn't get turned down to zero, or muted.**

   Both the GNOME and KDE desktops provide an icon in the system tray that gives you immediate access to the volume control for your sound system. Drag the slide bar up or down with your mouse to increase or decrease the volume level.

3. **Right-click the same speaker icon for more detailed volume adjustments. You can access a Volume Control application from the same speaker icon for both the GNOME and the KDE desktops.**

4. **Select the menu option to start the Volume Control application for your desktop.**

   Figure 13-1 shows the GNOME Volume Control.

Figure 13-1:
The GNOME
Volume
Control.

When this control opens, you can check your volume settings to help you solve your sound dilemma.

- *Master:* The main volume control corresponds to the volume slider on your desktop.

- *Headphone:* Adjusts the volume of the headphone jack on your workstation.

- *PCM (for Pulse Code Modulation):* Controls the volume for audio files stored on your computer.

- *Front:* Adjusts the volume of the front speaker(s) on your workstation.

- *Line-in:* Controls the volume for sound coming in through your sound card's line-in socket.

- *CD:* Controls the volume for sound coming in through your CD and/or DVD player.

- *Microphone:* Controls the volume for sound coming in through your sound card's microphone connector.

If you're working on the KDE desktop, you see the KMix volume control (Figure 13-2) when you right-click the speaker icon.

In KMix, you also see separate sliders for different elements:

- **Front:** Controls the volume for the built-in speakers in the computer. If stereo output is available, you'll see two Front sliders, one for the left channel, and one for the right channel.

- **PCM:** Controls the volume for audio files stored on your computer.

- **CD:** Controls the volume for sound coming in through your CD and/or DVD player.

- **Headphones:** Controls the volume for the external speaker jack in your workstation.

The Capture check box allows you to change the slider's meaning. Instead of controlling the CD volume, it controls the volume of any recording you perform from that device.

When you're comfortable with what you're looking at in the GNOME or KMix control, look for one of these two major clues as to what might be wrong:

- **Are any of the items you see muted?** You can tell by looking for red X's next to the volume icon underneath each section in the GNOME volume control, or for a checked Mute check box in KMix. In Figure 13-1, for example, Line-in and Microphone are both muted. Is the one you see muted responsible for your problem? For example, if you had head-phones hooked up to your Line-in jack and Line-in was muted, you'd hear nothing when you put on your headphones. To unmute, click the X and make it go away.

✔ **Are any of the volume sliders all the way down?** Again, Line-in and Microphone in Figure 13-1 are both slid down all the way. Using the same headphone example, even if Line-in wasn't muted, you'd hear nothing because the sliders were down. Slide them up and see whether you can hear anything.

If neither of these scenarios fits your problem, it may be something more fundamental. To investigate, find the Sound Preferences dialog box in your Linux distribution. For GNOME desktops, try this:

1. **In Ubuntu, choose System➪Preferences➪Sound; in Fedora, choose System➪Preferences➪Hardware➪Sound to see whether the card is correctly detected and plays test sounds.**

   You may be asked to enter your root (administrative) password before the Sound Preferences dialog box opens, as shown in Figure 13-3.

   In the Devices tab, you should see the driver that your Linux distribution uses to interact with your sound card for different types of audio. Usually this value is set to *Autodetect* so GNOME can use whichever driver is active.

2. **Click the Test button for each sound type's section.**

   You should hear a sound on the left, on the right, and in the middle. If not, select another driver for the sound card (if available) from the drop-down list, and then test again.

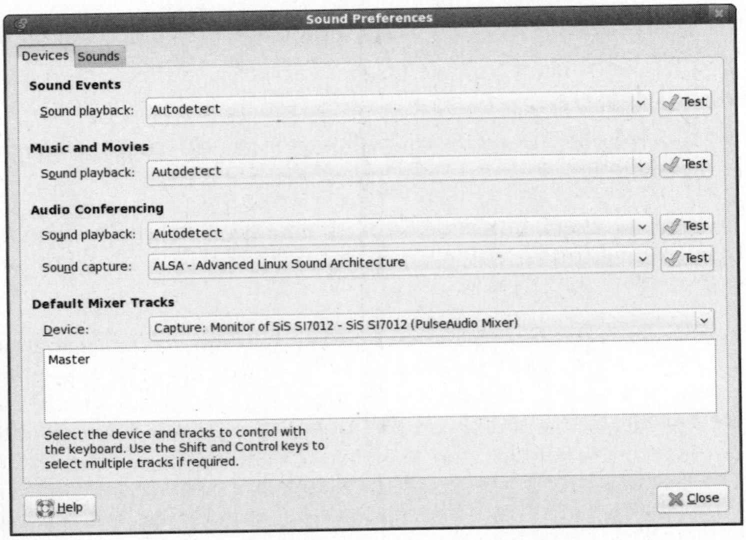

Figure 13-3: The GNOME Sound Preferences dialog box.

3. **If none of these actions helps, go to your favorite search engine and enter the make and model of your sound card and the word *linux*.**

   You may find some helpful information that way.

For KDE desktops, the sound settings can be found in the Sound section of the System Settings window.

Listening to CDs

If you have a CD/DVD player in your PC, you can play your audio CDs while you work (or play)! The application you use depends again on your desktop. The following sections walk you through the most common application used on each desktop — Rhythmbox for GNOME, and KsCD for KDE.

Rhythmbox

On the GNOME desktop, the first time you insert an audio CD, a dialog box appears and asks you what program you want to use to play the CD (as shown in Figure 13-4).

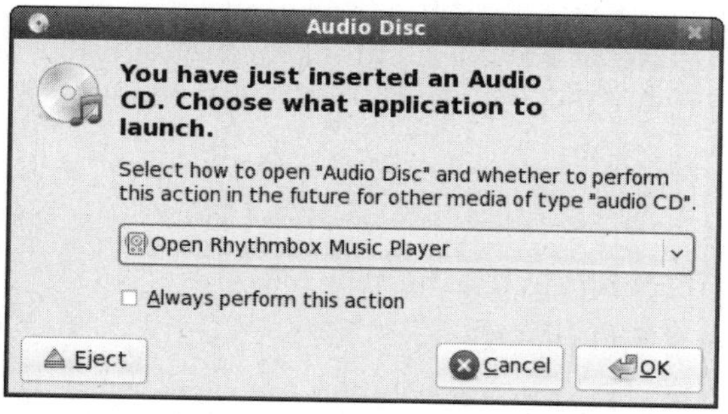

Figure 13-4: The Audio Disc dialog box.

Both Fedora and Ubuntu include the Rhythmbox application for playing audio CDs. Just select that option (it should be the default), and click OK. If you want your future audio CDs to start playing automatically, just select the check box that tells Rhythmbox always to perform this action *before* you click OK. Rhythmbox starts whenever you insert an audio CD.

Rhythmbox scans the CD, and displays the tracks and track lengths of the CD in the Music Player window. If your workstation is connected to the Internet, Rhythmbox also contacts a remote CD database to extract information about the CD — including the CD title, individual track song titles, and the album cover art for the CD if available. Figure 13-5 shows the Rhythmbox window after opening an audio CD.

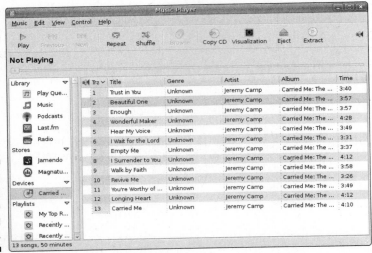

Figure 13-5:
Starting
an audio
CD using
Rhythmbox.

The main Rhythmbox interface is fairly straightforward. It lists the individual CD tracks in the main window area, along with the basic track information that it retrieved. The toolbar provides buttons for the basic functions you need if you're going to interact with a CD player, plus a couple of extras:

- ✔ **Play:** Start the current track.
- ✔ **Previous:** Jump to the previous track in the song list.
- ✔ **Next:** Jump to the next track in the song list.
- ✔ **Repeat:** Repeat the current track.
- ✔ **Shuffle:** Randomly play the tracks in the song list.
- ✔ **Browse:** Browse through the music tracks.
- ✔ **Copy CD:** Make a duplicate copy of the CD to a blank CD.
- ✔ **Visualization:** Display a screen saver image while playing the track.
- ✔ **Eject:** Remove the CD from the CD Tray.
- ✔ **Extract:** Convert the track on the CD to an audio file and store it in the music library in your home folder.

The Extract feature enables you to copy tracks from the CD to audio files on your workstation (called *ripping*), a process we look at more closely in the "Ripping Music Tracks from CDs" section later in this chapter.

KsCD

When you insert an audio CD while on your KDE desktop, you won't see anything happen. Instead, KDE quietly places it in the new devices applet in the panel (see Chapter 5). To play the CD, you need to start a CD player manually.

The tool for playing audio CDs in KDE is called KsCD. You can find it by choosing KDE⇨Applications⇨Multimedia. Figure 13-6 shows the main KsCD window.

Figure 13-6:
The main
KsCD
window.

Surprisingly, it looks like a real CD player! If you've ever used a CD player, you can probably guess what buttons to click to play your CD.

You probably also noticed that just like Rhythmbox, KsCD goes out to the Internet to retrieve the album and track names (if you have an Internet connection). That makes watching the KsCD interface a lot more interesting than staring at a boom box!

Listening to Downloaded Music

Downloading music from the Internet is a fun activity. A lot of people like to pretend that it's both legal and ethical, when, in fact, it's often theft, depending on where you grab the music. We leave that ethical issue between you and your belief system, but because our own ethics say that it's theft, we're going to focus on showing you music that you're *welcome* — legally and ethically — to download!

One source of legal songs is on artists' Web sites. Many popular artists offer free samples of their songs, and many new artists offer their entire songs free for downloading. In these situations, you're more than welcome to download and listen!

As you probably know by now, the program you use to listen to downloaded music depends on your desktop. Amarok can help you out on a KDE desktop, and Rhythmbox can help you out on a GNOME desktop.

TIP

A popular medium for playing songs on a Web site is the Macromedia Flash Player. This package plays songs directly in the Web page, without downloading the song to the computer's hard drive. You can add this functionality to your Firefox Web browser using the methods described in Chapter 14. This section specifically deals with playing song files that you download to your computer.

Amarok

In the KDE desktop world, the king of audio-file playing is the Amarok music player. Just about every KDE desktop installation we've run into uses Amarok to play audio files. Here's the drill:

1. **After you have Amarok installed, start it by choosing Applications⇨ Multimedia⇨Audio Player.**

   The first time you start Amarok, the First-Run Wizard launches, displays the Welcome screen, and then takes you to the Configure Collection section of the Configure screen.

2. **Expand (click the + symbols) and contract (click the − symbols) parts of the filesystem until you find the sections that contain your music.**

   When you display these folders (for example, /home/rich/Music), click their boxes to add check marks (see Figure 13-7). Leave (or put) check marks next to Scan Folders Recursively (which looks in subfolders) and Watch Folders for Changes (which picks up new files automatically). That way Amarok does most of the work.

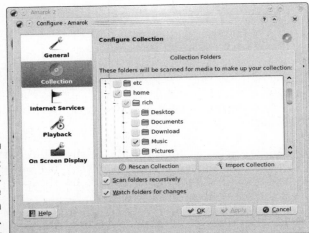

Figure 13-7:
The Amarok Configure Collection screen.

3. **Click the Import Collection button to import your existing audio files into the Amarok library.**

   The Import Collection Wizard starts.

4. **Select the site to retrieve track information for the audio file (such as artist name), and then click Next.**

   You can retrieve information from either the Amarok 1.4 Web site or the popular Apple iTunes site.

5. **Select a database system to use for the Amarok library, and then click Next.**

   If you're not a database guru, just select the default SQLite database system. This creates a single database file for your library. From this screen, you can also select to import the album artwork if it's available.

6. **Click Finish to complete importing your collection, and then click OK to exit the Configure screen.**

   The default Amarok screen displays, as shown in Figure 13-8.

Figure 13-8:
The main
Amarok
screen.

From here, you have to add music to the right side in order to play it. You can (for example) drag and drop files individually.

Along the left of the Amarok window is a collection of tabs. What you see and what we see might be different, depending on your version. Each tab offers a certain segment of functionality, and may change the interface to the left of the playlist. The tabs displayed in Amarok from top to bottom are

✔ **Files:** Browse through your filesystem to find individual songs that you want to click and drag into the playlist.

✓ **Playlists:** Here is where you create new playlists and access those that are already available. The Smart Playlists section offers you a variety of prebuilt playlists, such as All Collection if you want to listen to everything you have, 50 Random Tracks to let the player pick them for you, Genres (if you took the time to assign genre information when ripping your CDs), and more. Dynamic Playlists are different from Smart Playlists because they're constantly changing; the Random Mix dynamic playlist, for example, chooses music randomly from your collection and then keeps choosing it as you continue listening. For Suggested Songs, you put a few key songs in your playlist and then Last.fm (www.last.fm) builds you a personalized online radio station with music that it considers similar. If you're a big fan of online radio or are curious about it, then check out the Radio Streams section's Cool-Streams folder. Here you'll find lots of radio stations to choose from.

✓ **Internet:** If you have a connection to the Internet, Amarok lets you connect to popular Internet radio stations that provide streaming audio, search for books and audio recordings you can purchase online, or listen to podcasts.

✓ **Collection:** Shows your music collection. Above the listing, click the Search Preferences button to choose features (such as whether the collection is organized by group, album, and so on). You can search for a song quickly by entering it in the search text box. Click the Advanced button, and a Filter dialog box appears; there you can type keywords to determine what songs are displayed.

No matter how you get music into the playlist on the right, when it's there, you can click the Play button at the top-left side of the pane to play the selected track. You can also double-click a track to play it. The volume slider is on the top-right side of the pane.

There is much more to Amarok. Take the time to explore this program and really customize it to your satisfaction. When you close this program, the Docking In System Tray dialog box appears. It warns you that Amarok will continue to run and appear as a system tray icon on the panel. You can avoid this by choosing Actions⇨Quit rather than clicking the X in the corner of the application to close the program. If you leave the program on the panel, you can open it at any time by clicking the little wolf icon.

If you listen to your digital audio files using a mobile digital audio player (such as the popular iPod), you may be able to use Amarok to interface with your digital player. Amarok can detect digital players plugged into the USB port. If a digital player is detected, Amarok creates a Device tab in the main Amarok screen (see Figure 13-8). Select that tab to see whether Amarok can interact with your mobile digital audio player!

Rhythmbox revisited

The most popular tool for playing audio files on the GNOME desktop is Rhythmbox. That's right — the same tool we just finished looking at for playing audio CDs can also play audio files.

By default, the main Rhythmbox library area is the Music folder under your home folder. When you select the Music link in the Library section of the main page, Rhythmbox displays the files it finds in your library.

If you attempt to play an audio file that your Linux distribution doesn't have a codec for (such as MP3 files), it displays a warning message, as shown in Figure 13-9.

Some Linux distributions, such as Fedora and Ubuntu, provide additional codecs for various audio file types in their software repositories. If your workstation is connected to the Internet, click the search button in the warning message to attempt to locate an appropriate codec for the audio file type in the appropriate package repositories.

Linux is used in many different countries, so just because you find a codec for an audio file type you're interested in doesn't necessarily mean it's legal to *use* that codec in your country! For example, you'll easily find the MP3 file codecs in the Fedora and Ubuntu repositories, but decoding MP3 audio files without an appropriate license is illegal in the United States. (Now, that's a bummer.)

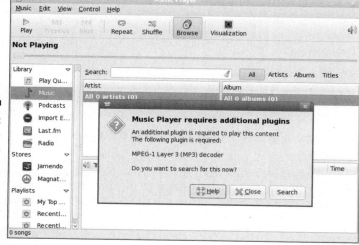

Figure 13-9:
The audio-file codec's warning message displayed in the Fedora distribution.

Ripping Music Tracks from CDs

Copying music from a CD to your own workstation is another topic that's impossible to cover without at least acknowledging that both ethical and legal issues are involved. We're not going to get into legalities here, but our personal ethics are that it's fine to rip (copy) music off our own CDs for our own use. If we want to pull our favorite songs off CDs that we purchased and set them up so we can listen to them collectively in a random playlist off our computer's hard drive, we don't see a problem with this.

That said, to rip tracks from your CDs in Linux, you need one of the popular ripping-software packages. You already saw how Rhythmbox can rip songs from audio CDs, so we take a look at a popular package — Sound Juicer — that specializes in ripping songs from a CD. Because it specializes in only one thing, it provides a few additional options for us.

The Sound Juicer package is available in most Linux distributions, including Fedora. If you don't see it in the Multimedia area of your menu system, check out Chapter 16 to install it.

Once you have Sound Juicer, it's easy to rip songs from an audio CD:

1. **Choose Applications⇨Sound & Video⇨Audio CD Extractor (see Figure 13-10) on the Fedora GNOME desktop, or Applications⇨ Multimedia⇨Audio CD Extractor on the Fedora KDE desktop.**

   Sound Juicer starts, displaying the tracks on the CD. If your workstation is connected to the Internet, Sound Juicer also displays the album and track titles.

2. **For each song that you don't want to rip, uncheck the check box next to the song.**

   The check mark disappears for each song that you don't want to digitize.

3. **Choose Edit⇨Preferences.**

   The Preferences dialog box appears, as shown in Figure 13-11.

4. **Select your preferred sound format in the Output Format drop-down list box.**

   If your available space is limited, we strongly suggest Ogg Vorbis (.oga) because this format is easily handled on Linux machines without any inherent legal problems, and is also better compressed than MP3 for equivalent sound.

   However, if you want higher sound quality for a home sound system, then FLAC (.flac) — another open format, but without any loss in sound quality.

Figure 13-10:
The Sound
Juicer CD
Extractor.

5. **Click the Folder drop-down list to choose where you want to save your music files.**

If the location you want to use isn't listed, select Other and then browse to the folder you want to use.

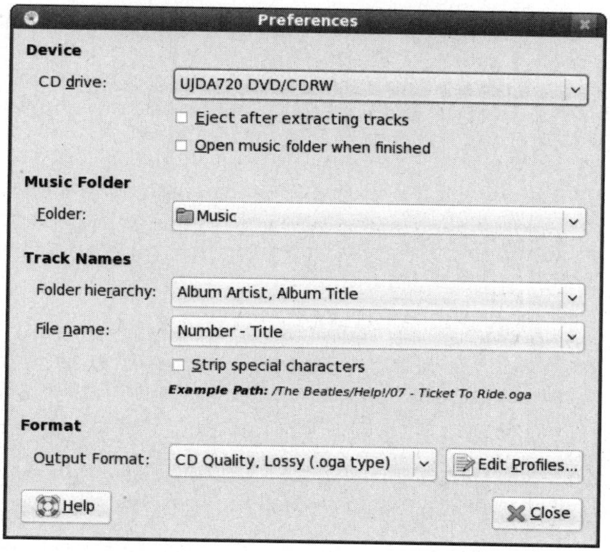

Figure 13-11:
The Sound
Juicer
Preferences
dialog box.

6. **In the Track Names section, select how you want Sound Juicer to name and arrange the files in subdirectories.**

7. **Make any other configuration changes you want to make.**

8. **Click Close when you're done making changes.**

9. **Click Extract.**

   The Sound Juicer window shows you a progress bar along the bottom, and it highlights the track it's currently working on. A dialog box appears when the extraction is complete.

10. **Choose Disc⇨Eject in the menu bar.**

    The CD tray opens.

11. **Remove the CD and close the tray.**

12. **Close Sound Juicer.**

Now you have your CD tracks stored as digital audio files. You can then import these files into your library (whether in Rhythmbox or Amarok), where you can listen to them without having to drag out the CD all the time.

Burning Audio CDs and DVDs

A CD and DVD burner is a great way to make data backups (especially if you're using rewritable discs), save and share your digital photos, and put together multimedia mementos and scrapbooks. But it's also great for creating audio CDs you can play on any type of CD player, not just on your computer. Many tools are available that let you record CDs under Linux.

For example, if you're using the GNOME desktop, you can record CDs and DVDs from audio files on your workstation by using the filesystem navigation tools discussed in Chapter 7, right-clicking the file you want to record, and choosing the proper options from the context menu.

However, this method often just burns the digital audio file onto the CD or DVD. This method won't work if you're trying to create an audio CD to play in an older CD player that doesn't recognize the digital audio file's format.

Here we focus on K3b, popular CD-burning software often found on KDE desktops, which can also run on GNOME desktops. The K3b software can create an audio CD from digital audio files on your system.

Choose Applications⇨Multimedia⇨CD & DVD Burning to open K3b from the KDE destkop, and the main window opens, as shown in Figure 13-12.

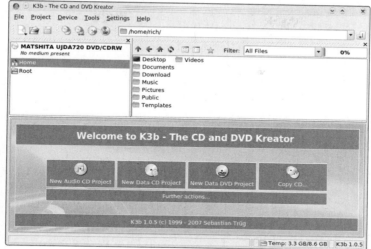

Figure 13-12:
The K3b CD
and DVD
Kreator
burner.

If all you want to do is create an audio CD out of music or audio files you
downloaded, do the following:

1. **Click the New Audio CD Project option in the main K3b window.**

   The Audio CD Current Projects dialog box opens (Figure 13-13).

2. **In the top section, click the folder button and navigate to the files you
   want to burn onto the CD.**

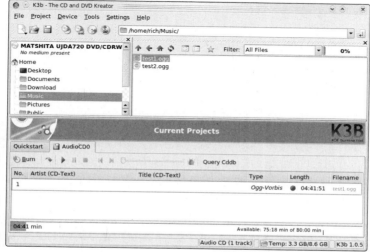

Figure 13-13:
The K3b
Audio CD
Current
Projects
dialog box.

3. **Drag and drop the files you want to burn into the lower section of the page.**

   As you drag files into the lower section, the status bar at the bottom grows, showing you how much space is left on the CD.

4. **When you're finished, click the Burn button in the lower section to start the burn.**

   The K3b Audio Project dialog box appears, as shown in Figure 13-14.

5. **Insert a blank CD, select the burn speed (if necessary), and click the Burn button.**

   The burn process starts copying your digital audio files onto the CD as analog audio files.

6. **Remove your new CD from the drive, and then click Close to close the burn information dialog box.**

7. **Click Close again to close the main burn dialog box.**

8. **Choose File⇨Quit to close K3b.**

Now you can take your audio CD to virtually any CD player to listen to your downloaded files!

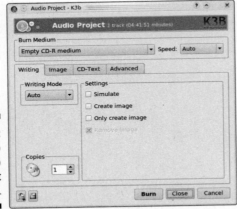

Figure 13-14:
The K3b
Audio
Project
dialog box.

Chapter 14

Messing with Video and Graphics

● ●

In This Chapter

▶ Watching online and downloaded videos

▶ Watching DVDs

▶ Creating and modifying high-powered graphics with The GIMP

▶ Playing 3-D games

● ●

Video killed the radio star.

— The Buggles

There's no question that video is one area in which Linux has been playing catch-up. The original Linux systems didn't even support a Windows-style desktop! In the early days of Linux, it was close to impossible to display any type of video, let alone play movies or high-end computer-graphics games.

Fortunately, things are much different nowadays. There aren't many things your Linux computer can't do in the video world (unless of course it's illegal, but more on that later). This chapter walks you through your Linux computer's video and graphics capabilities.

Watchin' Those Silly Web Clips

The Internet has become a clearinghouse for just about any type of video content you can imagine (and even some you couldn't imagine if you tried). From Google Videos to YouTube, lots of sites exist to keep you entertained.

Through the Firefox Web browser (see Chapter 9), your Linux system can display many different types of Web clips (although, unfortunately, not all of them by default).

Checking your plugins

Plugins are the key to displaying Web video content in Firefox. As discussed in Chapter 9, plugins provide additional functionality to the Firefox browser.

You can check to see what plugins are already installed in your Firefox setup by following these steps:

1. **Open Firefox by choosing Applications⇨Internet⇨Firefox Web Browser.**

   You can also start Firefox by clicking the Globe icon on the top panel on a GNOME desktop.

2. **Choose Tools⇨Add-ons; then in the Add-ons dialog box, click the Plugins icon.**

   The Plugins tab displays information about the current plugins installed, as shown in Figure 14-1.

Figure 14-1:
The Firefox
Add-ons
Plugins
dialog box.

The plugins you see depend on your specific Linux distribution and version. By default, the Fedora 10 Firefox installation includes the following plugins:

- ✔ **IcedTea Java Web Browser:** Provides support for running Java applets from Web pages, often used for animation
- ✔ **MozPlugger:** Plays QuickTime and Windows media file formats
- ✔ **QuickTime:** For playing Apple QuickTime videos in the MOV and QT formats
- ✔ **Totem Web Browser:** A full-featured video and audio player that can display AVI, ASF, WMV, OGG, and MPG video formats, as well as play WAV and MP3 audio formats
- ✔ **VLC Multimedia:** Plays most standard video formats, including the VLC format used by GoogleVideo
- ✔ **Windows Media Player:** Plugin for the Totem player that plays streaming video in Microsoft formats, such as ASF, WMV, and WVX
- ✔ **DivX Web Player:** For playing DivX-encoded AVI videos

Although it may seem, on the surface, that you have most of your Web video bases covered, you may be disappointed with your actual video results. Although Totem supports the popular WMV and MOV video formats, there's more to quality video than just supporting the right file formats.

The Microsoft and QuickTime video formats use proprietary encoding schemes called *codecs* that are strictly controlled under licensing agreements. Microsoft Corporation controls the WMV video format and (you guessed it) doesn't provide a license for using this codec with most Linux systems. As a result, Fedora doesn't support WMV video formats by default. The same applies to QuickTime MOV and QuickTime video files.

That said, some resourceful open-source programmers have reproduced the codecs for the Microsoft video format and created a software package called W32codec. Installing this package allows you to view almost every type of video available on the Web.

Because W32codec is not considered a legal software package in the United States, it is not included in the standard Fedora distribution. You can very likely find it by looking on the Internet, but don't say we didn't warn you.

If you want to view Microsoft video formats in the United States in Linux — legally — you can purchase the CrossOver Office commercial software for Linux. It provides the appropriate codecs for viewing Macromedia Shockwave, Windows Media Player, and Apple QuickTime movie formats, as well as the libraries required to run many Microsoft applications directly on your Fedora computer. You can find CrossOver Office at www.codeweavers.com.

Adding a plugin

If you don't see a plugin listed for a specific video format that you're interested in using, you can look to see whether one exists. The clearinghouse for Firefox plugins is located at http://plugindoc.mozdev.org (the Firefox Web browser is based on the Mozilla open-source browser). This site contains links to many different types of video-related plugins.

The Macromedia Flash video player is a popular plugin that supports the video format used on the popular YouTube Web site (and many others). Ubuntu installs the Shockwave Flash player plugin by default, but Fedora doesn't. Here's how to easily install it on your Fedora system:

1. **Open Firefox, and browse to plugindoc.mozdev.org.**

2. **Click the Linux (x86) link at the top of the page.**

   If you happen to be running on a 64-bit Linux distribution, select the Linux (x86 64) link instead.

3. **Click the Flash Player link.**

4. **Click the Download Macromedia Flash Player for x86 Linux link.**

   This link redirects you to the Web page for Adobe Flash installation.

5. **Select the version to download.**

   For Fedora, you can choose YUM for Linux. It uses the Fedora Software Manager (see Chapter 16).

6. **Click the Agree and Install Now button.**

7. **When the Firefox Download Manager dialog box opens, click OK.**

   The default action is to open the file automatically, using the Fedora Software Manager program.

8. **Click the Install button to install the package.**

9. **Click the Force Install button in the Missing Security Signature dialog box.**

   The Adobe Flash installation package isn't signed, but you downloaded it directly from the Adobe Web site, so it's safe.

10. **Type your root user account password to continue with the installation.**

11. **Click the Close button to exit the Software Manager.**

12. **After the installation finishes, open Firefox and view the Add-ons dialog box.**

You should now see that you have the Shockwave Flash plugin available. Now you can spend all day watching YouTube videos!

Getting even more video support

If you remember from Chapter 9, Firefox also supports a feature called *extensions*. Extensions are small applications that provide additional features to your Firefox browser. If you're looking for more video support, or just some fancy video features, plenty of extensions are available to help out. The official Mozilla site for extensions is `https://addons.update.mozilla.org`.

This site uses the secure version of HTTP, so you must use `https:` rather than `http:`.

You can also browse through the extensions directly from the Add-ons dialog box in Firefox.

One of our favorite extensions is Fast Video Download. Fast Video Download allows you to save embedded streaming-video content on a Web page (such as YouTube and MySpace) *and* as a video file on your computer. Here's what to do to load and install it:

1. **Open Firefox by choosing Applications⇨Internet⇨Firefox Web Browser.**

   You can also start Firefox by clicking the Globe icon on the top panel.

2. **Open the Add-ons dialog box by choosing Tools⇨Add-on; then click the Get Add-ons icon at the top.**

3. **Enter** Fast Video Download **in the search box.**

4. **Click the Add to Firefox button for the Fast Video Download Extension.**

   Because the Fast Video Download Extension is not signed, a dialog box appears asking you if you really want to install it, as shown in Figure 14-2.

5. **Click the Install Now button to install the extension.**

   When this process is complete, the Add-ons dialog box appears, showing that the installation was successful.

6. **Click the Restart Firefox button for the new extension to work.**

When Firefox starts, you should notice a new icon on the right side of the bottom status bar, and the Add-Ons dialog box appears, showing that the Fast Video Download Extension has been installed properly, as shown in Figure 14-3.

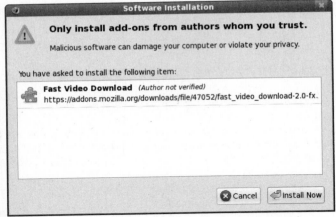

Figure 14-2:
Installing
the Fast
Video
Download
Extension in
Firefox.

Figure 14-3:
The Fast
Video
Download
Extension
installed.

To use Fast Video Download, navigate to a Web page that contains an embedded streaming video, and then click the New icon in the status bar. Fast Video Download scans the Web page, looking for video links; then it displays a dialog box that asks you where you want to save the file.

Just because you can download and save an embedded streaming video doesn't mean you have the rights to share it. Make sure you're not violating any copyright laws before downloading and distributing any online content.

Viewing Movie Files with Totem

With the popularity of DVRs (digital video recorders), it's not uncommon to receive a video clip of your niece's ballet recital in an e-mail message, or some other treasure from a file-sharing site. These files are often stored in a variety of video formats:

- ✔ **AVI:** Audio Visual Interleave format, a standard video format supported by most video software packages.

- ✔ **DivX:** A proprietary AVI video-compression format that must be licensed to work in Linux.

- ✔ **MPG:** Moving Pictures Experts Group (MPEG) standard format. This includes both MPEG and MPG formats.

- ✔ **WMV:** Windows Media Video format, a proprietary Microsoft format.

- ✔ **RM:** The RealNetworks proprietary video format that requires the RealOne video player.

- ✔ **MOV (and QT):** The proprietary Apple QuickTime video formats.

The default video-file viewer in both Fedora and Ubuntu is Totem. You can start Totem either by double-clicking a saved video file or by launching the viewer from the Panel menu (choose Applications⇨Sound & Video⇨Movie Player in the GNOME menu, or choose Applications⇨Multimedia⇨Movie Player in the KDE menu).

As with the Firefox video plugins, licensing restrictions limit the types of files that the default Totem installation can play. You can obtain the complete version of Totem, which supports more file types, by uninstalling Totem and then installing the original software package downloaded from the Totem Web page (http://projects.gnome.org/totem). Just follow the installation steps in Chapter 16 to install new software in Fedora or Ubuntu.

When you start Totem, the main viewing window appears, as shown in Figure 14-4.

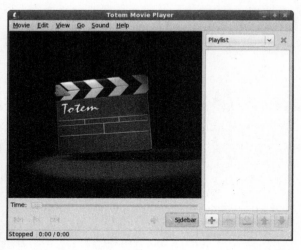

Figure 14-4:
The main
Totem
viewing
window.

The Totem menu bar provides several options for viewing your videos. The Movie menu provides options for loading movies into the Totem viewer:

- **Open:** Allows you to browse to a stored video file on your computer and load it into the Playlist.
- **Open location:** Allows you to add a video file from a remote Web location to the Playlist.
- **Properties:** Displays the properties of the video file, such as the format, and any embedded information such as the title, artist, and duration.
- **Eject:** Removes a DVD from the computer's disc player.
- **Play/Pause:** Allows you to start a selected file in the Playlist.
- **Quit:** Exits the Totem application.

The Edit menu controls how the movie is played:

- **Take screenshot:** Allows you to take a still snapshot of a scene in the video file.
- **Repeat Mode:** Repeats the video file until you stop it.
- **Shuffle Mode:** Plays video files in the Playlist in random order.
- **Clear Playlist:** Removes all files from the Playlist.

✔ **Plugins:** Controls the plugins used in Totem.

✔ **Preferences:** Allows you to set basic video and audio settings, such as setting color balance and audio-output format.

The View menu controls how the video is displayed on your screen:

✔ **Fullscreen:** Displays the video file, using the entire computer screen.

✔ **Fit Window to Movie:** Automatically alters the Totem viewing window to fit the default size of the video file; allows you to view the movie at 50 percent (a ratio of 1:2) of the default size.

✔ **Aspect Ratio:** Allows you to set the viewing mode to either standard 4:3 or 16:9 for widescreen videos.

✔ **Switch Angles:** Changes the camera view on DVDs that provide that feature.

✔ **Show Controls:** Displays the Play, Skip, and Location controls at the bottom of the viewing window.

✔ **Subtitles:** Displays subtitles if included in the video.

✔ **Sidebar:** Includes the Playlist sidebar window in the viewing window.

The Go menu controls which part of the video file is being played. For video files, it provides links to specific menus within the video, such as title menus, chapter menus, audio menus, and camera-angle menus. It also uses these generic options:

✔ **Skip To:** Locates a specific point in the video file.

✔ **Skip Forward:** Goes quickly forward in the video file.

✔ **Skip Backwards:** Goes quickly backward in the video file.

The Sound menu controls how the audio is handled:

✔ **Languages:** Plays alternative language audio tracks if they're available in the video file.

✔ **Volume Up:** Increases the volume level of the audio track.

✔ **Volume Down:** Decreases the volume level of the audio track.

The Help menu displays the Totem manual and information about the software version that you're running.

Watchin' DVDs

Watching a DVD in Linux is a bit of a legal quagmire if you live in the United States. The Digital Millennium Copyright Act (DMCA) and other issues make it tricky for any open-source program to navigate the licensing maze when it comes to movies that are encoded or protected in various fashions. However, not all DVDs have such countermeasures enabled: There are DVDs that Americans *can* watch under Linux with no trouble. (Note that we say *watch,* and not *copy* or *pirate.*)

For more on the DMCA and the problems that stem from it, go to `anti-dmca.org`.

To watch a DVD in Fedora, you can use Totem. However, as you saw when trying to view video files, the version of Totem that comes with Fedora is stripped down in terms of formats that it can support — again, this is a legal issue more than anything else. Often it's possible to replace this version with the full one by uninstalling Totem, adding software repositories that contain multimedia tools, and then installing the full version of Totem from those repositories (all these skills are discussed in Chapter 16). This is the solution we recommend for watching DVDs.

The Unofficial Fedora FAQ Web site (`www.fedorafaq.org`) provides some more tips on ways to view DVDs on your Fedora computer.

Creating and Modifying Graphics

The GIMP is a graphics program that's considered in many ways equivalent to Adobe Photoshop. Many don't consider The GIMP the friendliest program on the planet, but at the very least, it has enough features to keep you busily experimenting for weeks! To open The GIMP, choose Applications⇨ Graphics⇨GIMP Image Editor (in Fedora, it's listed by its full name — GNU Image Manipulation Program).

When you start The GIMP, you have to walk through its user-setup routine. Fortunately, you can just click Continue each time you're prompted, unless you're a graphics guru who has a particular reason for wanting to do things in a different way. After you've clicked past all these dialog boxes, a collection of one or more dialog boxes pops up, containing The GIMP main dialog box (see Figure 14-5) plus two additional tool dialog boxes. You can close the right-side dialog box that contains the Layers, Channels, Paths, and Undo functions. The Toolbox dialog box and the main dialog box are somewhat incorporated together. You can't close the Toolbox dialog box, but you can move it to another on-screen workspace by right-clicking the title bar and selecting the Move to Workspace Right option.

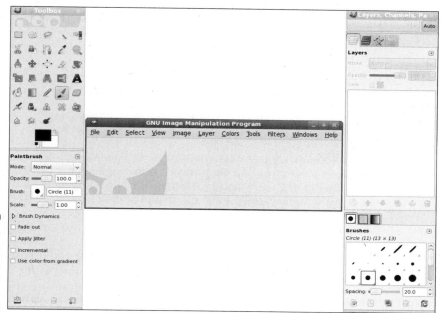

Figure 14-5: The GIMP's main dialog box in Fedora.

The GIMP is an incredibly complex program, with entire books written for the people who really want to use it heavily. Here are a few things to get you started.

The GIMP basic tools

The beauty of The GIMP is that all the tools appear in separate dialog boxes, allowing you to lay out multiple tools as you draw. The main dialog box allows you to coordinate between the different tool dialog boxes while editing an image.

The File menu allows you to open or acquire an image to work with. In The GIMP, you can edit images from five different sources:

✔ Start a new image from scratch on a blank canvas.

✔ Load an existing image from your computer. The GIMP supports all the standard image types, such as GIF, JPEG, TIFF, and others.

✔ Retrieve an image from a remote Web location.

✔ Retrieve an image from a scanner connected to your computer.

✔ Produce an image of a screen shot of your desktop or of a single application window on the desktop.

When you open an image, it appears in the main dialog box, within an editing window area. If you open more than one image at a time, each image opens in its own editing window. This feature allows you to work on several images at the same time; you don't have to flip from image to image in a single window.

The Toolbox dialog box contains all the image-editing tools you'd expect from an image editor. You get tools for selecting image areas; reorienting the image (by flipping and so on); drawing with a virtual pencil, paintbrush, pen, or airbrush; filling spaces with colors; and adding basic special effects.

For each tool you select, the bottom section of the Toolbox dialog box shows detailed settings for the tool. In Figure 14-5, the Paintbrush tool is selected; settings related to the Paintbrush (such as brush size and opacity of the color) appear in the middle section.

You can also keep the detailed settings for multiple options open as separate dialog boxes. The menu bar in the main dialog box allows you to select the editing features to open. Choosing Tools produces a list of the different tool dialog boxes you can have open on your desktop (as shown in Figure 14-6).

Figure 14-6:
The GIMP Tools dialog box list.

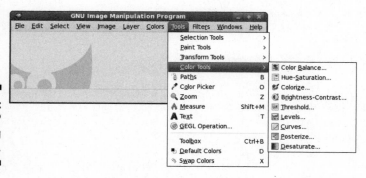

Below the tools in the Toolbox dialog box is an area to select the foreground and background colors (the black and white squares). Double-click the black square to set the foreground color; double-click the white square to set the background color for the image. Alongside that area is an icon you can use to make easy changes to the shape and size of the drawing instrument.

To demonstrate the abilities of The GIMP, the next section grabs and tweaks a sample image.

Capturing screenshots

To get an image to work with, you might as well test the Screenshot feature. Follow these steps to create a screenshot image:

1. **Open The GIMP by choosing Applications⇨Graphics⇨The GIMP (or whatever name your Linux distribution assigns to it).**

2. **From The GIMP menu, choose File⇨Create⇨Screen Shot.**

   The Screenshot dialog box appears, as shown in Figure 14-7.

   You can select to capture either a single application window or the entire desktop. You can also set a delay for when The GIMP takes the screenshot, allowing you time to set up the window just the way you want it before you take its picture.

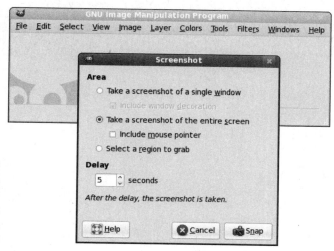

Figure 14-7:
The GIMP
Screenshot
dialog box.

3. **When the screenshot is taken, The GIMP opens the image in an image-editing window. Choose File⇨Save As to save the image file.**

   The GIMP allows you to save the image in most common image formats. All you need to do is place the proper file extension on the filename to specify an image format (such as `.jpg`, `.tiff`, `.gif`, or `.bmp`) when you save it. After you click OK, The GIMP may produce another dialog box that asks you to choose options specific to the image format you specified for the image.

You now have a saved image file that you can play with in The GIMP.

Editing an image file

Now open your saved image file and play around with The GIMP's image-editing features.

1. **Choose File⇨Open and select the image file you saved from your screenshot.**

   The GIMP opens the image in an image-editing window, as shown in Figure 14-8.

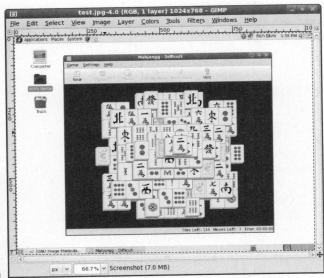

Figure 14-8:
The GIMP image-editing window.

2. **In The GIMP Toolbox, choose one of the selection tools (such as the rectangular box) and select an area on your image.**

3. **Again in The GIMP Toolbox, choose the Rotate tool (the icon with the two boxes and arrows), and then click in the selected area on the image.**

   The Rotate dialog box appears, allowing you to set the details of the rotation. As you increase or decrease the degree of rotation, you see the selected image area actually rotate in the editor. When you've rotated the image just the right amount, click the Rotate button to set the rotation.

4. **In The GIMP Toolbox, select the drawing instrument of your choice (paintbrush, pencil, and so on) and do some doodling in the image.**

   By default, the drawing color is set to black. To change the color, you can double-click the foreground area in The GIMP Toolbox. The Change Foreground Color dialog box appears, as shown in Figure 14-9.

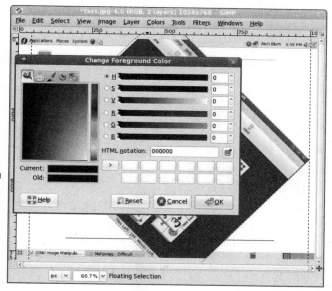

Figure 14-9:
The GIMP Change Foreground Color dialog box.

This tool provides an easy way to select just the right color for your drawings. You can point-and-click any shade of color you're looking for.

5. **Save your new creation, either under the same filename or under another filename (which creates a separate image file).**

That was some pretty basic stuff. You're probably thinking that you could do the same thing with some not-too-sophisticated tools, such as Microsoft Paintbrush. Well, you're right — in a way. The GIMP can do simple image manipulation — and a whole lot more. Here's a brief demo:

1. **If you've closed your image file, open it by choosing File⇨Open so it's in a new image-editing window.**

   The image-editing window has a few tricks of its own that you can use.

2. **Click the Filters menu and select a special effect.**

   The Filters section contains lots of special effects to enhance the look of your image. Figure 14-10 shows the result of the Whirl and Pinch effect (Filters⇨Distorts⇨Whirl and Pinch).

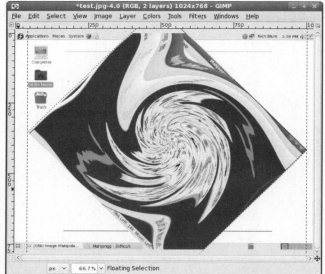

Figure 14-10: The image after applying the Whirl and Pinch effect.

Now you're starting to see the power of The GIMP.

Using The GIMP scripts

For those of us who are lacking in artistic ability, The GIMP tries to help out as best it can. Lots of artistic people have contributed scripts to The GIMP that provide more special effects than you see in a Hollywood action movie.

The key to special effects is being able to string together a series of special effects to create an overall effect. The GIMP allows you to string special effects together by using a *scripting language,* a series of GIMP commands that are run in sequence. Fedora includes both the Python-Fu and Script-Fu GIMP scripting languages.

The Python-Fu and Script-Fu scripts are accessible from the image editor's Filters menu. Each script has its own set of parameters; you can set them to alter its effects. Because scripts apply several layers of special effects to an image, they often take a while to apply.

The premade scripts included with The GIMP produce some pretty amazing effects. Figure 14-11 demonstrates the Weave Script-Fu effect on the saved desktop image.

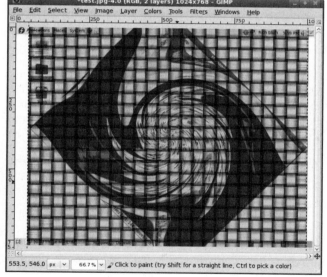

Figure 14-11: The sample image after applying the Weave Script-Fu effect.

That's pretty professional looking for a simple open-source program! Take the time to play around with the different script effects available in The GIMP. You'll be surprised at the quality of the special effects.

Most of the effects can be reversed by choosing Edit⇨Undo, so feel free to play.

Playing 3-D Games

One of the strengths of Windows PCs has been the support for advanced video games. These games utilize high-end graphics that often require specialized 3-D video cards to operate.

Again, this is another area where Linux had never quite caught up to Windows, until now. Two major 3-D video card vendors, ATI and NVIDIA, have released Linux drivers for their products, allowing game developers to enter the Linux market.

There's a catch to this, though: Both ATI and NVIDIA released Linux binary drivers for their 3-D video cards, but not the source code. A true open-source system must include source code for all the components included in the system. This has caused quite a dilemma for Linux distributions.

For a Linux distribution to include the ATI or NVIDIA binary drivers violates the true spirit of open-source software. But if a Linux distribution doesn't provide these drivers, it risks falling behind in the Linux distribution wars and losing market share.

Ubuntu handles this problem by installing the 3-D video card driver and notifying you that it installed a driver for a proprietary card. You can view the driver Ubuntu installed by choosing System⇨Administration⇨Hardware Drivers.

Fedora has decided to solve this problem by splitting the difference: Fedora doesn't include the ATI *or* the NVIDIA 3-D graphics-card drivers, making the distribution completely open source. However, if you still want support for your ATI or NVIDIA 3-D graphics cards, there's hope.

The `http://rpm.livna.org` Web site is a community-operated repository of non-approved Fedora software packages. Not only does it include software packages for many of the video codecs we've been discussing in this chapter, but it also includes software packages for the commercial ATI and NVIDIA 3-D graphics cards.

Installing commercial drivers for ATI and NVIDIA graphics cards isn't illegal, it just goes against the grain of the open-source movement. However, as we mentioned earlier, the codecs available do fall under licensing constraints, so be careful!

By default, the Fedora Yum software installer doesn't recognize the `http://rpm.livna.org` repository. The Web site includes instructions on how to add it to your repository list. After you do that, you're ready to install the ATI or NVIDIA 3-D graphics card drivers, but you have to use the command-line interface skills detailed in Chapter 17:

1. **Start a command-line prompt session by choosing Applications⇨ System Tools⇨Terminal in the GNOME desktop, or by starting the Konsole application in the KDE desktop.**

2. **Become the root user by typing** su **and entering the root password.**

3. **Use the** yum **command-line program to install the appropriate 3-D graphics card drivers on your system.**

   The ATI video driver is called kmod-fglrx, and the NVIDIA video driver is called, strangely enough, kmod-nvidia. The command to install the driver is

   ```
   yum install kmod-nvidia
   ```

4. **Shut down the X server by using the** init **command.**

   The command for this is

   ```
   init 3
   ```

5. **Enable the 3-D video drivers.**

   To enable the NVIDIA driver, type

   ```
   nvidia-config-display enable
   ```

   To enable the ATI video driver, type

   ```
   ati-fglrx-config-display enable
   ```

6. **Restart the X server by using the** init **command.**

   The command to do this is

   ```
   init 5
   ```

You should now have your 3-D graphics card working with Fedora! Lots of 3-D games are available in the standard Fedora software repositories:

- ✔ **freedom:** New episodes for the popular DOOM2 game
- ✔ **bzflag:** A tank-versus-tank battle game
- ✔ **openarena:** Based on the Quake III arena game
- ✔ **scorched3d:** Based on the Scorched Earth game
- ✔ **neverball:** A table-tilt ball game
- ✔ **neverputt:** A miniature golf game
- ✔ **ppracer:** Racing Tux the penguin down a mountain slope

If you prefer some more exciting games, many popular gaming sites (such as icculus.org) provide Linux versions of lots of graphical open-source games. Many of these games exploit advanced 3-D graphics to provide a realistic gaming environment.

If online 3-D games are your preference (or is that "addiction?"), you won't be left out in the cold with Fedora. Some of the most popular online 3-D gaming sites are starting to embrace the popularity of Linux and are providing Linux clients.

Unfortunately, even these days you'll still need to do a little more work to get these clients installed on your Fedora computer. This section covers the game Second Life as an example.

The Second Life online game is a virtual 3-D world entirely built by players. It uses the power of 3-D graphics cards to walk you through an array of locations and lets you interact with graphical "people" that represent other players. After you enter the Second Life world, you can interact with others to purchase or trade products, buy land, and even visit entertainment establishments!

To enter the Second Life world, you'll need the client software. The software is available from the Second Life Web site as an installable binary package. You'll have to do some extra work to get the client installed, but it's worth it:

1. **Open Firefox by choosing Applications⇨Internet⇨Firefox Web Browser.**

   You can also start Firefox by selecting the globe icon on the top panel.

2. **Go to the** `http://www.secondlife.com` **Web site.**

3. **At the bottom of the home page, click the Downloads link.**

4. **On the Downloads Web page, select the Download Now link.**

   The Web page detects that you're on a Linux platform, and it automatically downloads the Linux version of the installation program.

5. **Click to open the Second Life installation package automatically with the File Archive Manager application for your desktop.**

   The File Archive Manager application for your desktop starts (File Roller for GNOME, or Ark for KDE), showing the contents of the installation package.

6. **Extract the installation files into a folder.**

   The Extract window appears. You can select where to extract the Second Life client folder to (most likely you'll want to put it under your Home folder).

After you have the software installed, it's time to play. Find the Second Life folder you extracted from the installation package. In it is a file named `secondlife`. Double-click this file to start the client. The client connects to the Second Life site, and the game begins. Enjoy!

Chapter 15

Playing with Google Gadgets

No tyranny is so irksome as petty tyranny: the officious demands of policemen, government clerks, and electromechanical Gadgets.

— Edward Abbey (1927 – 1986)

*J*ust about every desk needs its gadgets. Whether those gadgets include a stapler, tape dispenser, or sticky notes, you just gotta have gadgets on your desk — if for nothing else, to help make you look busy! Your Linux desktop is no different. There are plenty of handy gadgets you can accumulate to make your Linux experience easier.

The Google Desktop project brought the world of desktop searching to the Windows computer — along with *Google Gadgets,* simple graphical utilities that provide information directly on your desktop. They became so popular that the Windows Vista operating system incorporated the same idea.

The Google Desktop consists of

✔ **The Google search bar:** Allows you to search not only the Google search archives, but also all the files that reside on your workstation, from a single place.

✔ **Google Gadgets:** A collection of small utilities that run on your desktop to provide information at your fingertips.

✔ **Google Apps:** A collection of full-featured office applications, including word processing, spreadsheets, and presentation graphics, all running from Google servers and accessed via the Internet.

Although Google Desktop Gadgets are popular in the Windows world, they haven't caught on as quickly in the Linux world. That may change with the increasing popularity of the gOS Linux distribution — which includes not only the Google Desktop Gadgets, but also links to the various Google applications online.

Finding Google Gadgets with gOS

The gOS Linux distribution includes the Linux version of Google Gadgets installed on a GNOME desktop, as shown in Figure 15-1.

Figure 15-1: The gOS desktop with Google Gadgets.

The Gadgets appear directly on the desktop, so you don't have to hunt through menus to start them. At the bottom of the gOS desktop is a separate toolbar that contains icons that start various applications you can use in gOS. This includes installed applications, such as the OpenOffice suite (see Chapter 12), as well as Google applications that you can access from anywhere you have an Internet connection (which we talk more about a little later).

Installing Gadgets in Other Distributions

If you don't have the gOS Linux distribution, you can still play with Google Gadgets. Depending on which Linux distribution you're using, you may or may not have easy access to the Google Gadgets. This section walks you through getting Google Gadgets installed on both the Fedora and Ubuntu distributions.

Installing the Gadget package with Fedora

The Fedora Linux distribution includes Google Gadgets in the main repository (see Chapter 16), so installing it is a breeze!

Open the PackageKit package-manager program, and look for Google Gadgets for Linux, as shown in Figure 15-2.

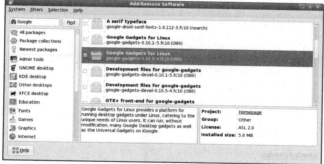

Figure 15-2: Installing Google Gadgets in Fedora.

Select the check box for the Google Gadgets for Linux package, and then click the Apply button. PackageKit retrieves the package and installs it for you. You should now see the Google Gadgets entry added to the Internet menu on your workstation.

Gadgets for all

If your Linux distribution doesn't include Google Gadgets as a software package (as is the case with Ubuntu), you don't have to change to the gOS Linux distribution to enjoy Google Gadgets on your Linux desktop. There's a Google Gadgets installation file that you can use for just about every Linux distribution.

The main Google Gadgets project site (http://code.google.com/p/google-Gadgets-for-linux/) contains the Gadget source code that you can compile on just about any Linux system, along with links to places where others have already compiled that source code and provided the binary executable packages to run.

In the case of Ubuntu, you can follow these steps to get Gadgets:

1. **Go to**

   ```
   http://www.getdeb.net/app/Google+Gadgets
   ```

2. **Select the link for the version of Ubuntu you have.**

   You can find out what version of Ubuntu you have by choosing System⇨ About Ubuntu from the top edge panel.

3. **Download the** .deb **package.**

   If you're not sure how to download a .deb package, see Chapter 16.

4. **Double-click the** .deb **package to start the Package Installer.**

   The Package Installer program (shown in Figure 15-3) automatically extracts the files in the software package and installs them in their proper location.

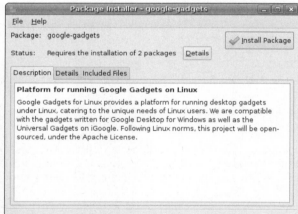

Figure 15-3: Installing Google Gadgets using the Ubuntu Package Installer program.

5. **Click the Install Package button to start the installation.**

   The Package Installer program determines if any additional software packages are required for the installation. If your Ubuntu workstation is connected to the Internet, it retrieves them automatically from the software repository and installs them.

6. **Close the Package Installer when it completes the installation.**

7. **Press Alt+F2.**

   The Run Application dialog box opens, as shown in Figure 15-4.

Figure 15-4:
The Run
Application
dialog box.

8. **Enter** ggl-gtk **into the Run Application dialog box, and then click Run.**

The ggl-gtk command starts the Google Gadgets application. You can also choose Applications➪Internet➪Google Gadgets to start Gadgets.

The Google Gadget icon appears in the top panel (it's the square with four colors), and the Gadget sidebar appears on the side of the desktop, as shown in Figure 15-5.

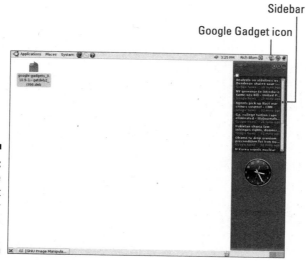

Figure 15-5:
The Google
Gadget
sidebar
running in
Ubuntu.

Using Gadgets

Having Gadgets at your fingertips isn't any fun unless you know how to use them. This section walks through how to use the Google Gadgets installed by default in the gOS desktop, how to customize them for your own environment, and how to add new Gadgets easily. These same instructions also work if you've installed Google Gadgets in another Linux distribution, although the default Gadgets may not be the same.

The default gOS Gadgets

The default gOS desktop contains several Gadgets that appear on your desktop (refer to Figure 15-1):

- **Battery meter:** Displays the charge status of your laptop battery.
- **Wireless signal meter:** Displays the signal strength of the wireless access point you're connected with.
- **Flower pot:** Pretties up your desktop; click the flowers to water them!
- **Google News:** Provides a brief synopsis of the day's news for those who need to stay informed.
- **Google Calendar:** Provides a quick glimpse of the monthly calendar, including holidays and special events.
- **Weather Globe:** Helps you keep tabs on the outside weather in your location.
- **Calculator:** Crunches numbers quickly on the fly.

The default Gadgets provide a small sampling of what's available. Some of these may not even apply to your particular situation. The Battery Meter and Wireless Signal Meter may not apply to your workstation. Likewise, unless you happen to live in Happy, Texas, you'll most likely want to change the default location set in the Weather Globe. The next section walks through how you can customize your Gadgets.

If you're not into desktop clutter, you can move the Gadgets into a sidebar area. You can then hide the sidebar, and only display it when you need to use a Gadget. Just click the Google Gadget icon in the top edge panel.

Customizing Gadgets

Each Gadget on the desktop includes its own control icon you can use to manage it. When you hover your mouse pointer over the Gadget, a little toolbar appears at its top, as shown for the Weather Globe Gadget in Figure 15-6.

The toolbar uses three symbols:

- **The double less-than sign:** Expands or collapses the Gadget window.
- **The down arrow:** Displays the Gadget menu.
- **The X:** Closes the Gadget window.

To remove a Gadget from your desktop permanently, just click the X to close the Gadget window. Not only does the Gadget disappear from your desktop, the next time you start your desktop, the Gadget won't start up. If you want that Gadget back on your desktop, don't worry; you can add it back by following the steps in the "Adding more Gadgets" section.

Figure 15-6: The Gadget control icon for the Weather Globe.

The Gadget menu differs for each one, but basically allows you to control the location of a Gadget, display information about it, and produce an Options dialog box for setting any additional features the Gadget may have. Clicking the Options menu for the Weather Globe Gadget (for example) opens the Options dialog box shown in Figure 15-7.

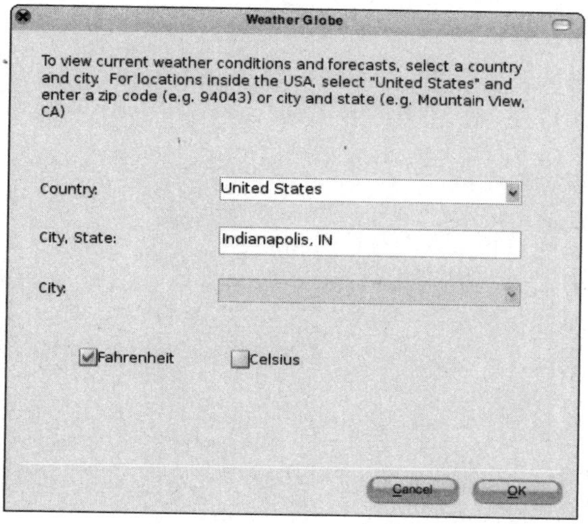

Figure 15-7: The Weather Globe Options dialog box.

Enter your country, your Zip code (if you're in the United States) or the name of your city, and whether you want to display the temperature in Celsius or

Fahrenheit. The Weather Globe Gadget saves this information; and now you'll
see the weather information for your location.

Adding more Gadgets

You're not just stuck with the Gadgets that gOS places on your desktop, there
are plenty more. The Google Gadget applet appears in the top edge panel as
the group of four colored boxes.

To add more Gadgets, follow these steps:

1. **Right-click the Google Gadgets applet icon in the top edge panel.**

   If you left-click the Gadget applet icon, all the Gadgets disappear from
   your desktop. That's a quick way to clear things off! Just left-click the
   Gadget applet icon again to bring them back!

2. **Select the Add Gadget option from the menu.**

   The Gadget Browser, shown in Figure 15-8, appears on your desktop.

3. **Search the Gadget Browser for new Gadgets.**

   Gadgets are grouped into categories, and a search tool is available at
   the top of the browser to search for either a specific Gadget or Gadgets
   related to a specific topic.

4. **Hover your mouse pointer over the icon for the Gadget you want to
   add to your desktop.**

   An Add button appears beneath it.

Figure 15-8:
The Gadget
Browser
dialog box.

5. Click the Add button that appears for the Gadget.

The new Gadget appears on your desktop, ready for action!

Using Google Apps

Besides the Google Gadgets you see on the desktop, you probably noticed the array of icons that appear at the bottom of the gOS desktop. These icons provide quick access to several Google applications, detailed in Table 15-1.

Table 15-1	Google Applications
Application	*What It's Used For*
Firefox	The popular Web-browsing program.
Google Mail	A full-featured e-mail client.
Google Calendar	A full-featured personal calendar that you can also share with others.
Google Documents	A full office suite of products, including word processing, spreadsheets, and presentation graphics.
Google Maps	The popular worldwide street map that provides both map and satellite views of streets.
Google Reader	Gathers news from selected Web newsfeeds, and enables you to subscribe to your chosen newsfeeds.
Google News	Connects to the Google news Web page, providing up-to-the-minute news.
Google Product Search	Allows you to comparison-shop for products.
Google Finance	Connects to the Google Financial news page, providing stock-market news and information.
Blogger	Connects to the popular Google Blog Web site, where you can create and maintain your own blog.
YouTube	Direct access to the popular video-clip-sharing Web site.
Pidgin	Connects to popular Instant Messages sites (see Chapter 9).
Skype	Connects to Internet phone services (see Chapter 9).
OpenOffice Writer	A popular word-processing program (see Chapter 12).
OpenOffice Calc	A popular spreadsheet program (see Chapter 12).
OpenOffice Impress	A popular presentation-graphics program (see Chapter 12).

Google Applications have a unique feature in that they all run on Google servers on the Internet. You must have an Internet connection to use the Google Applications.

Documents that you create in the Google Applications servers are stored in your own private area on the Google network. You can choose to keep them private or to share them — either with the whole world or with just a few of your closest friends!

To use the Google Applications, you need to create a free account on Google at google.com. You can either sign up for a free Google Mail account that'll work for all the applications, or you can sign up for individual Google applications using your own existing e-mail address.

Part IV
Junior Administrator Boot Camp

The 5th Wave   By Rich Tennant

"Oh, Scarecrow! Without the database in your laptop, how will we find anything in Oz?"

In this part . . .

In this part, you take control of your Linux computer. You find out what all those weird file extensions are (`.gz`? `.tgz`? `.rpm`? Huh?) You find out how to install new software, update your system, and track down even more new software. Then you discover some of the arcane hand-waving involved in administering a Linux system. For example, maybe you want to make an account for your little sister so she doesn't access boy band forums from your account. You take a walk into the land of basic Linux security. (Just because you're using Linux doesn't mean that you can ignore the issue of security.) Finally, you see how to run other operating systems (or even other Linux systems) from within your Linux workstation.

Chapter 16

Adding Software to Linux

● ●

In This Chapter

▶ Recognizing downloaded software file formats

▶ Creating tarballs and archives

▶ Compressing files

▶ Opening tarballs, archives, and compressed files

▶ Installing and removing software packages

● ●

I will make you shorter by the head.

— Queen Elizabeth I

When you start using a new operating system, one of the most frustrating things is trying to figure out all the goofy file extensions. The Windows world has `.exe` and `.zip`. The Macintosh world has `.bin` and `.hqx`. What about the Linux world? It certainly has its fair share of bizarre extensions, but really, they make a great deal of sense after you know the programs that make them. In this chapter, you find out all about `.tar`, `.gz`, `.tar.gz`, `.tgz`, `.bz2`, `.deb`, and `.rpm` files. (Anyone up for a game of Scrabble with alphabet soup?)

After you have the letter jumble all figured out, you'll be happy to find that Linux offers a number of cool tools for working with these crazy files, updating your system, adding new software, and more.

Opening Downloaded Files

The Linux world is full of strange terms and acronyms. For example, if someone comes up to you out of the blue and starts talking about tarballs, you probably get a mental image of sticky, smelly balls of tar, maybe rolled in feathers. Yet a tarball is something you run into regularly in the Linux world, especially when you're looking for software or when you need to save yourself some space. A *tarball* is a bunch of files (and possibly directories) packaged together in a .tar file and compressed using the gzip utility; the tarball then contains the .tar.gz extension.

Fortunately, all you need to know is how to double-click the .tar.gz file, which consists of a tarball, in order to access the many files in any of the formats listed in Table 16-1. When you double-click the .tar.gz file, your desktop File Manager shows you what's inside.

Although Table 16-1 mentions specific programs used to handle the file types, as with everything else in Linux, there's often more than one way to handle these files. People tend to use whatever programs they're comfortable with, no matter what operating system they're on.

Table 16-1	Potential Formats for Downloaded Files	
Extension	**Meaning**	**Program(s) Involved**
.bz	An older form of .bz2.	bzip, bunzip
.bz2	Slower-but-more-efficient compression for some types of files, such as text files.	bzip2, bunzip2
.deb	All the files related to an application bundled together using a Debian-specific format, used in Ubuntu and gOS.	dpkg, apt-get
.gz	Typical compressed file for Linux and UNIX.	gzip, gunzip
.iso	A CD-ROM or DVD-ROM "image," which is a single file that holds the entire contents of a CD or DVD. You have to tell your CD or DVD burner software that this file is an image so it knows to create a disc from this file, not to just place a copy of the file on the storage medium.	See Chapter 3.
.rpm	All the files related to a single application bundled together using a format designed by Red Hat and used in Fedora.	rpm, yum
.tar	A bunch of files bundled together.	tar
.tar.bz2	A *tarball,* which in this case is a .tar file inside a .bz2 file.	tar, bzip2, bunzip2

Extension	Meaning	Program(s) Involved
.tar.gz	A traditional *tarball*, which is a .tar file inside a .gz file.	tar, gunzip, gzip
.tgz	A traditional *tarball*, which is a .tar file inside a .gz file.	tar, gunzip, gzip
.Z	An old-style UNIX compressed file.	compress, uncompress
.zip	A Windows .zip file.	zip, unzip

WinZip (www.winzip.com) can handle .gz, .tgz, and .tar.gz files (along with the .bz2 versions) for Windows users.

Compressing and Packaging Files to Share

Life isn't all about "take, take, take" (or at least we should hope not!). Sometimes you've just gotta give. Creating care packages to share with other folks involves telling your File Manager that you want to do so.

To package and compress files for sending off to other people, navigate to where you've stored the file(s) — see Chapter 7 for how to move about in Nautilus or Dolphin — and then create your package, as follows:

1. **Determine whether you want to compress or package a single file, a group of files, or a whole folder.**

   If the files and folders you want to bundle together are flung all over the place in your filesystem, you may want to create a new folder and copy into it all the items you want to bundle — just for the sake of convenience.

2. **Select the item(s) you want to package.**

   If you want to select a whole folder, navigate to its parent folder and just select the folder's icon instead of opening the folder.

3. **Right-click the item(s) (or choose the Edit menu).**

   The context menu appears if you right-clicked, or, in Nautilus, the Edit menu opens.

4. **In the context or Edit menu, choose Compress (in Dolphin) or Create Archive (in Nautilus).**

   In Dolphin, an additional menu appears, allowing you to select the compressed file type. Choose the option labeled *Gzip-compressed tar archive* to create a tarball of the files in the same folder.

   In Nautilus, The Create Archive dialog box appears, suggesting a tarball (refer to Table 16-1) version of the file.

5. **If you want a tarball, leave it alone, or change the file extensions (as discussed in Table 16-1) to match what you want.**

6. **Click Create.**

   Nautilus uses the filename extension to determine what kind of compression to use.

7. **If you want to rename the file or change where it should go in your filesystem, do so now.**

   Leave the `.tar.gz` or `.gz` part alone. Just change the first part. For example, if you're archiving the Files folder, the suggested name might be `Files.tar.gz`. If you want to use `Files100305.tar.gz` for the actual name, just add the date to the existing name.

8. **Click OK.**

   The archive is created.

Keeping Linux Up to (Up)date

A vital feature of any operating system is the capability to update fast with minimum hassle. There are always new features, security fixes, and software bug fixes that should be installed to keep things running smoothly.

Most Linux distributions include a program for automatically updating the installed software on your system via an Internet connection. If your computer is connected to the Internet, then you can receive daily updates and up-to-the-minute patches.

Ubuntu, all its derivatives (including gOS), and Fedora include update programs to make it a snap to keep your system up to date. Fedora uses the `yum` program to manage Red Hat–based `.rpm` packages for installing software and updates. Ubuntu uses the `rpm` and `apt-get` programs to manage Debian-based `.deb` packages for its software and update installations.

These command-line programs (see Chapter 17) are great utilities if you're comfortable working in the command-line environment. If you're not, both Fedora and Ubuntu also include graphical programs:

- For Fedora, the PackageKit program. PackageKit interfaces with the `yum` program to manage the package database so you can easily install or remove packages.

- Ubuntu uses the Synaptic program, which interfaces with the `apt-get` program to manage the package database and make packages easy to install or remove.

The following sections walk you through how each of these programs works on your desktop system.

Keeping your Linux system updated is the first step in keeping it safe from viruses and exploits. See Chapter 19 for more information on keeping your Linux system safe.

Updating Fedora with PackageKit

Fedora, by default, runs the PackageKit program to automatically reach out to the Internet and check for available operating system and software updates. The PackageKit program is used on both the KDE and GNOME desktops in Fedora (although the KDE desktop version is called KPackageKit).

You can either wait on this utility to tell you when something new is available, or you can update your system manually. Most people do a mix of the two, accepting automatic updates when it's convenient, and refusing them if it's more convenient to go back later and get them manually.

Automated updates

If you're connected to the Internet and an update becomes available, a notification box appears on your desktop, proudly proclaiming "Updates Available" and telling you how many, as shown in Figure 16-1.

If security updates are available, the notification window has a bit of a warning feel to it (you can't tell from the black-and-white Figure 16-1, but the window frame is bright red).

You have the option to only install the security-related updates and come back later to install other updates, or you can choose to install all the available updates at this time.

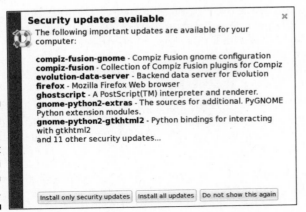

Security updates available ✕

The following important updates are available for your
computer:

compiz-fusion-gnome - Compiz Fusion gnome configuration
compiz-fusion - Collection of Compiz Fusion plugins for Compiz
evolution-data-server - Backend data server for Evolution
firefox - Mozilla Firefox Web browser
ghostscript - A PostScript(TM) interpreter and renderer.
gnome-python2-extras - The sources for additional. PyGNOME
Python extension modules.
gnome-python2-gtkhtml2 - Python bindings for interacting
with gtkhtml2
and 11 other security updates...

[Install only security updates] [Install all updates] [Do not show this again]

Figure 16-1:
The
KPackageKit
notification
window in
Fedora.

You may also notice that an icon appears in the panel on your desktop when
the notification window opens. KPackageKit uses a panel applet to display the
status of the update process. Different icons tell you what PackageKit is doing:

- ✔ **Red starburst:** One or more security updates are available.
- ✔ **Orange starburst:** One or more non-security package updates are available.
- ✔ **Box with a list:** Retrieving update file list.
- ✔ **Box with green arrow:** Downloading new updates.
- ✔ **Box with gear:** Installing updates.

If you click the panel icon, a dialog box appears, showing the status of the
process. When all updates are complete, the panel icon goes away.

Manual updates

If you closed the "Updates Available" box or just haven't tried to update
your machine in quite a while, you can start the updater manually. To do so,
follow these steps:

1. **Choose Applications⇨System⇨Update System in the GNOME desktop,
   or choose KDE⇨Applications⇨System⇨Software Management in the
   KDE desktop.**

   The PackageKit (in GNOME) or KPackageKit (in KDE) dialog box opens,
   as shown in Figure 16-2.

2. **Click the Software Updates icon on the left side.**

   You likely have to wait while the tool reaches out to the Internet and
   loads update information. When this process is complete, the progress
   dialog box closes and you can see all the available updates.

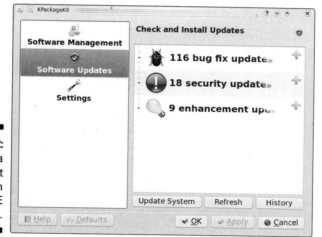

If, at this point, you're told, "Another application is running which is accessing software information," wait a few minutes. The utility that tells you when updates are available may be in the middle of scanning.

3. **If you want information on any of the individual updates, click the Review button, and then choose the desired item in the list.**

   Information about the update appears beneath the list of available updates, as shown in Figure 16-3.

4. **Click Apply Updates to proceed.**

   The Processing Tasks dialog box appears with a progress bar; the first time you update the machine, this process can take a while — there may be a hundred or more updates.

   When the tool is sure that everything that each program needs is taken care of, this dialog box closes. Another may appear, telling you that dependencies were added. (*Dependencies* are packages that another package has to have in place in order to install and run properly.)

   From here, you see a Downloading dialog box. A progress bar shows you how much longer it takes for all the updates to be downloaded onto your computer. After downloading is complete, an Installing progress bar appears. When the updater finishes installing the packages, an Information dialog box appears, stating that the update is complete.

5. **Click OK to close the updater, if necessary.**

Updating Ubuntu with Synaptic

The Ubuntu distribution runs the Synaptic program in the background at all times to check for updates. It uses a technique similar to the Fedora PackageKit program — it displays a dialog box telling you that there are updates available.

When you see the Synaptic dialog box appear, you know it's time to start downloading updates or patches. If you're in the middle of something important, you can choose to close the Synaptic dialog box and come back to it later. When you're ready to check for updates, follow these steps:

1. **Choose System⇨Administration⇨Update Manager from the top edge panel menu.**

   The main Update Manager window, shown in Figure 16-4, appears.

2. **Click the Check button to check for new updates.**

   The Update Manager checks the Internet for any updates to the installed packages on your system. If the panel applet has notified you that updates are already available, you can skip this step.

3. **If you want information on individual updates, select the update in the list, and click the Description of Update link under the listing.**

   The information about the update appears below the update list.

4. **Click the Install Updates button to begin installing the updates.**

   You're asked for your password to ensure that you have the proper security privileges to add updates.

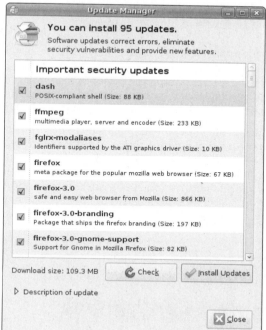

Figure 16-4:
The Ubuntu
Update
Manager
window.

5. **Click the Close button to exit the Update Manager dialog box.**

Now your Ubuntu system should be current with all the available patches.

Installing New Software

Both Fedora and Ubuntu contain programs that allow you to add new software to your Linux system. Software is bundled in two formats in Linux distributions:

- **Applications:** Software that contains multiple components, such as the OpenOffice.org package or software development platforms, can be installed as a complete application.

- **Packages:** Individual software programs that aren't part of a larger application, such as The GIMP (see Chapter 14), can be bundled in a package that just installs the one program by itself.

Because Linux provides two ways to install software, most Linux distributions provide two separate ways to install software:

- **Add/remove programs:** Programs that add or remove applications allow you to add new software as complete applications, with the order determined by the name of each complete application. Instead of having to install individual packages one by one, you can select to install the complete application.

- **Package-manager programs:** These programs install selected individual components *(packages)* of an application. They're the way to go if you just want to install an individual package because you need only a part of a complete application (or because a program isn't large enough to get its own entry in the add/remove program). This method is commonly used for installing individual components of larger applications, such as if you want to install Writer from the OpenOffice.org application.

This section walks you through using these tools in Fedora and Ubuntu to get new software on your system.

Adding complete applications

Add/Remove programs make adding complete applications no harder than updating your existing software: If your workstation is connected to the Internet, you just browse to the application you want to install, and then select it. The Add/Remove program automatically downloads and installs the necessary components from the Internet repositories.

Adding applications in Fedora

Follow these steps to install your new applications in Fedora:

1. **Choose KDE⇨Applications⇨Administration⇨Add/Remove Software for the KDE desktop, or choose System⇨Administration⇨Add/Remove Software for the GNOME desktop.**

   The Add/Remove Software window, shown in Figure 16-5, appears.

2. **Select the application category from the list on the left side.**

   You can also use the search text box above the category list to search for a specific application, or for a keyword within an application.

3. **Select an application to install from the list in the top-right window pane.**

   A description of the application appears in the lower window pane.

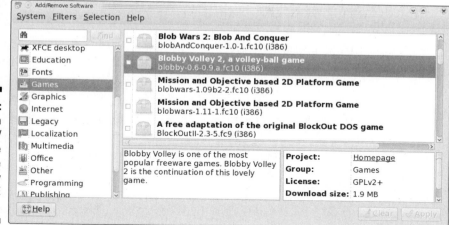

Figure 16-5:
The Fedora
Add/
Remove
Software
window
on the KDE
desktop.

4. **Repeat the process for any other application(s) you want to install.**

5. **Click the Apply button.**

Adding applications in Ubuntu

Follow these steps to get your new applications installed in Ubuntu:

1. **Choose Applications⇨Add/Remove Applications from the top panel menu.**

   The Add/Remove Applications program opens, as shown in Figure 16-6.

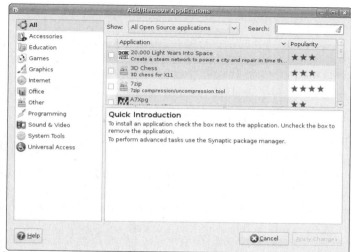

Figure 16-6:
The Add/
Remove
Applications
program in
Ubuntu.

2. **Select the application category from the left side list.**

   You can also use the search text box at the top-right side of the window to search for a specific application, or for a keyword within an application.

3. **Select an application to install from the list in the top-right window pane.**

   A description of the application appears in the lower window pane.

4. **Repeat the process for any other application(s) you want to install.**

5. **Click the Apply Changes button.**

In no time at all, the new application is available on your system. Usually applications are added to the Applications menu automatically.

Adding individual packages

Both Ubuntu and Fedora use a separate package-management program to install individual packages on your system. This section walks you through installing packages on both Ubuntu and Fedora.

Installing with PackageKit

The same PackageKit program used to install applications is also used to install individual packages in Fedora. This section walks through these uses of the KPackageKit application in the Fedora KDE desktop:

1. **Choose KDE Menu⇨Applications⇨System⇨Software Management in the KDE desktop.**

   The same PackageKit program is used to install both applications and packages in Fedora. The KPackageKit program for the KDE desktop provides icons for the different functions. The PackageKit program for the GNOME desktop handles applications and packages together.

2. **Select the Software Management icon in the left side.**

   The KPackageKit package handler opens, displaying the dialog box for adding and removing software (as shown in Figure 16-7).

3. **Select a package category from the drop-down list on the top-right side, select a filter from the Filters drop-down list, or enter a package name in the Search text box.**

   After selecting the filter criteria, all the packages that match the filter appear in the right-side window pane. It may take a little while for PackageKit to retrieve the packages from the Internet.

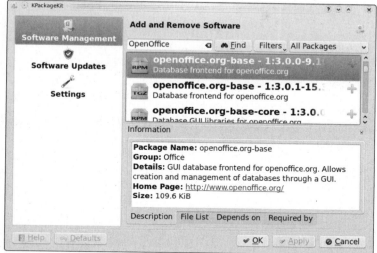

Figure 16-7:
The
KPackageKit
Add and
Remove
Software
dialog box in
Fedora.

4. **Click a package to display information about the package.**

5. **Click the plus sign on the packages you want to install.**

   When you click a green plus sign at the end of a package line, it turns into a minus sign. If you change your mind about installing the package, click the minus sign to remove the package from the installation list.

6. **Click the Apply button to start the installation.**

PackageKit downloads and installs all the packages you selected.

Installing with the Synaptic Package Manager

Ubuntu uses the Synaptic Package Manager to manage packages. This tool allows you to add, remove, and update packages manually from the same interface.

To add a new package in Ubuntu, follow these steps:

1. **Choose System⊅Administration⊅Synaptic Package Manager from the top panel menu.**

   The Package Manager displays the main window, shown in Figure 16-8.

2. **Select the category of the package in the left side filter list, or type the package name in the search text box at the top.**

   Packages matching the filter category or search keyword appear in the right-side list.

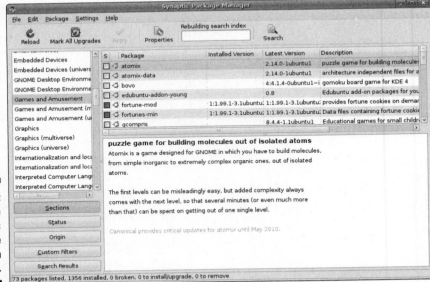

3. **Select a package from the list to view the details.**

   The details for the package appear in the lower window pane.

4. **Select the check box and choose Mark for Installation from the pop-up menu.**

5. **Click the Apply button to install the selected packages.**

Finding More Software

What if you can't find what you're looking for through the official (and not so official) sources discussed in the previous section? Those aren't your only options. Although we can't anticipate every situation you might find yourself in, we can at least give you some tips on how to find extra software — and how to install much of it.

Here are the general steps for finding new software:

1. **Check the Fedora FAQ (**www.fedorafaq.org**), the Fedora News (**www.fedoranews.org**), the Fedora Forum (**www.fedoraforum.org**), and other online sites that people might recommend.**

2. **If you don't know what you want, find out by opening your favorite Web search engine and searching on a desired feature, including the word *linux*.**

   For example, if you want something comparable to the program `irfan view` from the Windows world, you'd search on "irfanview linux."

3. **Sort through the search results and see whether a particular program is suggested. If not, add the word "equivalent" to your search — and run the search again.**

   So (to continue the example) you would search again, using "irfanview linux equivalent." Now you start to see a program called `xnview` mentioned.

   It wouldn't hurt to turn around and see whether Fedora's package manager PackageKit offers the program you're considering, before you bother installing it yourself.

4. **After you find a program that does what you want, do a Web search for it.**

   More often than not, you find the program's home page.

5. **Click through to that program's home page.**

6. **Click through the Download link on that page.**

7. **Locate and download the most specific version that matches your distribution.**

   You may be offered, say, Windows, UNIX, and Linux options; you'd choose Linux in that case. If offered Linux x86 versus Linux ppc, choose x86 unless you're using Linux on an Apple Macintosh computer (which is not covered in this book). If you're offered a specific distribution package or a tarball (see the beginning of this chapter for more information on these), choose the specific distribution package (such as `.rpm` for Fedora or `.deb` for Ubuntu).

8. **After you have the program downloaded, install it as follows:**

   - If the package has a filename extension of `.rpm` or `.deb`, open your file manager and double-click the download to install it. You can also install it from a command line (see Chapter 17 for how to open a command-line terminal). When you have the terminal window open, type **su** and press Enter. You're asked for your root password. Type it, press Enter, use the filesystem's navigation commands (see Chapter 7) to go to where you saved the file, and then type the following command to install or update the program as needed:

   ```
   rpm -Uvh filename
   ```

- If it's a tarball, open your file manager. Double-click the file to open it and look at its contents. There should be a file named README or INSTALL. This file contains instructions on what you need to do, and there may be more instructions available on the Web site itself. (Working with tarballs just requires practice; it gets easier over time, so extract the file and get to it!)

Upgrading Your OS

Typically, Fedora users upgrade by downloading the new version of the distribution, starting the installation, and then selecting Upgrade rather than a new installation from the installation menu. Ubuntu users have a cool way to upgrade an existing system easily: When a new version is available, the Synaptic Update System window displays a new button to select. If you click the button, Synaptic downloads all the upgrade files needed to completely upgrade to the new release (this most likely takes a long time, though, even on a high-speed Internet connection).

Usually, upgrading an existing system keeps all of the data stored in your home folders (see Chapter 6). However, nothing is perfect. It's always a good idea to back up your important data to a removable storage device such as a USB flash drive or a writable CD before trying to upgrade your system.

Chapter 17

Working without the GUI

Whom computers would destroy, they must first drive mad.

— Anonymous

Many computing old-timers speak fondly of the command line. Others who developed their skills by pointing and clicking refer to the command line as some antiquated tool used by crusty old-timers. The truth is that most skilled computing professionals recognize the merits of both the point-and-click graphical user interface (GUI) and the "lots of typing" command-line interface (CLI). You must understand that the command line provides a powerful force for operating your computer. If you ever watch over the shoulder of a skilled Linux geek, you notice that, after logging in, the geek doesn't take long to start tapping out seemingly cryptic instructions by hand.

In this chapter, we explore the Linux program that provides the CLI, which is called the bash shell. Although many shells are available for Linux, bash is the most common, and for good reason. Basically, the creators of bash rolled many good features of other shells into one terrific package.

Each shell has its own way of handling commands and its own additional set of tools. We start by explaining what a shell really is, and when you understand that, you're ready to get down and dirty with bash. We cover specifically what you can do with some of the best features of the bash shell. Then we continue with working in the command prompt and get into bash shell interior decorating.

Shells come equipped to perform certain functions. Most of these features have evolved over time to assist the command-line jockey with myriad tasks. Although we only scratch the surface here, you're encouraged to read the man page for the bash shell because it's likely one of the more complete and readable man pages in existence. You can read all about how to use man pages (the online Help system in Linux) in the "Using Help" section later in this chapter.

Playing the Shell Game

You need a way to tell the computer what you want it to do. In Linux, one of the ways to communicate with the computer is through something called the shell. A *shell* isn't a graphical thing; it's the sum total of the commands and syntax you have available to you to tell the operating system what to do so you can do your work.

The shell environment is rather dull and boring by graphical desktop standards. When you start the shell, all you see is a plain window with a short prompt (such as a $) followed by a blinking cursor that awaits your keyboard entry. (Later in this section, we show you a couple of methods for accessing the shell.)

The default shell used in Linux is the bash shell. This work environment is based on the original UNIX shell, which is called the *Bourne shell* and is also referred to as sh. The term bash stands for the *Bourne again sh*ell. The bash shell comes with most Linux distributions.

Getting a shell

You can start a bash session by using a terminal application in your GUI desktop. The terminal application you use depends (of course) on your desktop:

- **Terminal:** This is the default terminal used in the GNOME desktop. To start Terminal from the GNOME menu, choose Applications⇨ System Tools⇨Terminal if you're in Fedora, or choose Applications⇨ Accessories⇨Terminal in Ubuntu. Figure 17-1 shows the Terminal. Notice the prompt — that's the shell's command-line prompt. You enter your commands there.

- **Konsole:** This is the default terminal used in the KDE desktop. In the KDE world, choose K Menu⇨Applications⇨System⇨Konsole. The Konsole interface is shown in Figure 17-2. The command-line prompt appears in the window.

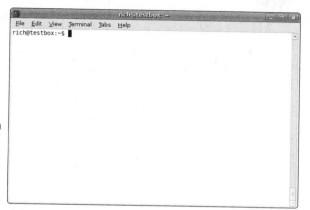

Figure 17-1:
The GNOME
Terminal
window.

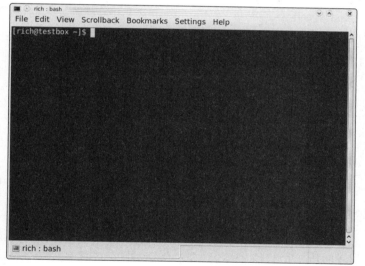

Figure 17-2:
The KDE
Konsole
window.

Both Terminal and Konsole have a few additional features that can come in handy, such as cutting and pasting text and changing the color of the text and the background. You can even go old-school and have green text on top of a black background — just like the computer terminals you see in old '70s movies.

If you use your shell prompt quite a bit like we do, it's handy to use what's laid out in Chapters 4 and 5 about adding the terminal window to your icons along the desktop's menu panel.

Using the shell prompt

Often your shell prompt includes helpful information. For example, if you're logged in as `rich` on the machine `testbox` in Ubuntu, your prompt looks like this:

```
rich@testbox:~$
```

The tilde character (~) indicates that you're in your home directory (see Chapter 6). The dollar sign indicates that the `bash` shell is ready for you to enter a command.

Opening a virtual terminal window

We need to tell you about another method for starting a shell session. You may not use it much, but you might find it helpful at some point.

First of all, notice that your shell prompt is merely inside a window that is part of your GUI desktop. Suppose you want your whole screen to be text-only. To switch to a text environment, press Ctrl+Alt+F2. Don't be alarmed when your familiar graphical desktop disappears. It's still running in the background, and you can get back to where you left off in a moment. But first, a few words about the boring text screen you're now looking at.

You're looking at a *virtual terminal,* a screen that imitates the way computer terminals looked in olden times before GUIs. It's one of several screens available with your default installation. You probably see something like this:

```
testbox login:
```

Go ahead and type your username and password, which you're prompted for. You see a message indicating your last login date followed by the `bash` prompt:

```
rich@testbox:~$
```

Notice the similarity between this prompt and the one you left behind in the open window on the GUI desktop. Both prompts indicate that you have a `bash` session open. Note that although it's accurate to say that both prompts result from using the `bash` shell, they're distinct and separate *instances* of the same program. In other words, the environment you're working with here is exclusive of (and independent of) the `bash` environment you still have open in the GUI terminal window.

Are you wondering where your GUI desktop has gone? Just to settle your nerves a bit, do some jumping around. The GUI desktop is located at virtual terminal (VT) number 7 by default. You now have VT-2 open. Position your piano-playing fingers and strike the chord Ctrl+Alt+F7 (if this doesn't work, try Ctrl+Alt+F8). Within a second or two, your screen should flash and return you to your graphical desktop. Neat, huh? And guess what? The bash session you left open on VT-2 is still there; you never logged out. Go back again by pressing Ctrl+Alt+F2. Voilà! — right where you left it. Feel free to jump back and forth a few times and try some other VTs (F1 through F6). Whoopee! This virtual-terminal stuff rocks.

If you use the Lock Screen tool for your desktop (discussed in Chapters 4 and 5), only your GUI session is locked. Anyone could use Ctrl+Alt to move to a virtual terminal. So make sure you log out of your virtual terminals before walking away from your computer.

Okay, when you've grown weary and bored with this little trick, exit (literally, type exit) to log out of each VT you may have opened and return to the graphical desktop and your bash prompt.

Understanding bash Command Syntax and Structure

Many people happily skip through their Linux use without understanding the fundamentals of commands in the bash shell. Note that this approach makes you lose out on some cool capabilities available in bash. The more you know about how this shell's "language" works, the more interesting things you can do with it.

The basics of using bash at the command prompt often involve typing a command and any of its flags and values. For example, you can enter the ls -la ~ command to see a long-format listing of all files in your home directory, including those that start with a dot (.), which are *hidden files*. That other mysterious squiggle character (~) — technically called a *tilde* — is a bash shortcut character that points to a user's home directory. The ls -la ~ command merely lists the contents of your home directory.

You can break a command into three distinct components:

✔ Command name

✔ Options or flags

✔ Arguments

Consider this example. Start with a simple command. The du command lists the contents of the directory you're now in, along with its subdirectories and how much hard-drive space it takes up, with a total at the end. Try typing just the du command by itself. You see a long listing of files that looks something like this:

```
rich@testbox:~$ du
4        ./.local/share/totem
8        ./.local/share
12       ./.local
4        ./.config/gnome-session/saved-session
8        ./.config/gnome-session
8        ./.config/gtk-2.0
8        ./.config/totem
40       ./.config
44       ./.pulse
```

That's neat, but it probably raises more questions than it answers. The output gives you a long listing of data, but of what? Do those numbers represent bytes, kilobytes, or messages from outer space? To clarify, try adding a simple option to your command:

```
rich@testbox:~$ du -h
4.0K       ./.local/share/totem
8.0K       ./.local/share
12K      ./.local
4.0K        ./.config/gnome-session/saved-session
8.0K        ./.config/gnome-session
8.0K        ./.config/gtk-2.0
8.0K        ./.config/totem
40K       ./.config
44K       ./.pulse
```

You're still issuing the same command, but now you're providing an additional instruction about what you want displayed. The -h option tells du to show you the information in terms that humans can read more easily. Now *M*s, *K*s, and *G*s appear next to the numbers so you can see how big these numbers actually are. But wait — there's more. What if you just want to know the total amount of disk space this directory and its subdirectories are taking up? That calls for the -s flag:

```
rich@testbox:~$ du -s
24064       .
rich@testbox:~$
```

What if you want the total for a different directory? Or just for one of your subdirectories? The following command shows, in a human-readable way, how much hard drive space the Music directory takes up:

```
du -sh ~/Music
```

In this example, du is the command name, -sh indicates the flags (options), and ~/Music is an argument. The -sh flags can be accompanied by many more flags that provide various options applicable to the command.

TIP

Are you wondering where to find all the available options and arguments of a particular command? Most commands offer man pages, which are discussed in the "Using Help" section later in this chapter. Another good place to turn is the --help option, available with many commands. Note that --help displays a terse list of options, but it's nice and quick if you already know about an option but just can't remember exactly which one it is. Try it by entering the following command:

```
du --help
```

Cool, huh?

Starting Programs from the Shell

The most obvious, but perhaps not so apparent, use of the shell is to start other programs. Most utilities you use in Linux are separate and distinct executable programs. Users need a method to start these programs. In the GUI, you can associate an icon with a particular program, and the graphical environment has enough intelligence to start the program. Note that programs often require information drawn from environment variables, which are a part of the shell environment (and which get a more detailed treatment in the section "Working with Variables," later in this chapter). Because the variables are in the shell, the GUI often calls the intended program via the bash shell. So you see, even the GUI finds the shell a necessity — although the GUI does its best to hide this detail from users.

For example, type the following command at the prompt:

```
mahjongg
```

After a few seconds, the Mahjongg game is displayed in the GUI.

You can start any program from the command prompt if you know what the underlying program name is.

WARNING!

If you're in a virtual terminal (which you get to by pressing Alt+F1) rather than the GUI, you may see an error message. Here's why: Some programs require a graphical environment in which to run; a character-based terminal (obviously) doesn't have one.

Putting Wildcard Expansion to Good Use

Computing life would be tedious if you had to repeat the same command on multiple files. After all, aren't repetitive tasks what the computer was designed to do? *Wildcard expansion* refers to the capability of executing one command against many files without having to re-enter the command. The asterisk (*) and the question mark (?) are two wildcard characters that are used to match any filename, or a portion of a filename. For example, you can use the following command to see a long directory listing that includes only files that end with a .doc filename extension:

```
ls -l *.doc
```

The files listed may include resume.doc, cover_letter.doc, and to_editor.doc, for example.

The asterisk wildcard character can match zero or more characters. To match just a single character, use the question mark.

Working with Long Commands

As you become used to the command line, you should find some shortcuts to ease your typing chores. In this section, we show you some features of the bash shell designed to make your life on the command line as pleasant as possible. These features include automatic command-line completion, editing, and using the history of previously entered commands.

Asking Linux to complete a command or filename for you

Considering that you do much more typing on the command line in Linux than you may normally do in a GUI environment, a feature that provides typing shortcuts wherever possible is extremely handy. *Command completion* is a function of the shell that fills in the rest of the filename and system commands you start to type.

The capability of the Linux filesystem to deal with practically unlimited sizes of filenames means that many filenames can become huge. Typing these long filenames can become cumbersome and error-prone. Fortunately, with command completion, typing a command or a long filename is short work.

You may want to use command completion in two situations: to enter a command or to complete a filename.

Completing a command

Suppose that you want to type a command, but you can remember only that it begins with the letters up and is supposed to return the length of time that has passed since the system was rebooted. Type up at the command prompt and then press Tab:

```
rich@testbox:~$ up[TAB]
```

One of two things happens:

✔ If only one matching command is in the *search path* (directory locations for searching for programs; type echo $PATH to find out what yours is), your command line is completed with that command, and the system waits for you to press Enter to execute the command.

✔ If you hear a beep, it means that more than one command begins with up. Simply press Tab a second time, and all the possibilities are displayed. Locate the command on the list and continue typing it until the first letters are unique — at which point you can press the Tab key to complete the command. If nothing is displayed after you press Tab twice, there's no match at all.

Completing a filename

Command-line completion isn't only for commands; if you're typing a filename on your command line, you only need to type the first few characters and then press Tab. The shell usually searches the current working directory for filenames that match what you have typed and subsequently completes the filename on the command line. This feature behaves the same way as the command-completion feature in that, if more than one file contains the letters you type, you hear a beep and need to press Tab again to see a list of choices.

It takes a little getting used to, but after you have control of the Tab key and the shell command-line completion feature, you may wonder how you ever got along without it.

Accessing your command history

It's nice of the shell to remember what you have done, for better or worse. Having the shell keep track of the commands you enter makes it easy to return to those gawd-awfully long commands you pecked at a while ago — even days ago! Suppose that yesterday you managed to issue a command to find all the *core dump* files in your system (massive files containing debugging data that only an expert programmer or your computer can understand) and delete them. The command looked something like this:

```
find / -name core -exec rm {} \;
```

To re-execute the command, all you need to do is fish it out of your shell history and rerun it. The simplest way to do that (if you're repeating the exact same version of the command you used last time, which in this case would be the find command) is to add an exclamation mark in front of the command. Just type !find and press Enter. Doing so tells your system to look through your history and rerun the last instance of find in the list.

On the other hand, if you have run the find command more than once and want to make sure that you're re-executing the right version, you need to read through your command history. Type history at the command prompt, and your last 20 lines appear. Press the up-arrow key repeatedly until you locate the command you want to re-execute. Then just press the Enter key to run the command again.

If you want to see a longer list of past commands, use the cat command to view the contents of the file ~/.bash_history.

Working with Variables

Variables in the bash shell are words or strings of text that computers use to represent a piece of data. An example of using a variable is setting the variable fruit to contain the text apple. A number of standard variables contain information about your account and environment settings.

Variables versus environment variables

The first thing you need to know is that the bash shell has two types of variables:

- ✔ **Variables:** A variable can be referenced in a program or shell session, but it's visible and available to only that session or program.

- ✔ **Environment variables:** An environment variable can also be referenced by the shell or program. However, it has an added behavior: Its value is copied to any other program or shell created from its environment.

You can usually tell at a glance the difference between a variable and an environment variable in bash. The normal convention is to name local variables in all lowercase characters, like this, or in mixed-case characters, Like This. An environment variable, however, is usually always in all uppercase letters, LIKE THIS.

Checking out commonly used environment variables

The bash shell has many environment variables. You may be amazed at the range of items these variables store. The handy thing is that you can change anything that's stored in a variable to suit your needs. Table 17-1 lists the environment variables you're most likely to want to work with.

Table 17-1	Commonly Used bash Environment Variables	
Environment Variable	**Purpose**	**Value**
HISTSIZE	Determines the number of previously typed commands that are stored.	Number of commands
HOME	Sets the location of your home directory.	The path to your home directory
MAILCHECK	Sets how often the bash shell checks for new mail in your mailbox. If mail has arrived, you see a message similar to You have new mail the next time you do something at the command prompt.	Number of seconds to wait between checks
PATH	Sets the directories that bash looks in, and set the order to look in them to find a program name you type at the command prompt.	Colon-separated directories
PS1	Sets your command prompt.	Command and formatting characters used to form the prompt

Most environment variables are established for you by the system Administrator or perhaps by the shell itself. These variables are mostly read by programs to gather information. You don't need to change their values —

but you may want to alter the value of some environment variables. For example, in Table 17-1, the first entry, HISTSIZE, determines the number of lines of command-line history that are kept on file. By setting a higher number for HISTSIZE, you can save an even longer list of previously executed commands.

Storing and retrieving variables' values

To assign a value to a variable, you just type your chosen variable's name, followed by an equal sign (=), followed by the value you want to store:

```
MyVariable=MyValue
```

To retrieve the value represented by that variable, you need to precede the variable name with a dollar sign ($). Look (for example) at a variable created by the shell, which determines what your prompt looks like: PS1. First, you view the value being held in PS1:

```
echo $PS1
```

You likely see something like the following line:

```
[\u@\h \W]\$
```

Each of the characters preceded by a backslash represents a special instruction to the shell to return specific information when the shell prompt is referenced. Table 17-2 shows you examples of special slash characters you can use to customize your prompt.

Table 17-2	Pieces of the PS1 Puzzle
Component	*Result*
\!	Prints the position of the command in your history list.
\#	Prints the number of commands you've used during the current shell session.
\$	Prints a $ for user accounts or a # for the superuser.
\d	Prints the date in the following format: *day month date*.
\h	Prints the name of the machine you're logged in to.
\n	Moves down to the next line.
\s	Prints bash for the bash shell.

Component	Result
\t	Prints the time in 24-hour format.
\u	Prints your username.
\w	Prints the lowest current directory level.
\W	Prints the entire current directory.

Okay, on with the example: To change your shell prompt to something more amusing, enter the following line:

```
PS1='Hello \u, what can I do for you? => '
```

Note the single quotes ('). Immediately after pressing the Enter key, you see that your prompt has changed into something more inviting. Don't worry if you'd rather have the original prompt; you can either reassign the original prompt's value (which is stored in PS1) or close the terminal window and open a new one. Either way, you're back to familiar territory.

Are you wondering which other variables your system has in store for you? You can view all environment variables at one time by typing env. Note that you may not have any reason to access variables on the command line during casual Linux use. After you get more proficient, however, you may want to journey into the shell-programming capabilities of bash — in which variable storage comes in handy, just as it does in any computer-programming language.

What's with those single quotes? You have to be careful of some details when changing environment variables. If you're just assigning something to a number, you could just use, for example, HISTSIZE=250. However, if you want to use something with spaces in it, you have to use quotes. Which kind of quotes you use — single or double — depends on what else you want to do.

If you want to display *exactly* what you have specified, use single quotes to create a *literal text string*. For example, type the following line at a command prompt:

```
echo 'Hello, my name is $USER'
```

The output gives you this:

```
Hello, my name is $USER
```

Kinda goofy, huh?

Take a look at a different kind of string that the shell interprets differently: an *interpolated string*. An *interpolated* value is one in which the shell interprets special characters before processing the value. Rather than using single quotes, this time you use the same example with double quotes:

```
echo "Hello, my name is $USER"
```

Notice what the output is this time:

```
Hello, my name is rich
```

Instead of displaying the exact text you provided, the shell replaces the variable name, designated with a dollar sign, with the actual value stored in that variable.

Why did you use single quotes in the first example but double quotes with the second one? The items with the backslashes (\) are *interpreted* one way or another. However, if you use double quotes, they're interpreted only once, so the item that lists what directory you're in changes only the first time. If you use single quotes, the variables are interpreted every time you do something.

If you're going to play around with environment variables, start by using the methods we discuss in this section. After you're comfortable with any changes you have made, you can make your changes permanent by opening the `~/.bashrc` file and adding the same text there. The next time you log in, the changes go into effect. You can make changes for all your users' profiles in `/etc/profile` as well.

If you experiment heavily with these files, create a separate user account so that you can do whatever you want without messing up your own login. This advice especially goes for `/etc/profile`. You can damage everyone's logins with this one! To create a separate `/etc/profile`, you can make a backup by typing `cp /etc/profile /etc/profile.original`. Then edit `/etc/profile` all you like, knowing that you can always delete it with the `rm` command and use the `mv` command to rename `/etc/profile.original` to `/etc/profile`.

To create an environment variable from scratch, you typically name it with all capital letters and then you have to export it — like this, for example:

```
CUSTOMVAR="new variable"
export CUSTOMVAR
```

Don't be too discouraged if you don't understand all this variable stuff right now. As you become more proficient with Linux, you should explore *shell scripting*. Shell scripting is the art of creating computer programs with just the shell. Most Linux and UNIX administrators speak shell-script language as easily as you and I speak our native tongues.

Using Redirection and Pipes

Redirection and pipes facilitate the flow of information. A *pipe* is exactly what it sounds like: It directs the output of one program to the input of another program. A pipeline may consist of several utilities plumbed together by pipes. At either end of this pipeline is, optionally, a redirection.

Almost all Linux utilities that require input and output have been plumbed with the following common interfaces: stdin (standard input), stdout (standard output), and stderr (standard error). By having a common method to feed input to a program or read data from the output of a program, you can glue utilities together into sophisticated solutions.

Redirecting command output

We discuss redirecting command output here because it's by far the most common form of information detouring. One example of *output redirection* involves telling a command to send its results to a file rather than to the screen, as you've probably been used to seeing. Start in some familiar territory by typing ls -l and then pressing Enter, to produce something like the following:

```
rich@testbox:~$ ls -l
total 36
drwxr-xr-x 2 rich rich 4096 2009-05-20 18:56 Desktop
drwxr-xr-x 2 rich rich 4096 2009-05-17 14:09 Documents
drwxr-xr-x 4 rich rich 4096 2009-05-17 17:42 GNUstep
drwxr-xr-x 2 rich rich 4096 2009-05-17 14:09 Music
drwxr-xr-x 2 rich rich 4096 2009-05-17 14:09 Pictures
drwxr-xr-x 2 rich rich 4096 2009-05-17 14:09 Public
drwxr-xr-x 2 rich rich 4096 2009-05-17 14:09 Templates
drwxr-xr-x 2 rich rich 4096 2009-05-17 14:09 Videos
rich@testbox:~$
```

Want to send this information to a file instead? You can use the > redirection operator to tell bash to send the data into a file rather than onto your screen. Enter the following command to send the information to a file named listing:

```
ls -l > listing
```

Notice that nothing shows up on-screen, where normally you'd expect to see the output from the ls command. That's because the shell has rerouted the output to a file named listing. To verify that the directory listing is there, enter the following command:

```
cat listing
```

The cat command (and more) is explained in Appendix A.

Note that if you type ls -l > listing again, the data is overwritten, meaning that the file's contents are wiped out and replaced with the new output. You can avoid this situation by using >> as your redirection operator, which tells bash to add the command's output to the end of the specified file. If you type ls -l >> listing in the same directory after making no changes, the contents of listing are as follows:

```
rich@testbox:~$ ls -l
total 36
drwxr-xr-x 2 rich rich 4096 2009-05-20 18:56 Desktop
drwxr-xr-x 2 rich rich 4096 2009-05-17 14:09 Documents
drwxr-xr-x 4 rich rich 4096 2009-05-17 17:42 GNUstep
drwxr-xr-x 2 rich rich 4096 2009-05-17 14:09 Music
drwxr-xr-x 2 rich rich 4096 2009-05-17 14:09 Pictures
drwxr-xr-x 2 rich rich 4096 2009-05-17 14:09 Public
drwxr-xr-x 2 rich rich 4096 2009-05-17 14:09 Templates
drwxr-xr-x 2 rich rich 4096 2009-05-17 14:09 Videos
rich@testbox:~$
rich@testbox:~$ ls -l
total 36
drwxr-xr-x 2 rich rich 4096 2009-05-20 18:56 Desktop
drwxr-xr-x 2 rich rich 4096 2009-05-17 14:09 Documents
drwxr-xr-x 4 rich rich 4096 2009-05-17 17:42 GNUstep
drwxr-xr-x 2 rich rich 4096 2009-05-17 14:09 Music
drwxr-xr-x 2 rich rich 4096 2009-05-17 14:09 Pictures
drwxr-xr-x 2 rich rich 4096 2009-05-17 14:09 Public
drwxr-xr-x 2 rich rich 4096 2009-05-17 14:09 Templates
drwxr-xr-x 2 rich rich 4096 2009-05-17 14:09 Videos
rich@testbox:~$
```

Laying pipes

Another bash shell feature enables you to connect commands so that the output of one becomes the input for the next one. This feature is referred to as a *pipe*. Suppose you want to look over the details of all the files in the / etc directory in long-listing format. If you type ls -la /etc to do so, a massive listing appears, and much of the information scrolls right past you. Although you can back up a bit by pressing Shift+PageUp, you may not be able to see everything you want to see.

To see all the information, you can do one of two things:

✔ Send the data to a file with redirection by typing something like ls -l /etc > ~/etclisting — and then review the contents of ~/etclisting with your favorite editor.

✔ Pipe the output to the `more` command (see Appendix A) so you can view it on-screen one page at a time.

To pipe the output to `more`, type `ls -la` *directory_path* | `more`, where *directory_path* is the directory for which you want to list the contents. The | symbol (which on the keyboard looks more like two vertical bars stacked on top of each other than just one solid line) tells `bash` that you want to use a pipe.

Using Help

The *man page* system is the electronic manual for Linux (*man* is short for *man*ual), designed to provide users with a convenient reference to all the detailed command information. This information includes command-prompt options, file formats, and program function usage.

The syntax for opening a `man` page is `man` *<command name>*.

Don't know the command you're looking for or need basic information about using the `man` page system? Just type `man man` to get started. When you're finished reading the man page, press Q to exit.

Clearing the Screen

The `clear` and `reset` commands are handy to know about when you're working in a shell. The `clear` command simply wipes the `bash` screen clean. Don't worry — it doesn't delete any files or change any settings — it just tidies up so you can start dumping new stuff to the screen again.

The `reset` command is a little more interesting. Suppose you try listing a binary file to the screen with the `cat` command. After the computer finishes displaying the result of executing the `cat` command on a binary file, you may get lucky and still be able to read your prompt. More likely, your prompt has been rendered into box characters of no special meaning, and typing on the keyboard gives you more of the same. To get back to normal, just type `reset` and press Enter. Note that it doesn't look like you're typing the word `reset`, but rest assured that the computer understands the series of characters; after a couple of seconds, it should restore your shell environment to your native language.

Chapter 18

Basic System Administration

After one look at this planet any visitor from outer space would say "I want to see the manager."

— William S. Burroughs

Okay, so you have your Linux system running exactly the way you want it, with just the right combination of software packages installed. You're writing documents, creating fancy graphics, listening to music CDs, and even playing games. But don't sit back and relax: There's still more left to do.

You'll always need to tweak things on your system — whether you're allowing other people to use it, installing a new printer, or trying to figure out why a software program is running so slow (yes, even Linux programs can go bad sometimes). Keeping everything in order and running properly can be a full-time job. Even for a home Linux system, you may need to manage several user accounts and printers, as well as keep track of over a dozen programs running on the system.

Linux provides a few tools that help in the management process. No doubt you've seen the Administration section in the menu area on your desktop (see Chapters 4 and 5). Some of the items are fairly self-explanatory, such as Date and Time settings, Display settings, Keyboard settings, and the Language setting. However, other items aren't quite as easy to figure out how to use. This chapter walks through a few of the administration tools Ubuntu and Fedora provide to help make running your system a little easier.

Managing Users and Groups

Whether you support a Linux system with hundreds of users or you just have a user account for you and one for your cat, you need to know how to manage user accounts. Most Linux distributions include some graphical tool to help you manage your user accounts.

There are a few different user-management tools floating around the Linux world, but they all pretty much work the same way. Instead of trying to confuse the issue and describe different tools, we take you through a guided tour of how the Fedora User Manager tool operates. That should give you an idea of how to deal with user accounts using whatever tool your Linux distribution provides.

If you use the User Manager tool in Ubuntu, there is one oddity you should be aware of: By default, it only allows you to edit your own user account properties. To modify other user accounts or create new user accounts, you have to click the Unlock button to open the entire interface.

Choose System⇨Administration⇨Users and Groups from the GNOME desktop to start the User Manager tool in Fedora. If you aren't already logged in as the root user, enter the root user's password. The main User Manager window appears, as shown in Figure 18-1.

The main window contains two tabbed panes — one for managing users and the other for managing user groups — plus several helpful buttons in the toolbar.

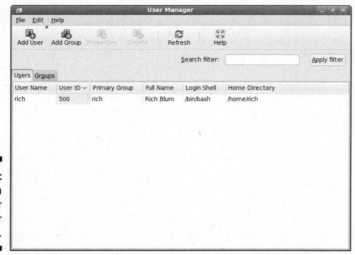

Figure 18-1:
The Fedora
User
Manager
tool.

The menu bar provides access to the same features available on the toolbar, plus one additional feature: preferences. Choose Edit⇨Preferences to open the Preferences dialog box, as shown in Figure 18-2.

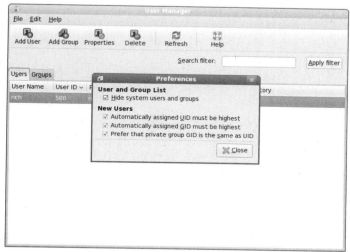

This dialog box contains settings that control the behavior of the User Manager tool itself:

- **Hide System Users and Groups:** The Fedora system requires a lot of additional usernames to control background system programs. Messing with these user and group accounts isn't recommended, so hiding them helps clean up the user's viewing area, and also helps prevent accidents from happening (such as deleting an important system user account).

- **Automatically Assigned UID Must Be Highest:** Fedora assigns each user account a unique *User ID number* (UID). The User Manager is more than happy to assign UIDs automatically to new users, or you can choose to assign your own UIDs manually. This setting ensures that if the User Manager assigns UIDs, the numbers are in order after the UIDs for any accounts you've already created. It's safe to keep this value set unless you're doing your own UID assigning.

- **Automatically Assigned GID Must Be Highest:** Fedora also assigns each group a unique *Group ID number* (GID). This setting ensures that any automatically assigned group numbers are in order at the end of the list. Again, it's okay to keep this setting enabled.

- **Prefer that Private Group GID Is the Same as UID:** This feature ensures that each user account's UID is the same number as the assigned Group ID. This helps simplify user management by ensuring that each user account belongs to its own group with the same number.

After you set your preferences for the User Manager tool, you're ready to actually start managing users and groups.

Adding new users

When you first installed Fedora, it created a user account for you. That account has its own home folder for storing files. If you are in an environment where others will use the same system, it's a good idea to create separate user accounts for each user. That way you don't have to worry about the cat accidentally deleting your important documents.

If you need to add additional user accounts, here's what you need to do:

1. **Click the Add User button.**

   The Create New User dialog box opens, as shown in Figure 18-3.

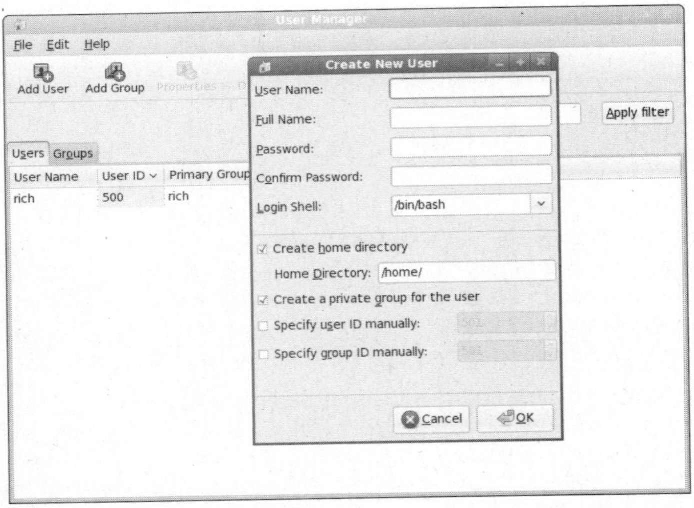

Figure 18-3:
The Create New User dialog box in the User Manager tool.

2. **Type a username for the user in the User Name text box. Type the full name of the user for documentation purposes in the Full Name text box.**

3. **Type a password for the user in the Password text box, and then retype it in the Confirm Password text box.**

For security, you should always use passwords that aren't common words, that contain a mixture of numbers and upper- and lowercase letters, and that are a minimum of eight characters long.

4. **Select a login shell for the user.**

Fedora Linux supports several different login shells; each allows you to work with text commands and scripts (see Chapter 17 for help with working with the login shell). The default login shell in Linux is the *Bourne-again shell*, called `bash`. Using this default is just fine.

5. **Create a home directory for the user.**

By default, the User Manager tool creates a directory in which the new user can store personal files — located under the `/home` folder, and named with the user account name. You can elect to not create a `/home` directory, or to create one in an alternative location. Unless you're running a huge data center that relocates `/home` folders to another disk drive, the suggested default location is just fine.

6. **Create a private group for the user.**

Each user must belong to a default group. Some Linux distributions create a single group that contains all users. By default, Fedora creates a unique group for each user, ensuring that users can't accidentally share files. It's fine to allow Fedora to do that.

7. **Specify a User ID manually.**

By default, the User Manager tool automatically assigns a UID for the new user account. If you prefer to use your own numbering system for UIDs, you can assign your own UID here.

8. **Click OK to create the new user.**

After the new user account is created, it appears in the user list under the Users tab.

Modifying existing users

A few user account settings are not assigned when you create a new account. You can get to those from the User Properties dialog box as follows:

1. **Either double-click a user account listed in the Users tab, or select the user account and click the Properties button on the toolbar.**

The User Properties dialog box appears, as shown in Figure 18-4.

Figure 18-4:
The User
Properties
dialog box
in the User
Manager
tool.

2. **Alter data on the User Data tab.**

   The User Data tab contains the same fields as shown in the Create User dialog box. You can alter the username, full name, home directory, or login shell here, as well as change the password for the user account.

3. **Click the Account Info tab to set an account expiration date or lock the account.**

   The expiration date doesn't mean the user has expired; only the login account has. The account's expiration date locks (but doesn't delete) the account when the date is reached, and the user is unable to log in. If you suspect unauthorized activity from this user account, you can also lock the account manually, preventing the user from logging in, but keeping the account still configured on the system.

4. **Click the Password Info tab to force password-expiration rules.**

   This section allows you to set whether users must change their passwords. There are fields for how many days can pass before users have to change their passwords, how many days before password expiration that the user is warned, and how many days after the password-change date the account is locked if the password is not changed.

5. **Click the Groups tab to assign the user account to additional groups.**

   When a user account is created, Fedora automatically creates a unique group for the user by default. Here's where you can assign the user account to other groups as well. All the groups defined on the system appear within the tab. Select each group the user account should belong to. You can also change the primary group the user account belongs to (by default, it's the same name as the user account).

6. **Click OK to accept any changes made to the user account.**

Any changes made to the user account take effect immediately. However, if you've added a user to a new group, permissions often don't work properly until the user has logged out and then back in again.

Deleting a user account

Although it's quite an ordeal to add a new user account, removing user accounts is a snap. Just select the user account you want to remove from the Users tab list, and then click the Delete button in the toolbar. A simple message appears, asking whether you're sure of your selection. After double-checking to make sure you're deleting the correct account, click Yes.

Adding new groups

Groups help you manage access to files and folders on the system. Each file and folder contains three sets of permissions — one set for the owner, another set for the group the file or folder is assigned to, and the last set for all other users on the system. By assigning a file or folder to a special group, you can allow all users that belong to that group to have full access to the file or folder.

Here's what you'll need to do to create a group in User Manager:

1. **Click the Add Group icon on the toolbar.**

   The Create New Group dialog box opens, as shown in Figure 18-5.

2. **Type the name of the new group in the Group Name text box.**

3. **Select the check box if you want to specify the Group ID manually.**

   By default, User Manager automatically assigns a unique Group ID number (GID) to the new group. If you prefer to use your own GIDs, select the check box, and then select an available GID from the drop-down list.

4. **Click OK to accept the settings and create the group.**

The new group is created, and it appears in the group listing on the Groups tab in the User Manager window.

Figure 18-5:
The Create
New Group
dialog box
in the User
Manager
tool.

Modifying groups

When you've created a new group, most likely you'll want to add some users to the group. (What good is a group with no members?) Do so by using the Properties dialog box:

1. **Double-click the group name from the Group tab, or select the group name from the listing and click the Properties button.**

   The Group Properties dialog box appears, as shown in Figure 18-6.

2. **Click the Group Data tab to rename the group.**

   If you want to rename an existing group while keeping the same GID, enter the new name in the Group Name text box.

3. **Click the Group Users tab to add users to the group.**

   The Group Users tab contains a drop-down list of all the configured users on the system (even hidden user accounts used by the system). Select the check box for each user you want to add to the group.

4. **Click OK to apply the changes to the group.**

You see any newly added user accounts appear on the Groups tab under the group name.

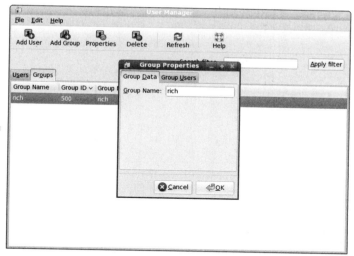

Figure 18-6:
The Group
Properties
dialog box
in the User
Manager
tool.

Setting Up Printers

Even though technology gurus keep predicting a paperless society, for now, we're still stuck having to print some things. In the past, printing was one of the dark areas in Linux. Trying to get modern printers working with Linux was quite the challenge. Over the last few years, however, some amazing advances have made Linux more printer-friendly.

Possibly the biggest advance in printing has been the Common UNIX Printing System (CUPS). CUPS provides a common interface between UNIX (and Linux) systems and printers. It runs in the background as a service, connecting to any defined printers, and waiting for applications to send print jobs. Because it runs in the background, it can talk with remote printers *and* accept print jobs from remote systems.

The Printer Configuration tool provides an easy way to configure both the CUPS server running on the system and any printers you've defined. Both Ubuntu and Fedora include the Printer Configuration tool to help you get a handle on your printing situation.

Choose System➪Administration➪Printing from the desktop menu to start the Printer Configuration tool on the GNOME desktop for both Ubuntu and Fedora. In the KDE desktop, choose Administration➪Printing. The main Printer Configuration window appears, as shown in Figure 18-7.

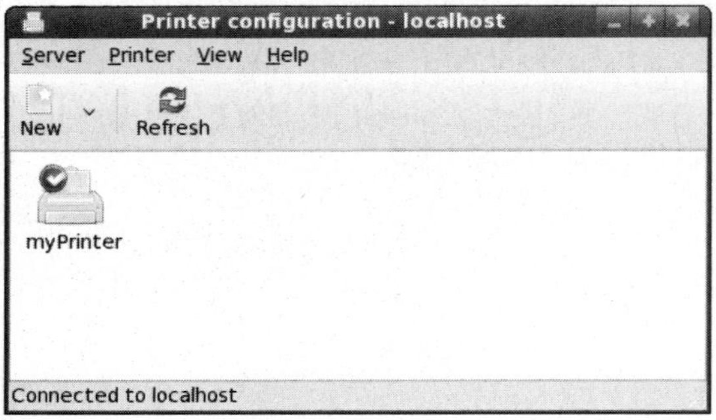

Figure 18-7:
The Printer
Configur-
ation
window.

You can control two settings from the Printer Configuration window:

- **Server Settings:** Use these to control how the CUPS server manages system printing features.

- **Local Printers:** Here you can change individual printer properties of all locally defined printers on the system.

The main window area displays icons for the local printers that you've configured (or that have been automatically detected by Linux). The New button on the toolbar provides two options for you:

- **New Printer:** Starts a simple wizard to guide you through adding a new printer to the system.

- **New Class:** Starts another simple wizard that guides you through grouping configured printers together to form a printer pool (called a *print class* in CUPS). Sending print jobs to a print class enables the job to be printed by any available printer in the class.

If you already have a printer defined in your system, right-click on the printer icon to access these features:

- **Properties:** Allows you to set features for the printer.

- **Rename:** Changes the system name of the printer.

- **Copy:** Copies an existing local printer definition to create another printer of the same make and model.

- **Delete:** Deletes an existing printer.

- **Enabled:** Allows print jobs to be serviced by the printer when checked.

- **Shared:** When checked, this feature advertises the printer on the network for other Linux workstations using CUPS to connect to.

- **View Print Queue:** Lists the print jobs waiting to be printed by the printer.

The following sections describe how to use the Printer Configuration window to set the CUPS and printer properties for your system.

Printer server settings

Choose Server⇨Settings to get to the Basic Server Settings window, shown in Figure 18-8.

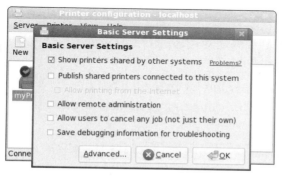

Figure 18-8: The Printer Configuration Basic Server Settings window.

There are a few different settings you can play with here to help out with your printer administration:

- ✔ **Show Printers Shared by Other Systems:** Displays printers found by browsing the network.

- ✔ **Publish Shared Printers Connected to This System:** Allows remote clients to connect to any of the local printers marked as shared (more on that later).

- ✔ **Allow Remote Administration:** Enables remote clients to connect to the CUPS server running on this system.

- ✔ **Allow Users to Cancel Any Job (Not Just Their Own):** By default, normal users can only cancel their own print jobs. Enabling this feature allows any user to cancel any *other* user's print job. Although this feature is handy, it can get dangerous in a huge multiuser environment (especially if your users like playing tricks on one another).

- ✔ **Save Debugging Information for Troubleshooting:** By default, the CUPS server generates a moderate amount of logging information to monitor usage or problems. If you're having trouble with a specific printer configuration, you can enable this feature to produce more (*lots* more) information in the log files.

After determining the settings appropriate for your CUPS server environment, you can move on to creating the individual local printer accounts.

Adding a new printer

One amazing feature of Fedora and Ubuntu is their automatic detection of printers connected via USB and parallel port cables. If you have one of these printers, you most likely don't need to add it to the system. It's automatically listed under the Local Printers listing. You can just move on to the next section to configure it.

If you're not fortunate enough to have a USB-connected printer, you have to add your printer manually. Here are the steps for doing that:

1. **Click the New Printer button on the toolbar.**

   The New Printer Wizard appears, as shown in Figure 18-9.

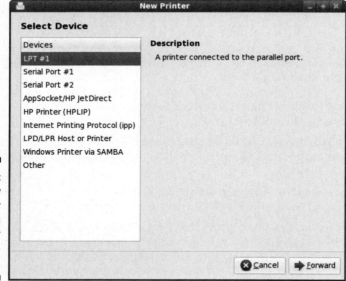

Figure 18-9: The New Printer Wizard in the Printer Configuration tool.

2. **Select the connection type of the new printer.**

   Although the printer is defined as a local printer, this utility also allows you to configure the types of printer connections listed in Table 18-1 to make a printer available to the system.

Table 18-1	Fedora Printer Connection Types
Connection Type	**Description**
LPT#1	A printer connected via the 25-pin LPT port on the local computer.
Serial Port #1	A printer connected via a 9- or 25-pin serial port on the local computer.
AppSocket/HP JetDirect	A printer connected directly to the network, using a network card and Internet software.
HP Printer (HPLIP)	A network printer using the proprietary HP network protocol.
Internet Printing Protocol (IPP)	A remote CUPS system, advertising local printers that can be used remotely.
LPD/LPR Host or Printer	An older UNIX standard for sharing local printers remotely.
Windows Printer via Samba	A Microsoft Windows workstation or server that advertises shared local printers.
Other	A specific Universal Resource Identifier (URI) used to map to a network printer.

As you select each connection type in the left side of the window, a different Properties area appears in the right side. For example, if you select the Windows Printer via Samba connections, text boxes appear in which you can enter the printer name, along with a User ID and the password required to access the network printer.

3. **Change any Properties settings, and then click Forward to continue on with the wizard.**

4. **Select the printer manufacturer or the location of the PPD file. Click Forward when you're done.**

CUPS uses standard Postscript Printer Description (PPD) files to handle formatting print for printers. These use the same concept as the standard printer drivers for Microsoft Windows that you're probably used to. Each printer must have a PPD installed for CUPS to know how to format text and graphics sent to the printer.

This wizard window allows you to select the PPD file to use for the new printer. You have three choices:

- Select the printer manufacturer from the list of installed drivers.

- Select to install your own provided PPD file for the printer.

- Search the Internet for a PPD file to download.

If you're lucky enough to have the PPD file for your printer, copy it to a location on your Linux system and then select the Provide PPD file option. Browse to the location of the file and select it.

If you don't have the PPD file for your printer, you can try to search the standard repositories for one. If you find the printer manufacturer listed, select it.

5. **If you selected a printer manufacturer, the next wizard window provides a list of specific printer models and PPD files. Select the printer model and (optionally) the proper PPD file. Click Forward when you're done.**

This wizard window asks you to select the specific model type for your printer. Hopefully your printer model is listed. If not, you must go back a step and find your own PPD file to install.

If your specific model is listed, select it, and a list of available PPD files is shown. Some models may only have one PPD file, but others may have two or more files to choose from. In that case, one is usually marked as recommended. Try that first: If it doesn't work, select a different PPD file.

6. **Create a unique name for the printer, and (optionally) enter a description and location. Click Apply on the summary window to create the new printer account.**

The new printer is added to the list of local printers (even if you mapped to a remote printer). You now see the new printer when printing from applications on your system.

Modifying printer properties

You can modify the properties of any printer on the system (whether Linux created it automatically or you created it manually). Right-click the printer you want to configure in the window, and then select Properties from the menu. The Printer Properties window appears, as shown in Figure 18-10.

There are five different areas that contain printer information you can modify. Those areas are Settings, Policies, Access Control, Printer Options, and Job Options. In the next few sections, we take a closer look at each.

If you make any changes in the Printer Properties dialog box, don't forget to click either Apply or OK to make the changes permanent.

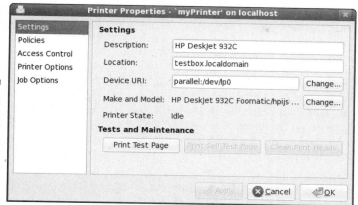

Settings

The Settings area provides some basic settings you can change for the printer. From here, you can change the description and location tags for the printer, the URI of the printer, and the PPD file used for the printer.

Under the settings are three buttons to help you test and maintain the printer: Print Test Page, Print Self-Test Page, and Clean Print Heads.

Policies

The Policies area contains three check boxes, plus four policies (or rules) that control printer behavior. The three check boxes enable you to control the state of the printer:

- ✔ **Enabled:** Allows you to take the printer offline if there's a problem.
- ✔ **Accepting Jobs:** Allows you to suspend the processing of print jobs temporarily.
- ✔ **Shared:** Allows you to set whether this printer is a shared resource on the network.

Two of the policies control banner pages for print jobs; the other two control how the printer operates:

- ✔ **Banner pages** allow you to print a special page describing the print job.
- ✔ The **Starting Banner** is a special page that prints before the print job begins; this option allows you to print a cover sheet for your print job. Theoretically it's supposed to provide some privacy, blocking people from seeing the first page of the job as the printer prints it, but really, who wouldn't just look under the banner page?

✔ The **Ending Banner** page allows you to print an ending page marking the end of the print job. If you're in a high-print-volume environment where lots of print jobs are pouring out of the printer, having a starting or ending banner helps keep everyone's print jobs separate.

There are two operation policies that you can set:

✔ **Error Policy:** Determines how the printer reacts to an error in the printing process. The choices are Abort the Print Job (giving up all hope of printing the job), Retry the Print Job (possibly trying again after manual intervention), and Stop the Printer (preventing all other print jobs from printing).

✔ **Operation Policy:** Determines the mode the printer runs in. At this time, the only setting for this option is the default.

Access Control

The Access Control area provides a method you can use to restrict access to the printer. There are two ways to do this:

✔ You can list every user account that the server will prevent from using the printer. This assumes that any user account not on the list can print, and any user account on the list can't print.

✔ You can list the user accounts that are allowed to use the printer. This assumes that any user account that isn't on the list can't print.

Obviously, which one of these you choose depends on whether you want to allow or restrict more people from printing.

Printer Options

The Printer Options area allows you to set some properties for the physical printer setup. The properties available for you to modify are based on information provided by the individual printer's PPD file and depend on the physical characteristics of the printer.

These properties are divided into separate categories, depending on the printer's capabilities. The options available for a printer are shown in Figure 18-11.

The General settings handle properties such as what types of paper the printer can handle, the print qualities it can produce, and the number and types of input trays. You can force the printer server to request a specific paper size for all print jobs, or even request which paper tray to take paper from.

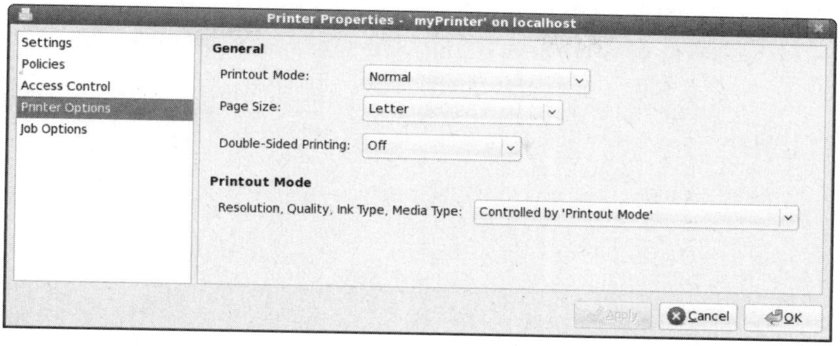

Figure 18-11:
The Printer
Options
area of
the Printer
Configur-
ation tool.

The Printout Mode setting specifies the default print quality used by the printer. Again, this setting depends on the capabilities of the particular printer, but usually there's a range of dots-per-inch (DPI) settings and color settings for you to choose from. A lower DPI number saves toner; a higher DPI number produces a higher print quality.

Job Options

The Job Options area allows you to set the default properties for print jobs sent to the printer. When you request an application to send something to the printer, a standard GNOME Print dialog box appears, as shown in Figure 18-12.

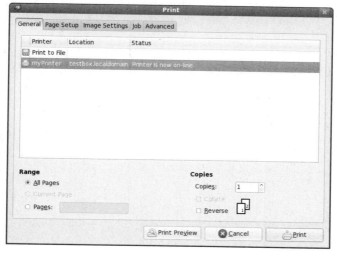

Figure 18-12:
The
standard
GNOME
Print dialog
box.

You can select several printing properties for the specific print job, such as whether to print in landscape mode, how many copies of the document to print, the paper size to use, and so on. If you prefer to use any of these settings by default, you can specify your preference in Job Options back in the Printer Configuration tool.

The process of setting Job Options is somewhat odd:

1. **In the Job Options area, enter the job option in the Other Options text box at the bottom of the window.**

2. **Click the Add button to add it to the list of available options to modify.**

3. **Change the default values for the option.**

The completed list of options appears within the Printer Properties window, as shown in Figure 18-13.

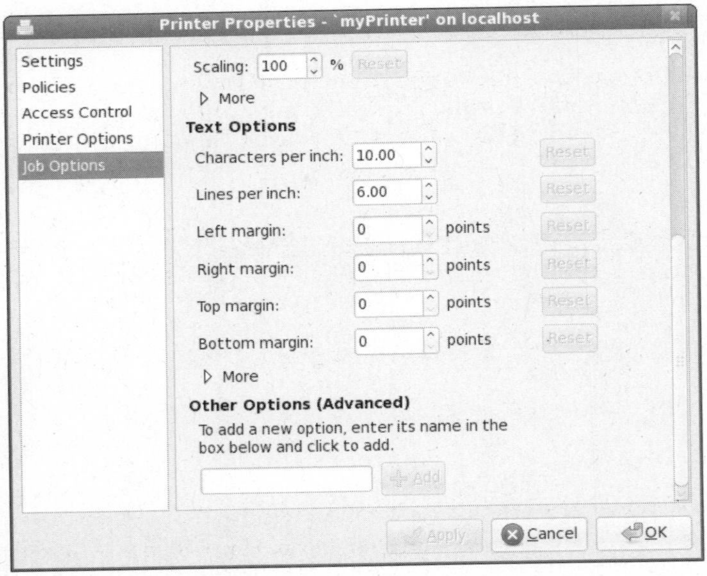

Figure 18-13: Job Options in the Printer Configuration tool.

If you decide to revert to the default setting for an option, click the Reset button. The option is removed from the options list.

Checking Out the System Monitor

Although things usually go well on Linux systems, sometimes applications can go awry. When that happens, it's handy to be able to watch what's going on under the hood of the operating system.

The System Monitor tool provides information about how the system hardware and software are working. It's often included by Linux distributions to provide a graphical peek at your system. Both Ubuntu and Fedora include this feature by default.

To start the System Monitor tool, choose System⇨Administration⇨System Monitor in Ubuntu, or choose Applications⇨System Tools⇨System Monitor in Fedora. The System Monitor includes four tabs:

✓ **System:** Shows the hostname, hardware information, and system status (available space on the hard drive).

✓ **Processes:** Shows information about programs currently running on the system.

✓ **Resources:** Shows information about CPU and memory usage.

✓ **File Systems:** Shows information about what hard drives are mounted on the system.

Of course, just having a bunch of information thrown at you doesn't help at all. You need to know what that information means so you can decide what to do about it. The following sections help you understand how to interpret the various pieces of information contained in the System Monitor.

Processes

Clicking the Processes tab provides an overview of the programs currently running on the system, as shown in Figure 18-14.

Processes — the Linux term for programs running on the system — are shown in a table format. The default view shows all the processes that are currently being run by your user account. Alternatively, you can watch all the processes — or just the ones that are actively working — by choosing View from the menu bar and selecting which option you want to view. You can base a sort of the table rows on any of the table columns; for example, to see what processes are using the largest percent of CPU time, click the % CPU column heading. The System Monitor sorts the rows automatically by percentage of CPU usage.

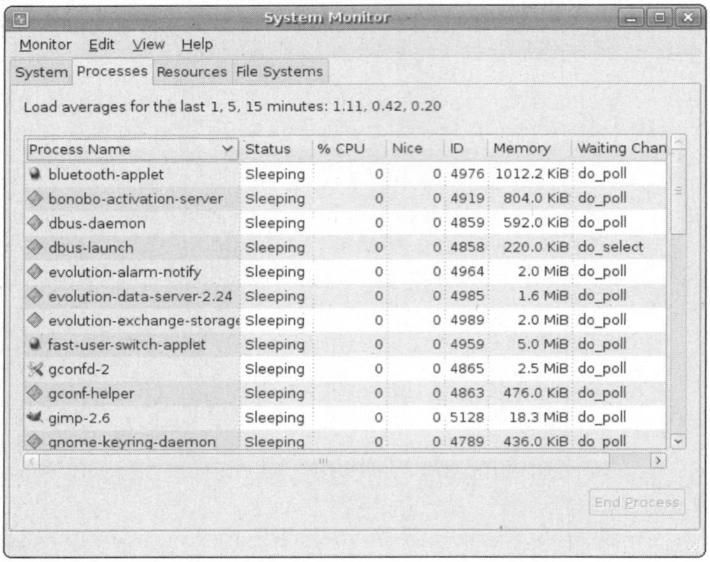

Figure 18-14:
The
Processes
tab in the
System
Monitor
tool.

Other columns are available for you to add. Choose Edit➪Preferences to open the Preferences dialog box for the Processes tab. Table 18-2 lists the data available to display in the Processes tab.

Table 18-2	System Monitor Process Table Columns
Column	*Description*
Process Name	The program name of the running process.
User	The owner of the process.
Status	The status (either sleeping or running) of the process.
Virtual Memory	The amount of virtual system memory allocated for the process.
Resident Memory	The amount of physical memory allocated for the process.
Writable Memory	The amount of memory allocated to the process currently loaded into physical memory (active).
Shared Memory	The amount of memory shared between this process and other processes.
X-Server Memory	The amount of memory the process shares with the X Windows (GUI) server.

Column	Description
%CPU	The percentage of total CPU time the process is using.
CPU Time	The actual CPU time the process is using.
Started	The time the process started running.
Nice	The system priority of the process. Higher Nice numbers have lower priority on the system.
ID	The unique process ID (PID) the system assigned to the process.
Security Context	The security classification assigned by the SELinux security system.
Arguments	The name of the command and any command-line arguments used to start it.
Memory	The amount of system memory that your running processes are using.

Here are a few other options you can set while you're in the Processes tab Preferences dialog box:

✔ **Update Interval in Seconds:** How frequently the System Monitor refreshes the table data.

✔ **Enable Smooth Refresh:** Gathers new process information before refreshing the table data, instead of refreshing table data as it gathers process information.

✔ **Alert Before Ending or Killing Processes:** Provides a warning dialog box ("just in case") before you're allowed to terminate a running process.

✔ **Alert Before Hiding Processes:** Provides a warning when switching to hide a specific process.

You can also control processes that you own directly from the Processes tab. Right-clicking a process produces a menu that allows you to stop, end, kill, or change the priority of the process.

Resources

Clicking the Resources tab provides a quick overview of the hardware status of the system, as shown in Figure 18-15.

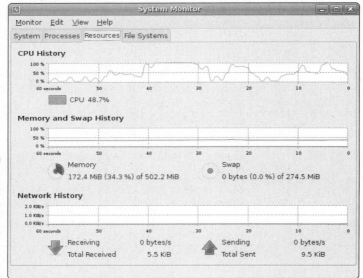

Figure 18-15:
The
Resources
tab in the
System
Monitor
tool.

Three real-time graphs are displayed:

- ✔ **CPU History:** Displays the running real-time CPU percent utilization. If the system contains more than one processor, each processor is shown as a separate history line.

- ✔ **Memory and Swap History:** Displays two running real-time graphs: one for the amount of memory used by the user, and one for how much virtual-memory swap space the user is taking up.

- ✔ **Network History:** Displays the amount of data sent and received from the network interfaces.

The Resources tab can give you a quick overall picture of how your system is doing. If you see that the CPU or memory usage is running high, you can flip over to the Processes tab and sort the listing based on that parameter.

File Systems

The File Systems tab gives you a quick look at the amount of disk space used on each mounted filesystem — see Chapter 7 for filesystems and mounting.

All hard drives and partitions are shown, along with the total disk space, free disk space, and used disk space for each one. You get a quick, accurate picture of how much free space you have left on your hard drive.

Chapter 19

A Secure Linux Box Is a Happy Linux Box

I am Inspector Clouseau, and I am on official police business.

— Inspector Clouseau

You don't leave the front door of your house open when you go to work, do you? How about leaving it shut and locked but with a few nice big windows open? The problem is that many people do the equivalent every day with their computers, and they don't even know it! This chapter takes a look at where your computer's open doors and windows are — and what you can do to secure them.

Every user's actions affect your overall system security. If your family members or officemates need access to your Linux machine, take the time to sit down and explain the facts of secure life to them.

Updating Your Software

All users can download and install new software. Of course, which programs they can install are limited by user permissions. Here — as with any operating system — be sure you don't get a version of a program that has been tampered with, and keep in mind that some are all-out fakes that try to trick folks into installing them.

Most Linux applications and other Linux software programs are distributed by way of the Internet. In fact, the development cycle of new Linux software — and updates to it — depends on the Internet for file exchange, e-mail, and forum or newsgroup discussions. Make sure that you and other users of your Linux system are comfortable with the Web sites they use and visit. You need to develop a *list* of trusted sites — those that provide you with the information you need and are not misleading in their presentation.

As a starting point, you can *trust* all the Web sites referenced in this book because we have accessed them all. If either you or a user of your Linux system is unsure about whether to trust a particular Web site, do some research and perhaps ask others for their opinions.

Chapter 16 details how to keep your distribution and its software up to date. Please, please, *please* do so! After all, as the person in charge, your job is to make sure that this computer stays intruder-free. In addition to making sure that you do all the things a user would do for both your user accounts and the superuser (root) account — such as making sure the passwords aren't compromised — you have one further mandate: No matter which Linux distribution you're running, you must keep up to date on emerging security problems.

Keeping Your Network Secure

On a Linux server or workstation — or any computer at all, using any operating system — you should not have any network services running that you don't intend to use. Think of each network program running as a glass window or sliding glass door in your house. Each network service is a weak spot, and many nasty folks are out there on the Internet who like to go up to all the houses and make note of how many windows and glass doors are on them, what kinds they are, and how easy they are to breach.

Controlling your services

The more software you've installed on your system, the more services it may have running in the background. Both Ubuntu and Fedora provide a utility for us to control which applications the system starts automatically.

In Ubuntu, you can see which services are activated by choosing System⇨ Administration⇨Services. The Services Settings window appears (shown in Figure 19-1). By default, you can only view the services; you can't make any changes to them. Click the Unlock button, and then enter your password to gain access to this utility.

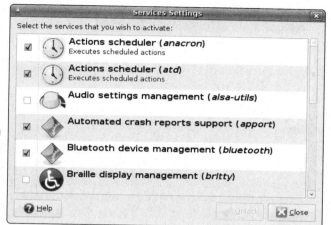

Figure 19-1:
The Ubuntu
Services
Settings
window.

The installed services are listed, each with a check box that indicates whether the service is currently activated. You can control several services from this interface:

- ✔ **Actions scheduler (anacron):** Schedules programs that run automatically on a regular basis, such as log cleaning scripts.

- ✔ **Actions scheduler (atd):** Schedules programs that run just once.

- ✔ **Audio settings management:** Controls audio settings using the soundcard drivers.

- ✔ **Automated crash reports support:** Generates reports if any application crashes.

- ✔ **Bluetooth device management:** Detects and configures Bluetooth devices on your system.

- ✔ **Braille display management:** Controls Braille terminal output.

- ✔ **Computer activity logger:** Generates log files to track users and programs.

- ✔ **CPU frequency manager:** Controls CPU access on laptop devices to save power while idling.

- ✔ **Graphical login manager:** Provides the graphical login page in Ubuntu (it's not a good idea to disable this unless you're using just the command-line prompt).

- ✔ **Hotkeys management:** Detects key combinations to perform common actions.

✔ **Multicast DNS service discovery:** Automatically detects network hardware, such as printers and shared drives.

✔ **Power management:** Controls battery use in laptops.

✔ **System communication bus:** Used for internal communications.

As you can probably tell, some services (such as Bluetooth support or laptop power management) are only used for specific situations. If your workstation doesn't need these features, it's safe to disable them.

In Fedora, to look at the services, choose System➪Administration➪Server Settings➪Services. (The Services option may be directly in the Administration menu; it depends on the collection of software you currently have installed.) Enter the root user password to ensure that you have permissions to mess with service settings.

The installed services are listed on the left side, as shown in Figure 19-2. Fedora starts the services with a green dot next to them at boot time. Services with icons next to them start only at specific run levels. Linux uses run levels to control what software starts when. Most of the graphical desktop-oriented software starts at run level 5. Software that runs in the background and doesn't require the desktop starts at run level 3.

You can turn a service on or off simply by clicking the service and clicking the Disable icon on the toolbar.

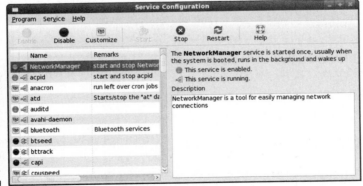

Figure 19-2:
The Fedora Service Configuration dialog box.

Services you may be interested in turning on or off include the following:

✔ **bluetooth:** This service isn't necessary if you don't have a Bluetooth interface on your workstation.

- ✔ **iptables:** This service is your firewall (more on the firewall in the section "Controlling and adjusting your firewall," later in this chapter). If you need to shut down the firewall briefly, you can do so using the Service Control dialog box.

- ✔ **ip6tables:** This service is for the new, improved IP version 6 protocol, which isn't being used in most of the world yet. You can most likely turn this off without breaking anything.

- ✔ **mdmonitor:** Shut this service off unless you implemented software RAID during your installation. (You had to go out of your way to do so, so if you don't know, you probably didn't!) If you change this service to on or off, make sure that mdmpd is also on or off (matching) as well.

- ✔ **pcscd:** This is the PC/SC smart card reader program. If you're not using a smart card to log in to your Fedora computer, you can turn this off.

- ✔ **sendmail:** Even though you're probably not in need of a full-fledged mail server, shutting this service off can have unintended consequences because it's used to handle internal mail on your system. Leave it on.

- ✔ **smartd:** If you're getting error messages for this one at boot time, shut it off. It only works with certain IDE hard drives, so if you're not using that type of drive, it kicks out a (harmless) error message.

- ✔ **spamassassin:** If you want to use this program in conjunction with your mail program, go for it! This program is used by default with Evolution in Fedora (see Chapter 10), so if you're using this combination of tools, leave this service on.

- ✔ **yum:** On Fedora, this program lets you run a nightly automatic update if your machine is connected to the Internet overnight.

In Fedora, when you select or deselect a service, make sure that it does what you intended — either does or doesn't turn on when you reboot. Use the Start and Stop icons in the toolbar to start or stop a service immediately; you can use the bottom-right part of the dialog box to see whether the service is running right now.

Controlling and adjusting your firewall

Even better than (but just as essential as) turning off unnecessary services is to make sure that you have a firewall in place. Using a firewall is like putting a big bunker around your house, with openings that only fit the visitors who want to do certain kinds of tasks. Friends could fit in through one door, family through another, and package deliveries through another.

In computer networks, each of the services discussed earlier always comes in through the same door (*port*, in computer-world lingo). You use firewalls to prevent anyone from being able to so much as touch a door (port) unless you've explicitly set it up so they can do so.

Both Ubuntu and Fedora install a firewall by default, but in Ubuntu it's not activated. The firewall package installed in Ubuntu is `ufw`. To activate the `ufw` firewall in Ubuntu, you need to do some work from the command line (see Chapter 17). Just follow these steps:

1. **Choose Applications⇨Accessories⇨Terminal from the top edge panel to start the Terminal application.**

2. **Enter the following commands:**

   ```
   rich@testbox:~$ sudo ufw allow ssh/tcp
   ```

   The output looks something like this:

   ```
   [sudo] password for rich:
   Rules updated
   rich@testbox:~$ sudo ufw logging on
   Logging enabled
   rich@testbox:~$ sudo ufw enable
   Firewall is active and enabled on system startup
   rich@testbox:~$ sudo ufw status
   Status: active

   To                Action      From
   --                ------      ----
   22/tcp            ALLOW       Anywhere
   rich@testbox:~$
   ```

   The first command enables secure connections on the SSH TCP port. The second command tells `ufw` to log any activity that it restricts in a log file. This enables you to see whether anyone is trying to hack into your system. The next command starts the `ufw` firewall, and the last command displays the status.

3. **Type** exit **to exit the Terminal session.**

Once you enable the firewall, it starts each time you reboot your workstation. Unfortunately, because `ufw` is a command-line program, you must use the command line to add or remove any further settings to the firewall.

Fedora, on the other hand, provides a handy graphical interface for configuring the firewall. If you ever want to make changes, choose System⇨Administration⇨ Firewall (you may be asked to enter your root password along the way). The Firewall Configuration window opens, as shown in Figure 19-3.

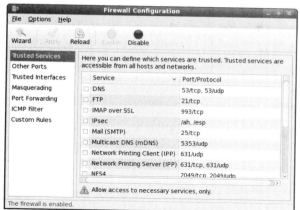

Figure 19-3:
The Fedora
Firewall
Configur-
ation dialog
box.

The Firewall Configuration window offers settings you can use to specify your firewall options easily. At the top is a toolbar that contains some quick actions you can take. You can even (for example) enable or disable the entire firewall feature by clicking the Enable or Disable icon, respectively, on the toolbar. If your computer is connected directly to the Internet — as most computers are these days — make sure you use Enable Firewall.

The only time not to have the Fedora firewall active is when you've already set up your machine(s) behind another strong firewall, or when you're using a critical application that won't work with the Fedora firewall in place. For just one application, though, that's one huge risk! You can find out how to open the proper doors in the firewall for that one program instead.

The Wizard icon on the toolbar provides a guided way to configure your system. It asks a few simple questions about your system and your network skill level, and then it provides options for setting your firewall features.

Beneath the toolbar is an area where you can configure specific firewall features manually. The left-side pane provides options for the following types of settings:

✔ **Trusted Services:** Allow or deny access on ports for common network applications, such as FTP (file transfers), HTTP (Web server), and SSH (secure interactive server).

✔ **Other Ports:** Allow or deny access on custom network ports for specific installed applications.

✔ **Trusted Interfaces:** Allow access based on an interface on a trusted network.

- ✔ **Masquerading:** Configure the firewall to allow connections from your local network out to the Internet.

- ✔ **Port Forwarding:** Redirect packets destined for one port to another.

- ✔ **ICMP Filter:** Block error message packets and network testing packets (such as ping) from your workstation.

- ✔ **Custom Rules:** Create your own restrictions in your firewall.

Here's a list of the most common network services. Select these items with extreme caution. For the most part, you should just stick with the trusted services:

- ✔ **WWW:** Web stuff; only needed if you're running a Web server.

- ✔ **FTP:** FTP server stuff; you don't need it if you're not running an FTP server.

- ✔ **Mail (SMTP):** Allows remote mail servers to send mail directly to your computer. If you use an ISP for your e-mail (as most users do), you don't need to enable this.

- ✔ **NFS4:** Network File Sharing. Enable this if you want to share folders directly with other Linux or UNIX computers.

- ✔ **SSH:** Select this one to keep open. We explain it in the next section.

- ✔ **Samba:** Allows remote Microsoft computers to share files and printers on your Fedora computer. If you're connected to a local Microsoft network, you may need to enable this to share files. If you're directly connected to the Internet, it's *not* a good idea to have this enabled.

Keeping an Eye on Your Log Files with the System Log Viewer

One other security issue you may want to configure concerns *log files.* Your network programs, kernel, and other programs all run log files, which contain records of what has been happening on your system. You may be amazed at just how much information gets put in them!

Most of your log files are in `/var/log`; take a look sometime.

Fortunately, tools are available that can help mere mortals sift through the wheat to look for the chaff of bugs and intruders. Both Ubuntu and Fedora provide the System Log Viewer, which allows you to easily scan through the major log files on the computer. Start the System Log Viewer by choosing System➪Administration➪System Log (see Figure 19-4). Enter your root password, as all log files are restricted to root-only access.

Different Linux distributions store log information in different log files. The System Log Viewer provides quick links to the major log files installed in your particular Linux system. If you want to view any other log files, you can do that by choosing File⇨Open from the menu bar, selecting the log file whose contents you want to view, and then clicking Open.

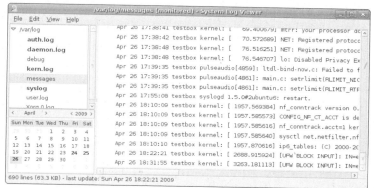

Figure 19-4:
The Ubuntu
System Log
Viewer.

As you can see, there are lots of log files to dig through. As mentioned earlier, different Linux distributions use different log files; what you see listed depends on your particular Linux distribution. Here's a quick summary of some of the log files you may run into:

- ✔ **messages:** This is the main system log file. It contains error and status messages from the operating system as well as many applications and services. All messages entered in the messages log file are in this format:

  ```
  timestamp system application: message
  ```

  You can use the filter feature to look at only messages from a specific application to help identify problems on the system. A sample entry looks like this:

  ```
  Apr  9 19:34:55 testbox dhclient: DHCPREQUEST on eth0
        to 192.168.73.254 port 67
  ```

  This entry shows that the eth0 network interface used the dhclient application to request an IP address via DHCP.

- ✔ **auth.log:** The auth.log file logs authentication attempts made on the system.

- ✔ **boot.log:** This log file contains messages generated from the boot-up process (most of which scroll by way too fast to read while you're booting the system). As applications and services start, they report their status in the `boot.log` file. The `boot.log` file uses the same format as the `messages` log file. This is a great place to look for answers if Fedora doesn't recognize any hardware on your system.

✔ **daemon.log:** The `daemon.log` file logs activity of programs running in background on the system.

✔ **secure:** The `secure` log file reports every instance of a security request on the system, such as when a user tries to log in or requests special privileges. Check this log if you can't log in to the system with a user account.

✔ **maillog:** The `maillog` reports error and status messages from the mail system. Each time a message is sent or received, a log message is generated and stored in this log file. Check here if you can't send or receive mail messages.

✔ **X.org.0.log:** This log file tracks the status of the graphical `X.org` server on the computer. The `X.org` server provides the windows environment for the desktop. Check here if you're having problems with the desktop display on your monitor.

In Fedora, the secure log file contains information about connection attempts and failed access attempts. It's a good idea to peruse this log file on a regular basis to watch for intruders. If you see a lot of denied access requests, you may have someone trying to hack into your system.

It also records each time a user requests root permissions. For example, when we started the System Log Viewer application, it required us to enter the root password. Doing so generated an entry in the secure log file:

```
Mar 20 13:38:22 testbox userhelper: running /usr/sbin/
          gnome-system-log with root privileges on behalf
          of 'rich'
```

This log entry identifies both the application that was run with root privileges and the user id that requested it.

It's also a good idea to peruse through the messages log file on a regular basis. If any system services fail to start, you'll find out from entries in this log file.

Chapter 20

The Virtual World

The real problem is not whether machines think, but whether men do.

— B. F. Skinner (1904–1990)

While the term *virtual server* sounds an awful lot like *air guitar,* virtual servers are actually a good thing. Virtual servers allow you to support multiple servers on a single physical machine, saving both space and money. They are quickly becoming all the rage in the corporate world, but they also have a place in the home environment. A virtual server allows you to install more than one Linux distribution on a single computer or to have Linux and Windows running on the same computer!

In this chapter, we detail exactly what a virtual server is — it's a bit more complicated than playing air guitar — and we show you how to install and use one virtual server, VirtualBox.

Understanding What Virtual Servers Are

In this fast-paced world of changing technology, nothing is taken for granted. In the old days, if you needed to run ten separate servers on your network, you had to go out and purchase ten separate systems, and then place them in a huge data center where they took up lots of space.

Nowadays, you have another tool at your disposal: the virtual server, software that gives you the same capabilities as all that hardware. With virtual servers, you can run all ten separate servers on one hardware system. You not only save on hardware costs, but you also save space in your data center, save on the cost of electricity and cooling, and (perhaps) even save on the cost of hiring a horde of people to support the servers.

Running virtual servers requires a software package that you use to create servers within a single host operating system. The host operating system takes care of interfacing with the hardware; the virtual-server software plays middleman between the host system and the virtual servers.

Each virtual server has its own area — a *sandbox* — to run in. The host server makes memory and CPU time available to the virtual server to use just as if it were running directly on the underlying hardware.

The trick to implementing virtual servers is all in the software. Several different virtual-server packages are around; the most popular in the Linux world are

- ✔ **KVM:** An open-source project, KVM (www.linux-kvm.org) plugs directly into the Linux kernel. It runs only on systems that have CPUs that can support virtualization — sharing the CPU between multiple programs.

- ✔ **VirtualBox:** A Sun-sponsored project, VirtualBox (www.virtualbox.org) installs in any Linux distribution, no matter what the kernel or underlying CPU type. Because it works with every Linux distribution, we show you how to use VirtualBox in this chapter.

- ✔ **VMWare Server:** A free software package provided by VMWare (www.vmware.com), VMWare Server is available in several different versions for different Linux distributions. It installs and runs as a Java Web application in a browser window.

You can install any of these virtual-server packages on a Linux host — and then you can run your virtual server with various operating systems, including Linux and Windows!

Installing VirtualBox

The first step is to install the VirtualBox software package. Depending on your Linux distribution, you may have this package available in the distribution software repository. For Ubuntu, the package name is virtual-ose. Find it in the Synaptic Package Manager (discussed in Chapter 16) to install it on your system. After you install the package, choose Applications⇨Accessories.

If your Linux distribution doesn't include the VirtualBox software, or if you just want to make sure you have the latest version, download it directly from the VirtualBox Web site. The VirtualBox Web site provides installation packages for many common Linux distributions (including Ubuntu and Fedora). When you download the VirtualBox software, it's important that you select the right version for your Linux distribution.

Here are the steps for downloading and installing the VirtualBox package from the Web site:

1. **Open a Web browser and go to the site** www.virtualbox.org.

    Although the VirtualBox project is sponsored by Sun, it has its own Web site — complete with download files, documentation, and a community-forum area.

2. **Click the Downloads link on the left side of the main Web page.**

    The Download VirtualBox page opens.

3. **Select the current version of VirtualBox for the Linux platform.**

    This is the host platform you're selecting. You can still run other operating systems, such as Microsoft Windows, within the VirtualBox software. We clicked the VirtualBox 2.2.2 for Linux link because that was the most current version of VirtualBox at the time of this writing.

    VirtualBox is available in versions for the Microsoft Windows and Mac operating systems. If you're squeamish about adding Linux to an existing Windows or Mac installation, you can install VirtualBox on the system and run Linux in a sandbox on the same system.

    The Download VirtualBox for Linux Hosts page opens.

4. **Click the link for your Linux distribution and CPU type.**

    VirtualBox has both 32- and 64-bit versions to support both Intel x86 (32-bit) and the newer AMD64 64-bit CPU platforms. If you're using the 64-bit installation of Ubuntu or Fedora, select the 64-bit version of VirtualBox.

    It's extremely important that you select the correct version of VirtualBox for your CPU.

    The File Download dialog box opens.

5. **Click the Save button to save the package to your hard drive.**

    The installation process is a bit lengthy, and it can crash. It's a good idea to download the entire package to your hard drive and perform the installation from there.

6. **Find the location of the installation package file using your File Manager (see Chapter 7), and double-click the package file.**

   Nautilus, Dolphin, and Konqueror all start the appropriate package-manager software to install the package. Then the package manager prompts you for an administrative password.

7. **Enter the password to continue the installation.**

   The package manager installs the VirtualBox software, then exits.

Here's how to find your new VirtualBox system:

✔ **In the desktop menu:** In the Fedora GNOME desktop, choose Applications⇨System Tools⇨VirtualBox, or choose Applications⇨System in the KDE desktop. In Ubuntu, choose Applications⇨Accessories⇨VirtualBox OSE.

✔ **In a Terminal session:** Open a Terminal session (or Konsole session in the KDE desktop) and enter the following command:

```
VirtualBox
```

Be careful to get the capitalization correct, or Linux won't find the VirtualBox program.

Figure 20-1 shows what the main VirtualBox window looks like after it starts.

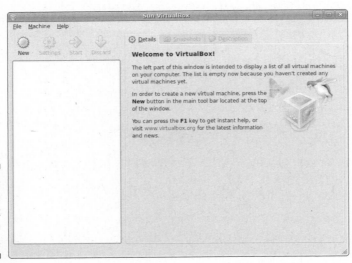

Figure 20-1:
The
VirtualBox
main
window.

Creating a Virtual Server

When you have VirtualBox installed, you're ready to create any number of virtual servers.

The next step in the process is to build a sandbox for your virtual server to run. You need to define two things for the size of the sandbox: the amount of disk space to allocate for the virtual server and the amount of memory to use.

These items are shared with the host system, so be careful how much you dedicate for the virtual servers! You need to leave enough for the host operating system to run on. You may have to experiment a bit to find out how much is too much or too little for your environment.

Follow along with these steps to create your first virtual server sandbox:

1. **Click the New icon on the VirtualBox toolbar, then click Next in the wizard's Welcome page.**

   A wizard opens, as shown in Figure 20-2, to walk you through creating the virtual server sandbox.

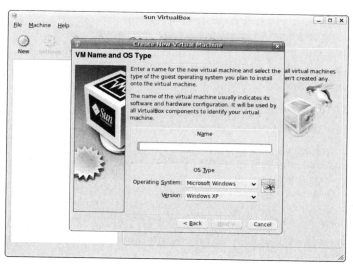

Figure 20-2:
The first screen in the VirtualBox new server wizard.

2. **Type a name for your sandbox in the Name text box, select the operating system you plan to install in the virtual-server area from the Operating System drop-down list, select a Version from the Version drop-down list, and then click the Next button.**

The VirtualBox software package provides a way to run multiple operating systems from inside a host system, but it doesn't provide any licenses for those operating systems. It's your responsibility to obtain a proper license for any operating-system software you install in VirtualBox.

3. **Either by using the Size slider or by typing a value, choose the amount of memory you want to dedicate to the virtual server; then click the Next button.**

   VirtualBox recommends an amount of memory to select, according to the operating system you selected and the amount of memory installed on the host system. You can increase or decrease that amount, either by using the slider or by typing the amount into the text box. If you're unsure of your virtual memory requirements, take the default value; you can always change it later.

   The amount of memory you dedicate for the virtual server is taken from the amount of memory available to the host server while the virtual server is running.

4. **Select a hard-drive emulation file for the virtual server.**

   VirtualBox emulates a hard drive by creating a large file on the host system. The amount of disk space you select for this virtual hard drive is created inside the file, so it can't be larger than the disk space available on the host system. We assume that you don't have a virtual disk file laying around and that you need to create one.

5. **To create a bootable hard drive for the virtual server to boot from, ensure that the Boot Hard Drive check box is selected, and then click the New button to create a new hard-drive file.**

   The Create New Virtual Disk Wizard starts.

6. **Click the Next button to continue.**

   VirtualBox can either create the entire hard-drive file at once (called *fixed-size storage*), or it can create a base file and expand it as the virtual server's operating system uses more disk space (called *dynamically expanding storage*). By creating the disk space all at once, you make disk access faster in the virtual server — but you also eat up more disk space on the host system that may not get used by the virtual server.

7. **Select the Fixed-Size Storage radio button, and then click the Next button.**

8. **Select a location (used as the filename) for the new hard-drive file, specify the size of the file, and then click the Next button.**

   You can place the hard-drive file anywhere you have access on the host system. Use the slider or the text box to set the size of the hard-drive file, as shown in Figure 20-3. VirtualBox selects a recommended size based on the operating system you selected earlier in the wizard. If you're installing a Linux virtual workstation, try to create at least a 5GB disk file.

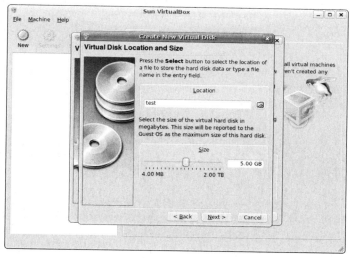

Figure 20-3: Setting the virtual server's hard-drive file's location and size.

9. **Review the settings for the new virtual disk drive file, then click the Finish button to create the file.**

   The wizard creates the file, and then it returns you to the original Virtual Server Wizard process.

10. **Ensure that the new virtual disk file appears as the selected virtual disk, and then click the Next button.**

11. **Review the settings you selected for the virtual server, and then click the Finish button to create the virtual server.**

When you finish the wizard, your new virtual-server entry appears on the main VirtualBox window, shown in Figure 20-4.

Figure 20-4:
The virtual-
server
entry in the
VirtualBox
window.

Setting Up Your Virtual Server

Before you can enter your virtual world, you need to set up your sandbox just a little more. The wizard sets up a generic sandbox environment, so you'll want to spruce things up a bit before using it. This section walks you through customizing the virtual server's sandbox and adding an operating system to your virtual server's operating system.

Changing settings

Each virtual server you create in VirtualBox has a set of configuration settings that determine just what VirtualBox emulates in the sandbox.

To get to the configuration settings, choose the virtual-server entry on the left side of the VirtualBox window (refer to Figure 20-4), and then click the Settings icon. The Settings dialog box, shown in Figure 20-5, appears.

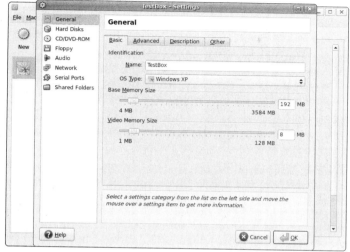

General

Figure 20-5:
The
VirtualBox
Settings
dialog box.

The Settings dialog box has eight setting categories, shown as icons with text on the left side:

✔ **General:** Sets memory and BIOS-emulation features. From here you can readjust the amount of memory the virtual server uses, along with setting the amount of memory dedicated for video memory. The Advanced tab allows you to configure BIOS-emulation settings, including the boot-device order, hard-drive controller emulation, and Clipboard sharing with the host system.

If you have to install the virtual server's operating system from a CD or DVD-ROM, make sure that the CD/DVD-ROM drive is enabled and that you place it above the hard drive in the boot-order list in the Advanced settings.

✔ **Hard Disks:** Manages the hard-drive files used for the virtual server. You can mount multiple hard-drive files to emulate more than one hard drive on the system.

✔ **CD/DVD-ROM:** Manages the CD drive hardware or access to the CD/DVD-ROM emulation file. Here's where you can allow the virtual server access to the CD/DVD-ROM drive on the host system. Another cool feature of VirtualBox is that you can directly mount an ISO image file already on the host system. This way you can install Linux distributions directly from the ISO image without having to burn them onto a CD. Figure 20-6 shows what this section looks like.

If you're installing the virtual server's operating system from a CD or DVD-ROM, be sure to mount the CD or DVD-ROM drive in these settings before you try to start the virtual server. It's not selected by default.

✔ **Floppy:** Manages the floppy-drive hardware or access to the floppy-drive emulation. Just as with the CD/DVD-ROM features, you can give the virtual server access to the floppy drive on the host system (if available), or you can mount a file that emulates a floppy drive.

✔ **Audio:** Manages access to the sound card on the host system. For Linux hosts, you can select the ALSA driver to allow the virtual server to send sound to the host Linux sound system.

✔ **Network:** The virtual server can tap into the network connection of the host system, and here's where you can configure that feature. The default NAT feature allows the host to act as a DHCP server, and it creates an internal network between the virtual server and the host. You can then access the host server's network by using the network interface on the virtual server. Figure 20-7 shows the standard settings for this section.

✔ **Serial Ports:** Manages access to the serial-communication ports on the host server (if available).

✔ **Shared Folders:** Allows you to create a folder that both the host system and the virtual server can access. This makes a convenient pipeline for moving files between the two environments.

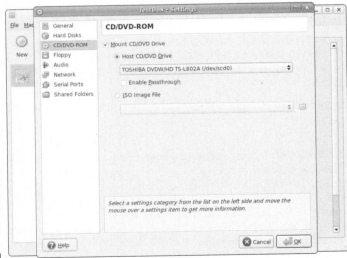

Figure 20-6:
The
CD-DVD-
ROM
section of
the Settings
dialog box.

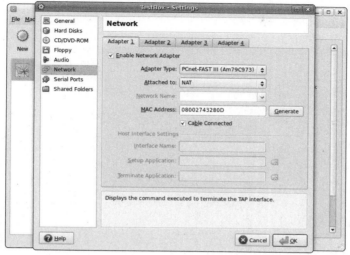

When you have your settings customized, click OK at the bottom of the dialog box to save them and return to the main VirtualBox window.

Loading an OS

With the virtual server's sandbox all customized for your new operating system, you're ready to install an operating system.

Before you start, make sure that you have the CD or DVD-ROM required for the OS installation.

When you have your installation disc in hand, follow these steps to get the OS installed:

1. **Insert the operating system installation CD or DVD-ROM into the CD/DVD-ROM player on the host system.**

   If your desktop opens a file-manager application automatically, close that app before proceeding. You may then see the disk mounted on the system and shown as an icon on the desktop — that's okay.

2. **From the listing at left in the VirtualBox window, select the virtual server on which you want to install the operating system.**

3. **Click the Start toolbar icon.**

The virtual server powers up, just as if you had turned on the power switch on a piece of hardware. The VirtualBox console-emulation window opens. Anything that would normally appear on the monitor appears inside this window, as shown in Figure 20-8.

Figure 20-8:
The VirtualBox console-emulation window.

4. **Proceed through the installation process for the operating system you're installing.**

   The virtual server should have booted from the operating-system CD or DVD-ROM you inserted (if not, refer to the General section of the Settings dialog box). Just follow the normal installation process for the operating system. The operating system should detect all emulated hardware you configured in the virtual server.

5. **Reboot the virtual server when the installation is complete.**

   Most operating-system installations reboot the system automatically. If this happens, the VirtualBox console-emulation window detects the reboot and stays open, allowing you to watch the reboot process.

The final result is a perfectly working operating system running inside your sandbox, as shown in Figure 20-9.

When you shut down the virtual server's operating system, VirtualBox closes the console-emulation window automatically.

Figure 20-9:
Running
the familiar
Microsoft
Windows
XP in
VirtualBox.

Working with the Sandbox

When you have your virtual server running, you need to become familiar with a few VirtualBox commands.

When you first start your virtual server, a set of icons appears at the bottom of the window (refer to Figure 20-8). These icons indicate when the virtual server is accessing hardware on the system. The icons represent

- ✔ The hard drive
- ✔ The CD/DVD-ROM drive
- ✔ The floppy drive
- ✔ The network interface
- ✔ The shared folder

The bottom-right corner of the window also contains a mouse icon, a key icon, and the phrase *Right Ctrl.* When you start the virtual server, VirtualBox takes control of the keyboard and mouse on the host system, and then it turns them over to the virtual server.

✔ If at any time you want to release control back to the host system (as when, say, you want to run another application at the same time), press the Ctrl key on the right side of the keyboard.

✔ To return control to the virtual server, just place the mouse anywhere inside the console-emulation window and press the right Ctrl key.

There are also two menu bar items — Machine and Devices — that can help you in your virtual-server environment.

The Machine menu

The Machine menu provides easy access to several common functions you may want to perform with your virtual server:

✔ **Fullscreen Mode:** Enlarges the virtual server's console-emulation window to take the full size of the host screen. To return to windows mode, hold down the right-side Ctrl key and press the F key.

✔ **Seamless Mode:** This is a special feature available with certain guest operating systems. VirtualBox allows you to install a video driver on the guest operating system so VirtualBox can display and control the guest operating system as a normal window on the host.

✔ **Adjust Window Size:** Changes the size of the VirtualBox console-emulation window on the host.

✔ **Auto-resize Guest Display:** Allows VirtualBox to size the window according to the video settings used on the guest operating system. If the display resolution set in the guest operating system becomes too large to fit in a desktop window on the host, VirtualBox creates scroll bars automatically so you can pan around the guest display.

✔ **Disable Mouse Integration:** Another special feature available with certain guest operating systems. VirtualBox allows you to install a mouse driver on the guest operating system, which allows better control over the mouse pointer in the console-emulation window. If this feature (called *mouse integration*) is enabled, this menu item disables it.

✔ **Insert Ctrl-Alt-Delete:** If you've installed a guest operating system that requires the old "three-finger salute" to reboot, but your host system also recognizes the Ctrl-Alt-Delete key combination, this option allows you to emulate the key combination.

✔ **Insert Ctrl-Alt-Backspace:** If you have installed a guest operating system that uses the X-Windows graphical manager (as most Linux installations do), and you're using a Linux host, you can't reset the X-Windows session on the guest by pressing the Ctrl-Alt-Backspace combination; if you do, the host system resets. This option allows you to emulate the key combination without having to press it.

✔ **Take Snapshot:** This is not related to taking a screen capture of the window. A snapshot in VirtualBox allows you to save a copy of the virtual disk file as it exists at the time. You can then start the virtual server using this copy of the virtual disk instead of the normal version. This provides a great way to perform backups of virtual servers at any point.

✔ **Session Information dialog box:** Provides basic information about the virtual-server session presently running, as shown in Figure 20-10.

The RunTime tab shows current statistics on the hard drive, CD-ROM, and network-adapter activity.

✔ **Reset:** Emulates pressing the Reset button on the workstation. This usually sends a shutdown signal to the guest operating system and restarts the virtual server.

✔ **Pause:** Places the virtual server in a suspended mode, but doesn't send any signals to the guest operating system to shut it down.

✔ **ACPI Shutdown:** Emulates hitting the power button on the workstation. This usually sends a shutdown signal to the guest operating system and stops the virtual server when the guest operating system has finished shutting down.

✔ **Close:** Closes the VirtualBox console emulation window. If you select this option with the guest operating system running, VirtualBox displays a Close dialog box. You can attempt to send the shutdown signal to the guest operating system, save the system state as a snapshot, or just perform a hard power-down.

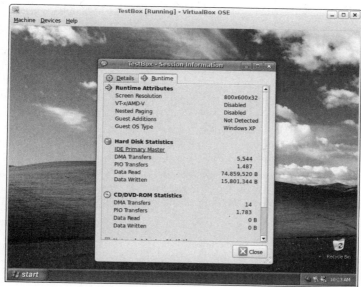

Figure 20-10:
The
VirtualBox
Session
Information
dialog box.

The Devices menu

The Devices menu allows you to control the status of the hardware devices being used in the virtual server. The options available in this section depend on which hardware devices you selected when you created the virtual server's sandbox. The available options are

- ✔ **Mount CD/DVD-ROM:** Allows you to connect the virtual server to the host system's CD or DVD-ROM drive or to an ISO image of a CD or DVD-ROM stored on the host system. This second feature is great for easily installing a Linux distribution from an ISO image without having to burn it onto a CD.

- ✔ **Unmount CD/DVD-ROM:** Releases the CD/DVD-ROM device or ISO image file from the virtual server.

- ✔ **Mount Floppy:** Allows access to the workstation's floppy drive (if installed) or to a file image of a floppy disk. Similar to the CD/DVD-ROM version, you can use a file on your host system to emulate a floppy disk.

- ✔ **Unmount Floppy:** Releases the floppy device or floppy image file from the virtual server.

- ✔ **Network Adapters:** Provides access to the emulated network adapters on the virtual server. You can either enable or disable the network adapter from this interface.

  A check mark next to an adapter means it's enabled.

- ✔ **USB Devices:** If you allow the virtual server to access your USB devices while you're setting up the virtual server, this option appears. When you plug a USB device into the host system, VirtualBox detects the new device automatically and passes it on to the guest operating system. To remove your USB device, disable the entry in this menu.

- ✔ **Shared Folders:** If you selected to create shared folders for the virtual server during the setup, use this area to enable and disable access to the shared folder.

- ✔ **Install Guest Additions:** You can download the VirtualBox Guest Additions CD from this menu entry. The Guest Additions CD contains specialized drivers you can install on guest operating systems to allow customized video and mouse interaction (see the section "The Machine menu" earlier in this chapter).

The Devices menu gives you full control over which hardware the guest operating system can access.

Part V
The Part of Tens

The 5th Wave — By Rich Tennant

"We should have this fixed in version 2."

In this part . . .

In this part of the book, we cover answers to the questions most frequently asked about Linux. We explain some key Linux installation and setup points, as well as share more routine troubleshooting tips and tricks. This is where to turn if you're having some trouble and need a helping hand, or if something is bugging you about your setup.

Chapter 21

Ten Steps to Setting Up a Samba Server

In This Chapter

▶ Introducing Samba

▶ Making a file server

▶ Troubleshooting

There are some things you can't share without ending up liking each other.

— J. K. Rowling, Harry Potter and the Sorcerer's Stone, 1997

*Q*uite possibly the biggest thing in local networking is file sharing. The sharing of files is a necessity in the business world, but it can also come in handy in the home network as well. Having a common place for everyone in the house to place pictures, music, or documents makes using floppies and flash drives almost obsolete.

There's no doubt that the Microsoft network environment is the most popular file-sharing system available. Any Microsoft Windows computers can connect together to share folders with one another. But just because you decided to use Linux doesn't mean you're left out in the cold. In this chapter, we walk you through the steps necessary to create your own file server on your home network that can be accessed from any Microsoft or Linux device on your network.

Dancing the Samba

Making your Linux computer talk with Microsoft Windows workstations and servers requires a special software package. Microsoft uses a proprietary (secret) network protocol to communicate between Windows devices on a network.

Fortunately, some enterprising open-source enthusiasts worked to reverse-engineer the Microsoft networking protocols and produced software to duplicate them. The result of this effort is the open-source package called *Samba*.

Both Ubuntu and Fedora include the Samba software to allow you to connect your workstation to an existing Microsoft network to share files. However, neither provides the software to create a Samba server — which is the way to allow Microsoft Windows workstations to read files and folders on your Linux system.

The Fedora distribution does, however, include a separate Samba package that provides an excellent graphical interface for creating and configuring a Samba server in your Fedora system. This allows your Fedora workstation or server to share your folders with other Microsoft Windows workstations on your network.

The Ubuntu Server Linux distribution provides the Samba server software, but it doesn't provide a graphical interface for configuring the server. You have to configure it from the command line.

The Samba server software allows you to define folders on your Linux system, which it then advertises on the Microsoft network. Remote Windows clients can browse and map to those folders just as if the folders were on a Windows system.

You can control access to the folders by using the standard Linux user and group permissions. Samba has the capability to allow Windows users on the network to access individual Linux user accounts. This feature allows you to use one set of user accounts on the Windows network and a different set of user accounts on the Linux system.

Step 1: Plan a Sharing Policy

Before you can start sharing, first you must decide what you want to share and who gets to share it. Mapping out a folder-sharing policy is a crucial element of creating a file server.

Even in small organizations, you must often restrict subgroups from accessing certain information. Whether it's separating teacher data from students, or keeping children away from parents' data, you often find yourself creating more than one group for sharing folders.

You can create as many *shares* (folders available to the network) on the file server as you need to manage the data groups. For each group that shares data, you must create a separate folder and define a separate group to place users in.

With all this information to keep straight, it's usually best to create a simple table, mapping out which users should have access to what data. When you can see the complete layout in front of you, it's easier to create the proper configuration. Table 21-1 demonstrates a simple shared-folder policy table.

Table 21-1	Mapping Out a Shared-Folder Policy		
Group	Folder	Share Name	Members
bowling	/bowling	bowling	fred, barney
shopping	/shopping	shopping	wilma, betty

Table 21-1 shows that each group is assigned a unique folder on the Linux system. To keep things simple, this example uses the same group, folder, and share names, but on a real system, this may not be possible. Making a table that maps out what's what can save you from lots of headaches later on in the project.

Step 2: Create Linux Groups

The next step in creating your file server is to create the necessary groups in Linux. The file server uses the Linux groups to control access to the individual shared folders that you'll create. For this step, you need to use the Fedora User and Group Manager:

1. **Choose System⇨Administration⇨Users and Groups from the panel menu.**

   Fedora asks you for the root password; then the User Manager window appears. This tool provides a graphical interface for creating and managing user and group accounts on the system.

2. **Click the Add Group icon to add a new Linux group.**

   The Create New Group window, shown in Figure 21-1 appears.

3. **In the text box, enter the name of the group you want to use to control the shared folder. Leave the Specify Group ID manually check box blank.**

   Fedora automatically assigns a unique group number to the group.

For example, create two groups — bowling and shopping. The new groups appear in the group listing under the Groups tab.

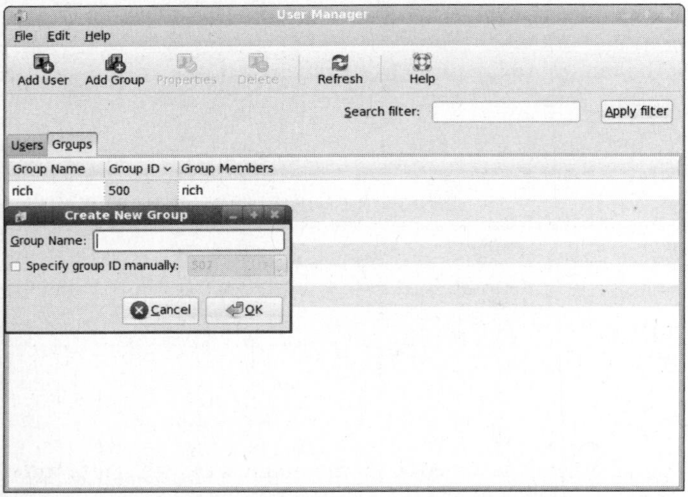

Figure 21-1:
The Fedora
Create New
Group
window.

Step 3: Create Folders to Share

After you've created the groups, you can create the folders you want to share.

For security reasons, it's not a good idea to create folders under an existing user's home folder, as that allows others access to your folder structure.

You should create your shared folders separately from the normal directory structure on the system. To do that, follow these steps:

1. **Choose Applications➪System Tools➪Terminal to start the command-line session.**

   See Chapter 17 if you need help with the command line.

2. **If you're not logged in as the root user, type the** su **command on the command line and press Enter to become the root user. Enter the root-user password when prompted.**

3. **Change to the root folder using the** cd **command.**

   The command to do that is

   ```
   cd /
   ```

4. **Create the folders using the** `mkdir` **command.**

   The folder names correspond to the groups you set up. For example, if you created bowling and shopping groups, the commands to set up the folders are

   ```
   mkdir bowling
   mkdir shopping
   ```

5. **Change the group of your folders.**

   The `chgrp` command is used to change the group that the folder belongs to. If your folders are bowling and shopping, the commands are

   ```
   chgrp bowling bowling
   chgrp shopping shopping
   ```

   This step allows members of the groups to have access to the proper folders.

6. **Type** `exit` **at the command-line prompt to exit root mode, and then type** `exit` **again to exit the Terminal session.**

Step 4: Set Advanced Folder Permissions

There is one additional trick you have to use to complete the permissions for your shared folder(s). When Fedora Linux creates a user account, it assigns each user account to a unique group (which happens to be the same as the username). Unfortunately, this causes problems in a shared-folder environment.

Even though your users are all members of the same group, their primary Linux group is still their unique group name. When a user creates a new file in the shared folder, it belongs to the user's primary group, not to your newly created group.

To solve this problem, you must tell the shared folder to use the folder's group, not the user's group, when users create new files. This requires a special Linux permission that is not available from a file manager.

You must manually assign this permission from the command-line prompt by using the Linux `chmod` command. Here are the steps:

1. **Choose Applications⇨System Tools⇨Terminal to start the command-line session.**

   If you're not familiar with the command line, see Chapter 17.

2. **If you're not logged in as the root user, type the `su` command at the command line and press Enter to become the root user. Enter the root user password when prompted.**

3. **Type the command** `chmod g+rws /foldername`.

   Replace `foldername` with the name of your specific group folder.

   If you created bowling and shopping folders, the command are

   ```
   chmod g+rws /bowling
   chmod g+rws /shopping
   ```

   The `chmod` Linux command changes the permissions on the specified folder. The individual options in the command are

   - `g+` specifies that the permissions be added to the group permission settings.
   - `r` specifies that the group have read permissions to the folder.
   - `w` specifies that the group have write permissions to the folder.
   - `s` specifies that the folder group setting be used for all files created within the folder.

4. **Repeat Step 3 for every folder you've created.**

   Now, whenever a user creates a file in one of the shared folders, the file's group is set to the special group name you specified instead of to the user's primary group.

   This process ensures that other members of the group can access files created by one member of the group.

5. **Type `exit` at the command-line prompt to exit root mode, and then type `exit` again to exit the Terminal session.**

Step 5: Install and Start Samba

Now you need to install the Samba server software. You can use the Fedora Package Management tool to do that, as follows:

1. **Choose System⇨Administration⇨Add/Remove Software.**

   The Fedora PackageKit software starts. You can easily add or remove software packages from here. If you're not logged in as the root user, it asks you for the root user password before you can continue.

2. **In PackageKit, select the Servers option on the left side. After the software package list populates on the right side, select the Server and Client software to interoperate with the Windows machines entry.**

   The Samba Suite package contains all the software packages required for the Samba server (see Figure 21-2). Select the check box next to the entry to select it for installation.

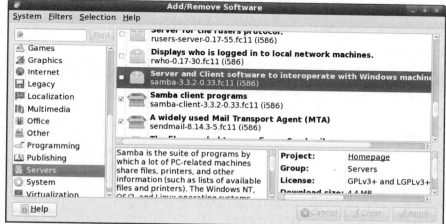

Figure 21-2: Selecting the Samba Suite package for installation.

3. **Select the Samba server-configuration tool package.**

   The Samba server-configuration package contains the graphical interface used to configure Samba easily. If you can't find it, type **system-config-samba** in the search box and click the Find button.

4. **Click the Apply button at the lower right to start the software installation.**

After you install the Samba software, you must decide how you want it to run on your server. You have two options:

- ✔ **Manually:** Choose this if you don't want the Samba server running all the time.

- ✔ **Automatically:** Choose this if you want the Samba server to start when the Linux server is booted.

For either option, you must use the Fedora Service Configuration window; follow these steps:

1. **Choose System⇨Administration⇨Services from the menu.**

   The Service Configuration window opens. Again, you must be the root user to use this tool, so if you're not already logged in as root, you're asked for the root password before you can start. When the Service Configuration window starts, you see all the services that are available on the Fedora system, as shown in Figure 21-3.

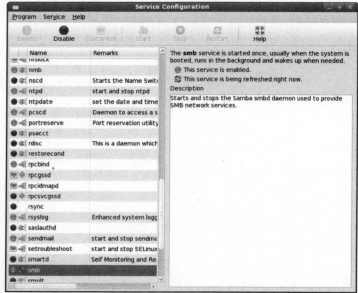

Figure 21-3:
The Fedora
Service
Configur-
ation
window.

The server automatically starts every service that has the green-dot icon when the system boots. You can also start, stop, or restart individual services by using the appropriate button.

The Services Configuration window labels the Samba service as smb. This service actually controls two separate Samba services:

- smbd: Controls client connections to the Samba server.
- nmbd: Controls advertising shared devices on the network.

2. **Select the smb service, and click Start.**

   When you start the smb service, both of the Samba servers start. You will see the status of the services in the right window.

3. **If you want Samba to automatically start at boot up, select the** smb **service, click the Enable icon, and then exit the Service Configuration window.**

Step 6: Configure Samba

There are two main features that you must configure to get your Samba server to work on your network:

- ✔ You have to specify the Microsoft network domain or workgroup name.
- ✔ You have to open the Samba server firewall port to network clients.

Here are the steps for configuring Samba:

1. **Choose System⇨Administration⇨Samba from the menu.**

   The Samba Server Configuration window opens.

2. **Choose Preferences⇨Server Settings from the menu bar.**

   The Server Settings window, shown in Figure 21-4, appears.

Figure 21-4:
The Samba Server Settings window.

3. **In the Server Settings window, enter the workgroup name for your Windows network.**

   Remember, all network devices that use the shared folder must use this same name. By default, Fedora uses the Linux hostname of your system as the Windows network device name on the network.

   You can also provide a brief description of your host in the Description text box provided. Network devices see the description along with your hostname when they browse the network.

4. **Click OK when you're done, and then close the Server Settings window.**

5. **Choose System⊏>Administration⊏>Firewall from the menu.**

   The Firewall Configuration window opens, as shown in Figure 21-5.

Figure 21-5:
The Fedora
Firewall
Configur-
ation
window.

You must be the root user to have access to this tool, so if you're not already logged in, you must enter the root password.

6. **In the Trusted Services area, select the Samba check box.**

   The Trusted Services area shows a list of common services that are configured on the system. Selecting the Samba entry marks it as a trusted service and allows network clients to connect to it.

Fedora uses the SELinux security to prevent unauthorized activity on your workstation. If the SELinux security software is enabled on your system, you have to tell it to allow Samba to operate. To do that, choose System⊏> Administration⊏>SELinux Management to start the SELinux Management tool. From there, select Boolean, and then scroll down to the Samba modules. From the Samba modules, select the Allow Samba to Share Any File/Directory Read/ Write check box.

Step 7: Create Linux User Accounts

When your Samba server is live on the network, you can turn your attention to setting up the shared-folder environment. You've already created the groups necessary to provide access to the shared folders, so now it's time to work on the user accounts.

Each user who needs to access a shared folder must have an individual Linux user account. Follow these steps to get that done:

1. **Choose System⇨Administration⇨Users and Groups from the panel menu.**

    After you enter the root user password, the User Manager window opens.

2. **Click the Add User button to create a new user.**

    The Create New User window, shown in Figure 21-6, appears.

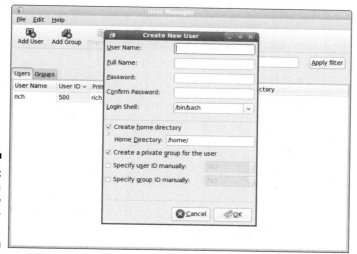

Figure 21-6:
The Fedora
Create New
User
window.

3. **Add new user accounts for each user who needs access to the shared folders.**

    Enter a username for the new user, along with the user's full name for documentation purposes (for example, fred, barney, wilma, and betty). Assign a password. You have to assign a password to the user account, but don't worry: Samba won't use this password to authenticate the remote client.

4. **Click the Groups tab to view the configured groups.**

    The Groups tab displays the groups that are configured on the server. You should see the groups you created in the "Step 2: Create Linux Groups" section.

5. **Add the new users to the appropriate groups.**

    Double-click the group name. The Group Properties window appears, allowing you to select the users that belong to the group under the Group Users tab. Select the users whom you want to belong to the group, and then click OK.

For example, if barney and fred are part of the bowling group, double-click the bowling group, and then select barney and fred from the Group Properties window.

6. **Repeat Step 5 for all your users.**

Step 8: Create Samba User Accounts

We mentioned in the preceding section that Samba doesn't use the Linux user-account password when authenticating remote clients. That's because Samba uses its own user accounts for that. Samba acts like a middleman between the remote Windows client and the Linux filesystem.

When accessing files and folders on the system, Samba uses the defined Linux user accounts. When communicating with remote clients, Samba uses its own internal user accounts. Because of this, Samba must use another group of settings you specify as root: You map the Windows user accounts to the appropriate local Linux user accounts. You do so in the Samba Server Configuration window, by following these steps:

1. **Choose System⇨Administration⇨Samba to start the Samba Server Configuration window.**

   As before, you need root permission to use this program, so if you're not already logged in as the root user, Fedora will ask you for the root password.

2. **Choose Preferences⇨Samba Users from the menu bar.**

   The Samba Users window opens, as shown in Figure 21-7.

Figure 21-7: The Samba Users window for adding new Samba users.

3. **Click the Add User button to add a new Samba user.**

   The Create New Samba User window appears. This window contains four areas where you have to enter specific information:

   - *UNIX Username:* A drop-down list where you can select the Linux user account to map.

   - *Windows Username:* A text box for typing the associated Windows network username that the remote client will use.

   - *Samba Password:* Here's where you enter the password assigned to the Windows network username (remember, this can be — and often is — different from the Linux password).

   - *Confirm Samba Password:* Here's where you retype the Samba password to ensure that you typed it correctly.

   You must match the Windows network username with the Linux username. In the example shown in Figure 21-8, Samba maps the Windows network username `fflinsto` to the Linux user account `fred`.

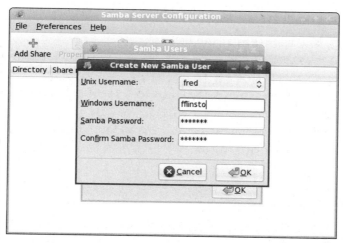

Figure 21-8:
Creating
a new
Samba user
account.

4. **(Optional) If you need to modify a Samba account, select the username of that account from the Samba Users list and click the Edit button.**

   After mapping the accounts, leave the Samba Server Configuration window open because you need it for the next step.

Step 9: Create Shared Folders in Samba

The final piece of the puzzle is to use the Samba Configuration window to tell Samba which shared folders you want to advertise on the network and allow network clients to connect to. Here's the drill:

1. **Click the Add Share button.**

   The Create Samba Share window appears. From here, you define the details of the shared folder:

   - *Directory:* Type the full pathname of the folder you want to share. You can also click the Browse button and browse to select the folder.

   - *Share Name:* Type the name you want Windows network clients to use when they connect to the share.

   - *Description:* Type a simple description that will be advertised along with the share name to remote clients.

   - *Writable:* Check this check box if you want to allow remote clients to write to the shared folder. You must also set the Linux permissions that allow them to write. This option is a handy way to stop allowing remote clients to write to the share in case of an emergency.

   - *Visible:* Select this check box if you want remote clients to see the share advertised when they browse the network.

2. **Enter the folder name for the directory in the Directory box.**

   As you type the folder name, Samba enters a suggested share name as well (which is usually the same as the folder name). Figure 21-9 shows an example: Configuring the bowling shared folder.

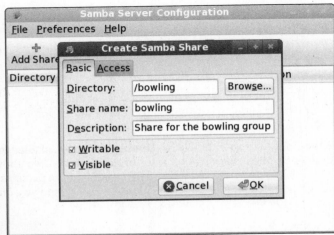

Figure 21-9: Sharing a folder in Samba.

3. **Click the Access tab and select which users have access to the shared folder.**

   Samba allows you to assign access for individual Linux user accounts configured on the computer. You can select the check box to allow access for all users, or you can select individual users from the list. Allowing all users isn't a bad thing because the Linux permissions still block out unauthorized users from the share.

4. **Click OK to accept the new shared folder changes, and then choose File⇨Quit to close the Samba Configuration window.**

Step 10: Map to Shared Folders

Now that your file server is complete, it's time to test it. There are a few different ways you can do this. The easiest is to test mapping a shared folder from a remote Windows client. For this test, we use a Windows XP Home Edition client:

1. **Open the My Computer window by double-clicking the desktop My Computer icon or by choosing Start⇨My Computer.**

2. **Choose Tools⇨Map Network Drive from the My Computer menu bar.**

3. **Click the Browse button to browse the network.**

   Under Microsoft Windows networks, the Fedora Linux server is listed as a network resource. Expand the resource to see the share names listed.

4. **Choose the share you have access to.**

5. **Choose an available local drive (by drive letter) to which you intend to map the network shared folder.**

6. **Click Finish to complete the mapping of the network shared folder.**

You can also map directly to the shared drive using the format \\server name\sharename. By default, your Windows window tries to log in, using your Windows username and password. If you want to log in using a different username and password, click the Different User Name link in the Map Network Drive dialog box, and then type the username and password you want to use, as shown in Figure 21-10.

That's all there is to it. You should now be able to see the shared folder in your My Computer area. Clicking the letter of the shared drive shows the contents of the shared folder on-screen. Due to your Linux permissions, you should have the capability to create, modify, and delete any files in that folder.

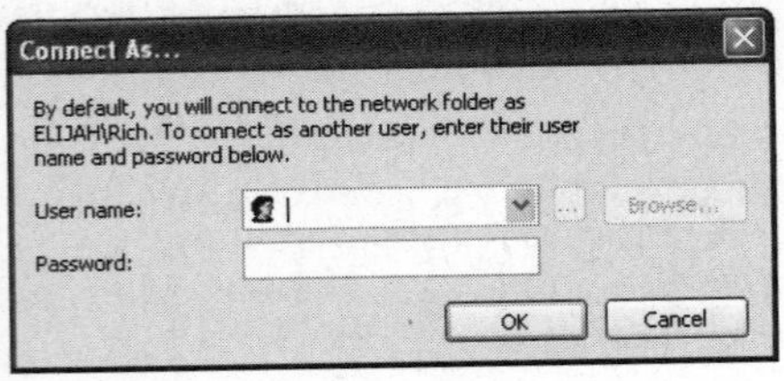

Figure 21-10:
Mapping to
the network
drive from
Windows
XP.

Troubleshooting

As with everything else computer-related, there are always ways things can go wrong while you're creating a file server. Here's a brief list of trouble-shooting issues that may crop up:

✔ **Users can't access their shared folders:** Check all the permissions. First, check to make sure that the proper Linux group is set for the folder. Then check to make sure that the group has the proper permissions for the folder. Finally, check to make sure that the individual users are members of the Linux group.

✔ **After you've verified that the Linux permissions are okay, look into the Samba permissions.** Check to make sure that the proper Samba user accounts have been given appropriate access to the share.

✔ **Users can't see shares when they browse the network:** Check to make sure that the Visible check box is enabled for the share in the Samba Configuration window. Selecting this check box allows Samba to adver-tise the share on the network. If this check box is not selected, the share will not be advertised — and it won't appear on-screen for clients when they browse the network.

The Visible check box can serve as an extra security feature. Hackers can't try to break into what they can't see. Valid users can map to the share manually by using the Microsoft network name in the following form: *servername**sharename*.

✔ **Users can't see the file server when they browse the network:** Make sure that the smb service is enabled in the Services Configuration window. If the smb service is not enabled, remote clients won't see the server on the network and won't be able to connect to it.

✔ **Users can see the file server, but they can't map to any shares:** Make sure the Fedora firewall settings have Samba enabled. If the Samba port is not enabled, Samba can send data through the network, but it cannot receive any data.

Chapter 22

Ten Troubleshooting Tips

*T*roubleshooting is like reading a mystery novel: You have some facts, symptoms, and details, but you don't know whodunit. You have to take whatever information you have, work with that data, weigh the various possibilities, and then narrow them to a single suspect. Finally, you need to test your theory and prove that your suspect is the guilty party.

Troubleshooting problems in Linux (or any operating system) can encompass many hardware and software issues. Whether the problem is the operating system, the hardware, or a service giving you fits, you can use some basic troubleshooting techniques to start your investigations:

✔ **Document the problem.** Write down any and all symptoms that the system is showing, including actions you can and can't do. Jot down any information you see in error messages.

✔ **Examine the Linux log files.** You can find most of these in the /var/log directory. Look for the word error.

✔ **Compare your problem system with a working system running the same distribution and version.** Sometimes comparing configuration files and settings may uncover the problem or narrow the possibilities.

✔ **Check connections.** Check to make sure that all the hardware is connected properly and powered on. Verify that all cables and connections are attached properly. There's always someone, somewhere, accidentally kicking a cable out of a wall connection.

✔ **Remove new hardware.** Remove any hardware that you have changed or added recently (before the problem started), and check to see whether the problem disappears. If it does go poof, you can probably conclude that the new or changed hardware (or its driver) is the culprit — and start researching solutions.

✔ **Reduce the number of active programs.** Stop running unnecessary services and applications that aren't related to the problem at hand. You may more easily figure out what's happening if other services and applications aren't getting in the way.

✔ **Check to see whether the problem is reproducible.** Does the same sequence of events produce the same problem? Suppose that when you try to print to a color printer, nothing happens. If nothing happens *every* time you attempt to print, then the problem is reproducible. If (instead) sometimes your information prints and sometimes it doesn't, then the problem pattern isn't the same, so it isn't reproducible — or it's caused by something more complicated than just clicking one button. Unfortunately, problems that are non-reproducible are more difficult to resolve; if no set pattern of events re-creates those problems, you don't know what to change.

After you've come up with a solution, take a few moments to document the situation. Note the symptoms of the problem, its cause, and the solution you implement. The next time you encounter the same problem, you can call on your notes for a solution rather than having to reinvent the wheel.

If you don't have any problems to troubleshoot (yet), document your environment *before* you do. Making a backup of your /etc directory and your /boot directory is a great place to start.

Tip #1: "The Linux Installer Froze"

When you're installing Linux, the installation process may just freeze. If it does, wait a bit (maybe even a few minutes) and make sure that the installation program really froze. (Sometimes the software just takes a while to process information.) If the software looks like it has frozen, there's no harm in rebooting your computer and starting over — just as you would do with any operating-system installation. Sometimes you can reboot and never have that problem again. At other times, the problem may happen twice in a row and then be fine the third time. Be sure to try several times before giving up.

If the installation still freezes at the same spot (or close to the same spot) in its process, go to the distribution's support pages (see Chapter 1). These pages may talk about some known problems and solutions that can help you — and should show you how to join discussion lists to get more assistance. Otherwise, diagnosing the problem can be tricky — and may seem more like voodoo than science. Here are some tips:

- ✔ **If this problem happens repeatedly at exactly the same spot, you may have a bad installation disc.** See the next section, "Tip #2: Checking Your Distribution Burns," and then return here if that technique doesn't solve your problem. Try the disc in another machine if possible; see whether the installation fails in the same place there. If you purchased this disc, contact the company's technical support team. If you got the disc with a book, contact the publisher's technical support team. If you burned the disc yourself, try burning a new disc at a slower speed.

- ✔ **If this problem happens repeatedly at exactly the same spot and you don't have a bad installation disc, the trouble may be with one of your machine's hardware components.** If you can, try trading hardware between machines. If not, you may need to choose a different machine on which to install Linux — or try another distribution.

- ✔ **If the problem seems to happen randomly, your particular Linux distribution may not be compatible with that particular machine.** Again, you can try trading some hardware around, installing Linux on another machine, or using another distribution.

If you're not sure whether your installer has frozen, try pressing various combinations of Alt+F#, where # corresponds to one of the function keys. Depending on the distribution, the installer may not have frozen completely if you can see different screens when you try this technique.

Tip #2: Checking Your Distribution Burns

Sometimes the problem with an installation is the physical CD-ROM or DVD-ROM. Some Linux distributions, such as Fedora, provide a utility in the installation process that allows you to check the integrity of the CD-ROM or DVD-ROM installation medium.

If your installation keeps dying while Anaconda (the installer program) is placing packages on your hard drive, follow these steps to try to fix it:

1. **Place the DVD-ROM (or the first of your distribution's CD-ROMs) into your drive.**

2. **Reboot the machine.**

3. **Wait until you reach the Media Check dialog box.**

   If you've changed your mind and just want to start the installation, press Tab or the arrow keys to select Skip and then press Enter.

4. **Tab to the Test button and press Enter. If you are using CD-ROMs and want to test a different disc, tab to the Eject CD button and press Enter.**

   If you chose the second option, remove the first CD-ROM from the CD-ROM drive and replace it with the CD-ROM you want to test. Close the CD-ROM drive and make sure that Test is selected.

5. **Press Enter to begin the media check.**

   The Media Check status box opens and shows you the name assigned to the DVD-ROM or CD-ROM along with how much progress has been made. At the end of the inspection, the Media Check Result dialog box opens.

6. **Look at the text after** `and the result is.`

   If the result is `PASS`, then nothing is wrong with the DVD-ROM or CD-ROM itself. Your installation woes are caused by something else. Return to the section "Tip #1: 'The Linux Installer Froze,'" earlier in this chapter.

   If the result is `FAIL`, then the DVD-ROM or CD-ROM you just tested is flawed. If you purchased this CD-ROM or DVD-ROM, talk to the company you purchased it from to see whether you can get a replacement. On the other hand, if you burned your own DVD-ROM or CD-ROM, try one of the following:

   - Burn the DVD-ROM or CD-ROM again, at a speed of 4x or lower.
   - Burn the DVD-ROM or CD-ROM again on a newer drive with BurnProof technology (`www.digital-sanyo.com/BURN-Proof`) or something similar.

If the DVD-ROM that came with this book is defective, contact the technical support address listed in this book. However, remember that the ISO installation files contained on the DVD-ROM must first be copied to your hard drive, and then be burned onto a DVD-ROM; you can't run the installation directly from the DVD-ROM supplied in the book.

Tip #3: "I Told the Installer to Test My Graphics, and They Failed"

The installer may have guessed wrong about what hardware you have. Double-check the settings as best you can. If they look right, try choosing a lower resolution for the time being, and test again; if that fails, try a lower number of colors and test again. You can then try setting things back the way you want them after the machine is fully installed and updated, when (hopefully) it will have a fix available for whatever the problem might be.

Tip #4: "The Installer Tested My Graphics Fine, but My GUI Won't Start"

If your Linux installation program showed you a GUI test screen saying that you were ready to proceed with the rest of the installation, you probably expected that the GUI would start with no problem. Unfortunately, that doesn't always happen.

If you boot your machine for the first time and see error messages when you're trying to enter the GUI automatically (or when you type `startx` to start the GUI manually), type `system-config-display` at a command prompt to start a program that will help you fix the problem.

Tip #5: "I Think I'm in Linux, but I Don't Know What to Do!"

Two different screens tend to cause panic to folks new to Linux. The first of these screens, shown in Figure 22-1, is in fact a sign that you installed the software and booted the machine successfully. Jump for joy! It's just that you're booting into the command-line environment rather than the GUI environment. If you reach a screen similar to the one shown in Figure 22-1, the computer is asking you to log in with the username for an account and a password that you created during the installation process.

```
Boot from (hd0,0) ext3    22c494a9-f926-4349-8e21-21eeea8b2eeb
Starting up ...
Loading, please wait...
19+0 records in
19+0 records out
kinit: name_to_dev_t(/dev/disk/by-uuid/a5fd48d0-ce82-4647-9a84-bf68ca0e5859) = d
ev(8,5)
kinit: trying to resume from /dev/disk/by-uuid/a5fd48d0-ce82-4647-9a84-bf68ca0e5
859
kinit: No resume image, doing normal boot...

Ubuntu 8.10 testbox tty1

testbox login: _
```

Figure 22-1: A Linux command-line login prompt.

TIP

In Fedora, you can log in as `root` and then manipulate what you need to on the system. Because Ubuntu doesn't use the `root` account, you can only log in as your normal user account, and then use the `sudo` command if you need to run any commands with root privileges.

After you enter the username and password, you find yourself at the screen shown in Figure 22-2, which just happens to be the second spot where people get worried. If you see this screen, then not only have you booted properly into Linux, but you're also logged in and are using the machine! Relax and give yourself a good pat on the back.

```
Loading, please wait...
19+0 records in
19+0 records out
kinit: name_to_dev_t(/dev/disk/by-uuid/a5fd48d0-ce82-4647-9a84-bf68ca0e5859) = d
ev(8,5)
kinit: trying to resume from /dev/disk/by-uuid/a5fd48d0-ce82-4647-9a84-bf68ca0e5
859
kinit: No resume image, doing normal boot...

Ubuntu 8.10 testbox tty1

testbox login: rich
Password:
Linux testbox 2.6.27-9-generic #1 SMP Thu Nov 20 21:57:00 UTC 2008 i686

The programs included with the Ubuntu system are free software;
the exact distribution terms for each program are described in the
individual files in /usr/share/doc/*/copyright.

Ubuntu comes with ABSOLUTELY NO WARRANTY, to the extent permitted by
applicable law.

To access official Ubuntu documentation, please visit:
http://help.ubuntu.com/
rich@testbox:~$
```

Figure 22-2:
Logged in at the Linux command line.

What do you do from here? Anything you want. Surf through this book for commands you want to run. Type `startx` to start up the GUI. If you didn't install any GUI (which means you selected a minimal install option with no graphical interface, or you actually unselected graphics), you may want to reinstall, or you have to add all the tools by hand (which is not a quick job!).

Tip #6: "I Don't Want to Boot into This!"

Are you booting into the command-line environment when you want to use only the GUI? Or are you finding that you're already booting into the GUI and you would rather boot into that nice, clean, black-and-white command-line screen? You're not stuck with either of these options. You can change them at any time.

You can press Ctrl+Alt+F# (F# refers to function keys F2 through F6) to change out of the GUI to a command-line terminal at any time — and then press Alt+F7 or Alt+F8 to switch back.

Tip #7: Changing Your Boot Environment "Permanently"

The word *permanently* is in quotes in the heading because you can, of course, go back and change this setting later if you want. *Permanently* just refers to the fact that after you've made this change, the system goes into the preferred environment automatically, every time you boot — until you change it.

You can't make this change in Ubuntu unless you want to boot into *single-user mode,* which is basically "safe mode" and not of much use. Well, okay, you can make the change, but you'd need a techie friend to set up a bunch of stuff for you if you actually want to *use* the system.

To make this change in Fedora, you have to edit what's called a *run level,* like this:

1. **In the GUI, open a command-line terminal.**

   If you're not sure how to do so, see Chapter 17. If you're not in the GUI and you're already logged in, type su - to become the root user.

2. **Type** cp /etc/inittab /etc/inittab.old **to make a backup.**

   Now, if something happens while you're editing the inittab file, you can always restart fresh with the old version.

3. **Open the** inittab **file in your preferred text editor.**

   Some Linux text editors are covered in Chapter 11.

4. **Scroll down until you find a line similar to the following:**

   ```
   id:5:initdefault:
   ```

   This line appears near the top of the file. What you're interested in here is the number. In most mainstream Linux distributions, the number 5 tells Linux to boot into the GUI, and the number 3 tells Linux to boot into the command line. The preceding example, therefore, boots into the GUI.

5. **Change the number in this line.**

   If it's a 5, change it to 3, and vice versa. Make sure that all colons and other items are left properly in place, or else your machine will have problems booting later.

6. **Save and exit the file.**

   The changes go into effect the next time you reboot the system.

If you do end up having problems booting the system, the Ubuntu or Fedora LiveCD can be used as an emergency boot disk.

At any time, you can have your Linux box switch between full command-line mode and full GUI mode.

To switch between modes, do the following:

✔ To change from the GUI login to the command-line login, open a terminal window and type (as root) `init 3`.

✔ To change from the command-line login to the GUI login, type (as root) `init 5`.

When you enter the `init` command, your system reboots into the mode you specify.

Tip #8: "I Want to Change Screen Resolutions"

Do you want or need to swap between resolutions in the GUI on the fly? Suppose you want to use 1,024 x 768, but you work on Web pages and want to be able to see how they look in a browser at 800 x 600 (or even 640 x 480). Your machine is very likely already set up to do this; you just need to know how to do it!

If your machine is set up for it, you can change resolutions by pressing Ctrl+Alt++ (plus sign).

Be sure to use the plus (+) sign on your number pad — you can't use the plus sign on the main keyboard for this one.

If you're using a keyboard without a number pad — as you will be if you're using a laptop — or your machine isn't set up to make changes on the fly, then you have to change your resolution through your display-configuration program (choose System⇔Preferences⇔Display).

Tip #9: "My GUI Is Hung, and I'm Stuck!"

If you're GUI isn't working, try pressing Ctrl+Alt+Backspace. If this doesn't do the trick, then your system is in really bad shape! Try switching to a virtual terminal by using Ctrl+Alt+F5. If this key combination also does nothing, you need to reboot the machine.

Tip #10: "Help, My Machine Hangs During Boot!"

When configuring a Linux machine, you may encounter problems with the GRUB configuration file. In Fedora, this file is the /boot/grub/grub.conf file. Ubuntu uses the /boot/grub/menu.1st file.

This file indicates the operating system or systems to which your system can boot, and the file also contains Linux start-up settings. In order to fix your computer, you can either try rebooting and selecting a different Linux boot option from the menu, or you could refer to Chapter 3 for instructions on using the rescue disk to boot into rescue mode. Consider this list of potential solutions if the GRUB configuration file makes trouble:

- ✔ If you have altered or added hard drives, you may need to change the boot line in the GRUB configuration file.

- ✔ If you haven't made hardware changes, check to make sure that your GRUB configuration file is referring to the correct location of the Linux image. (The program code that loads and executes at runtime is located in the /boot directory.)

- ✔ If the location under the /boot directory or the device for the root entry is incorrect, your system can't boot to Linux.

- ✔ If you're working with a multiboot (dual-boot or more) operating-system environment, be sure that your /etc/grub.conf file contains entries for each of your operating systems.

    Each operating system or Linux installation must have a separate entry.

- ✔ If your file contains entries to switch to a higher-resolution display and you have boot problems, try reducing the video setting to simple VGA.

Linux allows you to use spaces and other characters in filenames that you may or may not be able to use in filenames on other operating systems. However, some Linux applications may stumble when they encounter file or directory names containing spaces. Usually it's a safe bet to stick with alphanumeric characters and avoid spaces and odd characters (such as question marks and exclamation points).

And here's a bonus, all-purpose troubleshooting tip for an all-too-common situation . . . .

"Aaargh! I Forgot My Root Password! What Do I Do?"

Fear not — you have a way around this problem! You need to boot into *single-user mode,* which you can accomplish as follows:

1. **Reboot your machine.**

2. **When you see the blue screen with the words** Press any key to enter the menu, **press a key.**

   It doesn't matter which key you press at this point.

3. **At the GRUB boot screen, press E.**

   A configuration file opens.

4. **Use the arrow keys to go to the line starting with** kernel.

5. **Press E to edit the kernel line. At the end of the line, add the word** single.

6. **Press Enter to put the change into place, and then press B to boot the machine.**

7. **Type** passwd **and then enter the new password twice as directed.**

8. **Type** exit **and then boot the machine normally.**

Part VI
Appendixes

The 5th Wave — By Rich Tennant

"I'll be with you as soon as I execute a few more updates."

In this part . . .

This part adds some extra material to support the rest of this book. Starting with the ever-popular and useful Appendix A, you find a reasonably comprehensive and friendly compendium of common Linux commands, ready for use as a desktop reference. Appendix B shows you how to use the DVD included with this book.

Appendix A

Common Linux Commands

Computing novices often marvel at the keyboard dance that Linux experts typically perform. Sure, these experts know about modern advances like the mouse and the graphical interface, but these keyboard musicians prefer the home keys and find that they can work faster that way. It takes some time to reach this level of proficiency, but every expert was a novice at one time, and any novice can become an expert with plenty of practice.

In this appendix, you find the commands listed by themes, according to what they can actually do for you. So read on — and dazzle your friends with your command-prompt finesse. When they ask you how and where you figured out all those commands, just smile and mumble something about the voices in your head — and, of course, keep this section dog-eared and within reach of your computer.

Linux Commands by Function

Because every command serves a specific purpose, organizing these tools into groups according to their individual functions isn't difficult. If you know what you need to do but don't know which command does the job, flip through this section to start your search. From here, you can dig further by referencing man pages. To access a man page, type **man *command*** at a command prompt. For example, man ls shows you the help information for the file-listing command.

Getting help

When you're digging around for help on a command, you can call on an interesting range of shell commands for assistance, as shown in Table A-1.

Table A-1	Shell Help Commands
Command	*Purpose*
apropos	Looks for commands that contain a keyword in their man page descriptions.
info	One way of finding help information. You can find instructions for this tool at www.gnu.org/software/texinfo/manual/info/, or you can use the built-in tutorial by starting the info tool and pressing the H key when inside it.
man	The primary way of getting help in Linux and UNIX.
whatis	Gets and displays a one-line description of a command.

Locating details about the command-prompt options of a command is a never-ending pursuit. The man page system provides some helpful guides at your fingertips for rapidly finding this detailed information.

Archiving and compressing

Although disk space isn't as hard to come by as it once was, bandwidth and backup media are still at a premium. Subsequently, this group of commands provides a potpourri of tools for compacting and organizing data for storage, as shown in Table A-2.

Table A-2	Archiving and Compressing Tools
Command	*Purpose*
bzip2	Compresses files into .bz2 format. Used mostly for incredibly large sets of text files (which is what source code actually is).
bunzip2	Uncompresses .bz2 files.

Command	Purpose
compress	Compresses files into .Z format. Pretty old and not used much in the Linux world anymore.
gunzip	Uncompresses .gz files and .tgz files.
gzip	Compresses files into .gz format.
tar	Packages files together in a group called a *tarball*. The most common way of using this command is tar xvf *filename*, as in tar xvf download.tar.
uncompress	Uncompresses files from .Z format.
unzip	Uncompresses files from .zip format.
zip	Compresses files into .zip format.

Built-in bash commands

Some commands don't even seem to exist if you try to look up their help information in the man pages, and the commands themselves don't show up as files on your system. Remember, as you type commands at the prompt, you're communicating with a type of program called a *shell*. (The bash is the default Linux shell.) The shell has a set of commands that you can use to communicate with it, as shown in Table A-3.

Table A-3	Shell Commands
Command	**Purpose**
alias	Creates or lists command shortcuts.
env	Lists your current environment variables and their settings.
export	Whenever you're told to set an environment variable, create the variable and then use this command so that the variable will be remembered properly.
history	Lists the last 1,000 commands you've typed.
unalias	Removes command shortcuts.

If you try to view the man page entries for some of these commands, you find instead that the help information for BASH BUILTINS appears. To search through this manual, press the forward slash (/) key to open the man search interface — and then type the name of the command you want to search for.

Press Enter to start the search. The interface stops in the first spot where the term is found. If you want to try again, press the N key to proceed to the next occurrence of the word.

For example, you might be reading the massive bash man page (type man bash to access this page), but perhaps you're only interested in items related to *prompts,* which are the bits of text that appear to the left of your cursor in a text window. An example prompt is

```
rich@textbox:~$
```

You might type /prompt and press Enter to jump to the first instance of this word. If the text around the word doesn't reflect what you're looking for, press the N key to jump to the next one, and so on.

Files and the Filesystem

No matter which operating system you're using, it's hard to do anything without being able to find your way through and work with the filesystem. The utilities in the following subsections help you find your way.

File organization

Boxing, packing, sorting, shipping — you're probably always shuffling files around on your system. File organization commands provide tools for moving files and filesystem units around, as shown in Table A-4.

Table A-4	File Organization Tools
Command	*Purpose*
cd	Changes directories.
cp	Copies a file.
df	Shows partitions and how much space they have.
du	Shows how much disk space is being used in the current directory and below.
ln	Creates a shortcut.
ls	Lists the contents of a directory or information about a file.

Command	Purpose
mkdir	Creates a directory.
mv	Moves or renames a file.
pwd	Shows the path for the directory you're currently in.
rm	Deletes a file.
rmdir	Deletes an empty directory.

File attributes

Files are much like candy bars: The wrappers provide information about the ingredients, size, and package date — all descriptive of the tasty nugget inside. (Perhaps the wrapper is even childproof.) Files keep all this wrapper information in an *inode*. Along with the capability to change the file inode information, file-attribute commands can return data about the content of the file, as shown in Table A-5.

Table A-5	File-Attribute Commands
Command	**Purpose**
chgrp	Changes the group associated with a file.
chmod	Changes a file's permissions.
chown	Changes who owns a file.
file	Shows what type of file you're dealing with.
stat	Shows some statistics about the file.
touch	Creates an empty file of this name.
wc	Shows how many words, lines, and so on are in this file.

File locators

Where, oh, where can your file be? File-locator commands, shown in Table A-6, help you locate files in Linux's monster tree-structure filesystem.

Table A-6	File-Locator Commands
Command	*Purpose*
find	Heavy-duty filesystem search tool.
locate	Lighter-weight filesystem search tool.
which	Tells you the path for the program that would run if you typed this command.

File viewers

Text-file browsing is a favorite pastime of many a system user. These tools provide a variety of utilities for viewing the contents of readable text files of all sizes. Unlike the commands in a full-screen editor, none of these commands (shown in Table A-7) can damage the contents of a file. That's because they're just viewers, not editors.

Table A-7	File-Viewer Commands
Command	*Purpose*
cat	Dumps the contents of the file to your screen.
head	Shows the first ten lines of a file.
less	Shows the file a screen at a time.
more	Shows the file a screen at a time.
tail	Shows the last ten lines of a file.

Filesystem commands

Filesystem commands, listed in Table A-8, provide information or perform actions on the entire filesystem, from creation and tuning to repair and recovery. Some of these commands return data only, whereas others also provide you with surgical instruments for serious filesystem hacking.

Table A-8	Filesystem Commands
Command	*Purpose*
badblocks	Searches a partition for bad blocks.
e2fsck	Checks and repairs an ext2 or ext3 filesystem.
e2label	Applies a filesystem label to an ext2 or ext3 partition.
eject	Ejects a CD or DVD.
fsck	Can check and repair many types of filesystems.
mkfs	Creates a filesystem (format a partition).
mount	Loads a partition into your filesystem.
sync	Saves all information out of buffers onto disks.
tune2fs	Adjusts ext2 and ext3 filesystem parameters.
umount	Removes a partition from the filesystem.

mtools

The mtools suite of utilities provides a nice way to transfer information to your Microsoft friends. Although Linux has native support for Microsoft Windows and DOS filesystems, your Microsoft cohorts don't have access to Linux (ext2 and ext3) filesystems. To keep everyone happy, you can buy preformatted MS-DOS discs and use them with the mtools commands (see Table A-9) so you can swap files with your friends who are using Windows.

Table A-9	mtools Commands
Command	*Purpose*
mcd	Changes directory in DOS format on a DOS disk.
mcopy	Copies DOS files to and from Linux.
mdel	Deletes a DOS file.
mdeltree	Deletes a DOS directory and its contents.
mdir	Lists a DOS directory's contents.

(continued)

Table A-9 *(continued)*

Command	Purpose
mdu	Shows how much space is taken and available for a DOS partition.
mformat	Formats a partition for DOS.
mlabel	Applies a DOS volume label.
mmd	Creates a DOS directory.
mmount	Mounts a DOS disk or partition.
mmove	Moves or renames a DOS file or directory.

System Control

These commands provide system-wide information and control. Normal users can run many commands to obtain system information; however, commands that actively change the configuration of the system need to run while you are logged in as root — or have utilized the su command to become the superuser temporarily.

Administration

Some administration commands (shown in Table A-10) don't fall neatly into a category.

Table A-10	Administration Commands
Command	**Purpose**
passwd	Changes a particular user's password. Any user can run this command to change their own password. Only root can use it to change someone else's.
su	Switches to another user account without logging out of this one. The best way to use this command is su – so your filesystem path and other information are loaded.

Kernel-module handling

You may sometimes need to add kernel support for an additional device (software or hardware). When you do, you have a limited number of choices: You can rebuild the kernel or install a loadable kernel module. Although rebuilding a kernel doesn't exactly require a PhD in nuclear science, consider it a time-consuming nuisance that's best to avoid. The commands in Table A-11 enable you to include the kernel support you need while the system is running, without having to rebuild the entire thing from scratch.

Table A-11	Kernel-Support Commands
Command	*Purpose*
depmod	Regenerates your module dependencies.
insmod	Loads a module by hand.
lsmod	Lists the modules your kernel has loaded.
modprobe	Loads a module by hand, along with its dependencies and settings.
rmmod	Unloads a module by hand.

Processes

Most of your system activity requires processes. Even when your system appears idle, a dozen or so processes (programs) are running in the background. The process commands, shown in Table A-12, enable you to check under the hood to make sure that everything that *should* be running *is* running — and that you're not overheating or overtaxing your computer's resources.

Table A-12	Process Commands
Command	*Purpose*
crontab	Sets up commands to run at regular intervals.
kill	Stops a process by its number. Often used as kill -9 for a harsh stop if a process just won't die.
killall	Stops a process by name rather than number.

(continued)

Table A-12 *(continued)*

Command	Purpose
nice	Assigns a CPU use priority to a process.
pidof	Gets a program's ID number.
ps	Gets a lot of programs' ID numbers; normally you'll see it used as ps aux.
pstree	Shows the relationships between programs.
renice	Changes a program's CPU use priority.
top	Shows resource use over time.

Appendix B

About the DVD

The DVD-ROM included with this book contains everything you need to install and run either Ubuntu 9.04 workstation or Fedora 11. This is the equivalent of the LiveCD you'd have to download from the Ubuntu Web site, or the full Fedora installation DVD-ROM you would have to download from the Fedora Project's Web site. The DVD includes the following:

- ✔ **The Ubuntu Linux workstation LiveCD:** A Linux distribution that includes most of the common workstation applications. You can use the LiveCD to either boot directly from your PC's CD-ROM drive to test Ubuntu without having to load it on your PC, or load Ubuntu directly onto your hard drive.

- ✔ **The full Fedora full installation DVD-ROM:** A Linux distribution that includes just about every Linux application available. Since it's an installation DVD-ROM you can't run this distribution directly from your DVD-ROM device. When you boot from the full Fedora installation DVD-ROM, it automatically starts the Fedora installation program to install Fedora on your hard drive. Don't use this feature if you don't want to replace your existing workstation operating system.

- ✔ **KDE (the K Desktop Environment) and GNOME (GNU Network Object Model Environment):** The two leading graphical user interfaces for Linux. Ubuntu uses the GNOME desktop, but in the Fedora installation you can pick the one you like best!

- ✔ **Mozilla Firefox:** The best-of-breed Web browser for your Linux machine, just waiting for your surfing pleasure.

- ✔ **Samba:** The best way to integrate Linux servers with Windows users. Samba lets your Linux machine masquerade as a Windows server so that Windows users can grab files and print documents hassle-free.

- ✔ **Games!:** Tons of games; enough to help you procrastinate for weeks!

- ✔ **OpenOffice.org:** A full-featured and popular office suite.

If you don't have a DVD-ROM drive, you have a few options:

- If you want to try out Ubuntu, you can go to the Ubuntu site (www. ubuntu.com) to download the LiveCD and burn it yourself (as discussed in Chapter 3).

- If you want to install the full Fedora system, you have go to the Fedora Project site (http://fedoraproject.org) and download the CD images for Fedora 11 and burn them yourself. This is a lot of downloading, so that may not be your favorite choice.

- Go to the Fedora site and download the Fedora LiveCD image, which doesn't give you a full version you can install on your computer permanently, but is just one CD that you can boot directly into Linux without needing installation.

- Go to a site like CheapBytes (www.cheapbytes.com) and order the Ubuntu or Fedora CDs for around $10 — we can't anticipate what they'll charge, so don't hurt us if we're wrong.

If you download the CD images to burn, make sure that you tell your CD burner you're working with ISO images (usually the option has something to do with the word "image"). If you burn the CD and find that it contains just one big file (the ISO file), it will not work. The ISO image actually contains all the files that would be on the CD, so if you put the CD in and find that it contains many files, the CD was created properly.

System Requirements

Make sure that your computer meets the following minimum system requirements. If your computer doesn't match most of these requirements, you may have problems when using the contents of the DVD-ROMs:

- **A PC with an Intel-compatible Pentium-class processor:** We recommend a 400 MHz Pentium IV or better for using Graphical mode, although for a heavy-use desktop system, "more is better."

- **At least 256MB of RAM:** You need at least 192MB of RAM for Graphical mode. (Linux can handle as much RAM as you can fit into a typical computer, and more is almost always better than less.)

- **At least 1GB of hard drive space:** We recommend 10GB if you want to install all the software from the DVD. You need less space if you don't install every program, but you should go ahead and make more than 10GB of space available, to give yourself more options and room for file storage. Again, more is better.

- **A DVD-ROM drive — double-speed (2x) or faster:** The faster the DVD-ROM drive, the faster your installation experience.

 ✔ **Just about any VGA monitor:** Just about any monitor does the trick,
 but you want one that's capable of displaying at least 256 colors or
 grayscale.

 ✔ **Some kind of network connection:** Again, the faster your Internet connection, the less time it takes to update your installation to the most
 recent versions. See Chapter 9 on the various ways to connect to the
 Internet.

If you need more information on PC basics, check out *PCs For Dummies* by
Dan Gookin (published by Wiley Publishing, Inc.).

Using the DVD-ROM

The DVD-ROM included with this book is not bootable. To be able to include
both Ubuntu and Fedora on the same DVD-ROM, we created two ISO images:

 ✔ **ubuntu-9.04-desktop-i386.iso:** The 32-bit Ubuntu 9.04 workstation
 LiveCD image.

 ✔ **Fedora-11-i386-DVD.iso:** The 32-bit full Fedora 11 installation DVD-ROM
 image.

You need a CD/DVD-ROM burner installed on your computer to create a bootable Ubuntu CD-ROM or bootable Fedora DVD-ROM. Follow these steps to
create the appropriate CD-ROM or DVD-ROM to use:

1. **Insert the DVD-ROM into your computer's DVD-ROM player.**

2. **Open the File Manager for your operating system (such as Windows
 Explorer for Windows XP or Vista, Nautilus for the GNOME desktop,
 or Dolphin for the KDE desktop).**

3. **Copy the appropriate ISO image file from the DVD-ROM to your hard
 drive.**

 You won't be able to burn the image file directly from the DVD-ROM,
 even if you do have two DVD-ROM drives in your computer.

4. **Open a DVD-ROM creator program that supports burning ISO images.**

 Some free CD burning software doesn't support burning ISO images.
 For the Windows environment, one popular free package is the `iso
 recorder` package (`http://isorecorder.alexfeinman.com/
 isorecorder.htm`).

5. **Select the option to burn a DVD-ROM (or CD-ROM for the Ubuntu
 LiveCD).**

Be careful that you don't just copy the file to the CD-ROM or DVD-ROM. Make sure you select the option to burn an image.

6. **Insert a blank CD-ROM or DVD-ROM in your burner, and start the burn process.**

When you're done, take a look at the files on the CD/DVD-ROM. It should contain several folders and files, not just the .iso image file.

When you're ready to install Linux, place the CD/DVD-ROM disk in the CD/DVD-ROM drive, and then reboot your computer. You may have to select either a BIOS option, or press a key during the system boot on your computer to enable booting from the CD/DVD-ROM drive.

If You've Got Problems (Of the DVD-ROM Kind)

The DVD-ROM included with this book contains two ISO image files — one for the Ubuntu LiveCD, and one for the full Fedora installation DVD-ROM. When you place the DVD-ROM in your DVD-ROM, it should appear in your File Manager, and you should see the two files on it. You should be aware of a couple of issues before copying the files:

✓ **Disk space:** The full Fedora installation DVD-ROM image is quite large (it's a complete DVD-ROM image). Make sure you have enough disk space (close to 4GB) on your hard drive before copying it.

✓ **DVD-ROM speed:** If you have an older DVD-ROM drive, it may take a while just to copy the ISO image files to your hard drive. Please be patient.

If you still have trouble with the DVD-ROM, please call the Wiley Product Technical Support phone number at 1-877-762-2974. Outside the United States, call 1-317-572-3994. You can also contact Wiley Product Technical Support through the Internet at support.wiley.com. Wiley Publishing provides technical support only for installation and other general quality control items; for technical support on the applications themselves, consult the program's vendor or author.

To place additional orders or to request information about other Wiley products, please call 1-800-225-5945.

Index

• W •

• X •

• Y •

• Z •

GNU General Public License

Version 3, 29 June 2007

Copyright © 2007 Free Software Foundation, Inc. <http://fsf.org/>

Preamble

The GNU General Public License is a free, copyleft license for software and other kinds of works.

The licenses for most software and other practical works are designed to take away your freedom to share and change the works. By contrast, the GNU General Public License is intended to guarantee your freedom to share and change all versions of a program–to make sure it remains free software for all its users. We, the Free Software Foundation, use the GNU General Public License for most of our software; it applies also to any other work released this way by its authors. You can apply it to your programs, too.

When we speak of free software, we are referring to freedom, not price. Our General Public Licenses are designed to make sure that you have the freedom to distribute copies of free software (and charge for them if you wish), that you receive source code or can get it if you want it, that you can change the software or use pieces of it in new free programs, and that you know you can do these things.

To protect your rights, we need to prevent others from denying you these rights or asking you to surrender the rights. Therefore, you have certain responsibilities if you distribute copies of the software, or if you modify it: responsibilities to respect the freedom of others.

For example, if you distribute copies of such a program, whether gratis or for a fee, you must pass on to the recipients the same freedoms that you received. You must make sure that they, too, receive or can get the source code. And you must show them these terms so they know their rights.

Developers that use the GNU GPL protect your rights with two steps: (1) assert copyright on the software, and (2) offer you this License giving you legal permission to copy, distribute and/or modify it.

For the developers' and authors' protection, the GPL clearly explains that there is no warranty for this free software. For both users' and authors' sake, the GPL requires that modified versions be marked as changed, so that their problems will not be attributed erroneously to authors of previous versions.

Some devices are designed to deny users access to install or run modified versions of the software inside them, although the manufacturer can do so. This is fundamentally incompatible with the aim of protecting users' freedom to change the software. The systematic pattern of such abuse occurs in the area of products for individuals to use, which is precisely where it is most unacceptable. Therefore, we have designed this version of the GPL to prohibit the practice for those products. If such problems arise substantially in other domains, we stand ready to extend this provision to those domains in future versions of the GPL, as needed to protect the freedom of users.

Finally, every program is threatened constantly by software patents. States should not allow patents to restrict development and use of software on general-purpose computers, but in those that do, we wish to avoid the special danger that patents applied to a free program could make it effectively proprietary. To prevent this, the GPL assures that patents cannot be used to render the program non-free.

The precise terms and conditions for copying, distribution and modification follow.

Terms and Conditions

0. **Definitions.** "This License" refers to version 3 of the GNU General Public License. "Copyright" also means copyright-like laws that apply to other kinds of works, such as semiconductor masks. "The Program" refers to any copyrightable work licensed under this License. Each licensee is addressed as "you". "Licensees" and "recipients" may be individuals or organizations. To "modify" a work means to copy from or adapt all or part of the work in a fashion requiring copyright permission, other than the making of an exact copy. The resulting work is called a "modified version" of the earlier work or a work "based on" the earlier work. A "covered work" means either the unmodified Program or a work based on the Program.

   To "propagate" a work means to do anything with it that, without permission, would make you directly or secondarily liable for infringement under applicable copyright law, except executing it on a computer or modifying a private copy. Propagation includes copying, distribution (with or without modification), making available to the public, and in some countries other activities as well.

   To "convey" a work means any kind of propagation that enables other parties to make or receive copies. Mere interaction with a user through a computer network, with no transfer of a copy, is not conveying.

An interactive user interface displays "Appropriate Legal Notices" to the extent that it includes a convenient and prominently visible feature that (1) displays an appropriate copyright notice, and (2) tells the user that there is no warranty for the work (except to the extent that warranties are provided), that licensees may convey the work under this License, and how to view a copy of this License. If the interface presents a list of user commands or options, such as a menu, a prominent item in the list meets this criterion.

1. **Source Code.** The "source code" for a work means the preferred form of the work for making modifications to it. "Object code" means any non-source form of a work. A "Standard Interface" means an interface that either is an official standard defined by a recognized standards body, or, in the case of interfaces specified for a particular programming language, one that is widely used among developers working in that language.

   The "System Libraries" of an executable work include anything, other than the work as a whole, that (a) is included in the normal form of packaging a Major Component, but which is not part of that Major Component, and (b) serves only to enable use of the work with that Major Component, or to implement a Standard Interface for which an implementation is available to the public in source code form. A "Major Component", in this context, means a major essential component (kernel, window system, and so on) of the specific operating system (if any) on which the executable work runs, or a compiler used to produce the work, or an object code interpreter used to run it.

   The "Corresponding Source" for a work in object code form means all the source code needed to generate, install, and (for an executable work) run the object code and to modify the work, including scripts to control those activities. However, it does not include the work's System Libraries, or general-purpose tools or generally available free programs which are used unmodified in performing those activities but which are not part of the work. For example, Corresponding Source includes interface definition files associated with source files for the work, and the source code for shared libraries and dynamically linked subprograms that the work is specifically designed to require, such as by intimate data communication or control flow between those subprograms and other parts of the work.

   The Corresponding Source need not include anything that users can regenerate automatically from other parts of the Corresponding Source.

   The Corresponding Source for a work in source code form is that same work.

2. **Basic Permissions.** All rights granted under this License are granted for the term of copyright on the Program, and are irrevocable provided the stated conditions are met. This License explicitly affirms your unlimited permission to run the unmodified Program. The output from running a covered work is covered by this License only if the output, given its content, constitutes a covered work. This License acknowledges your rights of fair use or other equivalent, as provided by copyright law.

   You may make, run and propagate covered works that you do not convey, without conditions so long as your license otherwise remains in force. You may convey covered works to others for the sole purpose of having them make modifications exclusively for you, or provide you with facilities for running those works, provided that you comply with the terms of this License in conveying all material for which you do not control copyright. Those thus making or running the covered works for you must do so exclusively on your behalf, under your direction and control, on terms that prohibit them from making any copies of your copyrighted material outside their relationship with you.

   Conveying under any other circumstances is permitted solely under the conditions stated below. Sublicensing is not allowed; section 10 makes it unnecessary.

3. **Protecting Users' Legal Rights From Anti-Circumvention Law.** No covered work shall be deemed part of an effective technological measure under any applicable law fulfilling obligations under article 11 of the WIPO copyright treaty adopted on 20 December 1996, or similar laws prohibiting or restricting circumvention of such measures.

   When you convey a covered work, you waive any legal power to forbid circumvention of technological measures to the extent such circumvention is effected by exercising rights under this License with respect to the covered work, and you disclaim any intention to limit operation or modification of the work as a means of enforcing, against the work's users, your or third parties' legal rights to forbid circumvention of technological measures.

4. **Conveying Verbatim Copies.** You may convey verbatim copies of the Program's source code as you receive it, in any medium, provided that you conspicuously and appropriately publish on each copy an appropriate copyright notice; keep intact all notices stating that this License and any non-permissive terms added in accord with section 7 apply to the code; keep intact all notices of the absence of any warranty; and give all recipients a copy of this License along with the Program.

   You may charge any price or no price for each copy that you convey, and you may offer support or warranty protection for a fee.

5. **Conveying Modified Source Versions.** You may convey a work based on the Program, or the modifications to produce it from the Program, in the form of source code under the terms of section 4, provided that you also meet all of these conditions:

a) The work must carry prominent notices stating that you modified it, and giving a relevant date.

b) The work must carry prominent notices stating that it is released under this License and any conditions added under section 7. This requirement modifies the requirement in section 4 to "keep intact all notices".

c) You must license the entire work, as a whole, under this License to anyone who comes into possession of a copy. This License will therefore apply, along with any applicable section 7 additional terms, to the whole of the work, and all its parts, regardless of how they are packaged. This License gives no permission to license the work in any other way, but it does not invalidate such permission if you have separately received it.

d) If the work has interactive user interfaces, each must display Appropriate Legal Notices; however, if the Program has interactive interfaces that do not display Appropriate Legal Notices, your work need not make them do so.

A compilation of a covered work with other separate and independent works, which are not by their nature extensions of the covered work, and which are not combined with it such as to form a larger program, in or on a volume of a storage or distribution medium, is called an "aggregate" if the compilation and its resulting copyright are not used to limit the access or legal rights of the compilation's users beyond what the individual works permit. Inclusion of a covered work in an aggregate does not cause this License to apply to the other parts of the aggregate.

6. **Conveying Non-Source Forms.** You may convey a covered work in object code form under the terms of sections 4 and 5, provided that you also convey the machine-readable Corresponding Source under the terms of this License, in one of these ways:

a) Convey the object code in, or embodied in, a physical product (including a physical distribution medium), accompanied by the Corresponding Source fixed on a durable physical medium customarily used for software interchange.

b) Convey the object code in, or embodied in, a physical product (including a physical distribution medium), accompanied by a written offer, valid for at least three years and valid for as long as you offer spare parts or customer support for that product model, to give anyone who possesses the object code either (1) a copy of the Corresponding Source for all the software in the product that is covered by this License, on a durable physical medium customarily used for software interchange, for a price no more than your reasonable cost of physically performing this conveying of source, or (2) access to copy the Corresponding Source from a network server at no charge.

c) Convey individual copies of the object code with a copy of the written offer to provide the Corresponding Source. This alternative is allowed only occasionally and noncommercially, and only if you received the object code with such an offer, in accord with subsection 6b.

d) Convey the object code by offering access from a designated place (gratis or for a charge), and offer equivalent access to the Corresponding Source in the same way through the same place at no further charge. You need not require recipients to copy the Corresponding Source along with the object code. If the place to copy the object code is a network server, the Corresponding Source may be on a different server (operated by you or a third party) that supports equivalent copying facilities, provided you maintain clear directions next to the object code saying where to find the Corresponding Source. Regardless of what server hosts the Corresponding Source, you remain obligated to ensure that it is available for as long as needed to satisfy these requirements.

e) Convey the object code using peer-to-peer transmission, provided you inform other peers where the object code and Corresponding Source of the work are being offered to the general public at no charge under subsection 6d.

A separable portion of the object code, whose source code is excluded from the Corresponding Source as a System Library, need not be included in conveying the object code work.

A "User Product" is either (1) a "consumer product", which means any tangible personal property which is normally used for personal, family, or household purposes, or (2) anything designed or sold for incorporation into a dwelling. In determining whether a product is a consumer product, doubtful cases shall be resolved in favor of coverage. For a particular product received by a particular user, "normally used" refers to a typical or common use of that class of product, regardless of the status of the particular user or of the way in which the particular user actually uses, or expects or is expected to use, the product. A product is a consumer product regardless of whether the product has substantial commercial, industrial or non-consumer uses, unless such uses represent the only significant mode of use of the product.

"Installation Information" for a User Product means any methods, procedures, authorization keys, or other information required to install and execute modified versions of a covered work in that User Product from a modified version of its Corresponding Source. The information must suffice to ensure that the continued functioning of the modified object code is in no case prevented or interfered with solely because modification has been made.

If you convey an object code work under this section in, or with, or specifically for use in, a User Product, and the conveying occurs as part of a transaction in which the right of possession and use of the User Product is transferred to the recipient in perpetuity or for a fixed term (regardless of how the transaction is characterized), the Corresponding Source conveyed under this section must be accompanied by the Installation Information. But this requirement does not apply if neither you nor any third party retains the ability to install modified object code on the User Product (for example, the work has been installed in ROM).

The requirement to provide Installation Information does not include a requirement to continue to provide support service, warranty, or updates for a work that has been modified or installed by the recipient, or for the User Product in which it has been modified or installed. Access to a network may be denied when the modification itself materially and adversely affects the operation of the network or violates the rules and protocols for communication across the network.

Corresponding Source conveyed, and Installation Information provided, in accord with this section must be in a format that is publicly documented (and with an implementation available to the public in source code form), and must require no special password or key for unpacking, reading or copying.

7. **Additional Terms.** "Additional permissions" are terms that supplement the terms of this License by making exceptions from one or more of its conditions. Additional permissions that are applicable to the entire Program shall be treated as though they were included in this License, to the extent that they are valid under applicable law. If additional permissions apply only to part of the Program, that part may be used separately under those permissions, but the entire Program remains governed by this License without regard to the additional permissions.

When you convey a copy of a covered work, you may at your option remove any additional permissions from that copy, or from any part of it. (Additional permissions may be written to require their own removal in certain cases when you modify the work.) You may place additional permissions on material, added by you to a covered work, for which you have or can give appropriate copyright permission.

Notwithstanding any other provision of this License, for material you add to a covered work, you may (if authorized by the copyright holders of that material) supplement the terms of this License with terms:

a) Disclaiming warranty or limiting liability differently from the terms of sections 15 and 16 of this License; or

b) Requiring preservation of specified reasonable legal notices or author attributions in that material or in the Appropriate Legal Notices displayed by works containing it; or

c) Prohibiting misrepresentation of the origin of that material, or requiring that modified versions of such material be marked in reasonable ways as different from the original version; or

d) Limiting the use for publicity purposes of names of licensors or authors of the material; or

e) Declining to grant rights under trademark law for use of some trade names, trademarks, or service marks; or

f) Requiring indemnification of licensors and authors of that material by anyone who conveys the material (or modified versions of it) with contractual assumptions of liability to the recipient, for any liability that these contractual assumptions directly impose on those licensors and authors.

All other non-permissive additional terms are considered "further restrictions" within the meaning of section 10. If the Program as you received it, or any part of it, contains a notice stating that it is governed by this License along with a term that is a further restriction, you may remove that term. If a license document contains a further restriction but permits relicensing or conveying under this License, you may add to a covered work material governed by the terms of that license document, provided that the further restriction does not survive such relicensing or conveying.

If you add terms to a covered work in accord with this section, you must place, in the relevant source files, a statement of the additional terms that apply to those files, or a notice indicating where to find the applicable terms.

Additional terms, permissive or non-permissive, may be stated in the form of a separately written license, or stated as exceptions; the above requirements apply either way.

8. **Termination.** You may not propagate or modify a covered work except as expressly provided under this License. Any attempt otherwise to propagate or modify it is void, and will automatically terminate your rights under this License (including any patent licenses granted under the third paragraph of section 11).

However, if you cease all violation of this License, then your license from a particular copyright holder is reinstated (a) provisionally, unless and until the copyright holder explicitly and finally terminates your license, and (b) permanently, if the copyright holder fails to notify you of the violation by some reasonable means prior to 60 days after the cessation.

Moreover, your license from a particular copyright holder is reinstated permanently if the copyright holder notifies you of the violation by some reasonable means, this is the first time you have received notice of violation of this License (for any work) from that copyright holder, and you cure the violation prior to 30 days after your receipt of the notice.

Termination of your rights under this section does not terminate the licenses of parties who have received copies or rights from you under this License. If your rights have been terminated and not permanently reinstated, you do not qualify to receive new licenses for the same material under section 10.

9. **Acceptance Not Required for Having Copies.** You are not required to accept this License in order to receive or run a copy of the Program. Ancillary propagation of a covered work occurring solely as a consequence of using peer-to-peer transmission to receive a copy likewise does not require acceptance. However, nothing other than this License grants you permission to propagate or modify any covered work. These actions infringe copyright if you do not accept this License. Therefore, by modifying or propagating a covered work, you indicate your acceptance of this License to do so.

10. **Automatic Licensing of Downstream Recipients.** Each time you convey a covered work, the recipient automatically receives a license from the original licensors, to run, modify and propagate that work, subject to this License. You are not responsible for enforcing compliance by third parties with this License.

An "entity transaction" is a transaction transferring control of an organization, or substantially all assets of one, or subdividing an organization, or merging organizations. If propagation of a covered work results from an entity transaction, each party to that transaction who receives a copy of the work also receives whatever licenses to the work the party's predecessor in interest had or could give under the previous paragraph, plus a right to possession of the Corresponding Source of the work from the predecessor in interest, if the predecessor has it or can get it with reasonable efforts.

You may not impose any further restrictions on the exercise of the rights granted or affirmed under this License. For example, you may not impose a license fee, royalty, or other charge for exercise of rights granted under this License, and you may not initiate litigation (including a cross-claim or counterclaim in a lawsuit) alleging that any patent claim is infringed by making, using, selling, offering for sale, or importing the Program or any portion of it.

11. **Patents.** A "contributor" is a copyright holder who authorizes use under this License of the Program or a work on which the Program is based. The work thus licensed is called the contributor's "contributor version".

A contributor's "essential patent claims" are all patent claims owned or controlled by the contributor, whether already acquired or hereafter acquired, that would be infringed by some manner, permitted by this License, of making, using, or selling its contributor version, but do not include claims that would be infringed only as a consequence of further modification of the contributor version. For purposes of this definition, "control" includes the right to grant patent sublicenses in a manner consistent with the requirements of this License.

Each contributor grants you a non-exclusive, worldwide, royalty-free patent license under the contributor's essential patent claims, to make, use, sell, offer for sale, import and otherwise run, modify and propagate the contents of its contributor version.

In the following three paragraphs, a "patent license" is any express agreement or commitment, however denominated, not to enforce a patent (such as an express permission to practice a patent or covenant not to sue for patent infringement). To "grant" such a patent license to a party means to make such an agreement or commitment not to enforce a patent against the party.

If you convey a covered work, knowingly relying on a patent license, and the Corresponding Source of the work is not available for anyone to copy, free of charge and under the terms of this License, through a publicly available network server or other readily accessible means, then you must either (1) cause the Corresponding Source to be so available, or (2) arrange to deprive yourself of the benefit of the patent license for this particular work, or (3) arrange, in a manner consistent with the requirements of this License, to extend the patent license to downstream recipients. "Knowingly relying" means you have actual knowledge that, but for the patent license, your conveying the covered work in a country, or your recipient's use of the covered work in a country, would infringe one or more identifiable patents in that country that you have reason to believe are valid.

If, pursuant to or in connection with a single transaction or arrangement, you convey, or propagate by procuring conveyance of, a covered work, and grant a patent license to some of the parties receiving the covered work authorizing them to use, propagate, modify or convey a specific copy of the covered work, then the patent license you grant is automatically extended to all recipients of the covered work and works based on it.

A patent license is "discriminatory" if it does not include within the scope of its coverage, prohibits the exercise of, or is conditioned on the non-exercise of one or more of the rights that are specifically granted under this License. You may not convey a covered work if you are a party to an arrangement with a third party that is in the business of distributing software, under which you make payment to the third party based on the extent of your activity of conveying the work, and under which the third party grants, to any of the parties who would receive the covered work from you, a discriminatory patent license (a) in connection with copies of the covered work conveyed by you (or copies made from those copies), or (b) primarily for and in connection with specific products or compilations that contain the covered work, unless you entered into that arrangement, or that patent license was granted, prior to 28 March 2007.

Nothing in this License shall be construed as excluding or limiting any implied license or other defenses to infringement that may otherwise be available to you under applicable patent law.

12. **No Surrender of Others' Freedom.** If conditions are imposed on you (whether by court order, agreement or otherwise) that contradict the conditions of this License, they do not excuse you from the conditions of this License. If you cannot convey a covered work so as to satisfy simultaneously your obligations under this License and any other pertinent obligations, then as a consequence you may not convey it at all. For example, if you agree to terms that obligate you to collect a royalty for further conveying from those to whom you convey the Program, the only way you could satisfy both those terms and this License would be to refrain entirely from conveying the Program.

13. **Use with the GNU Affero General Public License.** Notwithstanding any other provision of this License, you have permission to link or combine any covered work with a work licensed under version 3 of the GNU Affero General Public License into a single combined work, and to convey the resulting work. The terms of this License will continue to apply to the part which is the covered work, but the special requirements of the GNU Affero General Public License, section 13, concerning interaction through a network will apply to the combination as such.

14. **Revised Versions of this License.** The Free Software Foundation may publish revised and/or new versions of the GNU General Public License from time to time. Such new versions will be similar in spirit to the present version, but may differ in detail to address new problems or concerns.

Each version is given a distinguishing version number. If the Program specifies that a certain numbered version of the GNU General Public License "or any later version" applies to it, you have the option of following the terms and conditions either of that numbered version or of any later version published by the Free Software Foundation. If the Program does not specify a version number of the GNU General Public License, you may choose any version ever published by the Free Software Foundation.

If the Program specifies that a proxy can decide which future versions of the GNU General Public License can be used, that proxy's public statement of acceptance of a version permanently authorizes you to choose that version for the Program.

Later license versions may give you additional or different permissions. However, no additional obligations are imposed on any author or copyright holder as a result of your choosing to follow a later version.

15. **Disclaimer of Warranty.** THERE IS NO WARRANTY FOR THE PROGRAM, TO THE EXTENT PERMITTED BY APPLICABLE LAW. EXCEPT WHEN OTHERWISE STATED IN WRITING THE COPYRIGHT HOLDERS AND/OR OTHER PARTIES PROVIDE THE PROGRAM "AS IS" WITHOUT WARRANTY OF ANY KIND, EITHER EXPRESSED OR IMPLIED, INCLUDING, BUT NOT LIMITED TO, THE IMPLIED WARRANTIES OF MERCHANTABILITY AND FITNESS FOR A PARTICULAR PURPOSE. THE ENTIRE RISK AS TO THE QUALITY AND PERFORMANCE OF THE PROGRAM IS WITH YOU. SHOULD THE PROGRAM PROVE DEFECTIVE, YOU ASSUME THE COST OF ALL NECESSARY SERVICING, REPAIR OR CORRECTION.

16. **Limitation of Liability.** IN NO EVENT UNLESS REQUIRED BY APPLICABLE LAW OR AGREED TO IN WRITING WILL ANY COPYRIGHT HOLDER, OR ANY OTHER PARTY WHO MODIFIES AND/OR CONVEYS THE PROGRAM AS PERMITTED ABOVE, BE LIABLE TO YOU FOR DAMAGES, INCLUDING ANY GENERAL, SPECIAL, INCIDENTAL OR CONSEQUENTIAL DAMAGES ARISING OUT OF THE USE OR INABILITY TO USE THE PROGRAM (INCLUDING BUT NOT LIMITED TO LOSS OF DATA OR DATA BEING RENDERED INACCURATE OR LOSSES SUSTAINED BY YOU OR THIRD PARTIES OR A FAILURE OF THE PROGRAM TO OPERATE WITH ANY OTHER PROGRAMS), EVEN IF SUCH HOLDER OR OTHER PARTY HAS BEEN ADVISED OF THE POSSIBILITY OF SUCH DAMAGES.

17. **Interpretation of Sections 15 and 16.** If the disclaimer of warranty and limitation of liability provided above cannot be given local legal effect according to their terms, reviewing courts shall apply local law that most closely approximates an absolute waiver of all civil liability in connection with the Program, unless a warranty or assumption of liability accompanies a copy of the Program in return for a fee.

END OF TERMS AND CONDITIONS